DERELICT LANDSCAPES

Geographical Perspectives on the Human Past

General Editor: Robert D. Mitchell,
University of Maryland, College Park

Derelict Landscapes: The Wasting of America's Built Environment
  by John A. Jakle and David Wilson

The American Environment: Historical Geographic Interpretations of
Impact and Policy
  edited by Lary M. Dilsaver and Craig E. Colten

Upstate Arcadia: Landscape, Aesthetics, and the Triumph of Social
Differentiation in America
  by Peter J. Hugill

DERELICT LANDSCAPES

The Wasting of America's Built Environment

John A. Jakle and David Wilson

ROWMAN & LITTLEFIELD PUBLISHERS, INC.

ROWMAN & LITTLEFIELD PUBLISHERS, INC.

Published in the United States of America
by Rowman & Littlefield Publishers, Inc.
8705 Bollman Place, Savage, Maryland 20763

British Cataloging in Publication Information Available

Library of Congress Cataloging-in-Publication Data

Jakle, John A.
  Derelict landscapes.

  (Geographical perspectives on the human past)
  Includes bibliographical references and index.
    1. Urban renewal—United States.   2. Rural renewal—
United States.   3. Landscape protection—United States.
4. Urban-rural migration—United States.   5. Land use—
United States.   6. United States—Industries—Location.
I. Wilson, David, 1956–   .   II. Title.
HT175.J35   1992   307.3'416'0973   92–5420

ISBN 0–8476–7735–4 (cloth : alk. paper)
ISBN 0–8476–7736–2 (pbk. : alk. paper)

Printed in the United States of America

 The paper used in this publication meets the minimum requirements of
American National Standard for Information Sciences—Permanence of
Paper for Printed Library Materials, ANSI Z39.48–1984.

For Cynthia Anne and Mary Anne

Those who survive for many years outlive
The landscape that they knew, which fades and flies.
Time makes a landscape ashes when it dies
And sifts them from a sieve.

Edgar Lee Masters
"Invisible Landscapes"

Sometimes it seems that more
has been lost than ever remains,
that we live in a slow passing
among indecipherable signs.

Michael Anania
"The Sky at Ashland"

Contents

Tables and Figures

Preface

One might assume from our title that this book concerns the values that underlie eroded farmland, toxic waste dumps, beaches closed by pollution, and abandoned strip mines. So it does, but emphasis is given to aspects of American environmental degradation as yet less widely discussed. Herein we focus on the dereliction of America's built environments, especially the degraded lived-in habitats of everyday life. As Americans squander natural resources so also do they waste cultural resources—specifically the raw material, energy, labor, intellect, and emotion invested and held in the physical infrastructures of cities, towns, and rural countrysides. Since World War II, forces have been at work to totally reorganize the nation geographically. Cities, for example, have been turned inside out as people, enterprise, and wealth have fled to suburbs. Whole regions have declined with loss of economic energy. Perhaps never before have Americans experienced change so rapidly. Unfortunately, not all change has been progress, for much waste has accompanied the nation's transformation. In this wastefulness, extensive areas of dereliction have accrued.

In this book we explore the spectrum of concerns variously ascribed to words like underutilization, disinvestment, vacancy, abandonment, and degradation. We seek to understand the complex forces that intersect to forge various kinds of dereliction types. We seek to enlighten on relevant social structures and human behaviors as they mesh to forge dereliction. To place in perspective the implicit processes of decline, we also explore notions of maintenance and orderliness—the counterforces operating to preserve rather than destroy places. What follows is an examination of America's changing cultural landscapes after World War II. Emphasis is placed on the decades of the 1950s, 1960s, and 1970s when an arrogant "throwaway" mentality dominated the nation's thinking as to what America ought to be.

Only in the 1980s did conservationists and preservationists accrue significant enough results to suggest that extensive, chronic dereliction need not be a permanent part of the American way. Purposely, we explore the rich texture of human intent that generates dereliction. An exploration; ours is not an attempt at definitive explanation. Rather, it is our purpose to raise questions about human intentionality as it relates to dereliction in the United States.

We adopt a perspective that recognizes the influence of active but bounded individuals. People are believed to be influential restructuring agents, but circumscribed by time and space in their options for action. This perspective, termed "structuration" by others (cf. Pred, 1984; Dear and Moos, 1986), accords influence to human decision making and constraining/enabling contexts. Landscape restructuring is seen to follow from the influence wielded by key decision makers within evolving social, economic, and political formations. Decisions simultaneously reflect individual initiative, as rooted in personal values, and the interpenetration of contextual forces formed around values publicly prescribed. Individuals produce and are penetrated by contextual processes that render them carriers of complex motives. The unique is thus emphasized, but as bonded to social context. This perspective integrates the polarities of structure and agency to more comprehensively understand processes like landscape dereliction (see Giddens, 1981, 1985). We emphasize that structuration is not a theory of explanation, but a framework to sensitize analysis. It is used to recognize dereliction as individually driven but within structured social contexts. As such, structuration is not designed to stand alone and explain events. Its "hollow core" necessitates more powerful theorization to inform analysis (Warf, 1989). Accordingly, we posit broad-based imperatives—like quests to accumulate and desires to obtain political legitimacy—as critical constructors of human intent. Human action takes place in structural contexts that constrain and enable. Such influences are filtered through local culture, politics, and biography to structure unique and personalized decision making.

Chapter One defines dereliction. Chapter Two focuses squarely on the cultural values that have underlain both personal and societal predispositions to be wasteful of places and landscapes. Chapter Three begins our assessment of dereliction types, focusing on the forces inducing deindustrialization, especially in the U.S. Middle West and Northeast. Chapter Four concerns America's changing central cities with focus on urban renewal, public housing, and the rise of an urban "underclass." The abandonment of central city neighborhoods is examined in Chapter Five, with racism spotlighted as the most insidious factor pushing mass exodus to the suburbs. Chapter Six treats dereliction in the countryside and in small towns to emphasize that decay and decline have not been limited to U.S. cities.

Indeed, rural decline is related directly to much urban dereliction. Chapter Seven examines successful experiments at reversing dereliction while Chapter Eight amplifies on these successes by highlighting the role of what we call "locality-based communities." Concluding remarks are offered in Chapter Nine.

The successes of World War II, and of the American world economic hegemony that followed, bolstered U.S. confidence to configure itself anew. Growth became a panacea to solve all problems, since the American engine for change appeared boundless. Institutions created to remedy the Depression of the 1930s, complemented by new initiatives fostering ascendant special interests (housing, automobiles and highways, and defense especially), set in motion a massive rebuilding that took little heed of the old, which, in general, was allowed to languish. By the 1970s, the very fabric of America's traditional cities and countrysides had begun to unravel. Behind the facades of modernity accumulated extensive decline and decay. In the 1980s, Americans found themselves with unprecedented blight. Americans faced an uncertain economic future exacerbated by overseas flight of jobs, budget deficits, and chronic balance-of-payment problems. Confidence in a constantly renewed and renewing America appeared to be waning. We offer here an overview of those problematical decades, approached through examination of derelict landscapes.

Our stance is that of cultural and urban geographers who believe that society can be known by the landscapes it creates and nurtures. Landscapes simultaneously structure and reflect human endeavor. They are recipients of forces whose implantation reproduces and rearranges society. Landscapes thus symbolize and construct, making ideal foci for social analysis. Understanding landscapes helps unravel the essence of society. The following questions guide our exploration: What is it that dereliction symbolizes in the American scene? What does it say about America as a society? How in the past have Americans been able to countenance the wasting of vast cultural landscape resources? Traditionally, Americans have been able to ignore dereliction through profound faith in an economy and system of governance perceived as rational and optimal. Does widespread, chronic dereliction in the built environment suggest basic flaws in the American system? In the values that underlie that system?

We write this book for educated lay readers and students of landscape who are interested in dereliction. We work from the premise that Americans generally ignore dereliction in commonly used places. As a result, Americans have come to accept whole categories of decline as somehow natural, when decline is in fact a societal construction. Individuals and collectivities drive initiatives to structure landscapes whether of prosperity, stability, or neglect. We believe that neglect is driven by the complex interconnections of uneven development, a supportive legal system, and basic cultural values that legitimize its perpetration. We explore these interlocking factors as they are played out to create derelict zones at a range of spatial scales. What follows is an overview of recent landscape change in America viewed through the important lens of dereliction.

1

Landscape Dereliction

Conflict and controversy continue to plague the contemporary major American city: prosperous cores embedded in dilapidated downtowns; blue-collar enclaves buffeted by slums; decay interspersed with affluence. The city continues to fascinate and provoke. Polarities seem at an uneasy truce: black and white, old and new, decay and modernity, grime and glitz. While some seize opportunities to forge prosperous lives, others are relegated to debilitating existences. Living amid dereliction, poverty, and nominal opportunity, they watch while others access urban amenities. As Michael Williams (1985) emphasizes, the contemporary urban problematic is a prevalence of opportunity with many denied access. Jobs, culture, and resources flourish amid uneven appropriation. The poor view the nearby trappings of affluence, their sensibilities attacked by the overt juxtaposition of wealth and poverty. Derelict landscapes emerge that reflect a failure to match urban resources with populations.

These dynamic landscapes are an unending curiosity to the authors. Our lived experiences in Detroit, New York City, Indianapolis, and elsewhere have led to a fascination in landscape change that is the heart of this book. Remarkable commonalities are reflected in these landscapes. Many are ominous. The uneasy transposing of consumption values on cities rooted in deprivation has created much tension. Neighborhood versus downtown, gentrification versus resident renewal, and developers versus the people have emerged as angry slogans. At the same time, an emergent postindustrial economy rooted in service jobs and employment in offices has masked industrial decline and resident suffering. Postindustrial ascendance has exacerbated resentment among low-income people who frequently lack the skills to participate in the newly emergent economy. These forces have

1

compounded urban social and spatial fragmentation. Decline and dereliction intensify in restructured cities that have generated benefits for only select populations.

Such problems are no longer confined to cities. They have increasingly filtered out to suburbia and beyond, to erode traditional urban–rural social distinctions. Previously insulated big-city suburbs, small cities, and small towns have experienced growing racial strife, ethnic polarization, and dereliction. Patterns of migration and information spread have been pivotal, with low-income suburbs steadily multiplying since 1945 (Muller, 1981). The poor have dispersed from traditional industrial corridors, bringing to the suburbs greater socioeconomic diversity. With this transformation, the city is no longer the exclusive domain for burgeoning low-income and troubled populations. Current data on crime rates support this position. Arrest rates in suburbs and in rural areas were 66.2 percent and 49.5 percent of cities in 1973. In 1978, these two percentages were 87.8 percent and 63.5 percent (Smith, 1988, p. 27). This convergence trend, slowing somewhat in the early 1980s, gained momentum in the late 1980s to further narrow areal differentials (ibid.).

Our aim is to unearth the roots of dereliction in contemporary America, to identify the forces that produce it. Derelict landscapes—contingent unfoldings neither predetermined nor inevitable—are, instead, fashioned by active and influential individuals. Such constructions symbolize society and its key decision makers. Whether unintended outcomes or deliberate outcomes, they reflect prevailing values, goals, and power relations. Derelict landscapes thus bear the imprint of human motive, reflecting human beliefs, predilections, and actions. To understand derelict landscapes, in essence, is to comprehend society.

DERELICTION RECOGNIZED AND DEFINED

How is it that scholars such as ourselves come to focus on dereliction? How is it that anyone awakens to dereliction as a profound fact of life, a pervasive aspect of landscape? For most Americans dereliction is something easily overlooked, or ignored if seen. Americans believe dereliction to be concentrated geographically in impoverished central cities or in isolated rural areas, and thus avoidable as most go about daily lives. Derelict zones need be of little concern. And then suddenly experience dictates that various forms of dereliction are really all around us. Suddenly we see dereliction vividly in places of emotional importance: places where we grew up, places where we visit frequently, places where we work, places where we live. It is then that the focus sharpens. Let us begin our intellectual embrace of derelict zones by sharing those moments of discovery that compelled us to undertake this project. We would ask that the reader personally retrospect to identify similar encounters and share our experience.

Perhaps, the easiest if not the best way to communicate a remembered place is through the medium of photography. Home from college for a May weekend in 1960, one author—John Jakle—took his camera to downtown Detroit. His favorite place was not Detroit's broad impressive Woodward Avenue, but rather the narrow State and Gratiot streets where they met in short blocks either side of Woodward. Here was a congested thoroughfare lined by the city's major department stores intertwined with lesser retailers (Figure 1.1). The view in the accompanying photograph is past J. L. Hud-

Figure 1.1   Detroit's downtown was alive in 1962 with much visual excitement to recommend it, and little evidence of the collapse soon to come.

son's on the right (then one of the world's largest department stores) and Kresge's large flagship five-and-ten. In the suburbanization of America already begun, Kresge's K-Marts would leave Hudson's behind in the quest for consumer dollars.

Going downtown in 1960, whether to work or to shop, was an event of importance. People dressed accordingly—men in business suits and women in fancy dresses accented by hats and white gloves. Downtown was a special place. Streets were congested with a busyness and vitality. In 1960, downtown Detroit appeared boisterous, bustling, and certain of its future. It was an exciting place for a student about to launch a career as a professional geographer to be looking closely at landscape. A quarter of a century later he returned, a university professor attending a professional meeting. From the new Renaissance Center hotel on the riverfront, with its glitzy skylights and fountains, a walk through Detroit's downtown resulted in the retaking of past photographs. In the second photograph, taken on an April afternoon, State Street was closed as part of a new Woodward pedestrian mall (Figure 1.2). Hudson's (now Dayton-Hudson's) stands mothballed and closed to shoppers, and the other stores, Kresge's included, are closed as

Figure 1.2   Twenty-five years later Detroit's retail center was terminally ill, victim of chronic underutilization, long-term disinvestment, widespread vacancy, and substantial demolition.

well. Many buildings have been torn down and the sense of enclosure once operative has been replaced by a foreboding emptiness. There was no longer variety in storefront and signage. And the people had disappeared! Only a few commuters wend their way toward nearby parking lots at what should be rush hour. Downtown Detroit had become but a shell of its former self. From a place alive and optimistically anticipating its future, it had become a ghost of times past shirking from the future. Few people bothered to dress up to go downtown. Few people bothered to go downtown.

What was at work here? Perhaps it was the poignant nostalgia of a person who had found that he could not go home again. A feeling of profound regret was inevitable as the camera imaged a partially abandoned downtown. Places change and often not for the better—a reality to which Americans have become quite accustomed. Belief that it could or even should be otherwise tends to be met with little sympathy in America today. Can progress bring with it anything less than the massive dislocation of capital, people, and things so evident in Detroit's evacuated downtown? We will argue that, indeed, there is something more than personal loss to report. Society at large loses when we wantonly discard the important places around which we have traditionally organized our lives. We all lose when we fail to protect our coveted landscapes inherited from our past.

Change—even negative change—gives the student of landscape clear rationale for critical scholarship. But, as time passes, one becomes painfully aware that much change—indeed too much change in America—pretends unrecoverable loss. American habitats are not only becoming different, but in many ways are becoming less satisfactory for more and more people. America is not just in transition, but may be turning into something less than it has been. The evidence for this negative change is all around us in our evolving landscapes. That is what this book pretends: its thesis, if you will. It is not enough for scholars like ourselves to report on changing places. It is time for us to suggest why places change, and to suggest whether the evolution is for better or for worse. It is time to focus on the processes of change and assess them from points of view of social awareness. Such was the message that John Jakle took from his emotive discovery of dereliction at Detroit's center.

For David Wilson, intrigue with dereliction grew out of an upbringing in metropolitan New York. In the middle 1960s the Bronx had already emerged as an entrenched slum. Vast acres of dilapidated and boarded-up buildings dominated a grey and bleak landscape. Pictured is a blighted street in the contemporary Bronx (Figure 1.3). Family would take frequent excursions to the North Bronx, the place of family friends and deeply rooted social ties. Fear and fascination were provoked by the seemingly endless neglect that passed by the car window. The North Bronx, by most accounts, was an island of middle-class residency amid a larger and menacing sea of poverty. Graffitied buildings and urban grittiness had replaced well-kept structures that his father had so fondly cherished in childhood. The texture and fabric of a once nurturing area had purportedly disappeared. Family was perplexed by the magnitude of devastation.

This fear and fascination turned to anger and bewilderment when this author moved to Philadelphia in the late 1970s. North Philadelphia—a daily destination from home in the center of the city—reflected intense

Figure 1.3   Graffiti in a New York City neighborhood where rampant unemployment and poverty coexist.

devastation. Rundown buildings and idle groups of youth gave to the area a sense of despairing poverty and hopelessness (Figure 1.4). The irony of nearby gentrification made the encounter with dereliction all the more vivid. The stark juxtaposition of vibrancy and squalor was there for all to see. Here in one setting were the most extreme living conditions that society could produce. And thus, an attempt to understand this divergent production of living conditions became this author's preoccupation during graduate school.

Slowly, a working definition for dereliction emerged as this book was conceptualized. Decline begins in landscape when structures, built to contain efficiently and symbolize prescribed functions, prove less efficient. Physical obsolescence may be at work to make a facility less useful. Or demand may have slackened in the face of new technologies, making a place functionally obsolete. Disinvestment results when maintenance is withheld in a building or area in the face of declining returns. Most costs of operating a commercial facility, for example, are fixed: generally speaking, interest payments, energy costs, taxes, labor costs. By deferring maintenance, which is not fixed, profit taking can be enhanced over a short run. Disinvestment means exploiting one's physical assets. Not only does this decrease a building's usefulness, it generates physical deterioration and

Figure 1.4   In the 1970s blight in central Philadelphia played out in derelict buildings.

blight. With increased return unlikely, disinvestment is a last effort to wring profitability from the parcel. Disinvestment is thus a form of profit taking that spurs neglect and decline. This was the kind of thing that we had seen in Detroit and in New York.

Underutilization and disinvestment often dissolve into vacancy. Buildings or areas are unoccupied. Not only are repairs left unmade, but places are left unsecured and vulnerable to intrusion, theft, vandalism, and arson. Short-term vacancy speaks of transition, often normal in the course of business events. But long-term vacancy speaks overtly of failure: the inability to revitalize, producing at best a kind of inanimate suspension. Vacancy also reflects speculation, the holding in abeyance in expectation of improved future circumstances. Speculators hold assets in anticipation of increased

Figure 1.5   St. Louis's LaFayette Square, although tawdry, was still physically complete when photographed in 1962.

value given technological or other changes expected. Irrespective, vacancy often leads directly into degradation.

In 1962 John Jakle visited the St. Louis neighborhood where his father had spent much of his childhood. The photograph, taken from the front door of what had been the family home, pictures part of the LaFayette Square neighborhood along Kennett Place (Figure 1.5). This was St. Louis's first exclusive residential area built just before the Civil War. After 1900, the more affluent moved away with dwellings either subdivided into apartments or operated as boarding houses. In 1962, residents were mainly migrants from the Ozarks of Missouri and Arkansas although here and there a residual German family remained from what had been a strong ethnic community around World War I. Houses were rundown in 1962. Rental and for sale signs were numerous and a few houses stood vacant.

Figure 1.6 shows the same street in 1971. Many houses had been removed with debris filling the vacant lots. A street once solidly lined by terrace houses now displayed profound gaps, like a boxer's grin with teeth missing. Most dwellings were vacant and mere shells of their former selves. Plumbing and electrical fixtures had been stripped away, doors removed, windows shattered, and walls graffiti laden. Landlords had walked away leaving properties abandoned to vandals, and to the City of St. Louis for

Figure 1.6   Nine years later, abandonment and gross dereliction prevailed on LaFayette Square's Kennett Place.

back taxes. Here was urban desolation looking as if street warfare had been fought. Degradation certainly dominated.

Dereliction is, of course, a state of mind. Like beauty, it varies with the eye of the beholder. Its outward symbols are the results of neglect and the unwillingness or inability to care for or nurture. The neglect may be benign, a failure to repair, to spare, or to steward. Neglect may be overt in the form of deliberate destruction, the work of vandals. Individual actions, of course, are never enough to explain dereliction, for social context must be considered as well. Nonetheless, a place may be considered derelict to the extent that the symbols of disinvestment, vacancy, and degradation dominate. Where disrepair, litter, emptiness, violation, and other signs of diminished habitat prevail, a derelict zone exists in mind if not in reality. Dereliction comes at the end of a cycle of birth and decline. It more than symbolizes transition. It symbolizes failure. Dereliction communicates that a place is less than it once was. In derelict zones, satisfactions are curtailed and quality of life is diminished. Decay is etched into the everyday local fabric that dominates thinking.

Derelict zones are disorderly in the sense that a previous order is unraveling. The previous order cannot be or, at any rate, is not being maintained. Or it is not experiencing an orderly transition to becoming something else.

Dereliction can be reversed, however. Order can be wrought out of chaos through heavy doses of caring, salvaging, and repairing. A maintenance ethic can be brought to the fore even in the most desperate of situations. Downtown Detroit in the 1980s was a derelict zone substantially mothballed from total collapse, a place awaiting rebirth once expectations rose and investments flowed. What remained largely a promise along Detroit's Woodward Avenue became reality in St. Louis's LaFayette Square. When in 1986 John Jakle again visited Kennett Place, the expectation of a neighborhood reduced to vacant lots clogged by cast-off bedsprings, abandoned hulks of cars, and other refuse of poverty was not evident. Obvious instead was a place rapidly undergoing revitalization. New investment had signaled the beginning of another growth cycle. This emergence was stunning and remarkable. Not only had old buildings been completely renovated, but new structures filled once vacant lots; lawns were well maintained and gardens bloomed (Figure 1.7). Sidewalks had been rebuilt, streets repaved, and trees planted along their margins. A sense of cleanliness prevailed. Order seemingly had emerged from disorder with a population concerned with revitalization newly dominant. And yet, only a few blocks away was sustained devastation.

Most Americans—including most of our readers, we suspect—have had similar personal experiences. We all are aware that places change and that,

Figure 1.7   By 1976, LaFayette Square had been revitalized, recaptured by a gentry population whose relative affluence permitted high levels of maintenance.

as frequently as not, change is for the worse. Sometimes we find places reborn, but that is the rarer phenomenon. Going back to revisit the past is usually an experience in regret. To many Americans the past means regret. Perhaps most Americans are ambivalent to the evidences of decline about them for this reason. Mindsets operate to obscure the implications of decay, dereliction being discounted as abnormal and a deviation from prevailing norms of growth. Vacancy and abandonment are believed transitional. Americans have an extraordinary penchant to ignore dereliction. When it is recognized, Americans have a wonderful ability to rationalize it away. So strong is the American belief in progress that evidence of decline is often transformed to represent growth only temporarily stalled.

As Americans we know dereliction but have learned to deny it. And then come those highly personalized experiences that click dereliction firmly into focus, that give it context and prove it to be more pervasive in our lives than we had dared suspect. The best of those experiences prove that dereliction need not be permanent even under the poorest of circumstances. The worst of those experiences depress and engender a loss of faith for ourselves and society. Discovery may come suddenly at the most unexpected of times in the most unexpected of places. Or it may evolve slowly as new places are absorbed and experienced. Dereliction's exploration then becomes compelling. In this book, we explore outward from our own discoveries to focus not only on the realities of landscape dereliction, but on the social production of that dereliction as well. We begin by tying dereliction to concepts of change.

DERELICTION AND CHANGE

Many economists and planners see dereliction as the last stage in a filtering down process whereby places and their resources are made ready for recycling (see, for example, Birch, 1971, p. 78; Colwell, 1976, p. 2). With such thinking dereliction signals a well-functioning market as abandonment sterilizes geographical space for subsequent reuse. Without such sterilization the costs of reforming the built environment stand noncompetitive. The recycling of places, they argue, demands the development of "unspoiled" spaces (Lynch, 1972, p. 37). Unfortunately, the process of desertion can be agonizingly slow and painful for those who reside there. Also, unspoiled land might be best reserved to uses other than the rebuilding of places spoiled elsewhere. The notion that dereliction is good and even necessary begs a frontier mentality that automatically sees abandoning the old as a necessary prelude to creating the new. Vacating land may, indeed, engender new rounds of investment, but it need not always be reinvestment's precursor.

The processes of underutilization, disinvestment, vacancy, abandonment, and degradation have been ever with us. Civilizations have been built on the dust of predecessor societies seemingly without end as archaeologists bear witness. Every archaeological site may be regarded as the skeleton of a dead community (Adams, 1980, p. 23). What are the signs of death in the archaeologist's landscape? As it was with ancient Ur, so yet it might be with the urban places of today's America. William Adams provides a check list of symptoms: physical contraction, lack of new construction, dilapidation, neglect of public monuments, disorderly new development, refuse accumulation, declining standards of craftsmanship, excessive diversity in artistic expression, neglect of the dead (p. 48). We have already made witness to many of these symptoms in cursory glimpses at Detroit, New York, Philadelphia, and St. Louis. Perhaps the apologists for dereliction are correct. Dereliction may be inescapable like death itself. As we always will have derelict zones, why fight them? Why not let them die their natural deaths? We will argue that change need not be so inescapably negative.

As some see abandonment as the necessary accompaniment to change, others see waste as the necessary companion of growth, with dereliction the common outcome. The American city is seen as vibrant with expansive energy. The city is never complete, but always changing with ongoing construction and reconstruction. Litter may be the symbol of the modern city's unending self-revision. Cities are prodigiously wasteful with overloaded trash cans testifying to the vigor of perpetual self-overcoming (Conrad, 1984, p. 300). Some artists scavenge in alleys and junk shops to symbolize the city with creations made of its refuse, dereliction made an amenity and symbol of place. Detroit, New York, Philadelphia, St. Louis, and other cities are consumptive machines and we should not be surprised to find refuse a principal urban outgrowth. As this thinking goes, urban economies define their residents as consumers who destroy in their consumption. American cities are engaged in famished consumption and excretion. And, as we are a very wasteful society, why not waste places as well as things?

Change is driven by people making decisions and taking actions within social contexts substantially structured to contain and direct initiative. Change is an all-encompassing term that signifies growth, modification, transformation. It may involve decline and decay or it also may involve growth and maturation. Irrespective, neighborhoods, cities, regions, and nations are transformed by bounded human agency. Individuals enact change bearing constantly the templates of cultural, political, and economic imperatives implicit in prevailing social organization. Landscapes change as developers, builders, realtors, city managers, bankers, and other players operate to define and manipulate the built environment as commodity. They dictate the location of growth and decline. Such individuals do not arrive naked to a decision content to be clothed only by social convention. Diverse values produce surprisingly complex decisions driving change in complex ways (Weeks, 1980; Thompson, 1980; Brown, 1980). Decision making defies the simple structuralist and functionalist logic. Change is never as foreclosed as it may seem.

How then does change play out as dereliction? When is dereliction purposeful, the result of the deliberate intentionality of individuals variously playing out social roles? When is dereliction inadvertent, the result of unforeseen responses to actions taken? In American society, who can we hold responsible for derelict zones? And how can we explain actions as producing dereliction as change? In America, which institutions are critical? And who in those institutions drive the action? Why do they do so? How, in other words, is dereliction created as a social product? As Arthur Brittan notes, "Man produces himself—he creates his own social objects, and in so doing is not a passive spectator—he is by his very social nature forced into an interactive relationship with his world" (1973, p. 16). What does dereliction produce in people? In institutions? These are all basic questions about change that our recognition of dereliction in landscape has engendered. Subsequent chapters further refine these questions in focusing on the more important agents of dereliction in American society.

Decay

In the change of things, decay is the antithesis of growth. Growth and decay are integrally linked, both going on simultaneously in most places. It is only when the rate of decay overwhelms the rate of growth that dereliction is seen as setting in. Americans readily see newness in landscapes. They are predisposed to valuing places actively evolving toward something new. Americans tend to ignore decay. Americans are obsessed by youth such that they often refuse to recognize age even when confronted directly with it. Dereliction is merely aberration, deviation from things becoming, and—as associated with aging—viewed as profound misfortune (Lowenthal, 1985, p. 125). When evidence of age (including evidence of dereliction) pervades a scene, the American eagerly seeks other messages. The devotees of antiquity, including the admirers of relics and ruins, may reorient to decay most successfully, but even they emphasize decay of clear aesthetic potential, ignoring all other. Most devotees of wear and tear confess their predilection "aberrant, embarrassing, and even perverse" (p. 143).

In recent decades a sense for "civilized decay" has achieved some popularity in the United States (Finkler and Peterson, 1974, p. 63). But an aesthetic of "oldness" has only begun to emerge—a valuing of places for the images of pastness that they convey. Appreciated is a weathered encrusting that connotes history as accumulation. Civilized decay results not so much from benign neglect as from conscious sparing below the level of overt rehabilitation. Places are allowed to grow old gracefully, and the grace emergent treasured for its distinctive quality of pastness. The Vieux Carré in New Orleans is such a place. Unsanitized, a patina of time has been encouraged in the look of buildings and streets. Minimally maintained in a benevolent holding action against time, the Vieux Carré's sense of becoming always seems at least one generation retarded. The place is not a museum and yet a sense of fossilization prevails. It is a kind of orderliness in which the sense of pastness implicit in controlled decay has been made the organizing idea. Limited maintenance contributes to the effect. Not only is dereliction avoided, but a sense of newness or modernity as well.

Growth and decline results from the unfolding of seesaw investment patterns. Capital zigzags in and out of regions in response to the need for continuous growth. Beyond the economics of decay stand social realities. Scholars have been reluctant to recognize the connection between growth and decline for ideology has submerged concern with the broader sweeps of change to focus on the parts. Scholarly conceptions of everyday life abstract individual elements from broad context. This atomizing serves to marginalize the links between things with life conceptualized as an array of nominally interrelated parts. Such thinking obfuscates the influence of totalities and produces easily comprehensible cause and effect relations as it emphasizes the unfettered freedom of individuals as actors. Decay is seen as reflecting pockets of individually driven neglect at various spatial scales. Decay purportedly emerges by localized processes. Local decay, for example, is seen less as symbol for societal process than indictment of cultures, groups, and specific kinds of people. Lethargic individuals and "deviant" subcultures have been frequently singled out as cause. The poor are seen as disassociated from a work ethic, act irresponsibly, and thus perpetuate decay outside of any concern for social norms. As Susan Fainstein (1974) emphasizes, pejorative social values are ascribed whose origins purportedly lie in self-affliction rather than societal circumstance. Creators of decay, the poor, are seen to be by choice unmotivated and unwilling to cleanse dereliction. Failure to link decay to broader processes substantially perpetuates misconceptions of decline.

Beyond the romance of decay stand the hard facts of economic reality. Decline and growth operate simultaneously as functions of investment and disinvestment respectively. Uneven investment at national, regional, and local scales generate both outcomes in often vivid juxtaposition. For select areas to prosper other areas suffer. Sunbelt replenishes at the expense of snowbelt; suburb at the expense of central city; gentrified neighborhood at the expense of slum. Uneven development is the hallmark of capitalist growth. Investors swarm to areas of optimal investment; residual scraps filter elsewhere. Investment and disinvestment are integrally linked. Landscapes that are heavily disinvested—cleansed or sanitized for reuse—become likely capital recipients for a new growth cycle.

At issue is the production of geographical space for economic expansion and capitalist sustenance. As geographer Neil Smith writes, "no corner is immune from the search for raw materials; every inch of the land surface, as well as the sea, the air, and the geological substratum is reduced in the eyes of capital to a real or potential means of production, each with a price tag" (1982, p. 143). Accumulation is the engine that powers growth; it continuously reshapes our landscapes. Accumulation requires the production of geographical differentiation. Simultaneous growth and decline assure fresh room for future growth and accumulation. The engine of capitalism cannot be allowed to falter. Capitalism can and does abide change as decay.

Pastness

"Whether it is celebrated or rejected, attended to or ignored," writes geographer David Lowenthal, "the past is omnipresent" (1985, p. xv). Sparing or preserving the sense of pastness in a place can enhance life. Lowenthal presents a litany of benefits derived (p. 38). Comfort lies in the familiar and readily recognizable. Associated meanings reaffirm and validate life's course, a sense of appropriateness fostered. Places rooted firmly in the past guide as they set strong templates for group activity and individual predilection. In a nation dominated by rapidly changing places, old places reinforce norms and traditions. Different lifestyles are configured around symbols of pastness. For most Americans who by choice seek newness, oldness offers occasional escape, an occasional adventure into worlds where different values and symbols prevail. Implicit in antiquity is the sense of precedence, lineage, antecedence. Important also is continuity: the notion of cumulative creation and conjunction. There is duration if not permanence by implication.

Pastness in place is a visible accumulation of overlapping traces from successive periods, each trace modifying and modified to form a collage of no single period (Lynch, 1972, p. 171). What remains is a sense of temporal depth comprised of varying vocabularies each differentially reflecting history. Designers can borrow upon these vocabularies to configure the future, but they can never re-create the past as ad hoc accretion. Once lost, continuity layered in a locality can never be regained except in shallow replication. Relics discovered and suitably praised enlarge today's landscapes with suggestions of pastness. The evidences of change are relished. If derelict, they may need rediscovery, a sense of history reattaching in the context of contemporary values. No longer just old, or just discarded, they are made historical or even historic. Surviving remnants of a period may be noticed for their rarity and made to stand symbolic for that which has all but completely disappeared. By size or texture, relics may be seen to stand apart in the modern context, their actual history little known or appreciated but their visual appearance too deviant to be ignored.

Nostalgia is the stuff of pastness. When things become rare they assume value for their rarity. They lend themselves to commodification on the basis of rarity. Value increases when sentiments attach, especially the emotions of a generation rediscovering the symbols of its youth or the symbols of a previous generation. Rarity can be collected and in the collecting preserved albeit usually in a museum or other place where things languish out of context as a kind of cultural flotsam. Preservation usually emphasizes the elite or gentry and the once fashionable over the ordinary or common and the never fashionable. Americans have a propensity to isolate history as display rather than embrace history an integral to contemporary life (Lowenthal, 1966, p. 27). The past is especially valuable when packaged as tourist attraction well apart from the cultural mainstream for the vicarious pleasures of tourism (Jakle, 1985, p. 286).

Inadvertently, the past pervasively penetrates everyday life in the inheritance of cultural values or norms. Pastness thus helps structure everyday reality, the past in most places reflecting layers of sedimented action with each layer modifying emerging economic, political, and social realities. Each layer reflects actions of bounded individuals making choices within socially constrained contexts. But the commodification of everyday life has rendered pastness a form of escape, oldness offering an occasional adventure into worlds where different values once prevailed. Demand for escapism has facilitated appropriation of the past for commercial gain. The past is commodified, made an artifact capable of being marketed to escapist populations.

Ruins

Ruins make ideal relics. Indeed, a building may be more memorable as a ruin than whole. Ruins speak of what used to be but can be no longer. They carry a sense of sadness for what is lost. However, they also speak with evocative power from a sense of mystery. They invite the romantic. The church pictured has fallen victim to a recent fire (Figure 1.8). It conveys a sense of violation in its ruined state. It elicits sadness and even wonder, but it does so weakly for we know all too well how the building met its fate. The church is merely derelict in its present state and demands to be reroofed or torn down. The church is ruined, but it is not a ruin. Ruins

Figure 1.8   Lost to arson, this church stood derelict
on the St. Louis northside until demolished in 1988.
There was little of the romantic in its wanton destruction.

represent a balance between architecture and nature seemingly achieved
without human intervention (Zucker, 1968, p. 2). The ruin must appear not
only accidental, but mysterious in its origin: decay dimmed by time. The
pillars pictured survive a Mississippi plantation house of the nineteenth
century (Figure 1.9). Here is the stuff of romance, half hidden in a copse
of trees. So old do these remains appear, so uncertain their fate, that at
superficial glance one is tempted to suggest the epic, and at close examination one is inclined to believe that its greatness must have been ravished
as elegance and privilege were being wrought asunder. The most effective

Figure 1.9   The ruins of Windsor Plantation near Port Gibson, Mississippi, do carry the stamp of romance, for a patina of time has accumulated with a century's persistence.

ruins are those of the stupendous past, the past of legend and myth (Macauley, 1953, p. 31).

Ruins are liberated of many restrictions applicable to whole buildings (Summerson, 1963, p. 236). The psychological barrier separating spectator and user has been removed, as the sense of outside and inside has been eliminated. "Space flows through the building; the interior is seen through the glassless windows and breaches in the walls. The building has become comprehensible as a single whole, no longer an exterior plus one or more interiors but a single combination of planes in recession, full of mystery and surprise" (p. 237). People have always been attracted to ruins for the visual delight and romantic impulses easily associated. "The literature of all ages has found beauty in the dark and violent forces, physical and spiritual of which ruin is one symbol" (Macauley, 1953, p. 20).

Ruins result from earthquake, flood, tornado, and all other violent forces of nature. Ruins are also made by human agency through neglect and care-lessness and overt assault. Pleasure, and oftentimes profit, may be had from the creating and looting of ruins. Indeed, the hand of the vandal may be found on most if not all ruins. Although fashion has from time to time inspired the building of sham ruins, ruins cannot be built up so much as worn down. Purpose-built ruins look artificial, although weathering and vandalism can reduce even them to the genuine article. No ruin, therefore, endures. Like everything else, it changes. The challenge, then, is to preserve ruins, and make them appear suspended between permanence and impermanence. But the capacity of any population to maintain ruins is limited, a function of its sense of history and ability to turn them to touristic or other purposes.

Ruins are rendered by humans through neglect, carelessness, and overt assault. Usually concealed behind such actions is the hidden hand of the accumulation imperative. Buildings are fundamentally fixed capital assets that store wealth. Accumulation through rental-free extraction or production of equity renders this a profit tool. Buildings that generate profit will be maintained. Those that do not will not be maintained in most circumstances. Declining profits necessitate disinvestment as capital pursues alternative courses. This investment–disinvestment continuum takes place in the context of uneven development. Some landscapes move toward decay while others move toward revival and resurgence. Ruins reflect once vibrant parcels caught in the vice of disinvestment, a useless shell replacing a once valuable building in an ironic turn of events often outside an owner's control.

Obsolescence

In a future-oriented society such as the United States, dereliction does not pretend the romance of ruins so much as mere obsolescence. Indeed, old places, derelict or otherwise, tend to be seen simply as obsolete when they do not fit the fashions of the moment. Obsolescence involves both diminished utility and physical deterioration. Physical obsolescence implies internal decline, the stuff of diminished repair and replacement. Functional obsolescence, on the other hand, is imposed from the outside as innovations elsewhere change competitive equations, local technologies being not as efficient as those elsewhere.

Through much of the nineteenth century (as in previous centuries) artifacts tended to be used until they wore out or fell apart (Fitch, 1982, p. 29). Final dissolution was postponed as long as possible through repair. Things were cannibalized and bits and pieces salvaged for new uses in new combinations. Until this century, obsolescence was primarily a physical phenomenon, the processes of aging determining an artifact's useful life. Today, obsolescence is primarily functional, induced by the marketplace. Most apparent physical deterioration results not from long use, but from abuse. If a building or an area retains its profitability as investment, then it also retains its physical integrity. But things can become obsolete literally over-

Figure 1.10 Functional and not physical obsolescence
rules today's world of discard. The sign draped across
this hotel reads: "It's check-out time." The building is
only two decades young.

night in today's America. Witness the hotel pictured (Figure 1.10). Physically the building is solid, but economically it is obsolete. Today, new
buildings can be as vulnerable to the wrecker's ball as old.

The older a place the more likely that ossification looms problematical
(Vernon, 1966, p. 4). Layers of pavement accrue as a street repeatedly is
resurfaced. Below-ground spaces are increasingly filled by cable, sewers,
water mains. Over time, buildings are enlarged filling adjacent lots more
completely, or small buildings replaced by large ones. Each expansion
tends to make the next expansion more difficult as physical densities in-

crease. Beliefs and attitudes may ossify along a street as well, diminishing people's inclination to change. Vested interests become increasingly reluctant to innovate. In the United States, relatively few places are designed to change easily. Buildings and their machines may not even be built to facilitate repair. People are not educated in change.

A central problem of modern capitalism is the need to stimulate consumption. Goods and services, and even places, have to be cycled toward sustained investment, the purpose of capitalism being profit (the bigger, the faster, the better). Thus we find ourselves in an age of planned obsolescence where things are engineered to fail, or ornamented to fall out of style. Planned obsolescence speeds discard toward accelerated investment and profitability. Popular writer Vance Packard (1960, p. 7) has labeled the engineers of this planned obsolescence "wastemakers," and our era the "Throwaway Age." We, as a society, need our material goods to wear out.

Wastemakers—through product design, advertising promotion, and credit sales—work hard at making Americans prodigal. As Willy Loman in Arthur Miller's *Death of a Salesman* laments, "Once in my life I would like to own something outright before it's broken! I'm always in a race with the junkyard! I just finish paying for the car and it's on its last legs. The refrigerator consumes belts like a goddamn maniac. They time those things. They time them so when you've finally paid for them, they're used up" (1973, p. 73). Ours is a society of debased products, from throwaway cameras to throwaway automobiles. The automobile industry has led the way. The yearly model change traditionally has accounted for one-quarter of what Americans pay for their cars (Wachtel, 1983, p. 148). American industry has stopped stressing durability and quality. Indeed, planned obsolescence is carried so far that some merchandise regularly fails to survive shipment to market. Repair is so difficult that replacement is usually easier and cheaper.

Functional obsolescence causes dereliction. Houses, industries, stores, landscapes, and regions are rendered obsolete under the vagaries of changing technologies, cultural predilections, and investment opportunities. With disinvestment physical decline follows. Lost utility means resource diversion, energy, capital, and technical expertise flowing elsewhere to nurture or create other landscapes. The mediary of the marketplace is crucial. The market defines landscapes of replenishment, stability, and decline. In the metropolis, outer suburbs are inundated with investment while central areas rapidly lose, dereliction emerging from investor neglect. Abandoned buildings, slums, and deindustrialized regions illustrate obsolete entities unable to attract investment to keep the pace of growth ahead of decline.

Powerful elements of society induce landscape obsolescence by sanctioning uneven investment. Planners, politicians, and economists voice the need to steer investment. The concentration of capital is purportedly economically prudent and efficient—it creates "positive fiscal impacting," "maximum leveraging," and "optimal resource targeting." These euphemisms are socially accepted slogans for replenishing selected landscapes and ignoring others (see Cybriwsky et al., 1986; Wilson, 1989). In New York City, the metaphors of "urban resurgence" and "progressive upgrading" have helped generate the Manhattan renaissance amid sustained decline in the outer boroughs. In Indianapolis, the "drive for livability" and "core replenishment" has permitted affluent downtown restructuring. Philadelphia elites have restructured much of the center city by reference to "downtown renewal." Examined closely, however, such investment concentration and associated rhetoric is a capitalist growth tactic. Room for expansion is necessary; uneven development differentiates geographical space to create growth outlets. Landscapes rendered obsolescent and in decay provide renewed opportunities for future accumulation, property devaluation setting the stage for future investment. The irony here is the important societal role that obsolescence plays. Obsolescence is often seen as lacking social value—but, in the wider view, is a necessary precondition for profit extraction.

DEPRECIATION AND IMPERMANENCE

Everything deteriorates and everything someday will be obsolete. That things decline should not be surprising. What does surprise is the apparent widespread reluctance in America to counter deterioration. Not only do we fail to renew or steward the resources of the built environment, but we have institutionalized the neglect. Tax laws and accounting procedures encourage waste. Over the past quarter century, commercial buildings have come increasingly to be financed on the accounting charges for depreciation. Depreciation has come to mean a deduction against taxes unreflective of a property's actual physical or functional reality (Sternlieb, 1980, p. 63). Depreciation charges now stand as incentives to investment rather than as sources of maintenance funds.

Until World War II, most buildings were assumed to have a 40-year useful life, and were depreciated, accordingly, at a steady 2.5 percent rate each year. Depreciation was viewed as a set-aside charge in anticipation of ultimate replacement. Beginning in the 1950s owners of new commercial buildings were allowed to accelerate depreciation in order to generate large tax deductions early in a project's life. Accelerated depreciation, coupled with Internal Revenue Service rulings allowing investors to deduct interest expenditures and real estate taxes directly from income, vigorously stimulated new construction at the expense of rehabilitating old. Only since the late 1970s have similar incentives been extended to selected categories of older building. For a new project 90 percent financed by loans in the 1960s, an investor in the 70-percent tax bracket investing $100,000 could recoup, even before construction began, some $77,000 through the federal tax system (Mayer, 1978, p. 338). Thus much new construction was begun not for the probable profits to be derived so much as for the certainties of tax advantage.

Depreciation charges taken for investment rather than for replacement purposes represents a disinvestment incentive built into new construction from the very beginning. Buildings are flimsily built on the realization that durability is superfluous to the investment cycle. Buildings that are intended to be written off quickly need not be durable. They need only function efficiently for the short run before capital gains are taken, and the cycle of tax incentives repeated elsewhere. Tax laws and related accounting procedures have not engendered permanency in the American landscape. Maintenance is postponed for an investment's duration; property may or may not be upgraded with a change in ownership as dictated by market expectations. Repair when it comes is cyclical or indefinitely postponed. Clearly, the original intention of the depreciation idea has been perverted. Rather than encouraging maintenance, depreciation allowances encourage neglect and dereliction. The system builds landscapes amenable to profit extraction rather than human permanency. Investment incentives foster fluid investment and often rampant speculation. Landscapes emerge as arenas for capital accumulation. Lost in the shuffle are "use values" whereby sentiments attach to a landscape through people living, working, or leisuring in a place.

Accelerated depreciation was introduced to stimulate new construction and, thereby, stimulate economic growth, the building industry having convinced Congress of its special role as economic catalyst. However, emphasis on new construction has meant a deemphasis on rehabilitation. Why upgrade old buildings when extensive tax benefits accrue from building new? Thus disinvestment and dereliction in the nation's older places, especially in central cities and rural areas, stand linked directly to shoddiness in new places, especially in big-city suburbs. Tax policies link actual and eventual declines in environmental quality in places old and new. Clearly, the principal objective of modern capitalists is not to build permanency at the landscape scale. The building industry, for example, functions not to produce human, durable environments, but only profitable ones. The shorter the cycle of investment and the more frequent the turnover of capital, the more potential profit there is to be made.

Depreciation refers to commodity loss of value. For our purpose, it signifies declining value of buildings, land, commodities. Implicit in the concept of depreciation is the treatment of landscape as "exchange value." As sociologists John Logan andHarvey Molotch (1987, p. 1) emphasize, a floor beneath, a roof above, and walls all around make for a commodity. Buildings—indeed, habitats generally—are places to be purchased and sold, rented and leased, pumped for profit and eventually discarded. This commodification of everyday life, so pronounced in American society, renders landscapes market constructions. There is little room for accumulated sentiment as attachment to place. Thus, depreciation is the downside of place commodification. It unfolds negatively for a place when entrepreneurs take their investment capital elsewhere, failing to renew or replace in place.

Scholars have long speculated on the seemingly inescapable cycles of life and death as societies, nations, and even empires have been seen to rise and fall. The world has always been a place of impermanence. Sociologist Daniel Bell (1978, p. 82) sees societies passing through specific phases toward decline: stepwise transformations from simplicity to luxury, and from asceticism to hedonism. In hedonism, people become competitive with one another for luxuries and lose the ability to share and sacrifice as community. They prove less able to control spontaneous impulse, thus less able to bring order and purpose into life. Historian Arnold Toynbee (1947, p. 578) sees a breakdown of creative power among society's elite, who then become merely a dominant minority; this results in a withdrawal of allegiance on the part of the majority, who then become merely the nemesis. Carlo Cipolla (1970, p. 9) sees an intractable resistance to change operating where success has bred conceit and self-complacency. Institutions then become rigid in their obsolescence. "More people think in terms of 'rights' rather than in terms of 'duties,' in terms of 'enjoyment' rather than in terms of 'work' " (p. 12). Increasingly, life becomes organized around old myths no longer applicable.

Decline in America may be rooted less in the unwillingness to change and more in the fact of too much change. And the rate of change is ever accelerating, producing what Alvin Toffler (1970, p. 11) has called "future shock": "the dizzying disorientation brought on by the premature arrival of the future." Life is increasingly transient being unanchored by enduring relationships. Everything seems ephemeral. The environment changes constantly both as container of activity and as social symbol. Change is institutionalized to the point of being America's most constant dimension. Change is universal. Change is omnipresent. Through tax laws, for example, physical depreciation is made reality, as a kind of self-fulfilling prophecy. These mechanisms promote impermanence such that impermanence seems natural in its expectation. America changes, but most Americans do not know why.

It may be that Americans have forgotten how to change with finesse in their quest for unending economic growth. We may be rigidly adhering to now anachronistic forms of change, comfortable and conceited in economic beliefs now anachronistic. We seem unable to resist the impulse of change for change's sake. Proponents of slow growth or no growth have been heard, but little heeded. Much of what we create we render obsolete almost immediately in the name of progress. Americans have forgotten how to create permanence, if ever they knew. They have forgotten or have never learned how to systematize renewal that allows incremental progress of a stable sort. Horizons remain horizons close at hand. Increasingly, the view is not the distant view. We depreciate quickly.

Impermanence is imprinted everywhere on our landscapes. Downtowns lose vibrancy, gentrifiers supersede the poor in some neighborhoods, the poor escape the total abandonment of other neighborhoods. Individuals respond in logical ways. Cycles of fashion become shorter as a sense of urgency and speed runs through much of modern urban life. "Each generation expects not to hand on a tradition but to be rendered obsolete, along with its artifacts and environments, by the next generation," writes Edward Relph (1987, p. 129). Each generation rejects the past and, in turn, expects to be rejected by the future. Generations consequently restructure landscapes to suit their own purposes. Accelerated change, coupled with pervasive disregard for the past and its symbols, demands that the world be remade to the moment. Thus the world is rendered an ever-changing entity with little sense of completeness allowed. The ephemeral remains as few landscapes mature to ultimate fulfillment. Americans are a people who never arrive. They only depart. The places that they create are evanescent. All seems impermanent; and in impermanence, much seems disordered.

THE CONTRAST OF MAINTENANCE

Permanence and order reside in maintenance. Maintenance is an act of keeping. Capital, time, skill, and energy are directed toward maintaining something in condition to perform efficiently the function for which it was built. Such expenditures do not increase utility, for that would be more appropriately called a "betterment" (Boyce, 1975, p. 135). Maintenance preserves value, ensuring a thing's intended useful life rather than extending it (Figure 1.11). When maintenance is deferred, usefulness declines due to physical impairment. Not only does a building or an area then meet its functional demands less successfully, but it appears to be less successful, its social symbolism changed. Negative cycles are set up between appearances and maintenance with low maintenance inviting even lower maintenance. Deferred maintenance creates clear visual signals that the future is uncertain.

Figure 1.11   Areas of high maintenance stand in sharp contrast to the nation's derelict zones.

Americans have long been able to avoid many of the realities of maintenance. We have been a people long used to deferring repair. William Burch writes, "There has always been a new valley over the hill, a new forest or a new waterfront to use up. When the forest was gone or the soil was lost, we simply left the mess for some unknown future" (1981, p. 11). Americans traditionally have sought to cleanse not by repairing the world around them, but by moving on to some unspoiled world, to a new utopia. Alexis de Tocqueville (1956, p. 68), that insightful nineteenth-century French visitor whose writings so stimulate scholars even yet, noted the American penchant for the ephemeral. In America, life was simply too decentralized to support high maintenance. As there was a lack of central authority encouraging orderliness, everything seemed always slightly out of control.

"Uniformity or permanence of design, the minute arrangement of details, and the perfection of administrative system, must not be sought for in the United States," de Tocqueville wrote. "What we find there is the presence of a power which, if it is somewhat wild, is at least robust, and an existence checkered with accidents, indeed, but full of animation and effort" (p. 68). Americans, he suggested, are "indifferent to the fate of the spot which they inhabit."

Maintenance is not an attempt to stop change for it is impossible to fossilize places completely. As repair seeks to conserve a preordained order, it must adapt continuously to changing uses and activities. Repair is an organic process embracing a gradual sequence of change—so gradual that a thing or a place only appears not to change. Maintenance seeks to keep an environment balanced, with attention to detail lying at the heart of the exercise. It is the constant attending to small matters that leads to the sense of homeostasis. Americans of the frontier mind have little attended to details. Change is allowed to take its course in both little and big jumps in apparent disequilibrium.

No modern commentator on the American scene has been so taken with the question of maintenance as Eric Hoffer (1969; 1982), the longshoreman of San Francisco's docks turned philosopher. To Hoffer, maintenance is a war with nature, with an aura of grandeur about it. There is grandeur in the intense trifling with detail. "The routine of maintenance: I see it as a

Figure 1.12   Without constant maintenance, dereliction is assured.

defiance of the teeth of time," he wrote (1969, p. 114). The built environment represents a separation from nature that has to be constantly maintained lest nature prevail (Figure 1.12). "At the edge of every human habitation, nature lies in wait ready to move in and repossess what man has wrestled from its grasp" (p. 116). To Hoffer (1982, p. 347), high maintenance levels reflect a community's vigor and stamina. "It is easier to build than to maintain. Even a lethargic or debilitated population can be galvanized for a while to achieve something impressive, but the energy which goes into maintaining things in good repair day in, day out is the energy of true vigor," he argued (1969, p. 114). Building is easy. Keeping something going is the difficult task.

The American frontier of seemingly unspoiled nature and infinite resources is long gone. Today we live in a finite world of shrinking resources; and yet, frontier mentalities regarding maintenance persist. The drive for change continues, insufficiently tempered by impulses to conserve and preserve. The quest for sustained growth continues to leave decay in its wake. Ultimately, of course, the nation will be forced to make the transition from a world of unbridled change to one of conservation through maintenance. This change, however, appears yet far in the future.

In the building trades, maintenance is considered inferior to new construction. Custodians, as a class, carry with them little prestige, and no glamour. Systematic maintenance as an engineering art is still largely restricted to the tending of machines. If factories in the 1950s began to place more emphasis on preventive maintenance, then the 1960s and the 1970s found more concern to design machines for maintainability. Not only are maintenance schedules more frequently built into equipment, but parts are standardized and made easily accessible. And repair procedures are made expedient in order to reduce lost operating time. "Terotechnology" (*tero* meaning to take care of) has come to the fore as a means of reducing operating losses and increasing profit (Srinivasan and Srinivasan, 1986, p. 15). Enhanced reliability results from attention to particulars: operating procedures clearly established and tolerances identified; probabilities of failure calculated and causes, effects, and frequency analyzed; performance documented through systematic inspection and testing; and repair tools and materials provided.

Cost effectiveness in the factory requires planning, estimating, scheduling, performing, reporting, and evaluating. After initial troubleshooting where imperfections are eliminated, repairs generally decline until the end of a machine's life cycle when breakdowns accelerate as it wears out. Functional obsolescence may abort physical repair where an old technology is no longer efficient, inviting betterment rather than maintenance. Where old technologies are retained, repair may require special skills and an even temperament. Maintenance tends to attract older, more experienced people who matured with the facilities they repair. The typical maintenance job is too small to require teams of journeymen variously skilled. Rather, maintenance usually necessitates wide-ranging abilities vested in individuals who operate alone. The effective maintenance person monitors, corrects, and periodically overhauls by bringing the requisite skills, tools, and materials together systematically.

Maintenance is a process of restoring. It reflects individual initiative at preserving value. It is often undertaken to preserve equity in property whether it be a single house or a neighborhood. Blight is, according to planners James Hughes and Kenneth Bleakly (1975, p. 57), the defect of modern society. It eats away regions, cities, and neighborhoods. Left unattended, it may prove contagious, diffusing across space to engulf vast land tracts with whole landscapes rendered uninhabitable. Such contagion is the American property owner's great dilemma. Fixed capital investments represent significant expenditures for most people. Maintenance must be continuous and substantive for property values to be sustained. Lack of maintenance may fuel a trajectory of decline that is geometrically self-reinforcing. Progressive deterioration compounds blight and disinvestment. It signals declining value and loss of energy to maintain. Without maintenance, dereliction looms.

Maintenance levels in America are not among the very highest in the world. Except in certain growth industries, business seems most inclined today toward deferred maintenance. In the public sector, streets, bridges, and other public utilities are in widespread decay. Whole areas are being abandoned in our older cities; agriculture is declining rapidly across a broad extent of rural America. Deindustrialization, central city decline, neighborhood abandonment, and rural decay are the emphases of this book yet to come. For now, we have been content to offer a definition for dereliction across the spectrum of underutilization, disinvestment, vacancy, abandonment, and overt degradation. We have explored dereliction's implications for change viewed through the lens of decay, pastness, ruins, obsolescence, depreciation, and impermanence. Against the negative impulses of decline, we have placed the positive impulses of maintenance.

Our purpose in the chapters that follow is to excite the reader's eye toward recognizing dereliction in the landscape, and, more importantly, to stimulate the mind toward understanding its meaning. What does it look like in its various manifestations? What does it represent for the people who create it, and abide it? We want to sensitize the reader to changes occurring in the recent past that pretend dereliction in the built environment. When

Americans look back to places important earlier in their lives, most find not only change, but decline. Clearly, there is a new sense of becoming in America. It is not the boisterous enthusiasm for a certain better tomorrow that was prevalent in the past, but a somewhat sober realization that tomorrow may be disappointing. Many suspect, and some pretend to know, that the nation's abilities to reproduce a new version of itself every generation may be on the ebb. What does the landscape tell us about all of this? What can we learn from America's derelict zones?

In this chapter we have begun to examine the forces that create and emerge out of landscape dereliction. These processes are seen as contextually driven, an outgrowth of a capitalist society. The form they take is locally specific. This recognition preserves the intentional character of human agency but embeds it within acknowledged institutional templates for action. The importance of individuals is retained even while identifying the context within which human action takes place. A causative whole emerges that recognizes a multiplicity of influences bound in time and space.

2

Underlying Cultural Values

Cultural values ascribe norms and meanings to everyday life as they infuse daily events with relevance and significance. Cultural values may be overtly expressed as ideologies around which people rally publicly for various purposes or they may be covert, held only in private and rarely expressed openly. Cultural values reference being in the world as a social animal as they assign relative worth and value. To the extent that they are widely shared across a population and structure values and norms, they carry power to organize the world conceptually. They raise whole categories of things to prominence, obscuring or rejecting other categories. Cultural values define the standards by which lives are lived.

Cultural values serve as a background against which individual and group actions may be examined. There is, of course, danger in overgeneralizing. Only the broadest value judgments widely shared can be identified. And how these values play out in any given social circumstance cannot be predicted with any certainty. Professed preferences do not translate directly into specific behaviors. They do, however, set standards against which real behavior can be evaluated. What people think and say and what they do rarely follow direct, simple, linear progressions. But knowing a group's shared beliefs and attitudes enables commentators to assign probabilities or establish expectations and evaluate behavior. Conflicting values can be identified and studied as a basis for comprehending social difference, social inequality, social deviance, social conflict.

Why should we be concerned with cultural values in a study of derelict zones? Having taken the stance of structuration theory, why do we outline selected cultural values seen traditionally to underlie America's concern for environment? Simply stated, cultural values structure everyday life. They filter the influence of general societal forces and imperatives by infusing them with meanings. Culture represents a lens that refracts general influences to define local norms, values, and expectations. Culture therefore both enables and constrains everyday life conduct as it provides the often unacknowledged boundedness that structures local actions. Cultural values, therefore, provide the "rationalization" by which social relationships become regularized as social structure. They represent the glue of social construction. Structuration theory provides a scaffolding for explanation that embraces both human agency and social structure. Concern with cultural values, we argue, is a necessary prelude to both considerations. This, then, becomes our principal question: which values seem to drive dereliction—either as individual initiative, or as defining context for such initiative?

Cultural values, of course, are molded within society's predominant institutions. In the United States, the market is a prime arbitrator of value. The engine of the capitalist economy as modified politically by government provides the grand, all-encompassing arena. It becomes our purpose, therefore, not only to identify significant cultural values driving and containing dereliction in America today, but also to identify the principal value manipulators—to signify which interests in society benefit from dereliction and thus promote it. How are professed values—especially ideologies—used to promote advantages for some Americans and disadvantages for others? What serves as gainful leverage for society's advantaged usually serves society's disadvantaged quite differently.

Professed cultural values can be invoked for a host of purposes. They can be used to categorize people, for example, as good or bad or as deserving or undeserving. They can be used to define problems by assigning blame. They can be used to invoke solutions by limiting options. They can be used to reward by assigning benefits. Rarely is a major initiative undertaken by business or government without an invoking of basic principles by way of justifying action. Actions launched are promoted and defended in terms of self-evident "truths" seen as setting contextual templates for action. Thus do some people create, sustain, and benefit while others often suffer. Truths that stand as obvious require little thought. Actions invoked for the sake of such truths—even extraordinary actions—are made normative. Frequently invoked values may become codified as a part of a society's mythology.

Myths provide a storehouse of adjustive responses whereby people relate to themselves and their environment. Myths simplify human socialization—and, thereby, environmental manipulation—by providing ready guidance. A myth is a frequently told story, referred to by label or allusion, that explains a problem (Robertson, 1980, p. 6). Very often the problem is paradoxical in its complexity, filled with inconsistencies that seemingly defy reason. But the retelling of the story, or the use of its labels, carries for those informed a satisfying sense that the contradictions stand resolved. Participation in the myth is taken to be an explanation, a structured understanding.

Cultural values are not static, summing to some manipulative sense of cultural imperative. There is no superorganic "culture," adherence to which governs one's outlook on life and thus one's behavior. Rather, values are constantly being negotiated as people use them in interacting with one another. Values change in the symbolic interactions of a community: the legislating and interpreting of news, the teaching of morals and ethics, the conducting of business, the raising of children, neighboring. Myths are sustained in a society to the extent that they successfully enlighten as easily remembered formulas. To the degree that adjustive responses fail to satisfy, new values may be embraced and new myths hammered out. Values denote a people's basic assumptions about good and bad, proper and improper (Turner and Musick, 1985, p. 4). They provide selective orientation toward experience, implying deep commitment or repudiation (Kluckholn, 1961, p. 18). Values are not held in isolation, but as components of value systems ordered in hierarchies of meaning (Barbour, 1980, p. 60). They form a set of rules whereby contexts for action are identified and choices ordered. Values direct people's thoughts about what should or ought to exist in a given situation, as well as their empirical beliefs about what actually does exist.

Values often clash. The individual in facing a problem or in anticipating an action will necessarily order his or her priorities, variously rejecting or compromising some values while embracing others. Psychologist Abraham Maslow (1968, p. 152) has suggested a basis for ordering values in a hierarchy of human need comprising survival, security, belonging, self-esteem, and self-actualization. Food, shelter, health, and protection from hazard are requisite to enhanced sociability as implied by social acceptance, ego enhancement, and fulfilled potentiality. Physical well-being must be satisfied before individuals can attend to such concerns as nature curiosity, creative activity, aesthetics, and intellectualization (Miller, 1971, p. 6). It is toward basic wants that human action is directed, competitive values shaping courses taken.

TRADITIONAL AMERICAN VALUES

Perhaps no other people in history so carefully expound their basic values as do Americans. Substantially codified into law, American values are subject to continued testing in the courts. Perhaps more important, so also are values brought constantly to the fore in the nation's marketplace—value allusion made a basis of salesmanship. Thus, certain myths have come to be widely recognized by most Americans as their society's traditional organizing principles (Therkildson, 1964, p. 15). The constant reassertion of these values provides a sense of cultural anchorage; they are touchstones of social legitimacy.

Self-improvement has been a primary motivating force in American history. Personal aggrandizement, whether for basic sustenance, safety, health, wealth, or religious fulfillment, propelled a largely European population to North America over nearly four centuries. Opportunity has been the byword. Although individuals formed communities to achieve their goals, the central idea was one of improving oneself as an individual; or at least that is how we tend to remember the American past today. Community, on the other hand, has been valued primarily as nurturing circumstance in proportion to an individual's, a family's, or, more recently, a corporation's ability to succeed. The primary impulse is to achieve success through one's own initiative and competence. Aside from the institution of black slavery, America was developed by people who were dissatisfied with life as they had known it elsewhere, and who, by moving, sought to improve life in a new place. America was and largely remains, in this view, a land of opportunity, although such an assertion is very much a cliché today—so mythlike has the idea of individual opportunity become. Equally as stereotypic is the "self-made man" (or woman), the American whose opportunities have been seized and fulfilled through individual initiative alone.

Freedom of action is seen as necessary to self-improvement, the individual requiring scope whereby expectations can be set and fulfilled. Freedom may be defined as an absence of external constraint (Barbour, 1980, p. 70). Eighteenth-century liberal thinkers interpreted freedom primarily as the absence of state coercion in private affairs. Authors of the U.S. Constitution were concerned to protect the individual against the power of government and thus to encourage individual initiative in economic affairs, especially through the use of private property. Freedom and the rights of private property are seen in the United States as closely intertwined. Freedom requires choice among genuine alternatives—a range of real options and the power to act on alternatives once chosen (p. 71). The relative absence of political restraint and the availability of economic alternatives of action traditionally have given Americans their sense of independence, especially in the buying and selling of property.

Civil liberty—the political circumstance of being free—involves both negative freedom (limits to the powers of government such as censorship, arbitrary arrest, and the taking of property without due process) as well as positive freedom (accessibility to government such as electing officials and influencing their decision making). Freedom of speech, assembly, and press are defended in the United States both as basic human rights and as necessary preconditions for democracy. Democracy is built around institutions for political self-determination through which all individuals may, if they so choose, have an influence on political decision making. Civil liberties are also necessary to a smoothly functioning competitive economy based on the private ownership of property and capital. People (and corporations) must have room to act imaginatively within circumscribed yet fluid political arenas.

Whereas Americans have been guaranteed degrees of access to political decision making, and enjoy a high degree of political equality accordingly, they have not been guaranteed equal access to the nation's economic resources. Wealth has been increasingly pyramided up the social hierarchy through an economic aristocracy's ownership and control of corporate enterprise. Yet, systems of advancement still function in most economic sectors, offering mobility to persons socially skilled if not technically competent. A myth of economic opportunity thrives, emphasizing American self-made men and women who are more economic animals than political. Perhaps this emphasis reflects the American penchant for the immediately useful, especially in a materialistic sense. Certainly, the dollar earned and invested or spent is more important than the ballot cast. Indeed, most Americans— for all their sense of independence—have been content to conform over the generations to rather narrow political consensuses, especially when galvanized by charismatic leaders.

Conformity has always been a part of the American character, even if not a professed value. Alexis de Tocqueville (1956, p. 18) wrote in the nineteenth century of the tyranny of the majority: barriers raised against individuals by prevalent forms of consensus. He saw a frightening oneness of thought in most political and even economic circumstances that led to a drab social sameness. "Men tend to be 'lost in the crowd' of their fellows; they lose respect for their own freedom and individuality, and so become grossly indifferent to the free expressions of individual thought, taste and desire on the part of all others" (p. 21). Democracy, as practiced in de Tocqueville's America, was a "great leveler." Divergent behavior was almost always viewed negatively. Geographer Wilbur Zelinsky (1975, p. 44) sees this drive to conformity, which persists today, as rooted in geographical mobility. Lacking a secure base in clan, neighborhood, or any other system of mutual dependence, the individual has been impelled to a series of political causes, clubs, fraternal organizations, professional societies, churches, jobs, and other shallow, transient associations. The American is a joiner. "Masses of insecure individuals find refuge and solace in mob camaraderie, in mass conformity within narrowly prescribed ranges of individualistic behavior" (Zelinsky, 1975, p. 44).

As an ideal, community has received short shrift in America. Certainly, the inclination to move constantly in search of economic opportunity has undermined community. To achieve *gemeinschaft* (society characterized by close personal connections among members) people need to be rooted in place over long periods of time. Instead, *gesellschaft* (society integrated by formal contract) dominates. More importantly, the heritage of individualism has emasculated the spirit of cooperation necessary for gemeinschaft. Thus, improvement in America has been a self-centered rather than communally oriented proposition. Private satisfactions have been preferred over public benefits.

In America today, success lies in the ultimate fulfillment of self. Although the measures of success are varied and applied only with difficulty, at base is the assessment of affluence or economic worth. Although individuals may exert little or no control over the forces of production as owners or managers of businesses, they can still function as consumers, and thus define personal well-being in terms of lifestyle. If one cannot emulate society's elites in controlling the marketplace, at least one can fully participate in that market as a consumer of goods and services.

There are, we believe, two principal ways by which Americans traditionally have sought self-fulfillment—a paradox of opposing values. The first, and by far the most important, is work embracing: the so-called "work ethic." Status is taken from diligent employment as well as from the results of that employment. The second is work avoiding: status that derives from achieving in reverse proportion to effort expended. The former is more a pursuit of competence linked to reward; the latter, more a pursuit of indulgence linked to leisure. Political liberty, and the economic individualism it has sustained, has been clearly linked to the work ethic—an impulse usually tied to Protestant Christianity's sense of divinely ordained "calling": diligence in work taken as a sign of moral and spiritual excellence (Cawelti, 1965, p. 168). However, work avoidance is also sustained by political liberty, and the outlook of individualism. In America, people are free not to work if they so choose. Those who do not work are free to consume in leisure to the extent that resources permit.

Work-embracing Americans have been viewed as pragmatic, concerned in de Tocqueville's terms not for "the lofty and the perfect, but for the quick and the useful" (1956, p. 18). They "prefer the useful to the beautiful and . . . require that the beautiful should be useful." From this utilitarian bent comes a mechanistic vision. Manipulating the physical world toward personal benefit is seen to have wrought a garden from the wilderness, and cities from the garden in the subduing of nature. Science has provided the organizing principles not only to engineer new physical habitats, but to engineer new human institutions as well, especially in the creation of public and corporate bureaucracies. The manipulative stance toward the world has bred an activism seen as traditionally central to the American being (Turner and Musick, 1985, p. 14). Problems are solved in the most rational and efficient manner possible, with restless dispatch. Manipulative rationality has led work-embracing Americans to seek change in a never-ending quest for progress. The motivating force is the persisting belief that environments and institutions can be improved toward greater efficiency and profitability. These Americans expect change and promote change for its own sake. They see themselves as agents of reform through change.

Americans long have considered themselves a moral people. Morality, of course, is seen to reflect in work; immorality, in laziness and leisuring. Americans have been quick to see such things in simplistic black and white: to see the inherent rightness or wrongness in situations, irrespective of complexities. There has been little room in American pragmatism for shades of grey (Turner and Musick, 1985, p. 17). Most Americans profess belief in a Supreme Being, and are nominally, at least, members of an organized church (Barbour, 1980, p. 74). Most work-embracing Americans see their country as progressive in its change, and their system of governance and related economic realities as inherently right—even divinely sanctioned. As an extension of the self-improvement bias focused on work, these Americans suffer a cult of "messianic perfectionism" (Zelinsky, 1975, p. 61). They would spread their values to others. They would share their gospel of achievement with the remainder of the world, often with missionary zeal. And indeed, the world beyond has proved very receptive to such American ideals (Figure 2.1).

Individualism and Community in America

The term individualism is relatively new. In Europe, it long remained synonymous with selfishness and social anarchy (Arieli, 1964, p. 193). In America, it has meant self-determination, freedom of action, liberty. Coined by the socialistic Saint-Simonian movement, it depicted for Europeans the conditions of industrial capitalism. Uprooted without common ideals and beliefs, workers were seen as ruthlessly exploited in the misery of their social fragmentation. In the United States, where the ideas of John Locke and other libertarians of the Enlightenment were given full sway, the quest for human dignity was translated into organizing principles for government whereby the rights of individuals were specifically protected from state abuse. Individualism meant the pursuit of individual happiness. Not until the American Revolution was the sovereignty of a people composed of free and equal individuals made the basis for the formation of a state and a nation. "And not until the Revolution was the idea of independence for the

Figure 2.1 Symbols of American liberty, freedom, and independence appear frequently in advertising not only in the United States, but abroad. Here a billboard in Ireland reminds those who have lost friends to American opportunities that America is but a phone call away.

individuals in a society made the goal of a whole nation" (Robertson, 1980, p. 71).

Thomas Jefferson's wording of the Declaration of Independence was the public statement of the complex ideas and feelings that governed the American idea of freedom. It summarized belief in the essential goodness of people, and the value of common sense. Benjamin Franklin's autobiography was the form the idea took when it was embodied in the story of an individual's life. It proclaimed the possibilities of the individual as organized into societies of his own devising. "Together, Jefferson and Franklin provided the outline for America's sense of universe, and man's place in it: the style, the myth, the dream, the official faith" (Carter, 1977, p. 30). Reason, moderation, decency, and civil behavior were the highest qualities of social being. "We hold these truths to be self-evident, that all men are created equal, that they are endowed by their Creator with certain unalienable Rights, that among these are Life, Liberty and the Pursuit of Happiness."

The successes of the American Republic led to a rethinking of individualism as a concept in nineteenth-century America. Ralph Waldo Emerson stood committed to the individual, and to individual self-improvement. Emerson justified democracy by focusing on the human potentialities that the system released. Government could perform no higher function than to elicit the best from its citizenry by allowing them to elicit the best from themselves. When coupled with Herbert Spencer's Darwinian views of society, such thinking justified the very economic circumstances that the Saint-Simonians decried. Individuals, equal before the law, were seen as locked in competitive struggle in the marketplace from which only the strong and truly gifted emerged dominant. Competitive enterprise was lionized, enabling elites to stabilize their position inside the framework of the new democracy. Individualism provided an ideology to explain success and its privileges while holding out the promise of success to others—even those trapped in economic relationships of little potential personal benefit.

No aspect of life in America escaped the cult of the individual. In religion, new beliefs of the heart came to the fore, diminishing the power of authoritarian churches. The individual was encouraged to look for spiritual guidance within himself or herself, enhancing the new mood of egalitarianism. Introspective preoccupation with self-wrought new sciences of human behavior invariably focused on the individual. As physical science analyzed nature according to its fundamental elements, so too society was viewed as composed of discrete, autonomously functioning individuals (Waterman, 1984, p. 10). Priority went to understanding the individual's quest for fulfillment, an intrigue given substantial momentum both in Europe and the United States by the writings of Sigmund Freud. "The self therefore became the central psychological construct with positive value attached to self-realization, self-control, self-esteem, and other ways of acting which reflect personal, internalized standards" (ibid.).

Nowhere was individualism more highly regarded than on America's nineteenth-century western frontier (Figure 2.2). An open country was seen to draw forth those with initiative and courage. The pioneering American was seen to draw on inner resources toward the shaping of personal destinies in a competition set up with self, with others, and with the environment. This kind of individualism was not to be mistaken for freedom to choose deviant political and economic practices. Individuals were expected to operate individually, but in similar ways. Everyone was to compete against everyone else, but for the same things. Out of this competition, communal good would follow naturally, as Adam Smith asserted in promoting laissez-faire economics. Communal good derived when successful competitors turned energy and initiative into creating economic opportunities for others. The entrepreneur was most highly prized—not only in the newly settled farmlands of the West, but in the burgeoning commercial and factory towns and cities nationwide, as well. The industrialist, who created

Figure 2.2   Perhaps the cowboy stands as the quintessential personification of American individualism. The cowboy strides into the American imagination as a lingering manifestation of an idealized western frontier.

new markets for new products, was perhaps the most highly prized entrepreneur of all.

Competitive individualism breeds loneliness and alienation in self-absorption. Americans have been taught to "do your own thing" and "look out for yourself." Cooperative effort and mutual interdependence in human relationships are devalued. The insecurities inherent in a competitive individualism have spawned a scarcity psychology. "There is always more to get, more to hang on to, and more to lose" (Parenti, 1983, p. 47). And the individual is the one who must achieve and defend.

Americans little think of themselves as rooted in a matrix of enduring social ties and relationships anchored in place. "Our view of self is that it is 'portable'; it can be carried around from place to place fully intact, and then plugged in wherever necessary" (Cochran, 1985, p. 9). Movement is a kind of magic that keeps expectations high, if not opportunities immediate. The functioning community is undermined by exaggerated mobility with its cycling of people through places. Commitments to public goals are prematurely terminated in the flux of ebb and flow. Paradoxically, people in new places do interact intensely, jockeying, if you will, to place themselves in new social contexts. The communal impulse was especially apparent on the isolated frontier, where individual initiative was combined with intense cooperation as people sought to establish themselves in alien environments. Cooperation was as much a legacy of the frontier as individualism—something the latter-day preoccupation with individualism has obscured.

Community is, of course, necessary to individual fulfillment. Without stable social context, there is no basis for competition; and without competition, no sense of success. Life is a constant round of negotiations other-directed. People are not isolates like atoms, but are bonded together in the molecular structures of social networks—the "structure" of society. Individualistic thinking, nonetheless, has come to dominate American political and economic thought. "Private man" has come to dominate "public man." People's wants are seen incorrectly as self-generated and autonomous.

Individualism is an ideology supportive of and, indeed, vital to modern capitalism. In today's United States, relations between people are largely those of mutual exploitation (Agnew, 1981, p. 458). People view themselves as competing for scarce resources. Others have value for what they can do to and for one another in the scramble for those resources. Such relations reflect in the fiction of "economic man," the belief that people rationally pursue self-interest such that satisfactions are maximized and dissatisfactions minimized. Although introduced by Adam Smith as a convenient analytical concept, this fiction is now accepted as dictum by many work-embracing, success-driven Americans (not to mention social scientists), who often make it a self-fulfilling prophecy in their lives (Miller, 1971, p. 57).

Apart from the military component, America's domestic economy is a commodity system based on the sale of products to a mass of private individuals. This system is fueled by individual profit taking. Entrepreneurs invest capital in productive enterprise, employing people at the lowest possible costs either through depressed wages, high levels of mechanization, or both. Entrepreneurs also seek to create the highest possible demand for their product—most through honest promotion, but some through deception in part. The very basic idea is to minimize the costs of production—including the costs not only of labor, but of investment capital, raw materials, and distribution, as well—in order to maximize income. Environmental and social costs frequently accrue outside the entrepreneur's accountability. Technologies may damage the physical environment, as when wastes are dumped in public streams; or communities may be disrupted, as when plants are closed and unemployed workers set loose in a depressed job market. The role of government is one of regulating private enterprise in an effort to remedy—if not prevent—worker abuse, consumer deception, and negative environmental and social impacts. Government's role in a capitalistic society is to referee private interests in their competitive struggle.

In today's America, demand for most products must be created artificially, consumption driving production. Billions are spent on advertising as competitors jockey to give their products a market edge. Much productive capacity is squandered in duplication and in needless variation. Such private waste goes hand in hand with underdevelopment of the public sector. Collective needs are neglected. Indeed, to the extent that individualized consumption dominates, the quality of collective existence usually atrophies. When the ideologues of a totally privatized economy take control of government, the neglect of the public sector goes beyond the sin of omission to that of commission. In competing one with another, private interests fight public regulation, and block expansion of social services. They undermine the communal impulse by promoting vigorously the ideology of individualism.

Despite their beliefs in the neutrality of government, businessmen do not hesitate to use government in promoting their private interests. In recent years, government has been called upon to protect domestic producers from foreign competition in order to guarantee markets. Government has been called upon to finance corporate reorganization in order to protect investments. Traditionally, government has been called upon to provide transportation and other utility infrastructures, thus to subsidize basic production and distribution. Pressure brought on government by environmentalists, consumer advocates, and those who advocate on behalf of the poor is resisted. A political environment is sought that nurtures the entrepreneur as profit taker while holding other interests in check. "The concept that what is good for business is good for the country is based upon the conviction that the business of the United States is business" (Rodnick, 1972, p. 25).

During the 1980s, the federal government extended as much as $100 billion in financial assistance to American business each year. Edward Meyers (1986, p. 60) estimated for 1984 some $67 billion in tax breaks (including accelerated cost recovery, preferential treatment of capital gains, investment tax credit, and expending of research and development costs), $14 billion in loans, and $18 billion in loan guarantees. In addition, some $14 billion was directed to selected industries. For example, farm support payments amounted to $6 billion, and research and development subsidies to nuclear and fossil fuel energy companies came to $1.8 billion. Meyers's litany did not include indirect subsidization as, for example, the billions of dollars in benefits derived by the building industry through home mortgage tax credits.

Privatization, based on the impulses of individualism, has wrought Americans many advantages. Privatization promotes innovation. Motivation follows from direct personal benefit—especially material benefit. Creativity stems from people being more on their own and having to rely on self-initiative. Creativity also stems from people being able to mix with diverse others of their own choosing (Popenoe, 1985, p. 122). Breaking away from the involuntary ties of family, neighborhood, or region can have profound personal as well as social benefit. "For the individual born of low status who wishes to escape, or born into a backwater area who wishes to migrate, a privatized society permits a fresh start in life and thus immeasurably advances the cause of human freedom" (ibid.).

Nonetheless, individualism taken to excess impedes the ability of communities to take collective action on common problems. Interest groups come to focus attention on limited agendas. The collective good is ignored or attenuated in the competitive climate created. The powerlessness of public planning in the United States, whether for health, welfare, land use, or environmental quality, is just part of the general pattern of weak community translated into weak government. Europeans are taxed at a much higher rate than Americans, with a higher proportion of the monies raised used to support local community facilities and services. While tax revenue as a proportion of gross national product ran at about 40 percent in Great Britain and Sweden in the 1970s, it ran less than 30 percent in the United States (Heidenheimer, Heclo, and Adams, 1975, p. 228). "The United States, with its public squalor, in a sense forces people to retreat into their private domains and to make those domains as spacious, attractive, and comfortable as possible" (Popenoe, 1985, p. 65).

Work versus Consumption in America

The work ethic may be traced back to the fourth century and rules that prescribed manual labor for monks in the Benedictine monasteries. The contemptuous attitude of the classical world toward work (as if only for slaves) became, thereby, a form of piety. It was not until the Protestant Reformation, however, that a reverence for work won widespread acceptance. Martin Luther's idea of man's sacred calling and John Calvin's doctrine of predestination infused new seriousness into life (Weber, 1930). Nonetheless, it was not merely the psychological effect of new religious ideas or doctrines, but the mass emergence of the autonomous individual, that proved the decisive factor (Hoffer, 1964, p. 29). Individual freedom generated the readiness to work, as work, within an emergent capitalism, reinforced and expanded the idea of freedom. Freedom emerged as feudalism eroded, driven by the rise of towns as commercial centers. Protestantism and capitalism rose in symbiosis.

Protestantism taught self-worth through humility, abstinence, frugality, thrift, and industry. It was an ethic of asceticism and hard work as opposed to idleness and indulgence. Indeed, luxury, greed, and avarice were condemned. Built in was an antipathy toward the aristocracy, viewed as nonproductive and superfluous, and disdain for the poor, considered lazy and corrupt in their deprivation (Campbell, 1987, p. 33). Pride in self, as displayed in hard work and frugal living, early underlay the philosophy of success, material affluence short of luxury marking a man and his family as successful. The first apostle of the self-made man established a rather tenuous balance between religious and secular values. The structure teetered on the diligent pursuit of one's calling as symbolic of moral and spiritual excellence (Cawelti, 1965, p. 168). But the balance depended on a static society in which the various occupations of the small farmer, artisan, and shopkeeper offered long-term security. Built into capitalism was a dynamic that made the new commercial towns and their hinterlands anything but static.

Protestantism stressed the individual's responsibility to achieve personal salvation. Christian perfection dictated charity as a primary virtue: the giving of self and one's goods to others. Giving to others without guarantee of return was, and is, difficult in a market-oriented society. This difficulty led to an insensible substitution of the minor virtues: hard work, thrift, sobriety, punctuality, honesty (Boulding, 1968, p. 203). Protestantism taught that pleasure should be postponed, and income saved and reinvested in one's livelihood. The acquisition of goods was not prohibited nor was comfort condemned, since goods and comfort carried much of the evidence symbolic of spiritual salvation. What was condemned was extravagant consumption for its own sake. However, as wealth in society increased, the new capitalists and the aristocracy found it increasingly difficult to refrain from extravagance.

English Puritans brought the work ethnic to colonial New England's shores. No other time and place in the American experience has been more thoroughly associated with its virtues and its vices. Sociologist Daniel Bell writes, "The core of puritanism, once the theological husks are stripped away, was an intense moral zeal for the regulation of everyday conduct, not because the Puritans were harsh or prurient, but because they had founded their community as a covenant in which all individuals were in compact with each other" (1978, p. 59). The individual had to be concerned not only with his own behavior, but with the behavior of his neighbors. One's own sins, including extravagance, imperiled not just oneself but the group. Failure to observe the demands of the covenant could bring down God's wrath on the community as a whole. The covenant was enforced through gossip and shaming and by public confession and repentance: methods effective in the relative isolation of the early New England frontier where communities were closed and inward focused. The idea of respectability (the distrust of leisure, pleasure, and lightheartedness) became so deeply ingrained as to persist long after the Puritan quest for Zion had dissipated.

Puritan New England was but one cultural shoal on which colonial North America was grounded. Political scientist D. J. Elazar (1972, p. 99) distinguishes "moralistic" New England from the "traditionalistic" South and the "individualistic" Middle Colonies. Each region spawned distinctive political cultures variously oriented to the emergent world market. Moralistic society was committed to the covenanted community, and thereby to active government intervention in the marketplace. Traditionalistic society emphasized deferential class and status relationships implicit in an established social hierarchy. Colonial government in the South was essentially the extension of elite economic interests, and their pursuit of economy hegemony. Thus, many southerners sought to live their lives in relative isolation beyond the influence of colonial government on a western frontier. Individualistic society embraced a free market with government's role held to minimal regulation.

Southern culture stood in stark contrast to that of New England. By and large, the southerner was not dedicated to a strict work ethic, nor to the conformities of imposed respectability that associated moralistic stances took. The southern gentry pursued aristocratic ideals, their wealth secure in land and slaves. Slavery dishonored labor. As de Tocqueville (1956, p. 41) recognized, it introduced idleness into southern society, and with idleness came exaggerated pride and preoccupation with luxury. Lesser classes emulated the elites vicariously. The South was stereotyped as a land not only of work avoidance, but of labor faking. Those who could not avoid gainful employment could at least avoid working in their employment. Those forced to work—especially blacks—carried strong social stigma as members of a lowly caste.

Some scholars have seen a decidedly "Celtic" temperament operating on the southern frontier (Furay, 1977, p. 91; Hawley, 1987, p. 32). Central was a "cult of chivalry" brought by Irish, Scots, and especially Scots-Irish. Besides an inbred resistance to authority, these groups were clannish, defining and defending their idiosyncrasies often violently. Emotion—passion for its own sake—tended to prevail over rationality. An assertive masculinity honored energy, but power even more. The southerner of the frontier pursued personal sovereignty. The southern man would be ruler of his own destiny and defender of his own person as he would honor, keep, and break the peace at his own will (Franklin, quoted in Hawley, 1987, p. 33). Pride and honor were the central planks in the southern platform of chivalry. Honor rested on an inner conviction of self-worth, its claim before the public, and the public's assessment in response (Hawley, 1987, p. 36). Reputation, in other words, was aggressively defended, leading outsiders to see frontier southerners as a quarrelsome lot.

Cavalier tendencies permeated the South's social hierarchy from high to low. Originally rooted in the ideal of the gentleman courtier, the cavalier was expected to be accomplished as a lover, soldier, and man of affairs. More important, he was expected to perform with a certain nonchalance indicative of style in lack of effort. "This ideal of a proud, independent and accomplished man, jealous of his honor, was almost entirely secular; religion was not a matter of great concern and there was little attempt to plumb the depths of the soul" (Campbell, 1987, p. 162). In close association with Europe's courtier class, there arose a second group comprised of men without aristocratic lineage yet who had obtained a privileged education. "They led the leisured life of gentlemen, often on borrowed money, and typically spent their time gambling, drinking, going to the theatre, doing 'the social round,' womanizing, or engaging in gentlemanly sports" (p. 167). Called "dandies," they devoted much time and money to clothes and general appearance, lacking real property and real position.

Dandyism emphasized refinement in dress and deportment. As such, it was work avoiding. Work was not only demeaning of character, but destructive of appearances. One not only avoided work, but arrogantly so. Dandyism was a reformulation of the traditional aristocratic role divorced from ancestral lineage and property. It was a promotion not of noble birth, but of noble self. It was a life of leisure, a pursuit of honor, and an enjoyment of bodily and intellectual pleasures. As work was taboo, the lifestyle was highly parasitic, dependent on those with wherewithal and social connection. The dandy, as a kind of cavalier, lived by his wits, concocting roles and guises to endear a constantly changing patronage. Dandyism reinforced conformity to social codes based on personal loyalty, and it reinforced the traditional standards of decorum, good form, and etiquette. The dandy lived a self-fulfilling fantasy through vicarious emulation where productivity was subsumed by consumption. Spawned by plantation society, the southern dandy was the eternal optimist in indulgent self-promotion—a distinctive kind of American individualist that we can find in America today.

The Middle Colonies probably contributed most to what would become the American cultural mainstream of the nineteenth and twentieth centuries. There society took neither the moralistic New England stance of the Whig capitalist concerned with community covenant, nor the traditionalistic southern stance of aristocratic privilege mixed with indulgent bravado. The mainstream impulse was more an individualism rooted in secular Hobbesianism. The individual was seen as having unlimited appetite that was restrained in politics by sovereign authority, but ran free in economics and culture (Bell, 1978, p. 80). A very cosmopolitan world, Pennsylvania had attracted migrants from various parts of Great Britain, and from the European continent as well. Dominated politically and economically by Philadelphia Quakers, colonial Pennsylvania was also influenced by Irish, Scots-Irish, Welsh, and Swiss and Germans, the latter combining a strong work ethic with community clannishness. Perhaps we should not be surprised that people in Pennsylvania mixed various definitions of community with various brands of individualism to produce a fluid cultural amalgam with which later nineteenth- and twentieth-century Americans could easily identify.

Westward expansion, industrialization, and urbanization wrought profound changes in nineteenth-century America. The rise of the factory system with its mass production, and the rise of corporate and public bureaucracies with centralization of administration, brought new meaning to work and employment. Personalized relationships of the workplace gave way to formality in the quest for efficiency. Human labor came to be viewed increasingly as a factor of production to be augmented by machine. Locality-based economies in which artisans and small businessmen earlier had thrived now gave way to national markets defined on specialized product lines controlled by large corporations and their financiers. Railroads came to tie the nation into a single economic unit, an integration intensified by the telegraph, telephone, rapid mail delivery, highways, air travel, radio, and television. Changed circumstances wrought new attitudes toward work. Only in certain sectors, such as farming and retailing, could individuals thrive under a guise of self-employment. By World War I, most Americans had come to view themselves as employees. Today the vast majority do so. We are no longer a nation of independent farmers and craftsmen; rather, we are a nation of functionaries. Our new communal orientation is the corporation, or its equivalent in the government bureaucracy.

Today few Americans emphasize work's public nature or societal contribution. Rather, the vast majority view work as a necessary means to a more rewarding private life through consumption (Popenoe, 1985, p. 113). "Personal identities are formed not so much by what one produces as by what one consumes. "Work is not an end in itself; it is a means to an end" (ibid.). What one consumes is dictated substantially by the media of the national market—now increasingly an international market. A consumer culture has come to the fore with both a materialistic and an experiential base. Americans surround themselves with novelties, and crave novel experiences. If cogs in a machine at work, they regain their sense of purpose at leisure. Puritan moralism has completely dissolved in favor of a "psychological eudaemonism" (Bell, 1978, p. 74). Moral obligations are framed according to the individual's sense of happiness or personal well-being. Stronger than ever is a kind of cavalier dandyism whereby Americans emulate lifestyles of society's influential not through personal contact, but vicariously through the media.

A new kind of capitalism has come to the fore which only weakly encourages a work ethic in the area of production, but strongly stimulates appetites in the area of consumption (Bell, 1978, p. 74). The consumer culture is not only a value system underlying a modern society saturated by mass-produced and mass-marketed goods, but also a new set of sanctions for elite control of society. While nineteenth-century elites ruled through traditional ethical precepts that they encouraged people to internalize, twentieth-century elites rule through subtle promises of self-fulfillment. The older system was individualistic and moralistic; the newer one is corporate and therapeutic. "Individuals have been invited to seek commodities as keys to personal welfare, and even to conceive of their own selves as commodities. One sells not only one's labor and skills, but one's image and personality, too. While the few make decisions about managing society, the many are left to manage their appearance" (Fox and Lears, 1983, p. xii).

In the emergent consumer culture, advertisers relate directly to basic American impulses at self-fulfillment. But whereas traditional individualism once spoke to moral values internalized, advertising speaks to a pervasive other-directedness. "A person's wants are not founded so much on a solid core of selfhood as on feelings of emptiness. The sense of self stands as an empty vessel to be filled and refilled according to the expectations of others, and the needs of the moment" (Lears, 1983, p. 8). Advertisers create appetites for commodities and services by championing emulation. Americans are invited to consume in a "follow the leader" game of self-aggrandizement. Significant others—elites of consumption—are thrust forward as role models to be emulated. The Marlboro man, among many other generic types, strides constantly through our lives, inviting experience and fulfillment through specific avenues of consumption (Salter, 1983, p. 43; Starr, 1984, p. 45).

Advertising's form of persuasiveness has changed through the twentieth century. Focus has shifted from presenting information to attracting attention. A new visual environment has been created where images of various kinds compete for attention. Therapeutic advertising has emerged as a kind of social control: a way to arouse consumer demand by linking products and services with imagined states of well-being. "To some advertisers, the implication was clear that the human mind was not only malleable but manipulable. And the most potent manipulation was therapeutic: the promise that the product would contribute to the buyer's physical, psychic, or social well-being; the threat that his well-being would be undermined if he failed to buy it" (Lears, 1983, p. 18). Marketers treat Americans as unthinking. In place of thoughts they substitute impulses, habits, emotions (Lears, 1983, p. 20).

Increasingly, Americans have come to view themselves more as agents of consumption and less as producers. Consuming has become a primary duty necessary to keeping the economy healthy as well as the individual fulfilled. As a result, Americans increasingly have abrogated their duties as citizens. Too many Americans have become passive observers of life rather than active participants in it, passive taxpayers rather than active citizens. "Management of society is left to the few. The many are left to manage their consumption" (Agnew, 1987, p. 78). An economy subject to popular will has been traded for increased personal affluence. The American is increasingly an individual lost in a mass society, the counterpart of the mass-produced object. The American is increasingly a cog in a machine of consumption, control over which he or she increasingly relinquishes. A political passivity has emerged sustained by a permissive morality of individual fulfillment.

During World War II, the nation rose as one to meet the challenge of tyranny abroad. But the spirit of cooperation was quickly emasculated by the consumption impulse, driven by the pent-up demand of savings accumulated during the war. Two possible courses of political action were brought to the fore. From the political right came a call for "normalcy": return to business civilization and a vigorous crusade against communism. From the political left came a cry to carry the New Deal forward through economic planning to full employment and social welfare reform. Instead of making a political choice, Americans opted for an economic surrogate: economic growth (Wolfe, 1981, p. 9). Economic growth helped liberals keep the support of their working-class and minority constituents through promises of employment. It enabled corporate interests to expand unhindered, not only at home but abroad.

Growth required substantial public subsidy. Federal monies were funneled into a reorganized and expanded defense establishment worldwide, new highway and air transportation infrastructures, a massive urban renewal scheme, a space program. The progrowth coalition was a brilliant answer to political stalemate. "So long as public works drove the economy forward, not only would the privileged obtain more privileges, but there would be benefits for the poor as well" (Wolfe, 1981, p. 91). The coalition was sustained only to the extent that economic growth was sustained. Once the economy began to falter in the 1970s, inherent problems loomed. The drive for growth had involved excessive fiscal irresponsibility, had embraced ideological eclectism, and had induced profound inequality (p. 96). Americans had mortgaged their future for reasons not totally rational or consistent, producing profound social injustices in the process.

The post-World War II political stalemate derived from the seniority system in Congress, use of the Senate filibuster, malapportionment in the House, and the disenfranchisement of blacks. All perpetuated rural control with effective power lodged in a shifting coalition of interest groups. In the 1950s, Congress was basically a turn-of-the-century institution (Udall, 1968, p. 20). It was antiblack, anticity, antieducation, anticultural, and incapable of defining national goals for full individual equality of opportunity. Into the breach stepped the Supreme Court, which induced partial resolution of some problems: for example, the long tradition of American racial inequality. The moralistic stance that the framers of the U.S. Constitution had taken in favor of the individual impacted American life belatedly not through legislative edict, but through court decision.

Consumerism involves a psychology of insatiability (Brittan, 1977, p. 63). Once exposed to the benefits of mass production and mass distribution, a population develops tastes that are incapable of satisfaction. Consumers spend their lives accumulating more and more goods and utilizing more and more services. The more one has, the more one wants, with the urge to increase consumption driven by advertisers. The individual, however, does not seek satisfaction from products and services so much as pleasure from the self-illusory experiences that they construct (Campbell, 1987, p. 89). The constant building of ego through consumption has produced what some critics see as an insipid hedonism in modern America. Exaggerated consumerism has perhaps blinded many Americans to problems of inequality and injustice, so content are they in the successes of their self-centeredness.

Although Americans traditionally have been viewed as pragmatic, as embracing the utilitarian in life and landscape, contemporary consumer culture has brought a new romanticism to the fore. Hedonism, Colin Campbell (1987, p. 77) asserts, tends to be both covert and self-illusory. Individuals use their imaginative and creative powers to construct mental images that they consume, like commodities, for the intrinsic pleasures they provide. People daydream, imagining themselves in idealized circumstances that may, as goals for future achievement, set off rounds of actual consumption. Crucial, however, is the sense of pleasure gained from the emotions aroused—daydreams created such that individuals react subjectively to them as if they were real (ibid.). Although images are generated for pleasure, they still contain elements of possibility, which separates them from pure fantasy.

Whereas work-embracing Americans traditionally practiced deferred gratification, consumption-oriented Americans occupy states of "happy hiatus" between desire and consumption predicated on the joys of daydreaming (Campbell, 1987, p. 86). The individual is both actor and audience in dramas of self-interest where wanting, rather than having, is the main emphasis. Thus, as Colin Campbell observes, the individual is "ever-casting daydreams forward in time, attaching them to objects of desire, and then subsequently 'unhooking' them from these objects as when they are attained and experienced" (p. 87). Many products and services offered in the market are consumed because they serve the construction of daydreams. Fashion and taste are largely a function of daydreaming. Once consumed, novelties may quickly lose image-building potential, and be abandoned in favor of new fads. Built in is a continual embracing of change for change's sake. Thus, the consumption-oriented American labors in continuing cycles of desire, acquisition, use, disillusionment, and renewed desire (p. 90). Although wants are constantly being indulged and rejected, new wants constantly are being created such that a sense of frustrated deprivation endures.

Narcissism enters when amplified wants build toward emotions of deprivation. Placed at the apex of existence, wanting venerates a kind of negative self-love. The world becomes a mirror of felt dispossession: the hero or heroine in the drama of life struggling sentimentally for fulfillments that always elude. The narcissistic personality, in Christopher Lasch's (1978, p. 5) view, ignores the future and trivializes the past in living for an emotionally charged present. The past does not provide a storehouse of memories with which to face a real world. Rather, it provides the templates of emotion whereby the individual clings to a present of self-deception. The real world stands as dull. The imagined world looms as exciting. Pleasure lies in the imagined realm where the individual indulges insatiable appetites romanticized.

America is not a hedonistic society where narcissistic individuals languish. The strongest indictment that can be made is that tendencies toward hedonism and narcissistic behavior appear more evident today than formerly. The work ethic seems to be losing its strength as an organizing template for action. A consumption ethic appears very much in the ascendancy, with greater emphasis placed on pleasure taking as a form of self-fulfillment. Today's individualist is less likely the self-confident mover and doer, and more likely the indulger of dreams. The pragmatic world of the realist appears to be giving way to the deceptive world of the fantasist. Americans seem to be intensifying their preoccupation with appearances. Obviously, the values of both work and consumption coexist in America today, but they produce more complex and more profound paradoxes in the behavior of Americans than ever before.

PROGRESS AS AN AMERICAN IDEAL

Perhaps no myth has informed the American experience so completely as the idea of progress. America is a new place of new beginnings. It is the New World. Self-improvement, freedom, liberty, equal opportunity are all pointed toward change as progress. Certainly, work-embracing Americans pursue a "cult of manipulation," in Paul Santmire's words (1973, p.

80). They manipulate their environment; they manipulate their social institutions; they manipulate their myths. Change is constant; the implicit sense of progress, an ideal. Life is viewed as a path with a particular direction. It is a path along which the individual faces ever forward in search of fulfillment. "Events low purposely and rapidly from a dim, unregarded past along a straight narrow groove toward an indistinct but brighter future" (Zelinsky, 1975, p. 54). It is, however, a short-run future where immediate expectations are fulfilled.

Americans discount the view of time as repeating cycle. The ebb and flow of nature in diurnal and seasonal rhythms does not provide life's organizing temporal matrix. The realities of life cycle—especially old age and death—tend to be ignored until personal crises force confrontation. Cycles of fashion are subsumed by the implicit sense of progression, fad following fad. The rise and fall of institutions and organizations—including nation-states—are viewed as peculiar events. Americans divorce themselves from the possibility that their nation and their society may be vulnerable to decline, that mechanisms internal to the thing called America may be operating in a cyclical manner. Always a youthful country of new beginnings in the past, America, it is assumed, will always remain so.

The idea of linear progress is rooted in the European Enlightenment. Whereas the rise of science taught the possible value of doubt and the value of mistrusting faith taken merely on authority, it also created a faith in its own method of knowing. Scientific truth seeking became the reliable authority of knowledge (Miller, 1971, p. 41). Thomas More, among others, brought utopian views of life suggestive that society in the future would be improved. Betterment lay in the future and not only in once golden ages. But not before Francis Bacon was it widely proclaimed that humans could steadily and indefinitely improve their conditions through their own unaided efforts (ibid.). The Judeo-Christian tradition saw mankind as naturally depraved, creatures of original sin. With the Enlightenment, the human animal was described as rational, and fit to govern himself without divine sanction in quest of self-fulfillment.

Growth—and often merely change—fulfills the progress prophecy. Implicit in growth is expansion both toward and away. By embracing the new one must necessarily release something of the old. In America each generation breaks away from older, established ways forcing obsolescence in the path of innovation (Reich, 1970, p. 2). Lives are thereby left in a never-ending state of tentativeness and uprootedness (Wachtel, 1983, p. 95). Ideally, the new is greater than the old by scale if not by kind. The new should not merely be different, but better. With growth change is truly progressive as more good accrues to more people, and human satisfaction is enhanced. So integrally linked are change and growth with progress that many Americans accept these terms as synonymous. Change is assumed to mean growth. Growth is assumed to mean progress.

Capitalism, of course, is the principal engine of change in the United States today. The stimulation of consumption through advertising propels cycles of investment. The constant generation of desire, envy, and discontent keeps the economy expanding. To do otherwise seemingly risks the confidences on which the system rests. Our economy is not set up to run a steady-state system. According to the common wisdom, the economy must expand or it will collapse (Wachtel, 1983, p. 250). The thrust of new productive technologies is usually in the direction of efficiency—especially labor efficiency. Whereas new methods may work to the profit advantage to entrepreneurs, they may also bring disruption as old methods are made obsolete, and laborers made redundant. Thus, cycles of investment are frequently disruptive of the social fabric of the communities impacted. Not all change is progressive under capitalism, from the point of view of community.

The word *progress*, Timothy Dwight observed early in the nineteenth century, is not of English but of American coinage (Ravitz, 1956, p. 63). Used as a verb in England, it became a noun in America. The restlessness of an America subduing a continent invited new uses of old words. Progress implied an embracing of new things toward betterment. It also implied a turning away from the past, and those who sought to retain past things by conserving or stewarding were not progressive. Americans assigned their country a youthful place among the nations. In America, youth was to be served toward new and better things. The ideal American became "an individual emancipated from history; happily bereft of ancestry, untouched and undefiled by the usual inheritances of family and race; an individual standing alone, self-reliant and self-propelling" (Lewis, 1955, p. 5). This autonomy was viewed as a birthright, each generation expected to reconfigure the nation in its own image (Lowenthal, 1985, p. 105). Each generation was given sovereignty to the American idea of progress.

The will to change is always countered by the impulse to retain the past, albeit a weakened impulse in America more like mere inertia. Indeed, adaptability to change requires such resistance. New experiences are assimilated by placing them in the context of old experiences. Thus, many Americans embrace the faddishness of the new by recognizing it basically as an extension of the old. Change, when it appears, arrives incrementally. As with the coming of the automobile, Americans ease into innovation by stages usually through an unplanned sequence of piecemeal adoptions. Once an innovation, technical or otherwise, sets a trajectory, society embraces it in fulfilling prophecies only partially disclosed and incompletely understood early on.

In landscape, new technologies usually do not require new forms, at least immediately. Buildings are left looking much as they have always looked, although their meaning may be changed (Relph, 1987, p. 120). Changes induced in landscape often provide few clues to the innovations at work since new construction often mimics old. The old therefore can disguise the new, making change seem less disruptive and less threatening. When the automobile arrived, it initially reinforced the fabric of the pedestrian city organized around streetcar lines and railroads. Who dreamt that widened streets, the elimination of curbside parking, the introduction of one-way streets, and overall higher traffic speeds and volumes would largely destroy the city as a traditional residential and commercial place? Who in the early years could have seen networks of freeways accessing business districts comprised substantially of high-rise buildings and parking lots? At first the automobile came unobtrusively to reinforce what had always been. But the automakers and the highway engineers proved to be disguised revolutionaries. America is a land of change as progress, but the change is not always immediately evident. Change—progressive or otherwise—does not have to be justified, or defended.

As landscapes change, so also do values. Indeed, values and landscapes change in mutual reinforcement, the whole manifesting a kind of cultural drift. Innovators invoke tradition in justifying change even to the extent of masquerading newness in traditional forms. Having invoked the past in their cause, they then move forward incrementally to embrace the new fully. Once the threshold of social awareness is reached, it is too late to reverse the process. The change stands as progress whether or not it is progressive given the old standards abandoned. Indeed, so gradual has the change been, that many people stand facing the future unopinionated as to the nature of past values, past landscapes, and the linkages between same. In this vacuum, change is given its own momentum, past values invoked and ignored in cycles that are made to appear cleansing, and buoyantly optimistic.

American values, like American landscapes, appear to be driven by technology. It is, perhaps, in technology that modern values and today's landscapes are conjoined. Ian Barbour (1980, p. 39) identifies four characteristics of modern technology inimical to human fulfillment: (1) uniformity; (2) efficiency; (3) impersonality; and (4) uncontrollability. As mass production yields standardized products, so the mass media produces a uniform national culture. "Individuality is lost and local or regional differences are obliterated in the homogeneity of industrialization" (p. 43). Interactions among people are standardized, human identity defined by roles played out to conform with the contractual rules of organization. Technology promotes efficiency through fragmentation, specialization, and speed pointed toward narrowly defined goals, the negative side effects of which are often ignored. "Quantitative criteria tend to crowd out qualitative ones. The worker becomes the servant of the machine, adjusting to its schedule and tempo, adapting to its requirements" (p. 43). Life is impersonal when relationships are specialized and functional. In bureaucracies, people tend not to take personal responsibility, and come to treat one another like standardized objects.

Most important, technologies form interlocking systems—mutually reinforcing networks that seem to lead lives of their own. "Technology is not just a set of adaptable tools for human use, but an all-encompassing form of life, a pervasive structure with its own logic and dynamic" (Barbour, 1980, p. 44). A sense of powerlessness easily derives as the individual faces monolithic systems too complex to understand, and too difficult to influence. The individual stands back and allows progress to take its course.

Certain basic values continue to propel American life, their importance as social arbitrator changed and changing over time. Americans tend to use the same traditional myths to organize their lives, but new variations on old themes come constantly to the fore. The drive to self-fulfillment continues to motivate most Americans, but just what constitutes fulfillment is open to increased debate. Freedom and liberty continue to be valued—some Americans inclined to extend these concepts into new areas of social concern, others to thwart extension. While some Americans abide by the social conformities of the past, others work at extending individual license. Values are molded in the political arena and the marketplace. Individualism still stands high in the pantheon of values as does the work ethic, although the latter has now been joined to a consumption ethic. Self-improvement now binds a sense of building up with a sense of using up.

Technological changes, especially in transportation and communications, have created social uncertainties at a new scale. Old myths persist in new forms, but with less unifying force. A kind of confused tolerance is widely practiced. Values are embraced expediently in social relations made increasingly anonymous and transitory. Mass consumption has brought widespread acceptance of the idea of change; and values—like the commodities one consumes—are expected to change, giving legitimacy to those who innovate. How this cultural drift impacts landscapes is a complex and difficult matter to unravel. Individualism, the work and consumption ethics, and the drive for progress reflect only covertly in landscape. They play out variously through the social institutions that organize and furnish places as contexts for socialization. Americans use their society's myths to inform their lives as circumstances warrant. Values are meanings always expressed in social context. Values are shared differently across age, class, and status groups, and reflect variously on people of differing political persuasions. But they are variously grasped as part of a shared culture driving the American experience.

How do America's traditional cultural values underlie landscape dereliction? The drive to self-improvement, the quest for freedom of action, the celebration of individualism, the promotion of work, and, more lately, consumption ethics have all fostered and been fostered by a capitalistic economy, the fundamental context for American life. Capitalism is deeply rooted in the American way. But from capitalism have come excesses of big business and big government largely responsible for dereliction in the American scene—dereliction, as we will argue, exacerbated by the undervaluing of community and its derived locality-based democracy. In subsequent chapters, beginning with a discussion of deindustrialization, we will show how traditional American values are used to both invoke and abide environmental change that is clearly negative. We show how espoused cultural values enable the few to dominate the many in the negative manipulation of the built environment from which derelict zones develop.

3

Deindustrialization

Most Americans readily accept capitalism as a driving force for change, but few tend to think critically of capitalism's impact on landscapes. Nowhere is dereliction more vivid than in old industrial areas, which are so clearly creatures of capital once at work, where underutilized and abandoned buildings stand as somber reminders of past prosperity now elusive. Capitalism's negative profile on the landscape is hard to ignore there. Brick and concrete, once symbolic of a nation's industrial might, signify obsolescence in an emergent "postindustrial" economy given less to manufacturing and more to service production (Dicken, 1986). The term *deindustrialization*, coined to describe this change, involves the systematic disinvestment of the nation's basic productive capacity (Bluestone and Harrison, 1982, p. 6). Short-term profit taking and its associated lack of long-term planning, corporate consolidation driven by tax and other financial considerations, capital flight overseas in search of cheap labor and new markets, plant closings and the resultant cadres of redundant workers (and, indeed, redundant communities)—these are all part of the story reflected in the dereliction of industrial landscapes today.

The history of capitalist societies is one of investments constantly shifting across economic sectors and regions. Industrialists grapple with one another for advantage in a transient economic order ever emergent. David Harvey (1981; 1985) concisely sums up the essential workings of a capitalist system, emphasizing the crisis-ridden nature of economies and the consequent maneuverings of investors to elude fiscal downturns. Under economically stable conditions, investment concentrates in manufacturing. Industry drives economies as commodities fetch prices conducive for continued investment. Problems arise, however, with unregulated capital flow. Periodic bouts of overproduction and underconsumption generate declining rates of profitability that increasingly render manufacturing investment unprofitable. Two global economic crises, in the 1930s and 1970s, were vivid illustrations of this. Following bouts of falling profitability, massive capital was diverted to other forms of investment (often real estate development, but also new forms of industrial investment) in order to avert crisis. Economists see capital diversion operating in business cycle fluctuations across a range of time scales. The two most influential—Kuznets cycles and Kondratieff cycles—occur roughly every 18–25 and 35–50 years, respectively (van Duijn, 1983; Sorkin, 1988). With capital diversion, spurts of urban and regional growth unfold. New housing, plants, infrastructure, parks, and the like emerge as built environments siphon capital away from old-line industrial investment. With capital pouring into selected regions, capitalist development negotiates a "knife-edge path" between preserving past investments in the built environment and destroying those investments in order to create "fresh room for accumulation." "Under capitalism there is, then, a perpetual struggle in which capital builds a physical landscape appropriate to its own condition at a particular moment in time, only to have to destroy it, usually in the course of a crisis, at a subsequent point in time" (Harvey, 1981, p. 113). The historical geography of industrial landscapes reflects vividly this internal capitalist contradiction. In order to create, investors inadvertently must destroy.

With industrialists in a continuous search for optimal profit environments, plant relocation has become common, ties to locality being far from certain in today's world. Industrialists stay in locations only so long as profit margins are sufficient. With declining profit rates, the search begins anew for locations offering cost savings in the form of lower labor costs, better access to raw materials, proximity to markets, and better tax benefits, among other advantages.

It must be noted that capitalism has never pretended permanence. (Nor, for that matter, has any other modern economic system.) Factories are not created to function indefinitely; instead, investments are expected to be amortized over time. They are programmed to die—a programming now greatly accelerated by recent tax laws. Workers may believe otherwise (as, indeed, whole communities may labor under assumptions of permanence), but investors know better. Under capitalism, investments occur where money can be made at acceptable rates of return. The primary concern is not to maintain the well-being of an industry, enhance workers, improve products, or please customers, but to generate profits. Thus, plant life expectancies decree both growth and eventual decay for communities in any given place.

Not surprisingly, deindustrialization reflects a loss of comparative economic advantage. Disinvestment triggers decline that increasingly renders once viable landscapes derelict and nonviable. The irony is that the level of disinvestment will substantially determine the degree to which a region will rebound in the future. As Neil Smith (1982) and Michael Storper and Allen Scott (1985) document, severe property devaluation and depression in local wage rates often create the necessary preconditions for future rounds of investment when current healthy regions lose their comparative advantage. Such uneven development may be envisaged as a seesaw investment pattern that is driven by the rhythms of capital accumulation.

The American political system is geared to protect the privileges of capital—to guarantee the fluidity whereby capital moves from investment to investment, place to place. But paradoxically, political institutions require infrastructures of cultural stability. In order for society to function, basic social relationships must be harmonious and predictable. Communities—especially political communities—must be supportive and docile (Padfield, 1980, p. 160). How is it that our system, functioning to program fluidity at the economic level, generates passivity at the level of community? The answer lies in the twin realms of ideology and state operations. In concert with local political operatives and growth coalitions, industrialists espouse the benefits of individualism, entrepreneurial spirit, and unfettered market operations. These tenets are cast as the backbone of American values. Deviation from them purportedly ushers in collective and vague decision making, constrained individual rights, and distorted (and inefficient) market dynamics. Wealth creation, it is contended, relies on entrepreneurial ingenuity. Such creative decision making is facilitated by competition. In this casting, community well-being is tied up with sustaining individual rights and the quest of entrepreneurs to accumulate. All classes could thus look forward to sharing in the benefits of an ever-expanding economy (Weinstein, 1968).

Everyday life in America has been penetrated by the rhetoric of individualism and capitalist market benefits. At the same time, government ensures a level of community happiness that engenders political passivity (see O'Conner, 1973; Clark and Dear, 1984). Social programs and policies assure suitable qualities of life. Housing, social welfare, and economic development programs seek to assist the poorest households by preventing them from falling below certain living levels. Regulation of the economy minimizes the devastating effects of sporadic economic downturns and recessions. The Federal Reserve, for example, carefully controls money supply to eliminate inordinately high or low interest rates. This activity ensures a sufficient enough production and consumption of commodities to sustain economic health. Redistributive schemes appear to foster an egalitarian economic structure, with the wealthy disproportionately taxed. All these diverse measures collectively acclimate residents to everyday corporate practices; everyday life becomes infused with rhetoric that generates harmonious and predictable human behavior.

GLOBAL CAPITALISM

The world economic system that emerged after 1945 was distinctive from past patterns (Dicken, 1986). The simultaneous sharp division between East and West and the harsh economic realities of the 1930s forged a new global perspective. An internationalization of economic activities unfolded amid increased interdependence, widespread removal of protective trade barriers, and the need for capitalist economic expansion. Spurred by the creation of the International Monetary Fund (IMF) and the World Bank (WB) in 1944, industrialists increasingly turned to markets abroad as a mechanism for economic growth. These acts served to stimulate a reconstructed world economy and growth in trade and production (ibid.). Such acts were simultaneously economic stimulants and political assertions. They fostered economic prosperity but also sought to expand U.S. influence for future market penetration. Amid this transition to global capitalism, a qualitative change in capitalist labor exploitation ensued. It involved increasingly bringing cheap foreign labor into the capital–wage labor relation. Worker pools in Asia, Africa, and Eastern Europe were actively tapped into the internationalized economy. An overwhelming majority receive wages far below that of comparable American workers (p. 210). At the same time, oligopolistic firms created structured relationships among themselves to unify markets and dominate firms that actually were operating competitively as suppliers or subcontractors. A dual labor market has been the result. Within oligopolistic firms, unionized labor has gained a relatively protected position. In competitive firms, typically less unionized workforces have experienced lower wages, poorer working conditions, and less job stability (Shakrow and Graham, 1983, p. 18). "The dominant corporations, exercising their monopoly power to secure favorable terms of trade in their dealings with satellite companies, capture higher levels of surplus value extracted from their lower paid employees" (ibid.).

Most large U.S. corporations have emerged as holding companies—conglomerates created through merger and buyout. Waves of merger and buyout have punctuated the U.S. economy. Peak periods are evident during economic slumps when small firm survivability is most problematic. As Peter Dicken and Peter E. Lloyd (1990, p. 199) note, large global firms have been able to produce commodities at lower cost than smaller firms. This cost savings has accrued to some degree because of cheap global labor and use of more efficient technologies. Moreover, larger firms can demand lower prices when buying raw materials in volume and obtain credit more cheaply. To compound the large versus small firm inequity, enlarging firms can exploit opportunities of "vertical integration," which involves corporate purchase of distribution and retailing networks. In short, the emerging size and assets of large firms increasingly differentiate them from smaller, struggling industries. Higher priced producers, as history has shown, are often driven out of the market. Selected firm growth in the context of more widespread industrial failure has created monopolistic market conditions. Where smaller industries have struggled but persisted, their deathblow is often delivered by industrial buyout and merger. Giant corporations unfold that transform the nature of competition and the role of markets (see Gordon, 1978; Storper and Walker, 1983).

Buyout and merger of smaller industries are often motivated by the simultaneous desire to eliminate competition and to acquire a larger pool of surpluses that can be reallocated toward maximizing short-run returns. In the latter, emphasis is placed in financial innovations that enhance capital mobility. Included are the machinations of short-run accounting procedure, tax avoidance, and litigation. Ways are sought to maintain or increase firm profits while avoiding the cost and risk of investing in new products or processes (Reich, 1983, p. 140). Often it is a matter of imposing losses on others—for example, the taxpayers (to the extent that the social costs of plant closings and the like are not covered) or the shareholders (to the extent that dividends are reduced and surpluses accumulated). As with independent suppliers, surplus value can be extracted from subsidiaries that are treated like subcontractors. Conglomerates relate to subsidiaries like investors seeking to spread speculative risk.

When a corporation's stock price falls below book value, the firm can post significant gains on its balance sheet by acquiring undervalued companies and consolidating the two sets of books (Reich, 1983, p. 145). If a firm has lost money, the acquiring conglomerate can use losses to reduce tax liabilities. U.S. Steel's purchase of Marathon Oil reduced corporate taxes some $500 million in the first year and saved at least $1 billion more over the productive life of Marathon's major oil field. Because U.S. Steel could take new depletion deductions against high-valued property, reserves were worth far more to it than to Marathon, which had exceeded its tax deduction potential (p. 147). In such circumstances, asset values lose their links with actual productive activity. As economist Robert Reich concludes (p. 153), Americans operate increasingly in a "symbolic economy" in which resources circulate endlessly among giant corporations, investment bankers, and lawyers. Little new is produced. By 1980, American corporations were spending as much as $40 billion annually in acquiring one another (Bluestone and Harrison, 1982, p. 41).

Until the 1980s, American corporations focused acquisition efforts overseas. From the Bretton Woods agreement of 1944 until 1971, the United States was the world's reserve-currency country. Each nation was expected to keep current value within 1 percent of its par value by buying or selling their currencies on international exchanges. The United States, by creating large trade deficits, forced foreign central banks to buy excess dollars with their currencies to decrease dollar supplies in global circulation (Agnew, 1987, p. 84). Thus, American corporations were provided with the foreign currencies requisite to buying assets abroad. In so many words, foreign central banks were placed in the self-effacing position of financing the takeover of their own industries. American corporations were able to make massive foreign investments in new plants as well as purchase already established plants in ready-made subsidiaries. Not only were foreign markets more readily served, but cheaply produced products could be exported back to the United States—a situation encouraged by the high-valued dollar.

Corporate investments abroad expanded from 21 percent to 40 percent of total investments during the 1960s (Castells, 1979, p. 107). Corporate overseas bank deposits increased from 30 percent of total deposits in 1965 to some 70 percent in 1972 (ibid.). Between 1950 and 1980, direct foreign investment by American businesses increased 16 times from approximately $12 billion to some $192 billion (Bluestone and Harrison, 1982, p. 42). At the same time, gross private domestic investment grew only half as rapidly, from $54 billion to about $400 billion. As economists Barry Bluestone and Bennett Harrison note (ibid.), total overseas output of American multinational corporations was larger in the 1980s than the gross domestic production of every nation in the world except the United States and the Soviet Union. Overseas profits have accounted in some recent years for 40 percent of the overall profits of the largest multinational corporations (Illinois Advisory Committee, 1981, p. 12). The record of specific corporations is instructive. General Electric, for example, increased overseas capacity by 400 percent between 1949 and 1969 by building 60 of 80 plants abroad (Agnew, 1987, p. 85). During the 1970s, General Electric added 5,000 workers to its payroll worldwide, adding 30,000 foreign jobs and eliminating 25,000 in the United States.

American manufacturers, constantly searching for favorable profit opportunities, were attracted abroad by foreign markets, cheap labor, absence of environmental regulations, and tax advantages. Many firms sought to evade trade barriers. In addition, companies sought to spread risks geographically. Declining capital for domestic investment followed. In 1957, the 298 largest American multinational firms invested nine cents for new plant and equipment overseas for every dollar domestically invested. By 1971, this had reached 25 cents (Illinois Advisory Committee, 1981, p. 12).

During the 1970 and 1980s, the rate of U.S. capital formation was consistently lower than most industrialized countries, reflecting low rate of savings (around 4 percent of disposable income for Americans as opposed to 14.5 percent for British and 20 percent for the Japanese) and a maturing American industry (Agnew, 1987, p. 148). Nonetheless, of investments actually made, some one-tenth or more were invested by American companies abroad. In 1979, American corporations made almost 10 percent of total plant and equipment expenditures in foreign countries as compared to less than 3 percent for West Germany and France and less than 2 percent for Japan (Agnew, 1987, p. 148).

Investment abroad has meant domestic job loss. Rather than importing cheap labor from overseas, American machines are taken to laborers abroad. Incomes once earned in the United States are earned elsewhere, thus supporting foreign ancillary economic activities. Between 1966 and 1973, the United States experienced a net loss of 1.06 million jobs because of corporate movement overseas (Illinois Advisory Committee, 1981, p. 12). Flight overseas has wrought substantive decline in the domestic clothing, consumer electronics, and small appliance industries. In contrast, the Japanese have, until recently, largely avoided transferring jobs to other countries. They have preferred automation as a means of lowering labor costs.

Failure to modernize at home and the licensing of technology abroad have wrought a general loss of technical advantage for American firms. Aging plants are not as competitive due to obsolescence and high repair costs. Higher per unit costs place antiquated facilities at immediate competitive disadvantage with those abroad both American and foreign owned. In addition, many American firms not electing to expand overseas pursue short-run profits by licensing their technologies to foreign companies. Whereas licensing technology is an easy way of paying off development costs and making quick profits without additional capital investment, it is also dangerous since licensees are given start-up technologies that enable them to become competitors. Japanese and German companies appear to be much more conservative in their licensing practices, being more concerned with the long term.

Federal programs have contributed to shifts of American investment and jobs. Riders on annual foreign-aid bills require that aid money be spent with American corporations, if any, in the countries aided. This annual rider, in effect, subsidizes American facilities abroad at the expense of facilities at home (Prouty, 1987). More than $200 billion has been spent in foreign aid in the past quarter century (Parenti, 1983, p. 22). In addition, federal tax policies have contributed to the corporate transfer of investment capital overseas. Through the 1960s and 1970s, American corporations were allowed to credit—rather than deduct—foreign tax payments against domestic tax obligations. Moreover, they were allowed to postpone tax payment until actual repatriation of profits earned overseas. Corporations could juggle internal accounts to take advantage of international differences in business-tax rates—a practice called "transfer pricing" (Bowles, Gordon, and Weiskopf, 1983, p. 69). In 1972, American corporations paid only $1.2 billion in taxes on foreign earnings of $24 billion—an effective tax of just 5 percent (ibid.).

American banks have also been active investors abroad. In the 1970s, America's eight largest banks lent more than 100 percent of their stockholder's equity to companies (including subsidiaries of American multinationals) and governments in but four nations: Mexico, Brazil, Venezuela, and Argentina (Agnew, 1987, p. 149). Should these countries default on payments (as various nations threatened through the late 1980s), the banks would have instant negative equity. In the 1970s, foreign investment looked more attractive than domestic investment. Lacking legal restraints on foreign lending, big banks—like big corporations—contributed substantially to U.S. capital out-flight.

Corporate concentration has favored some parts of the world over others. North America, Western Europe, and Japan retain a "core" distinction. These are the areas of most intensive and most sophisticated capitalization. Profits made elsewhere flow to these areas. "Peripheral" regions are used by the industrial and financial centers primarily as reservoirs of labor and primary materials. Nineteenth- and early-twentieth-century systems of European colonial extraction established in the European empires of the nineteenth and early twentieth centuries continue, but without the overtones of political control. Core–periphery relationships also can be identified within countries. In the United States, regional inequalities are quite evident when comparing Appalachia—a largely raw-material and surplus-labor producing area—with the highly urbanized "megalopolis" of the Northeastern Seaboard.

National Defense and Pax Americana

Capitalistic economies tend to be afflicted by stagnation, demand for products and services growing less rapidly than production. Lacking central planning and control, market economies experience periodic recessions and depressions marked by high unemployment, falling profits, and business failures. For America, defense expenditures have promised a partial solution. A permanent military sector has been rationalized as providing state-stimulated economic demand free of cycles. Military hardware is expensive to develop, test, and maintain; and the constant push to upgrade technology makes much of it quickly obsolete, requiring total replacement at frequent intervals. Most of the nation's largest corporations engage in defense contracting since it provides a safety valve, given the hazards of selling consumer and other products in competitive markets. After all, the overproduction of automobiles or refrigerators can lead to a falling rate of return as markets are glutted. With war material, however, technical innovation creates a built-in obsolescence and an endless demand for more expensive and sophisticated weapons.

The defense economy in the United States is a colossus. In 1970, the accumulated value of military equipment and fixed installations reached $214 billion (Agnew, 1987, p. 82). In that year, the total assets of all American manufacturing corporations was $554 billion, making the military infrastructure by size some 38 percent that of all of America's industry (ibid.). Between 1976 and 1980, defense spending totaled some $595 billion, increasing annually at rates somewhat higher than inflation; however, between 1981 and 1985, defense spending totaled nearly $1.2 trillion, increasing more than triple the rate of inflation (Meyers, 1986, p. 7). In 1982, the Pentagon projected a five-year military buildup costing more than $1.5 trillion, or 60 times the cost of the Vietnam War—as much as was spent in all the years since World War II (Meyers, 1986, p. 94). One estimate placed the amount that every American family paid each year to the Pentagon at $3,000 (ibid.). What if this money had been spent in ways more supportive of the nation's built environment?

An assumption might be drawn that, since military expenditures benefit corporate America, they also help drive a healthy economy and thus a healthy landscape. Such is not the case. A 1982 study concludes that each $1 billion in tax money spent on military equipment causes a net loss of 18,000 jobs— employment that could have been saved if consumers had spent the money on nonmilitary expenditures (Turner and Musick, 1985, p. 33). Profits earned in defense work are in part reinvested, creating new jobs; but the multiplier effects are not so great as with nonmilitary production. Nuclear warheads, missiles, aircraft, and naval ships cannot be used to create further productivity in the way that machine tools, farm implements, highways, and buildings can. As military spending decreases emphasis on the domestic economy, American firms lose capacity to compete. Money is diverted from research and development. Rather than stimulating the economy, Pentagon spending has had a dampening influence. One study shows that for each dollar spent on the military between 1939 and 1968 there was $0.163 less spent on consumer durable goods, $0.110 less on producer durable goods, and $0.114 less for homes (Russett, 1970, p. 140). Technological leadership has passed to foreign hands, especially in nondefense research and development. The American patent balance with West Germany turned negative in the mid-1960s, and with Japan in the mid-1970s (Agnew, 1987, p. 139).

Military spending has contributed substantially to the nation's federal budget and trade deficits. Increased defense spending, coupled with tax cuts and lowered tax revenues from a deep recession in the late 1970s, created annual budget deficits of more than $200 billion (Turner and Musick, 1985, p. 367). Since 1945, federal tax policy has consistently shifted the tax burden from big business onto individual taxpayers. Although corporate America has been left with more capital to invest, the federal government has been deprived of funds to cover escalating costs—especially military costs. In order to cover deficits, the federal government raised interest rates in the 1970s, attracting large amounts of foreign capital and strengthening the dollar. This action cut down deficit-induced inflation, but the strengthened dollar hurt American manufacturing by making foreign goods relatively cheaper both at home and abroad. By the mid-1980s, the annual trade deficit was running in excess of $100 billion. American multinational corporations increased their investments abroad while closing facilities at home.

American corporations are as deeply into deficit financing as the federal government. Since World War II, the private sector has relied less on internal funds and stock issues, which are not debts, and more on bonds, mortgages, and bank loans, which are debts (Harris, 1981, p. 64). Since 1950, corporate debt has increased 14 times, while the federal debt has increased only three times (ibid.). When, as a result of falling productivity, a firm cannot pay off a loan out of income, it must borrow to cover what has already been borrowed; and a spiral of short-term financing develops. "Premium rewards go to executives who are adept at meeting short-term obligations rather than to those who want to lay the basis for sound profitability in the years ahead" (p. 73).

During the 1960s, overall real economic growth in the United States averaged 4.1 percent per year. As a result, gross national product expanded by 50 percent over the decade, permitting the average family to enjoy one-third more real, spendable income (Bluestone and Harrison, 1982, p. 4). But during the 1970s, gross national product grew by only 2.9 percent per year, leaving the average family with only 7 percent more real purchasing power (ibid.). By 1980, Switzerland, Sweden, Denmark, West Germany, France, the Netherlands, and Belgium, among other countries, had surpassed the United States in per-capita gross national product. America's share of the world's manufactured exports fell from approximately 25 percent in 1960 to about 17 percent in 1980, the trade deficit with the Japanese alone reaching $10 billion (ibid.). In 1960, American automobile makers controlled 96 percent of the American market for cars, but in 1979 only 79 percent (Agnew, 1987, p. 162). The American steel makers' share of the domestic market fell from 96 percent to 86 percent, the footwear maker's share from 98 percent to 63 percent, the consumer electronic maker's share from 94 percent to 49 percent (Agnew, 1987, p. 162). In 1982, American investments abroad exceeded foreign investments in the United States by $196 billion; in 1985, foreign investments in the United States were $82 billion greater (p. 156).

Americans have attempted to build a "pax Americana" on a diminishing resource base. Since the 1960s, the United States has become increasingly dependent on foreign sources of raw material and energy due to depletion at home and corporate investment abroad. After 1973, when the larger oil-producing nations organized the Organization of Petroleum Exporting Countries (OPEC), oil prices jumped twelvefold before falling, triggering a deep recession (Agnew, 1987, p. 154). Whereas Japan and many other industrial nations were able to offset higher oil prices by increasing manufactured exports, especially to oil-producing countries like Saudi Arabia, the United States was not.

Some critics have blamed the victims for America's economic decline, noting a decay in traditional values among American workers. Advertisements in popular magazines warn that the average American has "turned away from hard work, saving, entrepreneurship, self-discipline and deferred gratification—the values and behavior traits that historically underlie our progress" (Smith-Kline Forum, 1980). Productivity measured on a per-worker basis has declined since World War II. Calculated as total output in the economy divided by the number of hours worked, productivity increased by an average of 3.2 percent per year from 1948 to 1965, but only 2.4 percent between 1965 and 1973, 1.1 percent between 1973 and 1978, and -0.8 percent between 1978 and 1980 before rebounding to 1.2 percent per year from 1980 through 1984 (Agnew, 1987, p. 138). Amitai Etzioni (1983, p. 232) reports that an average automobile worker in Japan produces 40 to 50 cars per year, against 25 for his counterpart in the United States, while an average Japanese steelworker produces 421 tons a year, against 250 tons for his American equivalent.

The costs of maintaining pax Americana—the keeping of the Western economy open to American business—has wrought repercussions at home that were little anticipated. Massive military expenditures, many of dubious defense value, comprise a huge investment of taxpayer money in activity destructive to the American domestic economy. While creating jobs and distributing billions of dollars in income, investments in defense produce little that absorbs the spending power generated. The manner in which corporate enterprise does business has been affected in very fundamental ways. Less is invested in basic research and development beneficial to the domestic economy, which is the real bulwark of national security. Defense spending and the costs of military intervention in Vietnam, the Middle East, and elsewhere in the world have contributed directly to budget and trade deficits. In sum, pax Americana—rather than securing American economy hegemony worldwide—may have made American business less competitive in world markets. Rather than sustaining the American economy as a base for a stable built environment, it may have fostered instability and outright dereliction in landscape.

Plant Closings

The 1960s and 1970s were decades of massive displacement as industrial facilities were closed, especially in the old "manufacturing belt" of the Northeast and Middle West. Approximately 32–38 million jobs were lost nationally as a direct result of American business disinvestment during the 1970s (Bluestone and Harrison, 1982, p. 9). New U.S. jobs created exceeded those lost, with some 3.2 million jobs destroyed each year amid 3.6 million newly created jobs between 1969 and 1976 (p. 29). With this net gain, however, many negatives emerged. What of the hidden social and economic costs of workers spatially dislocated—many into more routinized and lower paying jobs? What of the effects on communities faced with high unemployment and declining tax revenues? What were the impacts on small industrial towns whose social fabric was oriented to industries? The discussion that follows addresses these fundamental issues.

Plant closures affected different parts of the country differently. The Northeast, for example, lost 35,000 jobs between 1970 and 1975 while the South was gaining 3.3 million jobs (Sternlieb and Hughes, 1977, p. 8). Manufacturing employment declined 9.9 percent in New England and 13.7 percent in the Middle West alongside increases of 43.4 and 67 percent in the Southeast and Southwest between 1969 and 1976 (Illinois Advisory Committee, 1981, p. 9). Job loss by industrial relocation was compounded by increased substitution of capital for labor in all regions. Between 1967 and 1978, equipment investment increased approximately 60 percent, 178 percent, and 349 percent in the Northeast, Middle West, and South, respectively (ibid.). The goal of industrialists was to decrease reliance on labor—an input into production often perceived as unstable and burdensome.

The ideal environment for the industrialist involves low wage rates, a relative lack of unionization, low workmen's compensation insurance rates, and low unemployment benefits. The antithesis of this has been the industrialized North where unions are well entrenched and thus entrepreneurs bound by more strict union rules as well as minimum wage rates, fair labor standards, occupational health and safety provisions, equal employment opportunity rules, and extended unemployment benefits (Edwards, Reich, and Weisskopf, 1978). Generally, organized labor has been seen to limit management ability to extract full worker productivity, the union shop transforming the employer's wage bill from a variable to a fixed cost. In order to make labor once more a variable production cost, corporations have sought to disarm unions of such weapons as the grievance process and the ability to strike. As Bluestone and Harrison write, "What makes the disarming process possible is the enormous increase in corporate manager abilities to physically relocate production: that is, to move the locus of production or disperse it, and to inexpensively coordinate spatially dispersed production from a central headquarters" (1982, p. 95).

Job shifts to the South and West have also been explained by lower tax rates tied to less government spending. As the Illinois Advisory Committee (1981) poignantly notes, however, less state and local spending generally has reflected an area's ability to attract a glut of federal dollars. The sunbelt has benefited substantially through differential flow of federal monies associated with military procurement, agribusiness, major public works, and oil production subsidies. In 1976, the northeastern and midwestern states contributed some $33.5 billion more to the federal treasury than they received in federal spending, while the southern states received a surplus of $21 billion. In other words, the frostbelt received 81 cents for each dollar sent to Washington, while the southern sunbelt received $1.25 (Illinois Advisory Committee, 1981, p. 22). Sunbelt ability to attract federal dollars decreases reliance on local spending.

The geography of production, M. J. Webber (1982, p. 6) argues, involves spatial patterns laid down in succeeding rounds of investment, with each investment round concentrated in one or more select regions according to need and opportunity as defined by product. But all products, in turn, pass through cycles of development (Vernon, 1960). At each cyclical stage, the factors of production relate differently. Initially, new products reach the market as an experiment, with production unstable as new technologies are worked out. Inputs are not fixed and price elasticity is low. Uncertainty encourages concentration: activity hinging on the immediate face-to-face communications of personalized management. With product maturation comes acceptance of general standards, decline in innovation, and outright routinization of production on a large scale. Increasingly, management moves toward least-cost production in order to optimize market penetration. Highly standardized products of high price elasticity are produced using cheap labor in intensely capitalized and bureaucratically managed plants. Each stage dictates different conditions of competition within respective industries.

As product lines of northern industries matured after World War II, pressure grew to transfer activities southward where labor costs were lower and unions weaker. More recently, firms have looked beyond the traditional manufacturing belt and overseas where labor costs are cheaper and unions frequently nonexistent. Thus the peripheries have attracted much day-to-day firm operations producing standardized products on highly mechanized assembly lines. Coordinate management and planning, on the other hand, has remained in the North to access capital markets, professional services, the federal bureaucracy, and other corporate headquarters.

Government intervention has spurred this industrial mobility. Far from being a neutral observer, programs have assisted the out-migration through generous provision of subsidies. Most notably, federal tax codes of the 1960s and 1970s provided investment incentives in new equipment, plants, and new locations. Investment tax credits helped defray new facility costs with start-up costs at new locations also made tax deductible. Accelerated depreciation allowances on new facilities further provided incentive to transfer operations to new locations favored variously by lowered production costs, and, conversely, to abandon old locations. "The federal tax structure encourages corporations to write off old plants, counting the cost of relocation as a business expense and allowing generous investment tax credit for plant and equipment, tax policies helping to refinance runaway shops" (Tabb, 1984, p. 13).

Arguments for and against plant closings first entered popular awareness through media coverage in the 1970s. Today, those favoring unfettered capitalism speak of investment transfers between industrial sectors and between regions as necessary economic stimulants. These apologists start by denying the severity of deindustrialization and casting it as a minor dilemma. They contend that deindustrialization's magnitude has been exaggerated. While large plants have been prone to relocate to areas of greater anticipated profitability, smaller plants have tended to stay put because of loyalty to the community, allegiance to the workforce, and corporate attachment to place. Locations are purportedly influenced by but not determined by cash flow considerations. The typical small plant operator consequently deems profit at present location "sufficient" rather than "optimal" and remains. As critics like David Gordon (1980) note, however, these small plants in the 1970s accounted for only a small proportion of U.S. industrial investment and gross national product. Gordon believes that the role of small plants in the economic sphere continues to shrink as large corporations assume dominance via merger and takeover. Moreover, he believes the influence of noneconomic factors to be exaggerated. Plants that remain in place frequently lack the capital that would permit the building of factories elsewhere. With greater resources, Gordon contends, more small plants would relocate to suburbia and other regions.

Advocate Charles Schultz (1984, p. 158) takes the position that deindustrialization imposes only minor problems for the nation. During the 1970s, the United States outperformed major European countries and Japan in generating new jobs. Total U.S. employment grew 24 percent, with the next best performer—Japan—increasing 9 percent. Whereas the proportion of total employment accounted for by manufacturing fell steadily after World

War II, productivity or output per person did not. Indeed, a skilled and educated labor force permitted American capital to concentrate on high-tech industries with new products produced in nonroutine ways (Branson, 1984, p. 183). Thus, high-technology countries are seen to develop new products; but when they become standardized and their production routinized, manufacturers necessarily shift factories to areas with low-skilled workers and low wages. "When the economy is adjusting smoothly, jobs lost in declining industries are lost to firms, but not to workers—who move on to other jobs that are opening in expanding industries" (p. 189).

Capital and worker mobility are thus seen to go hand in hand. Unemployment-induced migration is seen merely as an individual worker problem. Through wages paid to workers and taxes paid to governments, businesses contribute to host communities. "Through personal savings," Richard McKenzie argues, "workers can secure their own individual futures against job displacement" (1984, p. 209). Indeed, wages tend to reflect the risk of plant closings: the greater the risk—everything else being equal—the higher the wages. Governments might set aside contingency funds or purchase insurance against risk of plant closures. But corporations should not be burdened with community problems even when they result from corporate action. To be thus burdened, McKenzie maintains, would diminish competitiveness and the entrepreneurial ability to create new jobs. McKenzie bolsters his argument with the observation that relatively few firms actually move production facilities great distances. Between 1969 and 1975, only 2 percent (6,639 manufacturing plants out of 326,125) changed location. The number of jobs displaced represented only 1.6 percent of all manufacturing jobs (McKenzie, 1984a, p. 23). These relocations he sees as playing a very minor role in reallocating manufacturing employment among regions, given the net effects of starts, closings, and stationary plants. When relocations do occur, the majority involve short-distance, intrastate moves in the direction of less urbanized areas (ibid.).

Lester Thurow (1980) further defends deindustrialization by arguing that eliminating low-productivity plants raises productivity. Plant closings ensure that capital and workers are available for reinvestment in new activities. Paradoxically, therefore, the essence of investment is disinvestment. Thurow accepts that capitalism is, after all, a doctrine of failure. "The inefficient (the majority) are to be driven out of business by the efficient (the minority), and in the process productivity rises" (p. 80). He suggests that the United States needs the national equivalent of a corporate investment committee, based on the Japanese model, to redirect investment flows from "sunset" to "sunrise" industries.

In these arguments, plant closings may be made to appear necessary as a means of promoting economic growth. But up close, looking at the communities and the people who suffer, a different view emerges. Amid this "efficient" economic reorganization, communities are battered and beaten. Jobs, investment, and energy are systematically withdrawn—shattering lives, upending careers, and uprooting families. Municipalities, moreover, are cut off from their major tax providers, eroding the tax base. Lost revenues hinder the provision of critical services like police protection, fire protection, and local housing-improvement programs at the very time of emergent community vulnerability. Residents with the least opportunity to out-migrate bear the burden of this community disintegration. They find themselves taxed at higher rates for declining services. This burden is borne in the name of "economic efficiency," which leaves in its wake unemployment, poverty, and substandard communities.

Two assumptions made by deindustrialization apologists have recently been questioned. First, workers have been presented as mobile actors easily capable of adjusting to plant relocation. It is believed that workers from menial to managerial levels can easily participate in interregional migration. They unproblematically divorce themselves from community ties, have sufficient resources to relocate, are knowledgeable about optimal regions for relocation, and migrate. Implicit is that individuals have transient connections to community and willingly relocate in response to evolving regional economies. Second, jobs created through the operations of a postindustrial economy are substitutable for manufacturing employment. Growth in retailing and service sectors, it is contended, represents viable employment alternatives to displaced factory workers. Wages, status, and sense of fulfillment are approximately equal in both instances. Critics like David Perry (1987), Norman Glickman (1987), and Richard C. Hill (1983) note the fallacy of these assumptions. They believe that, with both assumptions, worker needs are discarded to buttress an ideological position: that general economic growth is critical and requires efficient spatial organization. In effect, these apologists posit that industries should be given a free hand to go when and where they desire because of their growth-inducing societal role. These points become palpable if workers can be depicted as minimally hurt by the process and able to adjust to its footloose rigors. To critics, concealed in this rhetoric is the fact that, first, workers are often profoundly constrained from following industry across regions and, second, job loss from deindustrialization is frequently replaced by low-wage part-time work.

No declining industrial city has received as much attention as did Youngstown, Ohio (Figure 3.1). At the end of the 1970s, three major steel mills closed, laying off some 10,000 employees: the Campbell Works with some 5,000 workers; the Youngstown Works with 3,500; and the Brier Hill Works with 1,500 (Lynd, 1982, p. 6). Most notorious was the Lykes Corporation closing of the Campbell mill—a textbook case of a company deliberately

Figure 3.1   At the center of Youngstown, Ohio—in the 1980s—stands a visible and ominous abandoned steel mill.

milking a facility. Lykes, originally a shipbuilder, expanded rapidly in the 1970s to gain status as a conglomerate. It spread across many industries to absorb Youngstown Sheet and Tube. Because of the high debt Lykes incurred in purchasing the company, profits from the Campbell Works were used to pay creditors, and no capital was available for plant modernization. "During every year from 1969 through 1976, the Youngstown Sheet and Tube Corporation reported an annual profit ranging from a low $8.7 million in 1971 to a high of $96.4 million in 1974. During this period the subsidiary provided cash flow of more than $650 million. But by 1977 Lykes' consolidated debt had risen to $659 million" (Kamara, 1983, p. 41).

National finance capital played an important role in the demise of the Campbell Works. Lykes financed its acquisition by borrowing $175 million, principally from Chemical Bank, Chase Manhattan, Citibank, Marine Midland, and the Philadelphia National Bank. Inability to modernize was tied to Lykes's failure to leverage additional creditor loans. Yet, during the mid-1970s Lykes's bankers substantially increased investment in the Japanese steel industry. Between 1975 and 1977, Chase Manhattan and Chemical Bank increased loans to Japanese steel makers 346 percent and 547 percent, respectively (Kamara, 1983, p. 41). Lykes attributed the Campbell Works closing to cheap imports, costly environmental regulations, and government price restraints. But the plant's closing was not the result of national market forces, unusual or unexpected foreign competition, or governmental regulation. The Anti-trust Division of the Department of Justice had advised against the sale of Youngstown Sheet and Tube to Lykes, stating that the takeover would leave Lykes so heavily in debt that it would not be able to finance modernization. It was predicted that the Campbell Works would be closed within a decade—a prediction off by only one year.

Steel makers in the 1960s and 1970s appeared to be giving up the steel business altogether in favor of investments in other industries where profits were higher. Employment in the industry declined by about 100,000 jobs or 20 percent, and production fell 25 percent (Harrington, 1984, p. 16). Not that steel making was unprofitable. Indeed, the American steel industry may well have been the most profitable in the world, despite steel-maker assertions of noncompetitiveness. "In 1977 the Federal Trade Commission found that for the period 1961–1971 the United States had the highest profit rate, Japan second highest, and the European Community the lowest, when profit was measured by net income as a percentage of sales. When profit was measured by net income as a percentage of equity, U.S. and Japan profit rates were approximately equal. The European Community was the lowest" (Lynd, 1982, p. 208). Nonetheless, steel profits over the short run were lower than those of other industries.

The U.S. Steel Corporation (now USX) accelerated its diversification in the 1970s. Between 1976 and 1979 the corporation's nonsteel assets grew 80 percent to $4.7 billion, while steel assets increased only 13 percent to $5.9 billion (Lynd, 1982, p. 209). In 1979—the year U.S. Steel closed its Youngstown Works—the company opened a new shopping center near Pittsburgh containing Pennsylvania's largest mall, and the company joined with others to build a vast chemical works near Houston in Texas. U.S. Steel's chairman of the board reaffirmed in 1981 that new spending would go to businesses that provided the highest rates of return. Thus, in that year, company disinvestment in steel climaxed with the $6.3 billion purchase of the Marathon Oil Company.

What was the impact of mill closings on Youngstown? Closure of Lykes's Campbell Works prompted some 35 percent of its workers to opt for early retirement, the vast majority at only half of previous salary. Two years later, 15 percent were still unemployed and looking for new jobs, and 10 percent had moved. Of the remaining 40 percent who had found new employment, most had taken large pay cuts (Hayes, 1982, p. 102). In addition to the approximately 5,000 former Lykes employees, as many as 12,000 other workers were affected. Local retail sales dropped $12 million to $23 million annually in subsequent years (Bluestone and Harrison, 1982, p. 49).

Tax receipts fell off as public expenditure need rose. Within two years of closing the assessed value of Campbell Works had fallen from $13.7 million to $8.3 million with a decline of more than $300,000 in tax revenue accordingly (Bluestone and Harrison, 1982, p. 72). An estimated $70 million was paid out in various relief programs in slightly over three years following the closing, very little of which was paid for by Lykes (p. 69).

Plant closings like those at Youngstown in the 1970s are anything but catastrophic events dictated by uncontrollable circumstances. Most plant closings result from deliberate decisions to reallocate capital by failure to maintain and replace obsolete equipment. Management typically uses both operation profits and depreciation reserves for investment elsewhere. "Of course this type of capital reallocation produces a self-fulfilling prophecy. A plant that is not quite productive enough to meet the profit targets set by management will very soon be unable to make any profit at all" (Bluestone and Harrison, 1982, p. 7). Acting out such prophecies takes time, and may inflate undeserved confidence. The dashing of expectations ultimately revealed as false can be catastrophic.

Plant closings mean unemployment and economic loss for a place or region. The U.S. Bureau of Economic Analysis estimated that, with each unemployment percentage point increase in 1980, gross national product declined $68 billion and tax revenues fell $20 billion. Moreover, expenditures from unemployment insurance benefits, food stamps, and other forms of public aid rose $4 billion (Bluestone and Harrison, 1982, pp. 11 and 77). But what of personal loss to workers made redundant? M. Harvey Brenner (1976, p. 282) estimates that each percentage point increase in unemployment brings 37,000 additional deaths, including 920 suicides and 650 homicides. Mental hospital and prison populations jump by some 4,000 and 3,300 people, respectively.

Mobility, forced through job loss or otherwise, has become an American way of life. Between 1965 and 1970, 47 percent of all Americans changed their place of residence (Newman, 1980, p. 10). America had become, in essence, a nation of industrial refugees. In the 1970s some 7 million people moved to the South and some 5 million people moved to the West primarily from the Northeast and Middle West (Bluestone, 1982, p. 48). Thus, the geographical center of the U. S. population moved 58 feet to the west and 29 feet to the south each day (Lewis, Pollan, and Etheridge, 1987, p. 61). The average American family now moves about four times during the course of a marriage, and roughly one in five households moves every year (Mayer, 1978, pp. 5 and 62). David Rodnick likens America to a giant Alice in Wonderland tea party "where one moves to new place settings as soon as the old cups become dirty" (Rodnick, 1972, p. 106).

The average American holds ten different jobs before retirement, the duration of time that a worker stays with a job declining from 4.6 years in 1963 to 3.6 years in 1980 (Reich, 1983, p. 163). One-third to one-half of all managerial and white-collar employees leave their jobs each year, as opposed to only 12 percent in Europe and 6 percent in Japan (Hall, 1980, p. 60; Cole, 1979, p. 60). Worker mobility, built into the system, is aggravated by plant closures. Yet, constant disinvestment—and the ability of firms to close rapidly and move—leads managers and workers alike to short-term career horizons. Capital transfers and plant transfers force executives always to maximize short-term bottom line figures. Impermanence breeds impermanence.

Unemployment exerts psychological strain that often translates into physical disability. Job loss is tied to increases in gastrointestinal problems, more infections, and higher blood pressure. Severe medical problems associated with plant closures are hypertension, sleeplessness, alcoholism, ulcers, increased uric acid, weight loss, dyspepsia, and alopecia. Paradoxically, many lose health insurance coverage with joblessness, increasing economic and psychological burdens in a vicious circle of unemployment and poor health. An estimated 36 percent of U.S. workers and their families are uninsured (Reich, 1983, p. 204). Unemployment, moreover, brings self-doubt. Emotional response often corresponds closely to classical grief syndrome: denial, anger, guilt, depression, confusion, and lethargy (Raines, 1982, p. 282). Among blue-collar workers, job loss not only means immediate loss of income, but may mean loss of job opportunity for future generations. Sons and daughters cannot follow their parents' footsteps to build on the goodwill generated within a given firm. Alienation from life becomes more pronounced. For most middle-class people, hope means change; but for most working-class people, hope is when things stay the same (ibid.). When things do change, there develops a sense of impotence from not being influential in the change. Insecurity arises where there is little sense of permanence and where there is little opportunity to form deep attachments to trusted people in places familiar.

Although the American dream is one of economic progress, ever forward and upward, new jobs generated in a locality following plant closing usually translate into lower wages, especially for older workers. In the 1970s, real wages of Americans declined more than 20 percent (Parenti, 1983, p. 20). Nowhere were declines more evident than in the industrial Northeast and Middle West. True, the rise of service-oriented jobs paralleled declines in industrial employment. This substitution, however, was unequal. Service occupations paid less, offered less security, and provided fewer benefits. In Philadelphia, for example, the average manufacturing wage in 1980 was $265, but retail clerks and bankers earned an average of $124 and $174, respectively (Adams, 1982, p. 29). Moreover, such full-time service occupations provided substantive health-care benefits only at additional cost.

Workers displaced from industry to service occupations consequently suf-fered losses in wages, status, and health-care coverage. Lessened wealth imposed hardships on meeting mortgage payments, purchasing food, and saving. Reduced purchasing power hurts local businesses and city capacity to generate revenues.

Industrialists realize the necessity of community stability. Family, church, clubs, and schools help forge cultures of contentment that permit workers to accept everyday work practices. The sharing of common experiences and values promotes an acceptance of menial and difficult work tasks. Workers are thus inculcated with mindsets that foster subordination, allegiance, and efficiency as work requisites. Diverse personalities thus become unified in pursuit of common goals within the stable social contexts crucial to indus-trial success. Ironically, industry must disavow the need for strong commu-nity bonding when industrialists feel compelled to relocate. Communities that were previously presented as interwoven into the corporate fabric now become secondary to the felt need to act "economically" and "rationally." Community concerns are cast aside in favor of optimal profit strategies. Communities quickly become breeding grounds for anger and discord as charges of abuse and manipulation follow on the heels of corporate depar-ture (see Perry and Watkins, 1977; Beauregard, 1989).

In America, community (people related through the interaction of local-ity) is valued less; the individual—or the surrogate of the individual, the corporation—is valued more. Free-market ideology is based on the premise that motivation in human behavior is primarily based on selfishness: the individual seeking to maximize satisfactions and minimize dissatisfactions, or the corporation striving to maximize profits and minimize losses. Whereas selfishness is an important motivator (perhaps the most important motiva-tor), its worship tends to blind us to our continuing sociality, our depen-dence on others. "Free market ideology encourages a short-sightedness that does not tally the costs of human connectedness" (Raines, 1982, p. 304). Without a healthy community, there cannot be a healthy worker. Employees will likely not embrace a strong work ethic if they see their work adding to little save short-term sustenance. If they do not see their efforts cumu-lating over time in a strengthened family nurtured by a strengthened com-munity, then, in John Raines's words, "there can be no business efficiency, but only the encouragement of disillusioned workers exploiting managers and managers returning in kind" (ibid.).

Increasingly, capitalism's apologists have institutionalized the tunnel vision of individualism. Community has been denigrated in very high places. The Commission for a National Agenda for the 1980s, appointed by President Jimmy Carter in 1979, surveyed a wide range of economic and social prob-lems to advise a redirection of federal urban policies away from "place-oriented" aid to "people-oriented" projects. Aiding communities, especially through local governments, was seen as nonproductive. "According to the report, 'cities are not permanent' and policies which treat them as permanent are doomed to fail because they run against the tide of market forces. Instead, the federal government should 'let the market function and then assist people to adjust' " (Adams, 1982, p. 17). As in the nation's exploitation of its natural resources, Americans seem convinced that local communities are expendable. The redundant worker, the temporarily failed individual, is thus expected to face the future largely alone without the support apparatus that local communities have traditionally provided. This coping with the threat of human obsolescence by intensifying dedication to laissez-faire ideology may be a form of denial. "In essence, this posture constitutes a mind set against cognition of the forces impinging upon it, like the denial of death in a dying patient" (Padfield, 1980, p. 164).

Deindustrialization is a fundamental struggle between capital and community. Industrial dereliction and devastated communities attest to the dominance of capital. John Friedmann (1982, p. 20) casts this conflict in terms of "life space" versus "economic space." Life space represents the terrains of everyday existence. Its heart is the lived worlds of people and their emotional attachment to place. Economic space, in contrast, is the milieu of profit surfaces. Landscapes here are entities to be restructured for profit opportunities. Economic space, to Friedmann, ruthlessly subjugates life space. It restructures opportunities for subsistence, generates ideologies that guide everyday life, and commodifies communities. Industrialists, in effect, mobilize individual, organizational, and class resources to dominate landscape construction. Their influence is reflected in local government programs, planning policies, redevelopment initiatives, and media hyperbole. The ability to influence local organizations emerges from the dependency that localities forge with industry. As critical generators of jobs and tax dollars, community well-being is frequently seen as tied up with appeasing and nurturing industry. Place is manipulated through power and resource differentials that render landscapes economic productions.

Plant closure creates social costs that accrue to communities, costs that are rarely assumed by corporations responsible for the closure. Social costs are hidden in at least four ways. First, infrastructural costs are shifted from entrepreneur to community. Upkeep of streets, sewers, schools, and facilities fall on taxpayers. Second, social costs are transferred from rich to poor. The indigent are least able to participate in a relocation that promises economic benefits. They are left behind to pursue everyday life in a community bereft of opportunities and resources. Third, social costs are transferred from present to future. The degrading of lives and landscapes left behind becomes a social and economic burden borne by future generations. Poverty and decay are problems inherited by future residents. Fourth, social costs are transferred geographically. Regions of economic viability become focal points for capital and resource concentration at the expense of eroding regions. The polarities of vibrancy and neglect emerge that consign inadequate qualities-of-life to vast land tracts.

Rarely is there full accountability for plant closings. Almost always a profound incongruity exists between those responsible and those who suffer. The moral disparity should be obvious when a corporation executive can receive a prison sentence for embezzlement or some like white-collar crime but be rewarded for closing profitable plants. That the absolute cost to society of the plant closing may be infinitely greater than an embezzlement is not usually deemed relevant, however. Today there is an almost universal tendency to maximize self-interests and a widespread willingness to shift production costs to society to promote those self-interests (Moncrief, 1973, p. 37). The attitude toward community (and the built environment) is much the same as the attitude corporate America has traditionally held regarding the physical environment. Resources in landscape, whether physical or cultural, exist to be exploited. In exploitation, dereliction looms.

CORPORATE RESPONSIBILITY

The recent epidemic of U.S. plant closures has precipitated renewed discussion of corporate rights and responsibilities. Five stakeholder groups are involved in corporate enterprise: shareholders, managers, employees, customers, and local residents. Management is, of course, the crucial element in determining corporate responsibility. Its goal is to respect shareholder equity, employee and customer rights, and local community needs. Unfortunately, ideas of stewardship implicit in these relationships are usually negated by the dictates of short-term profit taking. The quest for profit takes precedence in a system where industrial success and survivability are measured by profit margins. This behavior is also an outgrowth of an inconsistent legal system that treats corporations in an unbalanced fashion. Under U.S. law, corporations have the rights and privileges of individuals and are treated as persons in court actions, but are not held to individual responsibilities. Critics contend that corporations, like individuals, should be held to good citizen conduct (Tuleja, 1985, p. 30).

Most corporations promote themselves as good citizens. Many give money, employee time, and equipment to community projects. Some have financial and organizational partnerships with local governments designed to facilitate local improvements. Plant closings, however, truly test the corporate conscience. Corporations like the International Business Machines Corporation

(IBM) have sought generously to subsidize employee and local community adjustments in the wake of facility shutdown. IBM had operated in Greencastle, Indiana, for 33 years. Plant closure meant loss to the town of a $38-million payroll. The company chose to give the city $1.7 million to offset lost taxes and continue for three years its annual $120,000 United Way contribution. Its 350,000-square-foot plant was also donated (Kleinfield, 1988). Employees were given the option of transferring to other company locations or taking early retirement, with IBM buying the houses of transferees. Corporate subsidy fostered creation of a local Economic Development Corporation, which in one year was able to attract six new local companies. But, as encouraging as the Greencastle case might be, it is unrealistic to assume widespread emulation.

Critics of plant closings began vigorously in the 1970s to advocate remedial legislation at both state and federal levels. Recognizing two major areas of concern—economic and psychological trauma to individuals and the fiscal problems of impacted communities—proposals called for a range of actions. Advance notice from six months to two years would provide time for communities to plan and implement adjustments. Severance pay to affected employees, incentives for employee ownership, subsidies for employee retraining, continuation of health insurance coverage, reimbursement of employee relocation expenses, and paid leave time prior to relocation would aid worker adjustments (Littman and Lee, 1984, p. 129). Local governments would be aided by direct financial assistance. Advocates also called for changes designed to minimize closings. Eliminating state and federal tax incentives that spur corporate flight, it was contended, was crucial. Strong takeover regulations were also proposed that would discourage conglomerates from seizing assets of small and medium-sized firms. Corporations might be required to show cause as to why profitable operations must be shut down.

Corporate defenders criticize such proposals as unduly interventionist. Normal market operations are purportedly thrown into disarray. Premature disclosure of intention to close plants damages relations with suppliers and customers who might seek alternative outlets and sources. In the wake of an early closure announcement that would demoralize workers, productivity could fall, with workers even engaging in deliberate sabotage. Subsidies to local government would compound unprofitable conditions, exacerbating rather than easing decline. Government intervention of this sort is purportedly another illustration of obtrusive and meddlesome government. Regulations impede economic efficiency, thwart "natural" market signals, and obstruct entrepreneurial acumen. The market, it is reasserted, is an effective self-regulator that requires only minimal tampering. Thus, such laws purportedly hasten corporate demise; they compound the very problem they seek to eradicate.

The closing of profitable plants will cease to be problematical when corporations perceive the practice as too costly. With minimal costs accruing, unrestricted capital mobility will continue to tear the financial and cultural roots out of working-class neighborhoods in big cities and small towns. Belief in work ethics, community stability, and individual determination are rendered cruel and illusory by the dynamic ebb and flow of job opportunities in such communities today. To embrace these beliefs in times of scant job opportunities is to induce pain and suffering. Hardship and feelings of inadequacy follow from inability to attain symbols of self-worth. To what extreme do we need to go to minimize profitable plant closure? John Raines believes in the effectiveness of a simple rewriting of tax laws: "We need to use tax laws to encourage corporations to update factories where they are. The human uses of extended family and of stable neighborhoods means new jobs need to be directed to already established industrial areas" (1982, p. 282). On the other hand, Richard C. Edwards, Robert Reich, and Thomas Weisskopf (1978) advocate a major societal restructuring where industry is collectivized to reflect the interests of people. Corporations need to act in the interests of community and workers when privatization hurts these groups; the public must seize corporate control. The fundamental capitalist impulses—the drive for profit, and community resource exploitation—render workers mere inputs in production. They are valued and treated as substitutable factors of production. The need is for a participatory form of corporation where equal material access among workers and owners is assured. This goal requires the obviously problematical abolition of private ownership to more equitably redistribute wealth.

BUREAUCRACY

Thoroughly rationalized by the profit motive, the management of the modern American corporation tends to minimize worker participation in decision making. American business (and government as well) has been substantially bureaucratized in the twentieth century, for the nation has experienced a "management revolution" with behavioralism providing the intellectual underpinnings: the belief that human nature can be molded through social engineering and that theories of human behavior can be applied universally. The machine, "streamlined, precise, engineered, devoid of superfluous parts," is the model for the new organizational efficiency (Reich, 1983, p. 57). Robert Reich identifies three principles at work (p. 64). First, work is made specialized through task simplification, enabling widespread use of inexperienced and unskilled workers at low cost. Second, predetermined rules are adopted to coordinate tasks; the workers related primarily through management hierarchies. Third, detailed monitoring of job performance invites formal, quantitative assessments rather than personalized qualitative evaluations.

Bureaucratic organizations necessarily tend to separate the thinkers from the doers. Feedback from operations to planning tends to be diluted through layers of responsibility lodged hierarchically. Authority is based not so much on knowledge-specific skills as on status defined in terms of influence. Careerism substantially affects decision making, decisions tending to reflect personal goals within organizations more than collective needs. Success, according to Reich (1983, p. 72), reflects the forcefulness of a manager's personality, his cleverness at analysis (especially at manipulating numbers), and his sense of detachment. The successful bureaucrat prides himself on making difficult decisions, and may even create difficulties for others in order to demonstrate self-worth. Layers of self-serving bureaucrats tend to make organizations "rigid, less able to make quick decisions, and to adjust rapidly to new opportunities and problems" (p. 143). In 1980, business administrative costs exceeded $800 billion, with $500 billion going to executives (Parenti, 1983, p. 17).

With widening gaps between managers and workers, organizations become increasingly reliant on quantifiable data. Managers concentrate on month-to-month profit figures, sales growth data, and return on investment. Less quantifiable information, such as product quality, worker morale, and customer satisfaction—although as important to a firm's long-term success— cannot be conveyed upward as efficiently through a hierarchy (Reich, 1983, p. 144). Subjective information does not invite quick, decisive action. "Soft" information may prove too bothersome, being vague and impressionistic or anecdotal, even though it may disclose deep problems and effective solutions to those problems. The use of formulas eases the manager's conscience in making the "hard" decisions that negatively impact others—even whole communities.

C. Wright Mills (1951, p. 1) coined the term *organization man* to describe the modern upwardly mobile manager. Like the small businessman before him, the organization man expresses allegiance to the work ethic with its virtues of initiative and thrift. As a member of a hierarchical system, however, he has become deferential to authority to the extent of surrendering idiosyncratic distinctiveness. "He is an accepted member of a miniature social system whose values of belongingness, togetherness, and scientism have narrowed his intellectual perspectives to the point where his judgements are singularly predictable" (Furay, 1977, p. 104). Hard work and frugality have been obscured by the drive to fit in. Getting along and being influential have become prime virtues—what Carol Furay (ibid.) calls a "personality ethic" with prescriptions for being liked and sought after by management superiors, business associates, and customers.

Vital to the workings of a bureaucracy are the functionaries who are in the organization but not really of it: the secretaries, the clerks, the salespeople, the computer operators, the mechanical technicians, the stagnated lower and middle managers. These are people who are going nowhere in the organization and know it. "Their efforts, if efficient, will win them raises, but not real prestige, for the reason that they do not have their feet on the established ladder of major advancement" (Furay, 1977, p. 104). They represent a silent majority contently going about their lives with varying degrees of competency, largely indistinguishable one from another. White-collar jobs are routine, affording little opportunity for initiative, close reasoning, or imaginative exercise. The white-collar worker may achieve competence in work, but his or her real interests lie elsewhere, especially in the leisure time pursuit of self-fulfillment. Valuing security, the white-collar worker adapts to the norms of the organization. The result is a rampantly conformist social setting that discourages diversity.

Factory work—what has been called blue-collar employment—is the most conformist of all. Workers are closely tied to machines in an interconnected system of production that requires careful timing for integration on rapidly moving assembly lines. Human labor is machinelike, being highly regimented if not outright monotonous. Work does not proceed at the worker's pace, but according to the celerity of the machine as gauged by the constant oversight of managers. Performing highly specialized tasks for which little or no skill is required, most factory workers are little more than machine tenders, their work meaningless in its immediate context save as a necessary means of making a living. Most factory and office work remains external to workers in that it does not contribute to an essential sense of being (Muller, 1971, p. 335). Through the machine and machinelike work relationships, workmanship has been reduced to "labor," a commodity to be bought and sold as any other in the marketplace, according to rules that largely ignore an individual's human value.

The bureaucratic organization of work operates to legitimize inequality as income and wealth are pyramided up hierarchies of organization and ownership. The wealth of America is not owned by a broad middle class. In 1980, some 1.6 percent of the population owned some 80 percent of all capital stock, nearly 100 percent of all state and municipal bonds, and 88.5 percent of all corporate bonds (Parenti, 1983, p. 11). In nearly every major industry, a few giant corporations controlled 60–98 percent of the business, some 200 companies accounting for nearly 80 percent of the nation's manufacturing resources (ibid.). As political scientist Michael Parenti emphasizes, almost all social institutions existing in America, along with the immense material and vocational resources they possess, are under plutocratic control, "ruled by nonelected, self-selected, self-perpetuating groups of affluent corporate representatives who are answerable to no one but themselves" (ibid.).

The typical American has not only a highly restricted but a highly fragmented view of life. One comprehends the narrow work niche bureaucratically configured from which economic sustenance derives, and a limited number of social niches often related to work or to the status of one's work. Americans are variously entangled in related sets of institutional participation—entailments that serve to restrict experience. Key to blue-collar or working-class America's sense of belonging are the relationships of family, neighboring, and such institutions as churches. The bureaucracies of work, for most, are inherently alienating.

People encountered day to day in settings bureaucratically organized reveal themselves only in specific capacities for specialized reasons. The overview of life—the big picture of how various niches fit together and what lies beyond—is come by with great difficulty. Individuals see life in isolated pieces. "The minimal consistency of experience and cohesion of cultural context necessary for the formulation of judgements—whether ethical, aesthetic or utilitarian—is hard to find" (Clark, 1960, p. 18). For many Americans, the inability to comprehend events—let alone conceptualize ways and means of influencing them—has led to apathy. Specialization has wrought widespread indifference and even cynicism. Apathy invites inertia when emotional biases stand against constructive action even in the face of pressing problems (p. 36).

Bureaucratic systems do more than organize work. They organize life. The management revolution has promoted efficiencies through specialization and hierarchies of control, but it has also promoted a fragmented view of life that tends to foster indifference. As power diffuses down the hierarchies of business and government, so wealth, influence, and prestige well up to the favor of owners and controllers. The values of elites hold sway, business people emphasizing profit through cycles of capital investment, with government facilitating, encouraging, and protecting investments. For the majority of Americans, who are functionaries within bureaucratized niches, one's lot is not to question but to accept.

The lessons of the machine were applied to human management–wrought efficiencies. Nonetheless, as big corporations have gained oligopolistic and even monopolistic control over whole sectors of the national economy, inefficiencies have come to the fore, inviting neglect of product, customer, worker, and even investor. When a nation's markets are dominated by two or three large firms, and foreign producers are excluded or disadvantaged through barriers to trade, then flabbiness should not be unexpected. Although American markets were opened to the world and, indeed, made vulnerable by a highly priced dollar through much of the 1970s and 1980s, a legacy of lethargic bureaucracy lingered on not only in corporate but especially in supportive governmental bigness.

Traditionally, big business has been expected to exploit labor by restricting wages. Big business has been expected to exploit the consumer by restricting production and raising prices in controlled markets. But what has not been appreciated until rather recently is the proneness to inefficiency and decay that oligopoly and monopoly represent. "The monopolist sets a high price for his products not to amass super-profits, but because he is unable to keep his costs down; or, more typically, he allows the quality of the product or service he sells to deteriorate without gaining any pecuniary advantage in the process" (Hirschman, 1970, p. 56). To most Americans, bureaucracy has come to mean inefficiency: organizations top heavy with personnel who are protected in formal relationships ossified in codification. Problems go unidentified; decisions are made slowly. Inefficient bureaucracy is seen to thrive where competition is lacking.

Big corporations have come to control the American economy through oligopolistic practices. The proportion of total manufacturing assets held by the 200 largest companies increased from 45 percent in 1947 to 60 percent in 1968 (Agnew, 1987, p. 16). By 1975, the 200 largest manufacturing firms had a greater share of all manufacturing, sales, employment, and assets than the top 500 had in 1955; by 1980, the 50 largest American manufacturers owned 42 percent of all assets used in manufacturing, and the top 500 owned 72 percent (Harris, 1981, p. 25). "Four or fewer companies dominate 99 percent of the domestic production of cars, 92 percent of the flat glass, 90 percent of cereal breakfast foods, 90 percent of turbines and turbine engines, 90 percent of electric lamps, 85 percent of household refrigerators and freezers, 84 percent of cigarettes, 83 percent of television picture tubes, 79 percent of aluminum production and 73 percent of tires and inner tubes" (ibid.). It is evident in most of these industrial sectors that quality of product has declined as price has increased. Not until the recent large-scale entry of foreign corporations into American markets have circumstances of real competition upset the oligopolistic tendency toward wasteful bureaucracy.

Clearly, much of the dereliction found in America's wasted industrial landscapes (those places reduced through deindustrialization) carries the imprint of bureaucracy. Bureaucratic insensitivity to the needs of workers, and to the needs of the communities that they occupy and sustain, sustains instead the triumph of capital mobility. Efficiency translated into profits—and usually short-term profits at that—renders the individual worker little more than a productive unit expendable in his or her redundancy. Lodged in the system, the individual's lot is not to question. Despite the glorification of the individual and individualism in America, it is in fact the worker's role to accept as inevitable the changes of deindustrialization.

INDUSTRIAL DERELICTION

Plant closings and related unemployment and underemployment translate eventually into communities with abandoned houses and empty storefronts. But nothing strikes a sense of pathos more than the ruined factory. Nothing seems so senseless as the neglected industrial plant rundown and abused. Perhaps it is scale. Massive walls and towering stacks, and other paraphernalia of industrialism, speak of technical and organizational sophistication. To see them derelict is to see failed dreams: prosperity gone awry not just for the entrepreneur, but for the collective of dependent individuals.

The evidences of deindustrialization are all about us. One can categorize the evidence residual in landscapes along a scale of dereliction. First come the facilities no longer active but mothballed in speculation of reopening. Critical machinery is given periodic maintenance and the plant exterior is

Figure 3.2   Much of America's basic industrial infrastructure lay underutilized or closed in the 1980s like U.S. Steel's Munhall Works at Pittsburgh. What once symbolized national strength had come to symbolize national weakness.

kept weather-tight. Security guards protect against fire and vandalism. But the plant is empty. As it stands idle, technical skills decline among idled workers and machinery grows obsolete. Metropolitan Pittsburgh has been a place to see the steel industry in such animated suspension. Reluctance to modernize in the face of foreign competition, and the determination to invest in other industries, resulted in mothballing the U.S. Steel Corporation's Munhall Works in the 1980s (Figure 3.2). Still impressive as gigantic architecture, the mill sits quiet as a cemetery. In such places, the week holds only Sundays. The demise of the American steel industry also reflects in the mothballed lake freighters at places like Superior in Wisconsin (Figure 3.3). Ships are no longer needed to supply the blast furnaces with iron, since the furnaces themselves are silent.

A second dereliction type involves active disinvestment and underutilization. A factory is no longer fully maintained although operations may continue. Lack of repair shows in chipped paint, dingy brick, and general accumulation of grit and grime in ceremonial areas of office and entrance. Debris accumulates in less public areas. Closure has been postponed as ongoing activity squeezes final value from the plant and only the date of the eventual demise remains in doubt. Danville, Virginia, is a place to appreciate benign industrial disinvestment. The city economy still hinges around to-

Figure 3.3   Reverberations from the steel industry's retrenchment were felt across the nation. Here at Superior, Wisconsin, much of the American Great Lakes freighter fleet lay dormant in the 1980s, awaiting salvage.

Figure 3.4   Largely vacated by the tobacco industry, Danville, Virginia's warehouses have enjoyed modest reuse, at least on the ground floors.

bacco processing and cotton textile manufacture, although new facilities for both activities now operate well beyond the old industrial zones. A walk through Danville's old tobacco district is to step back in time. Although some massive brick blocks now house retailing, most still function as warehouses, some as tobacco warehouses (Figure 3.4). Yet, much current activity is confined to ground levels in an era of forklifts and truck loadings. Only the upper stories reflect the effects of disinvestment. Expressionless windows hint of an emptiness hidden within.

A third dereliction type involves buildings structurally abused as new functions are fitted into spaces poorly designed to receive them. Buildings are stripped of machinery and fittings and marketed as vacant space. If a large complex, it may be divided and variously cannibalized, losing much architectural integrity in the process. Lacking sufficient demand, sections may stand vacant. Lack of paint, broken glass, and structural weaknesses abound. Vacant lots, decaying streets, and abused railroad tracks give the place a totally disordered look. Lawrence, Massachusetts, is a place to see such activity. Rooted in early nineteenth-century cotton milling, jobs began moving south in the 1920s and plant closings and runaway shops have been endemic since. Antiquated factories have served as industrial incubators,

Figure 3.5   The textile industry fled Lawrence, Massachusetts, decades ago for cheap labor markets in the South. Mill buildings, cannibalized for marginal activities, are rapidly approaching the point of forced demolition.

places where new firms could get established but where successful incubations did not tarry long. Old factories have also housed temporary contract activities where entrepreneurs, attracted to inexpensive rental space and unskilled labor, conduct temporary enterprises. Space is leased, machines are rented, unskilled employees are hired, and—once a contract has been fulfilled—such a shop is closed often after only months of operation. Such frequent turnover without long-term place commitment lends to rapid structural deterioration. Parcels along Lawrence's canals bear witness to such abuse (Figure 3.5).

A fourth kind of industrial dereliction involves abandoned structures without maintenance or direct supervision. The dereliction concept most clearly applies here, for owners have walked away completely to invest elsewhere. Buildings stand completely in ruin. Standard City, Illinois, exhibits a most striking relic of a long-abandoned coal mining operation that once sustained an entire town economy (Figure 3.6). The tall stack thrusts up above the prairie, too costly to demolish. The building surprises the visitor who is otherwise unaware of the area's past industrial dominance. To some, the romance of the ghost town attaches.

Figure 3.6   Industrial buildings, if left in a state of
ruin long enough, can assume an aura of romance.

A fifth order of dereliction is the factory under demolition. Change is
visibly ongoing. A building once useful is rendered useless by tangible
human action. Wrecking produces truly ephemeral land uses of disorder—
virtual theaters of controlled violence. Lacking a market for cannibalized
materials, an enclosure is reduced to rubble and cleared land. The parcel
becomes space clear and simple. Land is cleansed and made ready for new
rounds of investment unencumbered by the past. The industrial cities of the
Northeast and Middle West exhibit widespread factory demolition. Detroit,
for example, is a place actively disassembling its industrial infrastructure
(Figure 3.7). New York City demolishes more than ten industrial buildings
every month (Stegman and Hillstrom, 1984). Many are in the old South

Figure 3.7   Cleansing the land through demolition produces transient ruin, as in this Detroit downriver industrial district in the 1980s.

Bronx industrial core. This three-square-mile stretch of land once housed more than 400 industries in the 1940s. Philadelphia destroys 10–15 industrial buildings monthly, generating vast acres of downtown vacant land awaiting reuse. Nearby Camden, New Jersey, continues to bulldoze its antiquated industrial core; downtown is currently more than 40 percent vacant land.

Our present economic system invites short-term profit taking whereby maintenance in old locations is discouraged in anticipation of new investments elsewhere. Government policy assists this process. Plant owners are accorded the right to relocate. Tax policy encourages new plant construction. Workers are believed protected by their ability to migrate and follow employment patterns; footloose industrial practices are purportedly beneficial to economic productivity. They are, in effect, given a hand to plunder communities and labor on behalf of "the general economic good." In the process, landscapes are despoiled, built environments allowed to decay, and household subsistence made contingent on entrepreneurial profit decisions. The expansionary drive of capitalist firms has led to enormous economic growth in the United States. Wealth, goods, and services have multiplied in an unprecedented fashion. This growth, however, has been uneven spatially. Amid economic productivity, vast landscapes have experienced slow growth or economic deterioration. General economic expansion has arisen here at the expense of quality of life for many. Deindustrialized regions, once replenished by footloose capital, become devastated by the same process that brought prosperity.

Capitalism has produced impermanence in American landscapes. Since World War II, this trend has accelerated, with the growth of global capitalism hastening corporate dominance and the entrepreneurial ability to relocate. In this global process, U.S. industry has increasingly penetrated foreign markets and imposed the capital–labor relation on far-flung populations. In this capitalist encroachment, the emergent large corporation plays out intercontinental strategies of generating profits. Land, labor, capital, and raw materials are manipulated by production of landscapes. When landscape is obsolete for this purpose, relocation offers opportunities to reproduce these conditions elsewhere. The continued growth of business and government bureaucracies, moreover, legitimates the corporate relocation strategy. The cloaking of subjective and political decisions in verbiage of objectivity and rationality provides an arena for corporate legitimacy. Technocratic objectivity conceals the distribution of costs and benefits that relocation incurs. Relocation is cast as "efficient," "economically maximizing," and "value free." Technical expertise meticulously renders optimal corporate decisions. Critics of relocation policy are labeled well-intentioned but lacking technical knowledge and skills. The result is a corporate commodification of space. Left behind is the destruction of once productive industrial landscapes as profits are pursued elsewhere.

4

Central City Decline

It is difficult to reside in an urbanized America today and be detached from all the problems that are evident. A stroll through central cities reveals massive tracts of decay and deterioration. Abandoned buildings, litter-strewn lots, decaying sidewalks, and homeless people dot the urban landscape. Revitalized housing tracts, discerned only after experiencing areas of dilapidation, reflect a selective upgrading that directly benefits a small urban group. To glimpse the "urban renaissance" purportedly emergent downtown requires the sober recognition of sustained disinvestment. For example, large sections of Pittsburgh, Baltimore, and Philadelphia vividly reflect disinvestment, as the accompanying photographs depict (Figures 4.1–4.3). Social and physical ills continue to be concentrated in decaying central cities while most new investment continues to be made in suburbia. Most central city neighborhoods, certainly in the nation's older industrial centers, have been left to prolonged decay that persistently defies band-aid public improvement.

Conditions threaten to intensify. In these conservative times when egalitarian strivings are criticized as idealist or utopian, federal and state governments have all but abandoned the quest to reverse central city impoverishment. A history of failed government programs minimizes ameliorative efforts. The private sector, moreover, has systematically withdrawn urban resources to pursue profit in suburbia and beyond. In this context, periodic pleas for assistance generally have fallen on deaf ears. Urban advocates are widely perceived as practicing "poverty politics" and "welfare perpetuation." Liberal thinking and derived emancipatory politics, submerged under the criticism of naiveté and self-aggrandizement (see Short, 1987), have been ineffective against the power and the resources of the new conservatism. The 1980s emphasis on fiscal restraint and unfettered market benefits has marginalized urban unity and agendas under the weight of poverty and despair.

93

Figure 4.1   The riverfront of Allegheny City on Pittsburgh's westside was cleared through federally subsidized "urban renewal" in the 1950s. It lay largely vacant and underdeveloped for decades.

This chapter examines central city dereliction, with the neglect of central city neighborhoods at the expense of suburbia constituting the focus. We initially sketch central city decline in statistical form. Processes driving dereliction then comprise the emphasis, with competing explanations for dereliction explored. We examine poverty as a mechanism sustaining central city dereliction. At issue is the debilitating influence of poverty that has exacerbated and prolonged disinvestment. Governmental attempts at eradicating poverty and dereliction will be our final focus. Federal and local improvement schemes are evaluated to shed light on the government failures that have underlain the perpetuation of central city blight. Dereliction proceeds despite society's avowed responsibility to eliminate it and its debilitating consequences.

DECLINE IN STATISTICAL OVERVIEW

Demographic and other statistics enable one to sketch a concise outline of central city decline over past decades. Thus, in central cities, jobs increased 17 percent between 1960 and 1977 (from 23 million to 27 million

Figure 4.2   Baltimore's Bolton Hill had become badly blighted by the 1960s, with much vacant housing.

workers), but 95 percent in the suburbs (from 20 million to 39 million) (Illinois Advisory Committee, 1981, p. 6). Central city manufacturing employment declined from 33 percent to 26 percent of the national total between 1960 and 1978 (Morial, 1968, p. 32). A host of rustbelt cities illustrate this economic shift. Metropolitan Chicago experienced a 16-percent net decrease in number of manufacturing firms between 1966 and 1976; the suburbs realized a 41-percent growth (Squires, 1982, p. 65). Detroit lost more than 70 percent of its manufacturing jobs over a quarter of a century (280,000 jobs in some 3,300 firms in the late 1940s as compared to less than 100,000 jobs in fewer than 1,700 firms in the early 1980s) (Luria and Russell, 1984, p. 271). Philadelphia nongovernmental employment decreased 23 percent between 1953 and 1985 (Beauregard, 1989). The bulk of the 184,388 jobs lost relocated to suburbia and sunbelt states. The Pittsburgh region lost 35.8 percent of its durable manufacturing job base between 1980 and 1984 (Clark, 1989). Nondurable manufacturing jobs declined 11.1 percent in this four-year period.

Central city retail trade and retail jobs declined in response, with inability to retain jobs and affluent households diminishing purchasing power and retail viability. Chicago lost 15 percent of its retail establishments while suburbs experienced a 33-percent gain between 1970 and 1978 (Illinois

Figure 4.3   In Philadelphia's North End, much of the local retail infrastructure stood abandoned by the 1970s.

Advisory Committee, 1981, p. 3). Detroit had a 51-percent share of metropolitan area retail trade in 1958 that fell to 19 percent by 1977 (Morial, 1986, p. 32). Philadelphia decline was nearly as steep in the same period, from 51 percent to 29 percent (ibid.). St. Louis lost 6,000 retail businesses between 1948 and 1972, including 300 in the central business district; the remainder of the metropolis gained 4,500 (Schmandt, Wendel, and Tomey, 1983, p. xvi).

With declining central city employment, household incomes dropped. In 1983, median income for U.S. central city and suburban families was $22,286 and $29,397, respectively—a 32-percent difference (Meyers, 1986). This central city–suburban income disparity had been 18 percent and 28 percent in 1959 and 1979 (ibid.). Rustbelt cities, again, most vividly reflect these disparities. Between 1970 and 1980, New York City, Baltimore, Boston, Cleveland, and other cities had suburban per-capita income increases outpacing their central city counterparts by more than 5 percent (U.S. Census Bureau, 1980). In Chicago, Newark, and Detroit, this differential was more than 10 percent.

Unemployment and welfare dependency has soared in the nation's central cities. Unemployment has consistently run near or over 20 percent for inner-city blacks in such places as Detroit, Chicago, and Newark. Nation-wide, the unemployment rate among blacks was 15.3 percent in 1986, 2.5 times that of whites (Meyers, 1986, p. 3). More than 400,000 Detroiters—one of every three—were receiving some form of public assistance in 1981 (Luria and Russell, 1984, p. 273). Between 1969 and 1974 alone, the number of families in the Aid to Families with Dependent Children (AFDC) and General Assistance (GA) programs in Detroit increased some 187 percent, from 80,000 to 256,000 people (Hill, 1984, p. 320). In St. Louis, some 16 percent of the city's population was on welfare in the early 1980s, including 25 percent of those over 60 years old and 45 percent of all blacks (Schmandt, Wendel, and Tomey, 1983, p. xvi). By the late 1980s, one in every five central city residents lived in poverty—more than double the nation's suburban rate (Meyers, 1986, p. 3).

Central cities have experienced precipitous declines in population. During the 1970s, 84 of America's 176 cities with 100,000 or more people showed no gain in population, an estimated 31 percent showing decline between 1980 and 1984 (Morial, 1986, p. 32). During the 1970s, one-fifth of Detroit's population abandoned the city. Since 1950, the city declined by some 650,000 people—a population equal that of San Francisco. St. Louis declined from 880,000 people in 1950 to 453,000 in 1980 (Schmandt, Wendel, and Tomey, 1983, p. xv). For the 1970s, rates of population decline, city to city, include: –27 percent for St. Louis; –24 percent for Cleveland; –19 percent for Pittsburgh; –16 percent for Washington, D.C.; –14 percent for Newark; –13 percent for Philadelphia; –11 percent for Chicago; and –10 percent for New York City (Meyers, 1986, p. 31). In 1950, 59 percent of America's metropolitan residents lived in central cities and 41 percent in their suburbs. By 1980, the proportions had been almost exactly reversed.

Disinvestment, job loss, and the concentration of the poor has threatened most of America's older industrial cities with fiscal collapse. Welfare needs have escalated at the same time that property values—the traditional bulwark of municipal finance—have eroded. Cities have adopted income taxes and increased utility taxes among other measures in order to correct revenue shortfalls. Central city tax rates are high. On average, city residents pay 23 percent more in local taxes per capita than do suburbanites (Meyers, 1986, p. 3). In the 1970s, Detroiters came to shoulder a tax rate four times that of the average city in Michigan (Hill, 1984, p. 320). Despite higher taxes, tax receipts fell. In St. Louis, returns from property taxes decreased 10 percent between 1972 and 1978 (Schmandt, Wendel, and Tomey, 1983, p. 9). Between 1966 and 1977, the assessed valuation of real property in St. Louis dropped from $1.59 billion to $1.37 billion (p. 11).

In 1970, central cities held a 148:144 seat advantage over suburban interests in Congress; but in 1986, 19 congressional districts were urban, 228 suburban, and 128 rural (Meyers, 1986, p. 5). Strapped financially by falling local revenues, American central cities found themselves less able to obtain relief at the federal level. In the Nixon years, the growing suburban–rural majority turned its back on the central cities. The administration's New Federalism called for general revenue sharing, rather than programs specifically targeted at central city problems. Federal monies were distributed alike both to poor cities and to rich suburbs, and elected officials could use this funding as they saw fit without direct community involvement. Most central city politicians used revenue sharing to finance central business district development in efforts to improve local tax bases and accommodate real estate and banking interests (Tabb, 1984, p. 4). This trend continued through the Reagan administration. Total urban aid was cut more than 20 percent between 1980 and 1988 (see Feagin, 1984). In this period, Section 8 funding (administered by HUD) for new construction and substantial rehabilitation decreased from $10.2 billion to $1.5 billion, with construction/rehabilitation units declining from 141,530 to 10,032 (Zarembka, 1990). Block grants—the major redevelopment subsidy to central cities—declined more than 30 percent in this period. This program, moreover, was often used to subsidize affluent redevelopment at the expense of improving indigent housing and job opportunities (see Wong and Peterson, 1986; Wilson, 1989). Conspicuous consumption malls, hotels, and sports arenas were frequent block grant recipients, to the detriment of housing and neighborhood improvement schemes. While jobs were undoubtedly created, many were part-time and low-wage occupations (see Beauregard, 1989). The urban poor have been hit hard by this neglect. As of 1985, almost 9.9 million such households could not afford to pay anything for housing and still pay for other basic necessities (Zarembka, 1990). Consequently, despite there being only 1.3 million public housing units nationwide, an estimated one-half million families currently wait for such housing.

CENTRAL CITY DERELICTION

An array of competing notions have been advanced to explain central city decline and dereliction. These notions present causal mechanisms that can be arrayed on an explanatory continuum ranging from unfettered agency to structural determination. Individuals have been presented as ranging from autonomous voluntarists to passive bearers of materialist forces. On the one hand, individuals have been removed from wider economic and political contexts—choices seen to reflect unbounded personal predilections. On the other hand, choices are seen to be subsumed under structuralist imperatives—underlying societal drives exerting causal influence through the medium

of individual actions. These polar opposites have, quite surprisingly, dominated attempts to explain contemporary central city dereliction. A middle
ground between these extremes has been sought but has proved surprisingly
elusive. The discussion that follows reviews these competing explanations.

Social-technological theorists have advanced the most commonly accepted
explanation for central city decline and dereliction (see Adams, 1970; Muller,
1981; Tobin, 1976). Decline here is believed to emerge from increasing
suburban dominance and the technologies that have facilitated population
dispersal. These theorists depict central city dereliction as logical amid
technological advances and individual desires to live outside cities. On the
one hand, innovations in transportation and technology have allowed residency to spill outward from city centers. One could live on the ever-expanding urban periphery and still maintain central business contact. Four
distinctive periods of transport innovation are noted: the walking-horsecar
era (1800–1880), the trolley era (1880–1920), the recreational automobile
era (1920–1945), and the freeway era (1945 to the present). At the same
time, a deeply ingrained rural ethic has motivated households to take advantage of transport innovations and out-migrate. The tenets of Jefferson-
ian democracy with its emphasis on agrarian living, combined with such
powerful anti-urban images as congestion, social pathologies, and class di-
visions, fuel the desire to leave. In characterizing this ethic, Peter Muller
(1981) describes the city as a symbol for corruption, social inequity, and
disorder. From the very beginnings of our cities, he suggests, "a strong wish
persisted to make these economic centers noncities, and the parallel emergence of suburbia represented the continual attempt to recreate the agrarian ideal and its lifestyles in a metropolitan setting" (p. 23). In this view,
urban society appropriated technology to meet pent-up demands for a suburban society.

Social-technological theorists posit a controversial view of urban change.
Implicit is a neoclassical perspective that applies consumer-dominated tenets to the examination of urban land markets. Everyday change gets mediated through a neutral and value-free marketplace. Consumer choices are
expressed and society allocates resources to permit realization of preferences. Social harmony rather than conflict characterizes the market. Constraints on access, including position in the housing market and institutional
barriers, are subsumed under household wishes. Diverse market agents ostensibly allocate resources to meet consumer preference; they are apolitical
operatives that conform to a societal role. Suburbanization unfolds as a
consumer-directed process informed by a repugnance for urban living. Thus,
banks, lenders, realtors, government officials, and the like are essentially
harmonious actors that seek to please constituencies. They help build transport systems to satisfy consumers; developers build housing to meet con-

sumption desires; residents choreograph such actions through expression of consumption preferences. The fact that a select range of actors has stood to benefit primarily by suburbanization is less important. It follows that the influences of builder profits, realtor commissions, and bank lending practices are marginal relative to the guiding hand of consumer tastes.

This model has been criticized on grounds of idealism and simplicity. To critics, suburbanization was catalyzed by institutions that profited enormously from it. Builders, developers, banks, and landlords were purportedly more than passive resource providers intent on satisfying consumer tastes. Such actions are believed to be important, because they substantially structured the environment in which consumer decisions were made, housing choices realized, and housing constraints imposed (Bassett and Short, 1980). Land, for example, was an essential prerequisite for housing development that was often meticulously controlled through local zoning regulations, landowner predilections for development, availability of capital to build, and realtor "steering" actions. They contend that to dismiss the complex institutional context within which suburbanization was filtered through is to present a romanticized view of metropolitan development.

Critics also note that the technological determinist model treats urban change as gradual, evolutionary, and predictable. Outcomes seem determined (Gordon, 1978). The market, by implication, generates desired suburbanization and needs minimal government regulation and interaction. To counter this idealized vision, critics note that central city change is contingent and often carefully directed. As mediators of urban change, markets are thus not merely "meetings between producers and consumers, whose relations are ordered by the impersonal 'laws' of supply and demand" (Logan and Molotch, 1987, p. 11). Change, it is believed, gets filtered through a local political lens where some groups exert disproportionate influence. Growth and transformation involve a complex local web of interest-group interactions. Most importantly, local elites comprised of large developers, builders, city government, and the media seek to choreograph growth through manipulation of local policies. The poor frequently organize to counter this growth agenda but are usually unsuccessful. Conflict that follows is asymmetrical, where differently equipped contenders mobilize organizational resources. Processes like central city decline emerge as anything but value-free and neutral processes; an array of costs and benefits are incurred that fall on different population groups differentially.

Industrial-materialist theorists explain central city dereliction and decline in a more holistic context. David Gordon (1978), a major proponent, takes as his starting point the pervasive influence of accumulation in North America that penetrates everyday life (see also Mollenkopf, 1978; Perry and Watkins, 1977). Gordon argues that the process of capital accumulation has been the most important factor structuring urban change, with the logic of capitalism restructuring cities in response to prevailing accumulation modes. The city is believed to be an apparatus that functions to generate wealth. Its role as sustainer of capitalism is crucial: it is here that land, labor, and capital can be efficiently harnessed to facilitate wealth production. Three stages of capital accumulation are presented: the commercial, industrial, and corporate eras. Each era defines evolving urban form only to become systematically restructured to accommodate new accumulation practices; spatial barriers to accumulation are systematically destroyed by government and private-sector initiatives. For example, aging industrial and retailing parcels, once viable but rendered antiquated and standing in the way of new production forms, become redevelopment foci. Other marginal buildings that occupy increasingly valued land need to be demolished. They may impede land being used in its highest and best use. Slums, moreover, may threaten perceptions of an emerging downtown renaissance and require displacement to less visible locations. These accumulation barriers must be removed if the city is to continue as an accumulation container.

Central city dereliction here has its roots in the early twentieth century, where the antecedents to advanced corporate accumulation took hold. In particular, increasing urban strife of the late nineteenth century posed a clear threat to corporate legitimacy. Workers increasingly confronted abusive labor practices and poor living conditions by strikes and walkouts. Industry, however, frequently lacked the financial resources to flee the city for more "serene" environments. Consequently, owner–worker tensions in Chicago, New York City, Baltimore, Boston, and elsewhere were seen fearfully and controlled through a combination of worker concessions and stiff union opposition. For many industries, suburban out-migration was fiscally untenable. This resource lack begins to change, however, in the 1920s and 1930s when massive U.S. merger and buyout created a pronounced centralization of capital. The eradication of many small industries to the benefit of enlarging corporations meant a greater pool of resources at the corporate disposal. This process permitted a large-scale corporate exodus to suburbia post-1945 that increasingly rendered the inner city a derelict environment. Suburban relocation became a corporate strategy spurred by the drive to produce accumulation conditions. Docile and nonunionized workers, cheap land, and efficient transport systems were obtainable here. The job dispersal that followed induced massive population suburbanization in a classic leader–follower sequence. It must be noted that Gordon (1978) rejects the notion of a massively engineered and calibrated class conspiracy in favor of comprehending the logic of accumulation dynamics. In this thesis, central city dereliction emerged from the economic need to reorder urban landscapes.

A number of penetrating criticisms have also been leveled at the industrial-materialist model. Critics have focused on its implicit reduction of urban individuals to passive carriers of structuralist directives. While acknowledging the capacity of labor to strike and otherwise confront capital, the model supposedly casts such actions in a larger teleological script where accumulation imperatives guide conflict, political differentials determine capital as victor, and city form continues to be structured by materialist conditions. In this casting, corporate managers unabashedly seek to suppress labor in following the dictates of accumulation. Benevolence becomes subordinated to the thirst for profit. A shallow, greedy bunch of managerial automatons emerge that seek to exploit conditions for personal gain. In the final analysis, concepts like capital and mode of accumulation are endowed with a power to direct and guide (see Duncan and Ley, 1982). These wholes shape the course of urban history. To critics, theses like Gordon's ostensibly posit an urban condition whose emergence seems inevitable and predetermined. While Adams (1970) falls prey to this by asserting inevitable agrarian predilections, Gordon (1978) substitutes an all-powerful accumulation logic. Its influence permeates everyday life as an all-encompassing causal variable. In the final analysis, capitalist imperatives ineluctably render cities disinvestment shells. Urban impotence unfolds as capitalists withdraw resources guided by the hidden hand of capitalism.

Richard Walker (1981) offers a similar historical-materialist interpretation of central city dereliction. His starting point is, like Gordon's, that suburbanization is linked to capitalist urban processes. Unlike Gordon, he places suburbanization in a deeper economic context that itself reflects tensions in the spheres of production and social reproduction. At the broadest level, suburbanization is cast as reflecting the spatial division of labor. Metropolitan areas are systematically fragmented to isolate labor into small, sustainable pockets. This environment socially reproduces white-collar workers, with suburbanites bearing the imprint of their prescribed spaces and resources. Inner-city landscapes, too, are set aside by complex institutional interactions but for a very different population: the poor. This group plays a crucial role in local economies, and like white-collar workers must be socially reproduced into the next generation.

In this context, urban development is presented as a convulsive process expanding unevenly across landscapes. Urban growth—that is, new urban investment—occurs in spurts as capital finds the city differentially profitable for investment. Investment flow here is most intense when industrial downturns necessitate capital withdrawal from production and require its placement elsewhere. Peaks of urbanization appear as uneven overlays of 3- to 5-year cycles (kitchen waves), 15- to 20-year cycles (Kuznets waves), and 50-year cycles (Kondratieff waves). It follows that central cities expand unevenly as capital moves into landscapes amid bouts of industrial over-accumulation. Cities and suburbs are, in short, escape valves during economic downturns. They absorb excess investment during periods of capital glut in production. In this context, suburbanization absorbs excess capital at a time when cities are unprofitable for investment.

Suburbanization emerges in response to the dual need to reproduce labor power and open up new investment opportunities. On the one hand, suburbs promise vast open space for the construction of communities where old capital–labor relations can be remade. There, finely articulated communities can separate people by income, leisure time, work tasks, status, wealth, and education, nurturing social relations that minimize capital–labor conflict. On the other hand, "the suburban solution" also has offered unparalleled opportunities for profit. Cheap land and the production of demand for suburban housing can yield unprecedented real estate profits. Capital, in rejecting urban renewal—its costliness, conflict, and intense politicization—favors a slash-and-burn profit strategy. The city is left to rot while accumulation is more easily facilitated at the periphery. Capital, therefore, has found it easier and more profitable to start anew in open territory at the suburban fringe rather than remake the social and physical environment of the old city. In the final analysis, cities have been devastated by this process. They have experienced intensive job loss, exodus of the affluent, and capital out-migration.

In this general sweep of competing theories on central city dereliction, two points emerge as being most heatedly debated. The first—the role and power of consumers—involves the degree to which they embody causality. Technological theorists posit consumers as atomistic causal agents that drive the provision of resources by espousing tastes and preferences. Supply-side agents (banks, realtors, developers) are depicted as passive resource allocators conforming to consumer wishes. Materialist theorists, in contrast, depict consumers as essentially epiphenomenal actors. Their tastes and preferences represent social constructions that permit others to realize capital accumulation. Consumers appear to drive the market but are guided by ideological constructions serving the interests of others. The second debated issue—how the private market functions—involves competing notions of market operations. On the one hand, technological theorists posit a self-regulating apparatus. The market mediates consumer demand and resource supply; prices are determined by demand–supply intersections in accordance with household preferences and marginal productivities (Lake, 1983). Materialist theorists counter by presenting a manipulated marketplace. This apparatus represents a vehicle for powerful agents to realize accumulation objectives as political processes punctuate the market aimed at influencing market dynamics for personal or class gain. In sum, these competing perspectives embody a conflicting array of assumptions and beliefs. This seeming incompatibility makes integrationist attempts difficult. In the face of this grim reality, studies of urban dereliction continue to marginalize the pursuit of a middle ground.

POVERTY AND LANDSCAPE CHANGE

Poverty is a dominant sustainer of contemporary central city dereliction. Minimal financial resources reverberate throughout the urban arena to perpetuate central city disinvestment and decline. Most visibly, homeowners and landlords in this condition lack the resources to repair structures, plunging housing through courses of disinvestment. Retail strips, moreover, erode and lose tenants in response to decreasing local purchasing power. Shops already undercapitalized and unable to relocate are most vulnerable to closure. Poverty also sets in motion the locating of unwanted land uses whose existence compounds disinvestment. Poverty simultaneously catalyzes the encroachment and growth from within of locally unwanted land uses. Investors become increasingly repelled by burgeoning deterioration that signifies trapped investments. In a final irony, city attempts at alleviating dereliction become problematical amid shrinking tax ratables. Local revenues are often inadequate to implement substantive reform programs like tax increment financing, tax abatement, sweat equity projects, and urban homesteading. Programs are often ineffective and piecemeal. The discussion that follows elaborates upon these issues to forge links between poverty and central city dereliction.

Sustained poverty most immediately renders large populations unable to repair neighborhoods. Homeowners problematically view increased maintenance of aging homes amid costs outstripping budgets. In time, deterioration becomes a fact of life, with scarce funds spent to assure functional viability. Decaying exteriors, sagging porches, and peeling paint are neglected in favor of repairing furnaces, structural foundations, and the like. These basic elements are also neglected with continued decline. Growing costs soon facilitate a forced displacement that renders buildings empty shells. Rental housing follows a similar fate. Inability to extract sufficient profit sets in motion a pattern of landlord disinvestment. Initially, incipient structural defects are either ignored or cosmetically improved. Their persistent return, however, initiates a calculated disinvestment response. Sustained disinvestment exacerbates structural defects. Landlords here typically seek to capture declining profits by subdividing buildings to higher density usage. Conversion and crowding, however, usually fail as compensatory tactics. Deterioration is compounded by increased wear and tear, with the worst of such buildings ultimately abandoned unless a new economic rationale is introduced. Short of anticipated gentrification or government improvement schemes, abandonment proliferates. This infection can quickly spread to adjoining buildings in zones of marginal housing and even to zones of sound housing.

Poverty has sustained dereliction in most North American central cities. New York City currently has more than 500,000 poverty households, many of them black and Hispanic. Their concentrations in the South Bronx and Central Brooklyn have perpetuated decline. With minimal purchasing power, this population has proved unprofitable to service. Housing and retail provision is inadequate and getting worse. These populations have been largely bypassed by the resurgence of the New York City economy. A permanent "underclass" has formed, denied access to upward mobility by inadequate public schools and spatial disassociation from entry-level clerical and other jobs (Warf, 1990). Investors have fled to provide shelter and quality-of-life amenities in environments where economic recompense is expected. Philadelphia has experienced the same crisis. North Philadelphia, a ten-square-mile area, has been ravaged by deindustrialization. Poverty rates are twice the city average and among the highest in the urbanized Northeast (Philadelphia City Planning Commission, 1984). Forty percent of residents and 33 percent of families lived below the 1980 federal poverty level of $7,421 for a family of four (ibid.). As the city has admitted, this poverty is a complex and formidable constraint on human and physical development. Housing investors are provoked to invest here by an array of subsidy programs that tax the average household more than $500 per year (see ibid.). As evidenced by entrenched dereliction, these programs have been a dismal failure.

Retail erosion is an outgrowth of entrenched poverty. Physical blight and frequent closure follow from diminishing profit margins that reflect decreasing purchase power. While selected retailers like fast-food restaurants and gas stations appear to benefit from this, they do so by succeeding essential goods providers that can no longer sustain operations. Regional grocery stores, hardware establishments, and banks most often close or out-migrate. They leave in their wake a gaping hole in the retail bundle that residents need to subsist.

Indianapolis illustrates the ills that poverty wreaks on retailing. Amid a four-square-mile area of poverty on the Near Eastside, two regional grocers currently serve a population of over 75,000. In 1960, there were more than 11 regional grocers. Six of the 11 buildings today stand abandoned, reminders of an era when residents did not have to travel miles on deteriorated streets to purchase food. The irony is that one of the current grocers opened in 1987 in response to emerging downtown gentrification. Low-income residents here have little alternative but to purchase its upscale offerings of fine cheeses, meats, wine, and the like. The importance of this store to the inner-city economy has not gone unnoticed by the owners. When it threatened to pull out of downtown in the late 1980s, the city offered a substantial tax subsidy for this grocer to stay. The subsidy, it was contended, was necessary to assure suitable cash flow. The store to date continues to provide high-priced items to both gentrifiers and the poor. While the affluent patronize out of discerning tastes, the poor do so out of necessity. Downtown Newark exhibits a similar pattern. Its once stable retailing core has long given way to marginal high-turnover establishments. Two regional grocers, presently contemplating out-migration, service over 55,000 residents. The city's historic retail spine, Broad Street, is dotted with board-ups. Burgeoning poverty has driven retailers away; the remaining establishments are overwhelmingly low order, and they provide nonessential goods.

Poverty is also destructive to downtowns in that it generates locally unwanted land uses (LULUs) that compound disinvestment. LULUs are undesired land initiatives—prisons, toxic waste sites, derelict buildings, halfway houses—that society must site somewhere. At the heart of LULUs are negative externalities (Popper, 1985). They may be dangerous (hazardous waste facilities), blighting (decaying buildings), polluting (factories), or noisy (airports). Abandoned buildings, closed factories, and boarded-up warehouses represent health hazards and symbols of decay. On the one hand, such structures are lethal playgrounds for children and youth. Drug trafficking, prostitution, and assault are disproportionally practiced there (Bleakly and Hughes, 1975). Police recognize these as magnets for such activities and implore municipalities to board up buildings quickly (Van Allsberg, 1974). Such land uses signal the onset of sustained decline. They convey deterioration, full-scale low-income invasion, and prevalence of poverty. Investors filter this perception through anticipated cash flow opportunities. If others are channeling capital elsewhere, what rationale is there for themselves to invest? Symbolism and metaphor become impediments to reversing dereliction.

Low-income zones are often areas of low political resistance, permitting municipalities to site toxic waste sites, prisons, halfway houses, and the like with least political repercussion. Political underrepresentation, minimal political clout, and unorganized or disorganized constituencies make such areas prime siting locations for these facilities. Suburban areas, in contrast, effectively fight LULU penetration through political mobilization and lobbying efforts. For instance, suburbs have been notoriously successful in shutting out public housing, a perceived heinous neighbor to most middle-class Americans. In 1984 alone, more than 25 new prisons were sited across the United States, many ending up in slum space (see Popper, 1985). Due to this siting tendency, sets of cities have emerged as "prison capitals." Such cities usually exhibit depleting job bases and begrudgingly accept such facilities.

Urban-industrial northern New Jersey currently heads the list of prison repositories. Although many central city residents oppose such facilities, there is usually widespread support for such initiatives in the belief that jobs will be generated in otherwise economically crippled localities.

Perhaps the most devastating impact of LULUs is their penchant for choking off repair and maintenance. The negative symbolism of unwanted land uses invites disinvestment. Spurred by LULUs, a bewildering transformation of once well-maintained buildings into empty shells can quickly follow, a contagious spread infecting buildings in wildfire fashion. Local governments, recognizing the debilitating influence of LULUs, have responded by enacting measures ranging from the calculated to the ad hoc. Planned responses have often taken the form of local urban homesteading, tax abatement provisions to restore substandard buildings, and tax increment-financing designation. In city after city, however, these responses have had little impact. As a consequence, cities like New York have shunned conventional approaches in efforts to stem burgeoning disinvestment. New York City's attempt literally to "paper over" abandoned buildings represents one of the more unusual approaches, reflecting the city's lack of maintenance resources and sense of desperation. In the early 1980s, proliferating board-ups in the South Bronx reflected a housing crisis. Much borough housing was lost to abandonment (Stegman and Hillstrom, 1984). To induce investment, the city decided to cover over abandoned buildings with murals depicting family scenes. Murals were imposed on board-ups visible from the West Side Highway. This major thoroughfare was used by thousands of investors daily. Many found the reality of the South Bronx repugnant for living and investing, and such murals were meant to convey an impression of a revitalizing locality. If the South Bronx was not attractive to investors, at least it could be made to appear attractive. Within two years, the program—at considerable financial expense—was scrapped, deemed misleading and even dangerous by critics and city planners.

In the final irony, poverty has also led to dramatic tax-base depletion, rendering government programs ineffective in alleviating dereliction. Poverty concentrations not only have limited resources, but limit the capacity of central cities to raise revenues to finance ameliorative programs. As Judd (1979) notes, the will to enact change is often present, the funds are not. Consequently, growth in city expenditures has constantly outpaced tax-base growth. Between 1965 and 1973, city expenditure growth in Baltimore, Buffalo, and Cleveland was 172, 135, and 67 percent, respectively. At the same time, assessed value growth here was +11, −1, and −2 percent, respectively (ibid.). Newark was unequivocally the biggest loser, registering a 135-percent growth in city expenditures but a −12 loss in assessed values over this period. Faced with fiscal woes, such cities have curtailed expensive redevelopment programs like tax abatements and tax increment financing and substituted less costly approaches. While New York City tinkers with funding family murals in disinvested areas, Chicago tries low-income historic preservation. Meanwhile, Newark establishes local enterprise zones; Baltimore enacts unfunded sweat equity programs; and Cleveland toys with cheap housing recycling approaches. At the heart of this experimentation are scarce funds that necessitate low-cost approaches to eradicating a complex problem.

In sum, the bulk of America's poor have accumulated in derelict central city zones. Critical masses of poverty, once in place, generate negative externalities that exacerbate urban dereliction. The compounding of job loss, retail erosion, LULU proliferation, and tax-base depletion reflect this. Poverty comes to both reflect and propel disinvestment. In so doing, it symbolizes and transmits destruction of human landscapes. Poverty is a societal outgrowth that, in emergence, represents a critical purveyor of destruction. Left in its wake are ruined lives, devastated infrastructure, and destroyed urban fabrics. It follows that poverty is less a passive outgrowth than a dynamic blighting agent. The irony is that poverty, as a societal construction, gains an internal destruction dynamic, appearing to be a localized outgrowth that removes it from its causal underpinnings. Once in place, moreover, its contagious spread engulfs vast land tracts in a local invasion–succession sequence. The casual observer witnesses a simple diffusion of dereliction that removes the process from its root causes: local, national, and international economic restructuring. Hidden behind the scene is the dramatic influence of postindustrial economic transformation, capital shifts across landscapes, and overseas plant migration. This common misconception casts dereliction as discrete and locally generated. Lost in the shuffle are the complex economic underpinnings that account for the process's origins.

THE UNDERCLASS

Some 13 million people were officially designated as living in poverty in America's central cities in the early 1980s (Meyers, 1986, p. 3). In total, some 34 million Americans were so categorized nationwide, or 15 percent of the population. Between 1965 and 1982, poverty increased, especially among blacks who came to comprise 37 percent of the total poor, Hispanics accounting for 30 percent (*Newsweek*, 1983, p. 17). In 1981, the U.S. Bureau of Labor Statistics had established $15,323 as the minimum income necessary for a family of four "to fully participate in American life at a lower level"—the cost, in other words, of a complete market basket of goods and services necessary to sustain a typical lifestyle (Beeghley, 1981, p. 26).

Only 25 percent of all white Americans lived in central cities while 58 percent of all black Americans and 50 percent of all Hispanic Americans did so (Morial, 1986, p. 34). Black median income in 1984 was just 56 percent of white income (ibid.). In 1988, 33 percent of all blacks were estimated to live below the poverty line, and 28 percent of all Hispanics (Chicago *Tribune*, 1988, p. 1-5).

Female-headed households—especially minority families—suffered the lowest income levels of any statistical group. More than 66 percent of all black children and 71 percent of all Hispanic children, who lived in female-headed households in the 1980s, lived in poverty (Morial, 1986, p. 33). This group had grown very rapidly. In 1983, nearly three-quarters of all black births in Chicago were out of wedlock, compared to only half in 1970 (W. Wilson, 1987, p. 29). Some 95 percent of all black teenage births in Chicago were out of wedlock in 1983, compared to 75 percent in 1970 (ibid.). Of the 25,000 families living in projects of the Chicago Housing Authority in 1983, only 8 percent were married-couple families, 80 percent receiving AFDC subsidy (p. 26). The 1981 poverty rate was nearly 28 percent for central city children under age 18. For female-headed central city families, the rate was 60 percent for children under 18, and 70 percent for children under six (Morial, 1986, p. 199).

When Aid to Dependent Children (now AFDC) was established in 1935, its mission was to protect deserving widows and their children. Between 1940 and 1950, the number of children born to unmarried women increased from 3.8 percent to 4.0 percent. But for 1950–1979 the rate increased four-fold to 17.1 percent. During that period, teenage mothers accounted for almost half of the out-of-wedlock births (Gilbert, 1987, p. 6). Currently, the AFDC program targets low-income mothers and children, the benefits in a given locality set by state government. Washington, for example, pays up to 78 percent of each state's payments to recipients and half of the administrative costs. Recipients must be destitute, which in the early 1980s meant a $1,000 limit on allowable family resources, excluding an occupied home and one automobile valued at less than $1,500. In 1986, the AFDC program provided assistance to some 3.7 million single-parent families (as well as an additional 250,000 qualifying families where both parents work) at a cost of approximately $14 billion, the average monthly AFDC payment varying from $92 in Mississippi to $499 in California (ibid.). Although targeting a needy population of largely central city poor, the AFDC program has been criticized for sustaining and not resolving poverty. AFDC gives poor persons an incentive not to work, an incentive to be totally rather than partially dependent (Beeghley, 1983, p. 52). The disincentives of AFDC complement those of other welfare programs as, for example, public housing.

Poverty translates into poor health. Adults in families with incomes less than $10,000 were found in a 1975 study to have a 19-percent higher incidence of acute disease (Beeghley, 1983, p. 108). People below the poverty line suffered chronic illnesses at two to three times the rate of incidence as those above. White males born in 1978 could expect to live 70 years on average, and black males only 65 years. In addition, the infant mortality rate among white children was 12 per thousand in 1978, but 21 per thousand for black newborns. Black infants were 75 percent more likely to die than white infants (ibid.). Life chances over a metropolis varied substantially. In Detroit in the 1970s, there was a fourfold range in infant death rates between certain central city neighborhoods of the near eastside and the eastern suburbs. Central city rates were comparable with those of underdeveloped Peru or Guyana, while suburban rates were comparable with the highest in the world, found in Scandinavia (Bunge and Bordessa, 1975, p. 1). On average, a suburban Detroit child's air contained one-fourth the dust and sulphur dioxide of that of the central city child (Jacoby, 1972).

Most Americans, Leonard Beeghley observes in *Living Poorly in America* (1983, p. 131), find it easier to think about their own successes and failures or those of other individuals than to examine critically the more general, structural characteristics of society that induce success or failure. An ethic of individual responsibility is ingrained in American thinking, and Americans come quickly to easy answers rooted in this ethic concerning the causes of poverty. "It is asserted that people live poorly because they are not very thrifty, because they are lazy and do not want to work, because the 'welfare' system takes care of them, because they do not have very much ability, and because they have loose morals" (ibid.). Missing is empathy with the social context that, indeed, invites if not promotes such individual failings. The values of work avoidance, indeed, have come to the fore. Welfare poverty pervades America's central cities. One must consider, however, the total circumstances where discrimination, lack of jobs, lack of proper schooling, poor health, and all the other correlates of poverty interact in circles of poverty's entrapment. Poverty is not just individual but social, in that social institutions exist to perpetuate poverty in such places as America's central cities.

Thus, an entrenched underclass has evolved in the United States, comprised of families abandoned by fathers, the rapidly increasing offspring of unwed teenaged mothers unemployed if not unemployable, street criminals, the mentally ill without benefit of institutionalization, the functionally illiterate, and undocumented aliens who necessarily avoid full economic participation in American life. These people are often caught in webs of violence including gang extortion, drug pushing, prostitution, and other forms of rip-off. Easily generated in such people is a low level of self-esteem, a restricted view of personal effectiveness, a sense of separation from society, a belief in life's total futility. Such self-depreciation is easily passed from generation to generation as negative values effectively isolating individuals from the American mainstream. Low commitment of parents to their children's education, poor hygiene practices, alcohol and drug addiction, the propensity to physical violence, and a general unwillingness to adjust to life's regularities set an underclass increasingly apart in the United States.

The problems of the underclass appear especially acute among impoverished blacks. As middle-class and working-class black families escape the central city for the suburbs, old neighborhoods are left without leaders, and without role models. In many central city neighborhoods, children seldom interact on a sustained basis with people who are employed or with families who enjoy a permanent breadwinner. "The net effect is that joblessness, as a way of life, takes on a different social meaning; the relationship between schooling and postschool employment takes on a different meaning. The development of cognitive, linguistic, and other educational and job-related skills necessary for the world of work in the mainstream economy is thereby adversely affected" (W. Wilson, 1987, p. 55). Central city schools struggle ineffectively to overcome the poverty syndrome. Of the 39,000 students enrolled in the ninth grade in Chicago's public schools in 1980, only 18,500— or 47 percent—graduated four years later. Of those, only 6,000 were capable of reading at or above the national twelfth-grade level (p. 56.)

In the 1960s, anthropologist Oscar Lewis (1969, p. 187) wrote of a "culture of poverty." Poor people displayed low levels of occupational aspiration, lacked commitment to work, held fatalistic attitudes about health, preferred a present-time orientation instead of planning ahead, approved of sexual promiscuity, and engaged in violence. The whole was presented as a culture of deprivation, the values of which were passed within families from generation to generation. William Wilson (1987) argues forcefully against such presumption. "Culture values emerge from specific social circumstances and life chances," he writes, "and reflect one's class and racial position. Thus, if underclass blacks have limited aspirations or fail to plan for the future, it is not ultimately the product of different cultural norms but the consequence of restricted opportunities, a bleak future, and feelings of resignation resulting from bitter personal experiences" (p. 14). The key theoretical concept, therefore, is not "culture of poverty," but "social isolation."

Poverty has its apologists. Business interests often value cadres of low-skilled workers who can be employed, if only temporarily, at unpleasant tasks at low wages, a "lumpen proletariat" that helps keep prices low. Since wages are depressed, an indigent class subsidizes the consumption of more affluent people. Clothes are cheaper, fuel less expensive, rents lower. A dependent poor creates jobs and income for functionaries who service their basic needs: police, lawyers, court clerks, social workers. The poor represent a market for previously owned or deteriorating goods, and for shoddily constructed merchandise unsalable to others. Others justify poverty on constitutional grounds. Those who pursue lives of work avoidance, they argue, have a right to do so, and should be left alone even if imperiled by impoverishment. Some apologists for poverty even assume that the poor are a necessary evil, conditioned on human deviance and impossible to correct. Such thinking blames the victim totally and ignores the structural realities of American society. Such thinking perpetuates myths calculated to sustain the privileges of society's well-positioned.

THE POWER ELITE

Whereas genuine concern to eliminate poverty has motivated the "renewing" of cities since World War II, much of it has been tragically misdirected. National leaders assumed that the traditional city, once built, could fend for itself. Central cities, it was supposed, could withstand any amount of abuse: urban renewal, freeway construction, central business district redevelopment. Central cities, it was projected, would survive the expansion of big city suburbs. Even at the local level there was little respect for the traditional city. Leaders assumed that essential infrastructure, such as mass transit, could be withdrawn from old neighborhoods and that they would continue to thrive. Urban boosters preoccupied themselves with big development projects in central business districts, and in tying these projects to the suburbs by freeways. City leaders believed older central city neighborhoods could abide the intrusions of massive public housing complexes. A cure for poverty lay, it was believed, merely in physically upgrading the built environment for profit.

Power struggles have underpinned the process. Political scientist Michael Parenti (1983) defines power as the ability to get what one wants, either by having one's interests prevail in conflicts with others or by preventing others from raising conflicting demands. "Power presumes the ability to control the actions and beliefs of others through favor, fear, fraud, or force, and to manipulate the social environment to one's advantage" (p. 6). Those with power wield influence to obtain agendas or goals. In every community, the influential are naturally drawn together in coalitions to consolidate exercise of power. This impulse operates at the international scale down through that of locality, the influences of power brokering levered in social hierarchies. So it has been from the nation's birth. When delegates gathered in Philadelphia to craft a new constitution, they were determined that persons of birth and fortune should control the nation's affairs. James Madison focused the issue. Michael Parenti described the problem as "how to keep the

spirit and form of popular government with only a minimum of the substance, how to provide the appearance of republicanism without suffering
its leveling democratic effects, how to construct a government that would
win some popular support but would not tamper with the existing class
structure, a government strong enough to service the growing needs of an
entrepreneurial class while withstanding the egalitarian demands of the poor
and propertyless" (p. 64).

The most powerful urban leaders are its capitalists, who control and direct
private investment. Next in importance are politicians, who establish (with
the electorate's consent) the ground rules for investment both private and
public, and the bureau chiefs, who provide public services essential to private initiative. While each have their own interests to advance, they draw
together in the exercise of power—a symbiosis that forms and dissolves
loosely structured groups of influential people around causes and projects
thought significant and timely. Profit from land and building manipulation
is a primary preoccupation. Thomas Dye (1986) sees community power
structures as composed primarily of landed interests whose goals are to
intensify the use of land and add value to it. "Community power structures
are dominated by mortgage lending banks, real estate developers, builders,
and landowners. They may be joined by owners or managers of local utilities, department stores, title companies, and others whose wealth is affected
by land use, but bankers, who finance the developers, are probably at the
center of the elite structure of most cities" (p. 30).

While urban elites exercise variable control over development, they constitute a cohesive circle of influential people who rule by maintaining control over public decision-making agendas. Except for politicians, the people
who comprise these coalitions of power are not elected by popular vote.
Instead, they are appointed by their predecessors and will, in turn, appoint
their successors. For their part, politicians favorably connected in power
coalitions find it easy to garner campaign funding, and are thereby in a
sense "selected" as well. Politicians representing other interests—especially
those in opposition to established power brokers—usually face great difficulty in sustaining support. Their constituencies tend to evaporate once specific
issues are resolved. The mid-1970s saw Americans generally disillusioned
with power brokers both national and local. In 1975, pollster Louis Harris
reported that 58 percent of the people polled on the assertion "people in
power are out to take advantage of you" agreed, up from 37 percent in 1966.
Sixty-three percent agreed that "the people running the country don't care
what happens to you," up from 33 percent nine years earlier. Forty-one
percent felt "left out of things going on around me," up from 9 percent
(Finkler, Toner, and Popper, 1976, p. 10).

Urban space is a scarce resource and, as such, is an object of profit and control. Therefore, the main issues can be expressed in two questions. Whose profit is it? And who is going to determine what the profits are? The modern city is not just a place for people to live. In the power elite's view, it is a machine rationalized to make money (Domhoff, 1983, p. 167). To them, a city is not a place to which people make emotional ties, so much as it is a container of spaces subject to constant revision for profit purposes. Exchange values supersede use values. Space in the city is a commodity to be bought and sold for profit. Capitalism here casts everyday life as a pervasive process of commodification, with everything potentially a commodity to be exploited, managed, and manipulated. Built environments have come to be valued not as human habitat so much as salable good to be consumed and discarded.

Cities function to fulfill the imperatives of capitalism, the most important being the circulation and accumulation of capital. A city's layout reflects the contradictions of a capitalistic economy that lead to friction and conflict between interests. Friction intensifies as cultural landscapes are continually altered. "Residential neighborhoods are cleared to make way for new office developments; disinvestment in privately-rented accommodation leads to dissolution of inner-city communities; while the switch of capital to more profitable investment in private housing leads to an expansion of the suburbs; and so on" (Knox, 1982, p. 297). Urban elites function to provide stable and predictable political environment for business whereby the continual tearing down, re-creation, and transformation can continue. Change, benefiting powerful local interests, becomes the only constant valued (Hartman, 1984, p. 320).

In examining real estate development in San Francisco, Chester Hartman (1984) writes of the "golden rule": "Those who have the gold get to make the rules." With economic resurgence dependent on private market forces, large businesses usually appear to provide the only game in town. Their decisions become primary reference points for urban development. Governments, charged with promoting general public welfare, leave themselves with little choice other than to follow corporate initiatives. "With few or no alternatives envisioned, the imperative is to take what is offered, try to wrest some concessions in the process, and accept the concomitant social costs" (p. 320). Government here serves a narrow constituency. Through elected and appointed officials, government legitimizes development and aids in private capital accumulation. It establishes ground rules for development and provides basic support infrastructure to facilitate private market functioning. Government legitimizes priorities by managing conflicts between specific interests, providing incentives to some and compensations to others. "In a sense, modern government is about pushing and pulling levers—increasing tax incentives for one activity, adding tax disincentives to another, encouraging some forms of competition, discouraging others, setting in motion some bargaining processes, stultifying others, subsidizing some activities and withdrawing subsidies from others" (Stone, 1986, p. 107).

Of course, politicians and bureau chiefs also act in their self-interest: to remain in office, if not rise within political and bureaucratic contexts. In most cities, people elected and appointed to major positions in city government—at city hall, the planning commission, or the redevelopment board, for example—come overwhelmingly from or are closely connected economically or socially with the business community. Thus, business purposes and needs directly influence government. When positions advocated by business are challenged, the threat of capital flight with attendant job and tax revenue loss serves quickly to discipline (Hartman, 1984, p. 321). Individuals in government who would challenge directly business's domination find their degrees of freedom substantially constrained. Personal success in politics and government service usually means abiding an elite consensus once it is formed within a specific developmental context.

One primary function of community elites is to prepare land for capital. Preparation involves clearing and assembling large land tracts or providing good transportation facilities, obtaining utilities such as water, gas, electricity, and sewers, and securing municipal services such as fire and police protection. It also involves elimination of harassing business regulations and reducing taxes to the lowest possible levels. The construction of pro-growth, prodevelopment ideologies is crucial. The rhetoric of value-free development and benevolent middle-income restructuring is usually involved. The ills of profligate and corrupt welfare agendas are publicized while middle-income development is presented as publicly beneficial. In this process, terminology, symbolism, and metaphor are used to favor some development perspectives and stigmatize others. Widespread acceptance of livable city growth, for example, has been facilitated by promises of aesthetic renewal, downtown reawakening, and cultural resurgence. Opposition to this growth is seen as anticity. Redistributive development, in contrast, typically involves government sacrifice and welfare provision. Resources are often "wasted" and "nonstimulative." Elites effectively define growth debates to structure constituent demands.

San Francisco's Yerba Buena has received much attention in recent years from scholars interested in how power elites function. The project leveled a district of residential hotels, boardinghouses, and businesses that once catered largely to single men. Workingmen, immigrants, transients, hoboes gathered "to live, work, or just while away their time between opportunities" (Hartman, 1984, p. 53). As originally planned, the half-billion-dollar project was to encompass twelve city blocks, displacing 4,000 residents and

700 businesses (Ley, 1983, p. 314). A convention center, sports arena, hotel, and office and retail facility were to be constructed. The Bank of America, Bank of California, Crocker Bank, Wells Fargo Bank, Del Monte Corporation, Pacific Gas and Electric, Pacific Telephone and Telegraph, and Southern Pacific Railroad joined in financing the plan. Other supporters included hoteliers, restauranteurs, and other members of the tourist industry, construction unions, and both city newspapers.

Businessmen, city officials, planners, and newspaper editors began to speak of the development zone as skid row, and of its inhabitants as bums, winos, and drifters. Pejorative social values were ascribed in a pattern of distortion and bias. Their problems were purportedly tied to self-affliction rather than societal circumstance. They were by choice unmotivated, happy to live off the public dole, and constrained only by their lethargy. Urban elites thus played on class prejudices. They presented themselves as providing economic revival through construction jobs and increased tourist and convention business while clearing away slums. Such labeling permitted the power elites, and the public at large, to disregard the injustices done to those displaced. In the words of the director of the San Francisco Redevelopment Authority, "This land is too valuable to permit poor people to park on it" (Ley, 1983, p. 317). Yet, alternative housing at affordable rent was not available for single men elsewhere. Nor was the mix of support institutions that this population came to rely on.

Feasibility studies remain an important tool used by developers to manipulate public opinion and coalesce political support. Such studies purportedly provide technical information on which to base objective decision making. In reality, they often do little more than rationalize already foregone conclusions by giving them an aura of objectivity. The consultants selected are often those who can be relied on to share elite views. It is the rare consultant who risks losing future contracts by producing discordant results. Feasibility studies tend to provide great quantities of information without establishing relevance. Reports hide weak assumptions and methodologies behind a blitz of statistics and equations. Dazzling graphics exaggerate a utopian view of intentions based on changes presumably justified. Feasibility studies thereby tend to validate elite agendas. One of the most important forms of power that a local elite can exercise is the ability to limit public debate to "safe" issues. Feasibility studies serve to focus public attention in ways that are safe (Adams, 1982, p. 8).

The projects that power elites fashioned in the United States in the decades after World War II are numerous. Nearly every large American city has been affected, as, for example, Detroit with its Civic Center and adjacent Renaissance Center (Figure 4.4). A plaque lists the organizations in-

Figure 4.4   The Renaissance Center towers over Detroit's Civic Center. Built in response to the destructive riots of the late 1960s, the imposing new center has never been successful financially—and yet the focus on big mega-projects continues in the declining Motor City.

volved in the Renaissance Center development, including the Ford Motor Company, Ford's Manufacturer's National Bank, various parts suppliers to the automobile industry, and companies such as Amoco, Goodyear, and the Automobile Club of Michigan. Another mega-venture was Baltimore's Charles Center and the adjacent Inner Harbor redevelopment (Figure 4.5). It integrated old and new design to create a massive middle-income playground downtown. Conspicuous consumption shops, upscale restaurants, and expensive boutiques replaced acres of moderate-income housing and commercial land uses. Into such giant projects as these, America's cities poured redevelopment monies during the 1950s, 1960s, and 1970s, as opposed to funding central city residential neighborhoods. Such schemes were pronounced economically rational by local elites. Their logic as economic stimulants was irrefutable, public technicians purportedly applying the tools of science and rationality to draw their conclusions. Instrumentalist planning reduced political issues to rational matters, thereby generating support for class-biased development.

Figure 4.5   Perhaps the most visible and touted downtown redevelopment in the United States has occurred in Baltimore—specifically, the Charles Center (on the right) and the Inner Harbor (on the left). Both projects sought to reinforce the traditional business district, rather than replace it.

CENTRALIZED CITY GOVERNMENT

As power is centralized in corporations, so also is it centralized in government. There are some 80,000 separate governments in the American political system, but one of them—the federal government—collects some 68 percent of all tax money (Dye, 1986, p. 30). The 50 states collect some 20 percent, but all local governments combined collect only 12 percent (ibid.). By holding the nation's purse strings, the federal government exerts influence directly and indirectly over central cities. In addition, municipal governments themselves are centralized, with a powerful city hall controlling local tax revenues and federal grants at the expense of local neighborhood autonomy. City governments, bureaucratically organized, have come to function substantially divorced from the felt needs and inclinations of citizens defined at the neighborhood level. Big government parallels big business.

During the twentieth century, the focus of urban political attention moved from the neighborhood to city hall. Numerous correlates accompany this concentration of power. Most important is the rise of government bureaucracies based on the scientific management concepts pioneered by corporations. The implied idea is that governmental function is largely technical, a matter of effectively managing public enterprise. Citizenry should necessarily play a minimal role, functioning largely as a source of social value. Values, once translated into policies by elected politicians, are then implemented by appointed officials expert at their specialized tasks. Such a view depreciates the kind of deep civic attachment and public-spiritedness that many feel to be requisite to a viable political society. In this managerial view, political obligation is grounded primarily in calculated utility. Peter Steinberger writes, "According to such a perspective, the polity is—at least in principle—reduced to a benefit-generating enterprise in which customary, traditional, and moral attachments are relatively superfluous" (1985, p. 59). An ideology of managerialism invokes standards of efficiency and effectiveness as measured quantitatively, usually in economic terms. Qualitative measures concerning such abstractions as freedom, moral autonomy, community, or individual dignity are made at best secondary, and at worst irrelevant.

Centralization through growth of civil bureaucracies has been encouraged by the rise of government professionalism. By emphasizing group credentials through special training, certification, and organizational memberships, planners, social workers, teachers, police officers, and other functionaries work to increase their status and economic power. Citizens are reduced to mere clients for public services when professed experts define citizen needs in terms of professional standards. Professionalism implies that services should not be negotiated with citizens so much as imposed on them for their own good. Professionalism depends on the elitist view that some members of society are—by inherited temperament, training, or both— more capable than others not only of guiding governmental action, but of governing. "It is a theory of technocracy, government by experts, rather than democracy, government by people" (Steinberger, 1985, p. 39). Expertism tends to be rigid, and very difficult for citizens to influence. Bureaucracy with its complex rules and standard operating procedures not only alienates the citizen, but insulates the decision makers, making them less sensitive to needs defined locally.

Bureaucrats can be authoritarian and even totalitarian in their functioning. Levels of outright arrogance easily surface where rigid, depersonalized rules and regulations become ends in themselves. Frequently, rules are created not to facilitate a public agency's service mission, but merely to promote the agency as the vested interest of its functionaries. Jurisdictional disputes both between and within agencies can drain governmental effectiveness, especially when decisions are based on rules created to further the goals of the organization as opposed to the goals of the community. Individuals overly preoccupied with personal career advancement can lose track of community needs as personal expediency subsumes public dedication. Besides being cumbersome, rigid, and remote, municipal bureaucracies can become dysfunctional in the sense of being alienated from citizen needs.

The rejection of local politics is a second corollary to governmental centralization in American cities. Early in the twentieth century, progressive reformers fought the corruption of machine politics by dismantling neighborhood-based political patronage systems. In order to rescue service delivery from the depredations of political self-interest, reformers placed political power in the hands of "neutral" administrators serving on boards and commissions or otherwise well insulated from the politics of the street. Authority and autonomy was taken from the neighborhoods and vested in governmental agencies. With the coming of the New Deal and federal programs directed at urban problems, local politics was again rejected in favor of centralized administration. Washington's influence was especially direct in public housing and urban renewal programs begun by federal initiative. "Service arrangements that were once negotiated by street-level employees and citizens were now often redefined by directives from Washington and were expanded, reorganized or superseded by new service delivery mechanisms as a result of more distant bargaining processes among federal, state, and local officials" (Yin, 1982, p. 74).

In rejecting local politics as unsavory, bureaucrats came to reject locality as irrelevant. Government dismissed the political coherence of neighborhoods and other locality-based communities as having little administrative value. Often government agencies divided cities into differing sets of administrative jurisdictions, the operational zones of different agencies enjoying only random geographical overlap. Service boundaries came to divide localities that previously had enjoyed a strong internal sense of cohesion. City people found themselves in school districts, police precincts, fire districts, and political wards, none of which related geographically to their sense of neighborhood. Even where the rudiments of the traditional ward system survived (a city divided into discrete political and administrative regions), individual agencies often failed to coordinate activities within regions. The American city was fractionalized. "Intellectually, the importance of locality coordination is little recognized or acknowledged in city administration," Jane Jacobs (1961, p. 417) wrote in the 1960s.

Government was not understood as a process of negotiating conflicts between interests locally defined, so much as a mechanism for delivering public services according to the standards of professional codes. Government functioned not to steward community social order in divergent local forms; rather, it functioned to impose standard forms of order to the diminishment of locality-based community. Government operated not to encourage participatory democracy through local politics; rather, it operated to negate political machinations everywhere save at city hall. Law applying was emphasized over law making. As Peter Steinberger (1985, p. 61) notes, the managerialist considers law not as a restraint on government, a protection against arbitrary or capricious interference, but instead as a tool for government, a means by which programs can be instituted and results obtained. Big-city government has become an apparatus for solving problems. As a result, the deliberative, educative, communicative, and moral functions of government have tended to be underemphasized (p. 28).

The rising costs of services and declining tax revenues represent additional correlates of governmental centralization. Most of the activities engaged in by city governments are routine housekeeping functions acquired over the years largely because no private persons or organizations proved able or willing to perform them. The names of the agencies into which most municipal governments are divided reflect the nature of their activities: sanitation, police, fire, streets, housing. Although private organizations may also provide some services in competition with the public sector, they usually do little more than skim the cream off an affluent market able to pay a high tariff for better service, leaving public agencies to service those who can pay little or not at all. As a result, city governments have been pressed to streamline. This has meant encouraging economies of scale whereby minimal standards, increasingly defined at lower and lower levels of service proficiency, are applied in larger and larger contexts.

In most cities, little energy exists in the public arena to enhance directly the quality of urban life. Governmental initiatives at enhancement lead invariably to the private sector. Politicians and agency heads necessarily join businessmen in advocating civic improvements, the offices of government given to facilitating private initiative. Public agencies act primarily to solve problems, governmental action viewed primarily as corrective (Haworth, 1966, p. 43). Sanitation workers combat refuse in its various forms, police officers fight crime, firefighters fight fire, highway engineers combat traffic congestion, housing officials provide shelter for those who would otherwise be without shelter. Even planners—those presumably charged with scheming for a better future—devote most of their time to correcting urban deficiencies. Underlying all is the belief in minimal government. The notion prevails that government should do what private interests are unable to do—no more and no less. Municipal government in the United States has an improvised character. The limited energies available do not go to anticipating problems or reducing minor problems before they grow; rather, they go primarily to solving the major problems that have become too large to ignore.

Weak government has encouraged Americans to set low standards for their cities. As Stuart Udall (1968) points out, low standards have led to low citizen expectations regarding government efficacy. "Low expectations, in turn, led to weak leadership; weak leadership led to lack of control over growth, and onward to the waste of the resources and opportunities of cities. Finally, waste and improvidence led to supposedly 'insoluble' problems, and insoluble problems meant that cities were indeed 'ungovernable'" (p. 27). Thus, a self-fulfilling prophecy of governmental ineptitude was set in place in most American cities.

UNSUCCESSFUL GOVERNMENT INTERVENTION

An array of government approaches have characterized federal efforts to redevelop central cities since the 1930s. Overwhelmingly, dereliction has been seen as physical blight in need of eradication. Only rarely has it been seen as a social condition requiring social uplift in the form of employment and social encouragement. That government resources have concentrated in physical restructuring while ignoring the social roots of blight partially explains programmatic failure. Equally important, however, is an array of programs that compounded dereliction through inappropriate physical engineering. Poor design, poor execution, and inadequate specification of program beneficiaries (permitting program subversion) were some of the major culprits. Geographer John Short (1989) sums up such failure by noting three distinctive programmatic orientations: (1) cities created as if only capital mattered; (2) cities created as if only professionals mattered; and (3) cities created as if only some people mattered. The discussion that follows examines these city values in specific planning contexts.

Public Housing

Public housing represents an initial federal response to central city dereliction. Public housing was born in 1937, a child of the New Deal. Originally, it was intended to facilitate slum clearance, thereby generating jobs through new construction. Its secondary goal was to house the working poor who, without available private housing, would lack shelter. Faced with strong opposition from real estate, banking, and construction interests, public housing advocates settled for a program quite unlike any adopted elsewhere in the industrialized world. Public housing was not to compete with the private sector and was therefore designed only to meet basic shelter needs. Public housing units were purposely stripped of all but basic amenities; they were to be temporary quarters until private housing could be afforded by its occupants. Proponents operated on the assumption that changing the physical housing conditions of the deserving poor would positively impact their behavior—a kind of beneficial environmental determinism. Clean, orderly surroundings would excite ambition and high morals toward full participation in the private economy.

This public housing approach has proved durable across the decades. By 1965, every state had some public housing under way, the program sheltering more than 2 million people (Friedman, 1980, p. 473). By 1970, every city over 250,000 save one had a public housing program, the 800,000 units nationwide sheltering nearly one percent of the nation's population (Solomon, 1974, p. 203). In 1975, New York City operated some 116,000 units, Chicago 38,600, Philadelphia 22,900, Baltimore 16,200, Atlanta 14,700. In the 1980s, public housing constituted approximately 15 percent of the total housing stock in Atlanta, 10 percent in Baltimore, and 9 percent in Philadelphia (Meyers, 1986, p. 142). In the late 1970s, some 60,000 new public housing units were being built each year, the rate of new construction dropping precipitously to some 1,400 in 1985 (Meyers, 1986, p. 145). Increasingly, public housing clients have tended to be the very poor. National median income rose by 90 percent between 1960 and 1972; but for families in public housing, median income increased only 21 percent (Vaughan and Vogel, 1979, p. 91). In 1960, only one-third of the families moving into public housing were receiving welfare payments; it was nearly three-quarters by 1972 (ibid.).

As affluent households fled central cities during the 1950s and 1960s, public housing came increasingly to serve the permanently indigent, the emergent underclass. The new suburbanites, determined not to jeopardize their hard-won status (not to mention high property values), resisted attempts to locate public housing beyond the nation's central cities. By the 1970s, public housing had developed clear caste implications. "Public housing no longer meant homes for less fortunate friends and neighbors but, rather, intrusions of 'foreigners,' the problem poor and those least welcome 'forbidden neighbors,' the lower class Negro" (Friedman, 1980, p. 473). Vacant land could be used as public housing sites only if it happened to lie in an already poor black neighborhood; and accordingly, most public housing was tied to slum clearance. Public housing was more expensive to build at city center than in the suburbs since city land had to be bought and cleared of buildings before development. High land costs contributed substantially to the eclipse of low-rise two- or three-story public housing complexes, which predominated in the early years. By the 1960s, most buildings were high-rise affairs of 12, 14, and even 18 or 20 stories (Figure 4.6).

Most commentators agree that public housing has been a failure in the United States. The federal program has come to exacerbate rather than alleviate poverty. It has contributed to the growth of an urban underclass that now perpetuates itself across generations, in a kind of culture of poverty in isolation. It is a major contributor to urban community disintegration. Big-city

Figure 4.6   The same "international modernism" that brought downtown skyscrapers also brought, in stripped-down form, America's high-rise public housing. Shown here is New York City's Edgemere.

housing projects epitomize the modern slums. Social pathologies associated with public housing are legion. Lee Rainwater lists them:

- High propensity to drop out of school
- Low achievement levels while in school
- Difficulties establishing stable work habits
- High rates of dropping out of the labor force
- Apathy and passive resistance to programs of self-help
- Hostility and distrust toward neighbors
- Careless use of money
- High rates of mental illness
- High levels of illegitimacy
- High divorce rates
- Child abuse widespread
- Criminality
- Drug and alcohol addiction
- Carelessness and destructiveness toward both one's own and other's property (Rainwater, 1980, p. 599).

Such pathologies are spawned by debilitating social contexts. For the under-class warehoused in central city public housing, escape becomes increasingly difficult. Social disabilities are systematically sustained. Self-help values come not to apply. Poverty and despair come to constitute a norm.

Weaknesses of public housing have been many. As Anthony Downs (1981) notes, sense of community has been eroded by concentrating social pathological individuals in slum space. To Downs, "projects are not true 'neighborhoods' because not enough residents share the kind of values based upon mutual respect that are necessary for a fruitful common life" (p. 121). Families are admitted on the basis of financial distress and, prior to 1974, removed whenever incomes advanced beyond given thresholds. After 1974, people exceeding thresholds were permitted to stay if willing to pay commensurate rent increases. Most big-city projects, however, were so debilitated by that time that most who could afford alternative housing chose it. Public housing recipients tended to have undeveloped capacities, aspirations, educational backgrounds, and aptitudes. For those with ambition, there is a sense of being merely transient. Working hard to advance oneself leaves little energy to advance the collective good, especially in a situation perceived as impermanent. As tenants do well, their very successes have tended to force or incline them out of public housing, depriving projects of potential group leadership.

Misguided regulations have also prevented public housing tenants from asserting community initiatives. The typical tenant has few choices about how apartments are furnished, decorated, or maintained, the local housing authority having made most of these decisions as communicated through coded rules. Residents are told the length of time that houseguests may stay, the kinds of pets they may own, the paint colors appropriate to their walls, the schedules by which they may use laundry and other facilities. A sense of powerlessness and alienation pervades. "Decision makers, who are never seen and cannot be influenced—the archetypical they—make rules that invade the pettiest details of living in a home" (Ryan, 1971, p. 243). Public housing tenants are unable to use their residences to start businesses. That is, they are unable to store and display bulky goods, or to engage machines in piecework or craft production. As William Ryan reminds us in his book *Blaming the Victim* (1971, p. 251), public housing is a stigmatized commodity that involves means tests, eligibility requirements, and caste marks of suitability. It is doled out as a welfare commodity. Such projects are managed as custodial institutions for second-class citizens.

Very few housing complexes have been designed to fully serve residents' needs. Indeed, physical structuring frequently complicates family life and discourages positive social relationships. Functioning community may be made impossible. Today, single-parent families headed by unmarried women dominate most city public housing projects. In Chicago, three of four public housing families are headed by unmarried woman (Chicago *Tribune* staff,

1986, p. 247). Yet, many buildings are not designed with children—let alone single women burdened with children—in mind. A project on Chicago's south side containing some 7,000 children was provided one playground and two tot lots. As William Moore reports in his book *Vertical Ghetto* (1969, p. 11), children occasionally fall from apartment windows. These places are dangerous for children and inadequately designed. "The play of children stops; a dice game comes to a temporary cessation; a wino emerges from his hiding place, looks, and reinforces himself; and the mother, who is often the last to get the news, can be heard screaming as she attempts to reach her lifeless child" (p. 16).

Buildings do not function conveniently even when mechanical systems are operating properly. Elevators may be designed to stop on alternate floors. Incinerators may require a climb of several flights of stairs. Children who live on the first floor and who are assigned the chore of emptying the trash leave a trail of debris when they go to the second-floor incinerator (Moore, 1969, p. 16). There is a further accumulation of refuse around the trash chute because its doors are too small to consume the volume of regularly deposited debris. In most cities, projects are built in a bland "state vernacular" style of monotonous giant brick or concrete block boxes totally unadorned. Roofs are flat, with rooftop machinery usually showing. As at Chicago's Robert Taylor Homes, hallways in big-city projects are often open to the exterior to facilitate police surveillance from the ground (Figure 4.7). Cages of meshed wire complete the prison look. Congressional watchdogs prevented public money from being "wasted" on grass and trees, private balconies, air conditioning, or other amenities. Thus, public housing is consistently Spartan. It is depressingly ordinary. And the scale of the ordinariness is often massive. The Taylor Homes, an incredible 4,400 units in 28 identical 16-story buildings, sprawls over a site that is half a mile wide and two miles long. Its look-alike superblocks are grouped into U-shaped clusters, three buildings to a cluster.

Public housing is also shoddy. Apartments are furnished with cheap appliances quick to malfunction. Poor quality control has given almost every public housing project problems of ill-fitting windows and doors, leaking pipes, cracking and crumbling plaster. Poor quality cannot be laid to federal miserliness. In St. Louis, the Housing Authority paid for its projects at cost equal to or greater than the cost of luxury housing in the suburbs (Meehan, 1985, p. 293). Poor quality control and the cost cutting of builders led to abuses, proving perhaps that a profit-maximizing economic system also minimizes performance when public oversight is missing and the market is complacent or monopolized. Few public housing projects contain space for shops, entertainment and recreation facilities, churches, or day-care centers. There are few meaningful spaces for neighboring and other social

Figure 4.7   In 1964, Chicago's Robert Taylor Homes still had its "landscaping" of grass chained off from the sidewalks. Subsequently, asphalt was laid building to building.

interactions. As architect and urban planner Oscar Newman (1973) has written, most public housing buildings prevent residents from controlling public spaces. Hallways, stairways, and other areas are not structured to encourage resident surveillance of public areas or to encourage their assuming jurisdiction in matters of decorum and maintenance. The orderliness of public space is left wholly to project management. Thus in most projects, public space has become a kind of no-man's-land where vandalism and other criminality flourishes.

Maintenance in public housing declined precipitously after the Brooke Amendment was placed on the 1969 Housing Act. Housing authorities were prevented from charging rents in excess of 25 percent of a tenant's income. Federal subsidy was promised to cover the difference between tenant's allowable rent and an authority's normal break-even rent; however, Congress has never appropriated sufficient funds. In the 1970s, managers were left with little choice than to divert monies from maintenance. In project after project improvements ceased and repairs declined. High energy costs further diverted maintenance monies. Most projects were "master-metered," local utility companies delivering electricity and gas to a site where they were then distributed by the authority. Individual housing units were not metered, thus saving construction costs; monthly energy costs are built into rents, prorated across projects. Managers everywhere underestimated the capacity of tenants to waste energy and no mechanisms existed by which penalties for wastefulness could be imposed. Vandalized play equipment was removed and not replaced. Playgrounds were asphalted over. Graffiti were allowed to accumulate. Vacant housing units proliferated. Plumbing and wiring went unrepaired, and apartments were simply closed and left vacant as uninhabitable. Broken windows, missing light bulbs, and pilfered hardware went unattended. As vacancies increased income received from rents declined, further reducing operating monies. Managers found themselves in a spiraling circle of decline. A 1985 survey of 66 cities indicated that $1.7 billion was needed in those cities to bring public housing projects up to safety and other standards (Meyers, 1986, p. 142).

Public housing projects have seriously impacted surrounding neighborhoods. Population densities soar. In Brooklyn's Crown Heights, Albany Houses was built on a site that originally contained 120 families in about 60 duplexes. The project contained 4,000 families in 21-story buildings with ten apartments to each floor (Gold, 1980, p. 167). Project families flooded streets, schools, churches, parks, and outlying stores, with none of these facilities upgraded to meet the crush. Public housing depressed property values almost everywhere. Projects came to symbolize the stigma of caste that made adjacent localities undesirable residential environments. Lost tax dollars and declining public services followed.

By the 1980s, conventional public housing projects in most large cities warehoused the hard-core poor totally bereft of other residential options. The projects were the last resort for unmarried girls and young women with children. Entering most projects in the 1980s, visitors saw mostly women and children, with only a few men and adolescent boys loitering restlessly in small groups. Pregnancy and qualifying for public aid had become for teenage girls a rite of passage. "With her baby, she is no longer a cipher; she has become somebody. She has her own case file, her own apartment . . . and her own social worker" (Marciniak, 1986, p. 66). However, these young women have also become entrapped in a seductive welfare system that pays the rent, buys food and clothes, and covers medical bills. All the teenage mother has to do is continue producing babies. The syndrome has passed from generation to generation, with women who are grandmothers in their twenties, and great-grandmothers in their forties, not unusual.

Children growing up in public housing projects frequently lack role models that can encourage upward mobility. Children in such places tend not to profit from having a father at home. William Moores writes, "A boy (or a girl) could learn responsibility from watching a father provide the basic necessities for his family; he could profit from hearing a father make a decision or repair a broken window sash; he might learn more about the father role if he could see how a father fulfills the role both in times of triumph and in times of adversity" (1969, p. 490). Project children play in the no-man's-lands of the public spaces, the average project child learning to fight before he or she learns to play organized games. For boys there is a forced masculinity that evolves early. Aggressions mount, much of it released in physical violence directed at the environment: apartments, hallways, stairwells, elevators, and playgrounds. Vandalism also spills beyond the immediate projects. Such behavior accelerates human and environmental abuse that is propagated by unbroken poverty.

Perhaps the only success in public housing in recent years involves America's elderly. The Housing Act of 1956 allowed builders special premiums for constructing elderly housing. The Housing Act of 1961 provided local housing authorities extra stipends for accommodating the elderly. These bonuses were sweetened by the highly desirable characteristics of older people. They usually have no young children prone to vandalism or other violence, they themselves cause little wear or tear on buildings, and they tend to pay rents regularly. The elderly require small apartments and live readily in buildings. They are ideally suited to structures that occupy high-rent parcels. Moreover, older people are nearly universally recognized as deserving public assistance "for with few exceptions they are someone's mother or father and that, in the American scheme of things, guarantees virtue and deserving" (Meehan, 1985, p. 303). In St. Louis, for example, elderly households in public housing jumped from about 15 percent in 1955 to about 30 percent in 1970 to more than 55 percent in 1975 (p. 304).

By the 1970s, most large public housing projects had become slums worse than those they had replaced. They were warehouses for a rapidly growing population of deprived and self-depreciating people. The scale of the problem was immense. Approximately 145,000 people were official residents of Chicago's public housing facilities, with an estimated additional population of illegals numbering at some 100,000 (Chicago *Tribune* staff, 1986, p. 252). Here was a population approximating Illinois's second largest city, Rockford. On Chicago's south side, some 42,000 people lived in 65 buildings. This population equaled that of Santa Cruz, California, or Salina, Kansas, or Atlantic City, New Jersey. The 42,000 residents of Rapid City, South Dakota, for example, were spread over 16 square miles, living 2,700 to the square mile. But, on Chicago's south side, project residents lived 170,000 to the square mile (Bagdikian, 1978, p. 41). In 1980, ten of the 16 poorest U.S. neighborhoods were located in Chicago Housing Authority projects, six of them along three miles of the Dan Ryan Expressway south of the Loop (Chicago *Tribune* staff, 1986, p. 252).

Urban Renewal

Urban planning did not enjoy widespread popularity in the United States early in the twentieth century. Business interests tended to view land use planning, and even zoning, as unnecessary restraint of private enterprise. Only when capitalist urbanization became deeply troubled during the Depression did urban planning win widespread acceptance. Only when collective action could no longer be postponed with America's embracing of the automobile (to the general exclusion of other forms of transportation) after World War II did planning become essential. Today some 40 percent of the land in the average American city is given to freeways, streets, and parking lots. Today one out of six jobs in the United States is directly or indirectly related to the automobile: building, selling, and servicing them as well as building and maintaining the streets and highways to accommodate them. In the early 1980s some 10,000 new drivers and 10,000 new cars were being added to the nation's roads every 24 hours (Wachtel, 1983, p. 34). Between 1950 and 1980 the American population increased by 50 percent, but the number of automobiles by 200 percent (Jackson, 1985, p. 246).

Nowhere was the motor car more disruptive of life than in the central cities where residential neighborhoods designed around mass transit had to accommodate both resident automobile ownership and the traffic congestion of commuting suburbanites as well. Close to central business districts, extensive areas were blighted by parking lots. Encouraged by the motor truck, light-industrial, wholesaling, and warehousing functions intruded on residential areas, making them fit only for the poor who could not afford to live elsewhere. The automobile's impact was most intrusive after the 1956 Highway Act extended the interstate highway system into cities, and established the Highway Trust Fund to pay for that and other highway construction. The displacements engendered by the automobile forced collective action. Private interests could not resolve the difficulties created, forcing government and urban planning to the fore. Streets needed to be improved, expressways located, and blighted areas renewed. Most planners sought to strike a professional aloofness divorced from the political process. Borrowing heavily from social scientific theory, planners sought a value-free profession. In reality, municipal planning departments came to support the power elites and their programs, planning theory serving to rationalize the restructuring of the city to benefit the influential at the expense of the weak. Values merely went unexamined as planners sought to turn America's cities into better functioning machines for money making.

After World War II, when the federal government began to intervene directly in local affairs through single-purpose agencies, planning took on new dimensions. Although municipalities were required to create master plans to guide physical development, federal spending often brought uncoordinated development as different agencies with different agendas acted independently of one another to effect piecemeal change. The highway builders, for example, built roads and did not worry about the destruction of neighborhoods, the erosion of tax bases, the decline of public services, or the out-migrations of people to the suburbs. The single-purpose agency led inadvertently to unplanned, unforeseen impacts. Cities were not planned as unique places. Cities, aided by federal largesse, sought standard solutions to problems. Planners—a highly mobile cadre of technicians—sought professional resolves at the expense of solutions rooted in locality. Cities sought identities for themselves very much in the image of other cities, with the result that a universal modernism gradually came to submerge local initiatives everywhere. As Jane Jacobs bluntly put it, "Routine, ruthless, wasteful, oversimplified solutions for all manner of city physical needs (let alone social and economic needs) [had] to be devised by administrative systems which [had] lost the power to comprehend, to handle and to value an infinity of vital, unique, intricate and interlocked details" (1961, p. 408).

Perhaps no federal initiative impacted city planning more than the Housing Act of 1949. The act was intended to engage private enterprise in eliminating urban blight through the clearing and rebuilding of central city areas. The process worked as follows. To begin, a local urban renewal agency was created, an area designated as an urban renewal zone, and renewal plans approved with authorities in Washington. Then hearings were held where local renewal officials documented their case, and other interests, pro and con, allowed public comment. On approval, land acquisition began with properties obtained through negotiation with owners or taken through the use of eminent domain powers. Clearance started once an area was evacuated. Most renewal plans called for total clearance; and therefore, sound as well as blighted buildings were removed—the prevailing assumption being that new was inherently better than old and that places contrived all at once were better than those that evolved piecemeal over time. The cleared land was then refit with streets, sewers, and other public utilities at municipal expense and, as a final step, made available to private developers. Implicit was a "write down" of property costs as a direct subsidy to the developer, government paying the difference between the cost of acquiring and clearing blighted land and the income received when sold.

Few urban renewal projects achieved their goals as originally stated. Highway construction and federal mortgage insurance programs translated into exploding suburbs, which diverted investment from urban renewal projects despite the subsidies. The poor displaced by the bulldozers moved into neighborhoods adjacent to the urban renewal zones, precipitating overcrowding and the making of new blight in ever-increasing circles of decay. Many urban renewal zones languished for decades. The new urban fabrics ultimately forced on these areas tended to be mediocre—in some cities, mainly public housing. The instability generated in neighborhoods beyond was immense, leading not to the solving of big-city slum problems, but to their exacerbation. During the 1960s, federal legislation expanded private involvement by enlarging urban renewal to include community development. During the 1970s, the Housing and Community Development Act merged programs for urban renewal and community development with model city building, open space acquisition, housing rehabilitation, and water and sewer construction into a single entity, which then languished with the Reagan administration's cutback on domestic spending.

Between 1949 and 1967, more than 1,400 urban renewal projects were launched in some 700 cities. Although the 1949 act was prefaced by a statement urging that every American family be assured decent, safe, and sanitary housing, urban renewal resulted in the destruction of 383,000 dwelling units during this period, most of them occupied by the poor. This loss was offset by 107,000 new units, only 10,000 of which were affordable by the poor (Ryan, 1971, p. 177). By 1963, more than 600,000 people had been displaced by urban renewal, four out of five being black (Anderson, 1966, p. 496). Nearly 100,000 small businesses had been displaced, with perhaps as many as half of the businessmen affected electing to quit business. Government condemnation paid only for business premises. It did not pay for the loss of patronage resulting from the dispersal of customers. Symptomatic of urban renewal was the destruction of Boston's Italian West End, a neighborhood of 9,000 residents whose houses once covered 38 blocks or some 41 acres. The land was condemned and bought for $7.40 per square foot, revalued at $1.40 per square foot, and leased for a yearly rental at approximately 6 percent of the lower value to a housing syndicate (McQuade, 1966, p. 263). "The area was ruthlessly cleared to make way for a cluster of high-rise, high-rent apartment houses, a banal grouping of blunt, balconied towers on a treeless plain—and a bitter warning to all of the timeworn Boston neighborhoods of what renewal might mean to them too" (ibid.).

The Housing Act of 1949 resulted from a massive lobbying effort by big city realtors (especially the National Association of Real Estate Boards), the savings and loan industry (especially the U.S. Savings and Loan League), the U.S. Chamber of Commerce, and various other builder and business groups. Their advocacy of urban renewal was substantially a stance against public housing that seemingly threatened the private housing market. Paradoxically, public housing paved the way for urban renewal by eliminating many legal, political, and institutional roadblocks. Nearly every state by 1939 had passed enabling legislation and had it upheld in the courts, verifying the constitutionality of the use of eminent domain to clear blighted areas. Public housing had not only popularized the role of intergovernmental public action to clear slums, but had linked federal and local authorities directly, essentially bypassing the states. Both public housing and urban renewal were intended to fight slums. Slum formation was seen to be a social problem involving poor people in high densities: social pathologies resulting from overcrowding. Urban renewal, however, came to focus on blight that was not social but economic in concept. Essentially, blight meant declining property values such that the maintenance of property was made problematical.

Total clearance was not necessary to the renewal of cities, but it fit the tenor of the times. A generation frustrated by the economic Great Depression, but bolstered by the triumphs of World War II, little appreciated its inheritance from the past. Modernism had come to dominate architectural design. New buildings stripped of all past symbolism floated as isolated objects in space, contrasting boldly with their surroundings (Figure 4.8). Clearance provided open space. The design of buildings and landscapes called for complete clarity and extreme simplicity. The new cities were to be orderly even to a fault. Ambiguities were to be eliminated. A new bold symbolism was called to the fore, in which the past would not only be ignored, but destroyed. The slab office tower—a rectangle of metal and glass—found its counterpart in the urban renewal landscape of streets lined

Figure 4.8   Chicago's Lake Meadows on that city's near southside was the very epitome of what the modern city was supposed to be: buildings devoid of historical allusion, floating as isolated objects in open space.

by formal tree plantings setting off bald expanses of open space. By the 1960s, however, Americans were beginning to voice concern with the new order. As the popular writer Vance Packard concluded, "The challenge of tackling urban blight in the United States does not necessarily mean tearing down miles of buildings and replacing them with thirty-story concrete slabs jutting up from fenced-off grassland. Inhabitants would be happier if they could simply have their old neighborhood homes and streets spruced up, with some pleasant open spaces added" (1960, p. 301). What Americans had taken for granted, and had stood passively aside while watching it destroyed, began to appear nostalgically as once again desirable. Missed was the excitement of the ad hoc city accumulated over time with its sense of mystery and excitement.

Neighborhood conservation and rehabilitation came to the fore slowly. By 1964, there were 229 rehabilitation projects under way, but usually in conjunction with clearance (Slayton, 1966, p. 214). By the 1970s, the historic preservation movement had come to the fore as a redevelopment alternative. Arthur Ziegler (1971, p. 10) calculated that in Pittsburgh a quarter century of urban renewal had impacted only 2,000 acres out of 14,000 needing renewal, the city itself containing 35,000 acres ultimately renewable. Not one single urban renewal project had yet been brought to completion. Ziegler estimated that it would require 120 years to "renew" the city using clearance as originally implemented.

Merely designating an area as an urban renewal zone was enough to guarantee not only its conversion into a slum, but conversion of adjacent areas as well. Landlords had little choice but to disinvest properties since monies spent for repairs and improvements would be monies ultimately lost. As long as housing for the poor was in short supply, as was the case through the 1960s, it worked to the advantage of slum landlords to divide buildings into more housing units, and to charge rents exorbitant relative to the accommodations provided. Higher rents inflated property assessments for urban renewal land, taking as well as generating inflated profits over the short run before condemnation. The result was deteriorated and overcrowded housing that amplified the public resolve to "renew," leading to an ever-widening blight problem. Although the 1970s and 1980s saw few clearance projects initiated, the forces unleashed earlier could not be contained. The overbuilding of new houses in the suburbs opened up large quantities of older housing to the poor at an ever-accelerating rate. Urban renewal became not so much a cure for urban ills as a self-fulfilling prophecy of decline.

Planners, in embracing urban renewal, did not build carefully on the past. Instead, they advocated arrogant elimination of things old. They sought not to preserve the best that previous generations had produced, carefully enhancing same with the best that the future could suggest. Rather, they sought to start totally afresh, to reinvent the city in the vague imagery of modernism. The governing reality was the city as it might be or ought to be, and not the city as it was: a highly complex organism of people, institutions, and physical infrastructures that needed fine tuning rather than quick fixes. Big ideas weakly constructed on unproven assumptions governed in the place of small ideas carefully bolstered by observation and comprehensions as to what made cities vital. Jane Jacobs (1961, p. 440) took planners to task for not thinking carefully about processes of change and for failing to work inductively, reasoning from particulars to the grand rather than in the reverse.

Planners were quick to abstract the deteriorating central city as "space" inefficiently used, as a potential surface for redevelopment. They did not see communities where communities existed. They did not see neighborhoods as the homes of people. They abstracted away from peoples' lives. For those displaced came a loss of neighborhood as extended home. There came a loss of familiar setting and of the sense of stability, especially important in the lives of blue-collar workers and their families. Places have both a public and a private face. Buildings not only function publicly; they also stand symbolic of the private lives lived around them. Routines are fragmented when people are forced from a familiar place. People displaced lose much of their sense of continuity. Again, the upwardly bound middle and upper classes may relish change and move easily from place to place, but it is uncertain whether the lower classes do so.

Discontinuity can be stressful, as planner Marc Fried (1966) discovered in his now classic analysis of Boston's West End Italian neighborhood. Grief manifested itself in "feelings of painful loss, the continued longing, the general depressive tone, frequent symptoms of psychological or social or somatic distress, the active work required in adapting to the altered situation, the sense of helplessness, the occasional expressions of both direct and displaced anger, and tendencies to idealize the lost place" (p. 359). Fried advocated slowing drastic redevelopment and its associated displacement of people (p. 377). When people had to be displaced, he advocated relocating them in their old neighborhoods. When neighborhood displacement was necessary, then people should be relocated in new places where traditional attachments could be reestablished in old ways. It was but a short step to a logic of rehabilitation and an ethic of preservation. As Peter Marris counseled, "There is virtue in rehabilitating familiar forms which neither economic logic nor conventional criteria of taste can fully take into account, and we should recognize this, before we decide what to destroy" (1974, p. 150). In a sense, the rush of the affluent to suburbia was a quest for continuity. In suburbia were the overt symbols of traditional America rooted in the simpler past of small towns and farms. Here was the appearance of a pastoral place that would not suffer the instability and decline that the nation's central cities had come to symbolize. The dream, of course, was an illusion.

Block Grants and Housing Vouchers

The Community Development Block Grant Program (CDBG) arose under the Housing and Community Development Act of 1974 in response to perceived shortcomings of traditional "categorical" programs. Categoricals—like urban renewal, model cities, and public works loans—were increasingly perceived as bureaucratic and inefficient. To critics, their reliance on federal decision makers and regulations rendered them locally unresponsive. Local community needs were purportedly being subsumed under bureaucratic rules that stipulated specific spending goals. To counter this shortcoming, the Department of Housing and Urban Development (HUD) folded seven categorical programs—urban renewal, neighborhood facilities, model cities, water and sewer, housing rehabilitation, open space, and public works loans—into one multibased program. The stated objective was to expand local capacity to determine development needs, with local organizations projected as major decision makers. Block grants would purportedly trim government intervention, scale back bureaucracies, and make redevelopment more locally responsive (Bunce, 1980).

Over the years, general procedures have evolved that guide most city's CDBG decision making. In general, the city submits plans for spending priorities to a city council and public participatory body. After acceptance, citywide organizations are invited to submit proposals to receive funds for various purposes. Developers, nonprofit groups, and public–private partnerships seek funds on a competitive basis. City technicians and public participatory groups review proposal merits, based primarily on possibilities for successful completion of project and past track record of success. The final stage involves funding selected organizations who are mandated to adhere to proposal specifications.

Like its predecessor, categorical programs, CDBG has run into considerable controversy. Underlying much of this debate has been a bickering over political ideologies that emphasize different public agendas. Ronald Reagan, for starters, successfully converted block grants into a sharply partisan and ideological issue (Conlan, 1984). Categoricals were purportedly gross failures, reliant on a shortsighted vision of throwing money at problems to seek quick solutions. The only clear beneficiaries, to Republicans, were government bureaucrats who built bloated bureaucracies for self-aggrandizement. Democrats countered by focusing on basic programmatic flows. To Democrats, equity priorities were marginalized under a program that ascribed too much importance to nonredistributive economic growth.

Granting excessive flexibility to local officials and their political allies to define community need supposedly hindered local redistributive efforts. This program therefore shifted too many policy decisions from federal administrative agencies to local institutions. In the absence of strict federal regulations, it was contended, block grants became increasingly subject to local economic and political interests.

Academic studies on CDBG have borne out Democratic concerns. Kenneth Wong and Paul Peterson (1986) note basic flaws in block grant administration that stem from programmatic defects. In their study of Milwaukee and Baltimore, city officials used block grants to achieve desired personal goals. Given the power to define local needs, disproportionate funds were distributed to advance middle-income economic agendas that consolidated local political support. In this process, mayors and their key advisors used funds to reinforce their political position. Political leaders here were anything but mere brokers who resolve local issues placed before them. Developmental policies submerged redistributive programs under local growth concerns. Programs enhancing local economic position in its competition with other areas were given highest priority. Such programs rebuilt the local tax base and generated amenities to attract conspicuous consumers and more investment. In contrast, redistributive goals (the thrust of the former categoricals) were assigned low priority. They were deemed irrelevant to the pressing issue of economic growth and were believed potentially counter-productive by their attracting the needy and discouraging new investment. Political officials, therefore, eyed block grants as political resources whose "proper" use could make a social statement. They could produce widely publicized achievements that could translate into continued electoral support.

Similar results are uncovered by S. Catlin (1981), who studied nine cities in Florida. He suggested that with widespread spending discretion under CDBG only select cities lived up to the spirit of the Housing and Community Development Act of 1974. A retreat from a commitment to housing and public social services, he contended, was easily accomplished under vague federal guidelines and the empowering of local politicians to decide spending priorities. In Florida, the norm was to give scant dollars for redistributive purposes. This money, moreover, was usually targeted to secondarily declining areas over "too far gone" neighborhoods. Thus, vast slums in Miami, Jacksonville, Tampa, and other large cities were basically untouched by block grants. Catlin deems the apologist argument of prioritizing places by "probability of success in treatment" unacceptable. For one thing, he suggested, this strategy violates the intent of the program. More importantly, to Catlin, "this is like saying that if you have two patients seeking admission to a hospital with one being critically ill and the other in serious condition, we should treat the latter and allow the former to die." Catlin sees block grants as one more social initiative that reflects the gradual abandonment of black and poor Americans.

David Wilson (1989) reveals the problems implicit in the block grant approach when funds can be unproblematically appropriated by local power elites to foster middle-class forms of civic improvement. A Middle West case study put into focus the power of local elites in defining growth agendas and manipulating government resources. An alliance of mayor, city council, media, and local developers forged growth conducive to elite advancement (i.e., profitability) and political sustainability. Block grants unproblematically flowed to building shopping malls, sports stadiums, and gentrified housing amid a pronounced neglect of low-income neighborhoods. In this context, local politics cast the poor as undeserving welfare recipients. These were people who purportedly refused to contribute productively to the system and lacked a work ethic of upward mobility. Influenced by an elaborate ideological apparatus, middle-income residents grew insensitive to the indigents' plight. The boosterism of "livable city" penetrated everyday life to encourage citizens to tame a dark and wild inner city by imposing middle-class growth. In this ideological context, reforming block grant distribution failed. Public hostility and government insensitivity to change were critical impediments. The poor became a stigmatized minority ignored and forgotten by a citizenry caught in the frenzy of upper-class redevelopment.

Paralleling emergence of block grants was the expansion of housing vouchers—a controversial Republican housing initiative. This program, an experimental undertaking for 12 years, became embraced as the most appropriate government response to helping the poor acquire suitable housing. The program, simply put, provides those with low income with direct cash payments that are to be used for securing housing. Rental units, selected by eligible families, must meet decent and safe standards. Eligible families are those whose incomes do not exceed 50 percent of the median areal income. Government subsidies in monthly payments are based on the difference between rental fees and 30 percent of family monthly income. For qualifying families, preference is given those that occupy substandard housing, are displacees, or are paying more than half their income for rent.

While still controversial, the roots of housing vouchers extend back over three decades. This concept was called "rent certificates" in the era of its initial proposal and debate during the 1930s and 1940s (Zais, 1976). Its programmatic merits were debated prior to the passage of the Housing Act of 1987, the hearings before the Taft Subcommittee in 1944, and the Housing Act of 1949. The President's Advisory Committee on Government Housing Policies and Programs further debated the issue in 1953 but rejected it in favor of continuing the public housing program. The voucher approach, it was argued, would cause a vast number of families to go on relief, would not add to housing supply, and would be too complex to administer (ibid.). In December 1968, however, the President's Committee on Urban Housing issued its final report in which it gave strong support for housing vouchers. The committee recognized programmatic shortcomings but acknowledged an array of possible benefits. The committee urged immediate program adoption. In 1972 the Experimental Housing Allowance Program (EHAP) was implemented; it continues, in modified form, today.

Criticisms of the housing voucher program arose upon its implementation as federal policy. A major concern has been the emphasis on housing demand versus housing supply that neglects building production in favor of subsidizing building costs. The dilemma here was the inflationary spiral that was frequently generated in local housing markets. Put another way, it was probable that a market saturated with housing vouchers increases housing demand to a point where prices are artificially inflated. Housing supply, it was contended, cannot match increased demand to keep down inflation. Critics, moreover, contended that this process subverts program goals by subsidizing landlords and owners. Supposed beneficiaries—those with low income—get caught in a web of escalating housing prices while unintended participants—housing providers—reap the benefits of enhanced profitability. As James P. Zais argues, "because the housing market traditionally has been 'sluggish' in the speed with which supply follows demand, few would argue that the short-term response to housing allowances, in the absence of price controls, will not be inflationary" (1976, p. 233).

From a different perspective, housing vouchers have purportedly failed to break down patterns of residential segregation. One supposed benefit of the program, as articulated by its proponents, was the opportunity to promote integration that a "freedom of choice" program affords. To critics like W. Widrow (1987) and Arlene Zarembka (1990), however, housing vouchers have accomplished little in this area. The problem, to these critics, is a complex convergence of forces that sustain slums in the face of government eradication efforts. Realtors, developers, builders, and the like purportedly have a vested interest in sustaining slums: undesirable populations need to be funneled somewhere to contain their influence on local submarkets. These actors are not seen as operating in collusion, but rather as following individual patterns of intervention that promise optimal economic return. This materialist perspective recognizes the economic logic of slum persistence in capitalist societies. To integrate society is to dampen profit opportunities in local land and housing markets. Segregation is consequently reinforced and institutionalized in subtle ways. Zoning, homeowner protectionist beliefs, realtor steering, and low-income social stigmatization all serve to fragment urban residential space. In this context, housing vouchers are a band-aid measure destined to fail. In seeking to eliminate segregation but tackling symptoms rather than causes, it conceals the mechanisms that produce segregation. With this failure to integrate, segregation is made to appear a natural occurrence, inevitable and inexorable in form. Its purported inevitability and persistence eludes benevolent attempts at eradication.

THE BOLSTERING OF SUBURBIA

While federal and municipal government faltered in the revitalizing of America's central cities, the suburbs thrived. Development there was driven by other initiatives, many indirectly detrimental to central city neighborhoods. For example, federal housing programs subsidized suburban growth—especially the Housing Act of 1934, which established the Federal Housing Administration (FHA) and its program to insure mortgages held by qualified financial institutions. Subsequent legislation established, among other agencies, the Federal National Mortgage Association to harness the borrowing power of the federal government as a source of funds for financing housing, and the Veterans Administration (VA) to back mortgages for veterans returning from World War II. These were all "pump-priming" ventures designed to increase the flow of capital into the housing market. Programs benefited primarily the financial and real estate interests, and secondarily the nation's more affluent citizens who could afford single-family residences in the suburbs. Benefits were expected to "trickle down" to the poor in the form of old housing discarded by the affluent in the central cities.

By artificially stimulating new house construction in the suburbs, Congress sought to stimulate economic recovery during the Depression. Thereafter, an expansive construction industry came to be viewed as a major bulwark of a healthy economy. By the 1970s, the building materials and construction industries accounted for more than 14 percent of the nation's gross national product while construction employed nearly 5 percent of the nation's labor force (Solomon, 1974, p. 2). Federal housing policy ultimately lost sight of all but the affluent consumer for, by the 1980s, new housing was beyond the means of some three-quarters of the nation's families (Parenti, 1983, p. 122). Lavish assistance was provided upper-income homeowners in the form of low-cost credit, income tax deductions, and other subsidies. For example, in 1981, homeowner income tax deductions amounted to $31.8 billion (Goetz, 1983, p. 24). Only about one-eighth of American taxpayers with incomes below $10,000 received federal housing assistance either through HUD programs or tax deductions. In contrast, four-fifths of the households with income above $50,000 benefited through the tax code alone (Meyers, 1986, p. 140). Tax regulations encouraged families in high tax brackets to live on credit, including mortgage credit, while at the same time discouraging savings by taxing interest as ordinary income.

By the 1970s, the suburbs of most cities were overdeveloped, weakening substantially the housing markets of the nation's central cities. Between 1963 and 1973, 175,000 new housing units in excess of demand were created in metropolitan Chicago, prompting a very rapid shift of mostly white, affluent families to the suburbs. At the same time, only 27,000 new public housing units, mostly for blacks, were created in the central city (Center for Urban Studies, 1977, p. 78). Clearly, central cities were well along the way to becoming receptacles for all the functions that suburb dwellers did not want to support. At the same time, however, the public infrastructures of the central cities continued to support suburbanites. A study of Detroit in 1970 concluded that a suburban family of four received net benefits in services from the city that amounted to compensatory payments of as much as $50 per year. With 63 percent of the metropolitan Detroit population living in the suburbs, estimated transfer payments as high as $35 million occurred annually (Ley, 1983, p. 362). Suburban commuters used city streets and depended on city utilities and services while at work. Suburbanites used city parks, museums, libraries, hospitals, and other facilities conducive to an urbane life. The city was still very much central to suburban lives.

Central city decline is not inexorable. In the United States, central cities declined because economic and political interests, aided by tax codes and other legal mechanisms, willed it so. Central cities declined because influential people considered it in their best interest to sustain a system that made decline appear natural and inevitable. The remedies of the power elites were unsuccessful in solving basic urban problems; indeed, most programs only precipitated the spread of the very circumstances programs were designed to eliminate. Failure reflected the unwillingness of elites to define problems in terms other than self-interest. Public housing was designed not to solve fully the difficulties of housing the poor, but to ensure that the public sector would not intrude on the private housing market. Urban renewal was not designed to eliminate slums so much as to subsidize vested interests in recycling land for capital accumulation. Aided and abetted by centralized government, power elites turned the cities to their own needs.

Did distressed neighborhoods really need convention centers, sports arenas, and huge commercial developments? Certainly, they did need a stable real estate market and stable sources of capital for maintaining and improving old buildings. They did need improved public services to keep abreast of new suburbs. They needed enhanced entrepreneurial opportunities whereby local businesses could thrive in place. They needed the opportunity to manage themselves as distinctive places. Distressed neighborhoods, however, were not allowed the resources necessary for solving their own problems as communities of local interest. Autonomy was denied. In neighborhood after neighborhood, in city after city, residents were reduced to passive observers, and ultimately to victims, as experts at a distance decided their futures. The statistics of central city decline only outline the tragedy. They not only reflect the result, but hide the opportunities lost to make American cities truly places for human improvement. Americans have been so busy escaping the perils of urban instability that they have had little time or energy to contemplate a different life. In words of Herbert Muller, "The trouble remains that most Americans have little idea of what city life can be at its best and as limited an awareness of their own higher needs and potentialities" (1971, p. 260).

5

Abandoned Neighborhoods

Urban neighborhoods are increasingly sites for intense conflict. At issue are those who seek to commodify place versus those who try to protect suitable qualities of life. Neighborhoods have both use values and exchange values, providing entrepreneurs avenues for accumulation and residents opportunities to forge fulfilling lives. On the one hand, neighborhoods are places to satisfy essential needs, providing schools, social networks, and social spaces to humanize daily existence. In effect, lives are made in neighborhoods. On the other hand, these areas encompass land and buildings whose commercial exchange generates profit. Business interests strive for financial gain through buying, selling, and renting property. The conflicts engendered between those who would define neighborhoods as economic spaces and those who would define them as social spaces are very much at the heart of the urban dereliction problem.

Recent changes in our urban neighborhoods testify to entrepreneurs' ability to dominate use-value advocates. Spurred by government subsidies, favored political treatment, and disproportionate economic resources, "place entrepreneurs" have reconfigured urban form to maximize real estate investments. A vivid illustration is the emergence of gentrification. Place entrepreneurs have successfully restructured selected central city areas for market development, simultaneously removing land uses and populations potentially disruptive to a revitalization process. Outside investors effectively supplant low-income people by reordering the price and quality of housing. Displaced households overwhelmingly end up in nearby low-income areas. To Peter Marcuse (1986), low-income isolation has been as important to sustaining gentrification as has been the infusion of new investment.

The reproduction of segregation by class reflects the power of place entrepreneurs to dictate spatial forms. Cities continue to take the form of fragmented residential "islands," reflecting a socioeconomic stratification that allows realtors, banks, developers, and speculators to extract maximum profit from everyday housing transactions. Confidence thresholds are provided for speculator investing, bank lending, realtor intervention, and the like. Unprecedented rates of neighborhood dereliction have emerged from those processes. Amid islands of rejuvenating and stable housing, vast acres of urban land have been untouched by investors—a situation that serves to exacerbate erosion. Neighborhood decline unfolds logically from the partitioning of urban space into zones of vibrancy, stability, and neglect.

This chapter examines the dynamics of neighborhood dereliction, focusing on the neighborhood as a contested human element. We initially explore the range of current explanations for this phenomenon. Our focus then shifts to the empirical forms that create it: redlining, blockbusting, and government policy. The controversial roles of tenants and landlords are subsequently discussed, followed by examinations of abandoned housing and what some critics have called the American "throwaway society." Our final focus is the everyday treatment of the "underclass," a group stuck in derelict neighborhoods but accorded little societal assistance. Our belief is that neighborhood dereliction reflects an inequitable distribution of societal resources that, being humanly constructed, is not inevitable.

EXPLANATIONS FOR NEIGHBORHOOD DERELICTION

Social scientists have virulently debated the causes of neighborhood poverty and dereliction over the past 30 years, making the individual versus society issue the focus of contentiousness. Individual-based explanations have emphasized the free will and decision-making capabilities of the poor who purportedly make choices, act on predilections, and construct their own plight. This markedly conservative vantage point, drawing inspiration from the 1960s culture-of-poverty thesis, has emphasized individual capacities to overcome contexts of constraint. The poor are, by implication, accorded mechanisms that permit upward mobility and advancement if initiatives exists. Society is less constrictive than enabling, allowing the poor to choose a life path that suits their desires. At the other extreme, society-based explanations, taking a structuralist form, depict the poor as passive victims of oppression. Capitalist society is seen to be permeated by inequality, according unequal life chances and opportunities across populations. Society is less enabling than constrictive, imposing low-income social and spatial hardships that are entrenched and impossible to overcome. As in explanations for central city dereliction, neighborhood-based notions have marginalized attempts at finding a middle ground between these extremes.

Attempts to implicate either individuals or society in the production of poverty has retarded integrationist efforts. The discussion that follows briefly reviews these competing explanations.

Theorists emphasizing the influence of the individual have drawn inspiration from anthropologist Oscar Lewis (1959), the initiator of the culture-of-poverty school. Studies here have focused on the interconnections between cultural traditions, family history, and individual character (W. Wilson, 1987). Briefly, this group believes that inner-city residents, faced with dim opportunities for long-term material advancement, form their own value sets to adapt to marginal circumstances. The construction of different norms can permit residents to achieve goals and values, ones that are frequently impugned by the larger society. While resignation, passivity, fatalism, and powerlessness permeate the slum, these values are paralleled by failure of self-discipline, unwillingness to defer gratification, and marginalization of a work ethic. These two value sets, seemingly disparate, exist side by side to yield fatalistic, low-skilled workers. Such workers have difficulty holding jobs and perpetuate the poverty that reduces their life chances. Poverty is perpetuated by transmission of values across generations that lock low-income households into low-income castes. Thus, those submerged in welfare living tend to spread values of little ambition and lack of self-reliance (cf. Wilson, 1975; Gilder, 1981; Murray, 1984).

In its various forms—particularly versions offered by conservative theorists—the poor are treated as a monolithic population. They are ascribed pathological values whose roots lie in a variant subculture. A specific coping strategy is selected by the poor among a range of possible options. In confronting poverty, households could choose a path of self-help, communal efforts to rise above poverty, or other agendas. Instead, they choose to stay mired in poverty and construct perverse value orientations to minimize pain and suffering. Poverty is, at its core, a chosen way of life that infects generations of people unwilling to break its debilitating influence. In the final analysis, it is consciously chosen and nurtured through an unwillingness to tackle the difficult task of self-rehabilitation. In effect, the poor choose lives of poverty and deprivation. Constraints like racism and discrimination can purportedly be overcome with diligence and firmness of purpose. The power of such constraints, moreover, are believed exaggerated. Ed Banfield, for example, notes that "a wish to make amends for wrongs done by one's ancestors lead to a misrepresentation of the Negro as the near-helpless victim of 'white racism.' . . . That racial prejudice has long been declining at an accelerating rate counts for little if the Negro *thinks* that white racism is as pervasive as ever" (1970, p. 8). To such theorists, this active deliberation maintains a culture-of-poverty that persists through adaptation to local circumstances.

Criticisms of the culture of poverty thesis are many. Numerous critics have argued that it places blame on the victim and conceals the social causes of poverty (W. Wilson, 1987; Steinberg, 1981). To critics, slum residents in this thesis are granted an inflated causal role over the context of oppression within which they operate. The moral fiber and personal characteristics of slum residents become important relative to the denial of opportunity. Critics contend, however, that poverty is less chosen than socially constructed. Limited opportunities flow out of constraints imposed by local institutions—a fact ignored by culture-of-poverty advocates. White institutions constrict resources and life chances in prescribed areas. For example, realtors concentrate the poor, banks deny them upgrading capital, depleted schools constrict future employment possibilities, and society relegates them to inferior social status. With these actions, white society can preserve its privileged position. To these critics, white society is insensitive to the low-income condition because of a constructed myopia. To be sensitive and face the problem squarely is to jeopardize a privileged status. These everyday life constraints, moreover, are believed persistent, debilitating, and rarely capable of being mitigated through rational choice alone. Such constraints are not tenuous and superficial, but entrenched and constrictive.

A related criticism of the culture-of-poverty thesis has focused on its policy implications. This theory, by inference, believes that poverty is best eradicated by changing low-income motivations and attitudes. The need is to culturally rehabilitate the poor rather than restructure economic and political conditions. Critics, however, have identified this potential policy directive as misguided and ineffectual. Such actions have been labeled "crass social engineering" and ignorant of structural conditions that induce poverty. A revisionist notion, it is contended, must consider the lack of political, financial, and social resources that the poor have at their disposal to change conditions (cf. Judd, 1979; Cater and Jones, 1989; Piven and Cloward, 1977). For example, social and political institutions frustrate the poor through inadequate provision of jobs, education, and social status. Low-income contempt and aversion cast them as inferiors. Such barriers to upward mobility lock the poor into immobile situations. It follows that poverty is rooted in the dual spheres of powerlessness and economic deprivation. Poverty eradication, therefore, requires challenging institutional barriers and unequal opportunities rather than individual self-help (Perry and Watkins, 1977; Gale and Moore, 1975; Herzog, 1990).

Important new theories of poverty have recently surfaced under the structural constraint banner. These innovative theories, seeing the poor as essentially victims of an unjust society, have focused on causes for slum neighborhoods persisting in current times of massive urban restructuring. Neil Smith's (1982) rent-gap thesis has attracted much attention, highlighting the influence of uneven resource flows and political domination across urban space that rejuvenate small residential islands at the expense of promoting widespread poverty and deprivation. Smith's model, forged to explain uneven upgrading, has obvious implications for patterns of slum persistence. In this notion, slums persist by the playing out of two forces. First, upper-income-controlled uneven development revitalizes selected blocks amid larger tracts of sustained disinvestment. Government subsidies are targeted to induce upper-income restructuring while regulations fail to prohibit low-income residential displacement. Tax subsidies and block grants, for example, induce investment in targeted urban enclaves amid low-income inability to blunt forced removal. Poverty and dereliction arise from a resource void in declining areas. Second, poverty is sustained by low-income failure to be represented in the local political sphere. Political and ideological constructions favoring upper-income redevelopment suppress low-income dissent. On the one hand, the poor are denied the political mechanisms to contest lack of resources and inequitable development. On the other hand, conflict over local development and resource distribution is negotiated to the detriment of the poor. Public aversion to their goals and needs is nurtured through construction of "pro-growth," "economic efficiency," and "livable city" political ideologies. The public excoriates their "political agenda," deeming it "poverty politics," "welfare development," and "low-income self-aggrandizement."

The sphere of politics and economics interconnect here to produce uneven urban development. The poor are controlled through structural factors that minimize their purportedly destructive role on local housing markets. Real estate—a prime venue for accumulation—needs protection and nurturing from detrimental land uses or populations. Slums are devalued land districts that hold undesirable populations. Realtors steer those with low income here, inadequate schools provide marginal job skills, churches preach social passivity in the face of oppression, and city rhetoric renders political opposition ineffectual. The poor, locals believe, threaten the production of conspicuous consumption districts and need to be isolated. In the face of these forces, a poverty is nurtured and sustained that permits profit to be chased in other housing submarkets. Thus, for gentrification to exist, poverty and dereliction must be sustained. The strength of this thesis is its forging of connections between the construction of affluence and the emergence of poverty. These polarities, traditionally seen as separate development forms, are now linked.

This structural constraint model has been criticized on grounds of being too mechanistic. As Chris Hamnett (1984) notes, this model accords causal primacy to structural factors that overwhelm local capacities to produce pluralistic politics and meaningful local conflict. By implication, uneven development and slum persistence are cast as something that happens to us rather than something we make. The logic of accumulation permeates local politicians and planners, and guides them to advance materialist agendas; city form is appropriately restructured. Politicians, planners, the poor, and others are reduced to passive beings, acting out scripted roles whose inevitable outcome is poverty and dereliction. An inexorable logic therefore underpins local development, conditioning outcomes and spatial forms irrespective of human capacities to confront circumstances. Under capitalism, poverty and dereliction have to exist; structural forces choreograph change.

David Wilson (1991) expands on this critique by noting that this model downplays the restructuring influence of local culture, politics, and biographical idiosyncrasy. Because of this local filter, cities exhibit different intensities and patterns of poverty and dereliction. While one city may be substantially segregated with intense poverty concentrations, another may exhibit only patches of poverty and dereliction. Moreover, different power relations and cultural predictions across areas may offer divergent opportunities to consolidate and prolong poverty. In one city, cultural predilections may ascribe intensely pejorative values to the poor and socially stigmatize them. Common attitudes of aversion, antipathy, and repulsion may crystalize the underclass status that so dramatically constrains them. In a second city, local culture may be more sympathetic to the poor, seeing circumstance and context as major culprits in their plight. In this circumstance, the local political arena may offer opportunities to induce some positive social change. Smith's structural constraint model, in short, purportedly fails to consider the importance of local influences on promoting or retarding poverty and dereliction. To Wilson, the need is to more thoroughly sensitize the model to the particularities of place.

Richard Peet (1975) also offers a structural constraint model by conceptualizing poverty as outgrowth of capitalist labor requirements. Peet takes as his starting point the view that inequality is inherent in the capitalist mode of production. Inequality is "inevitably produced during the normal operation of capitalist economies, and cannot be eradicated without fundamentally altering the mechanisms of capitalism," he writes (p. 564). His argument centers around the notion of the spatial division of labor, where households are residentially stratified by class and job skills across neighborhoods. Urban fabrics are marked by patchworks of nominally connected neighborhoods differing in status, class, and labor skills. Thus, affluent enclaves, middle-income neighborhoods, and slums serve as labor repositories. This stratification—essential to reproducing local labor—is sustained through realtor steering, bank redlining, government constricting low-income social spaces, and so forth. While these actors do not conspire to promote residential differentiation, the short-term pursuit of profit collectively has this effect. Space, as socially constructed apparatus, encourages labor slot reproduction into future generations. Each isolated social group "operates within a typical daily 'prism,' which, for the disadvantaged, closes into a prison of space and resources" (p. 568). It is therefore "easy," Michael Dear adds, "to understand how an individual can carry an 'imprint' of a given environment, and how the daily-life environment can act to 'transmit' inequality" (p. 485).

Social and spatial isolation render those with low income unwitting societal victims. Mobility restrictions, nominal resources, inadequate infrastructure, and dominance of peculiar norms woven into local social fabrics impregnate youth with similar goals and values; such environmental deficiencies limit individual potentials and opportunities. The poor thereby reproduce themselves in an environment of attrition and denial, using their menial resources to raise the next generation of impoverished workers. In cities "a person may only exploit the social resources of a limited section of space in order to ready himself for the labor market. . . . Each age group, each social class, each racial group, each sex, has a different sized typical daily 'prism' in which to operate" (Peet, 1975, p. 508). For the lowest class and most discriminated against groups, prisons without walls retard their opportunity for upward mobility. Slums emerge as uniquely differentiated spaces, denied the resources and opportunities to nourish disadvantaged populations. They transmit inequality by their capacity to define and constrict everyday lives.

Criticisms of this model have focused on its functionalist nature. James Duncan and David Ley (1982), for example, reacted sharply in the larger context of critiquing structuralist Marxism. They contend that such models transform complex everyday worlds into sets of abstract, functional parts whose logic is understood by reference of causal wholes. In other words, such models view everyday reality as functional units tied part and parcel to the rhythms of capital accumulation. Social relations that create things like poverty and dereliction are understood only in functional terms, that is, how one form creates another. The world of agents is reduced to simple directives and logics that exist to exploit or be exploited. Thus, change as unintended outcome becomes inconceivable, lost under the logic and power of wholes. Such wholes, as reified categories, have a life of their own and a distinctive materialist purpose. These functional units reify entities like mode of production and capital and endow them with an inner logic divorced from human capacity to modify. Such functionalism, it is contended, has the additional influence of relegating human agency to unimportance. It "obscures the true underlying processes by which the action of individuals produce the structural conditions under which they act and through which those conditions may later become constraining or coercive" (Duncan and Ley, 1982, p. 37). In the context of Peet's model, capitalist wholes create a spatial division of labor, spatially and socially polarize the poor, and sustain poverty through the intervention of materialist guided agents. Power to modify or rearrange these forces is nonexistent, the political sphere being functionally controlled to limit low-income dissent.

A number of promising studies seeking a middle ground between structure and agency have recently unfolded in different empirical contexts. These studies offer insights into how such polarities may be collapsed in a study of neighborhood poverty and dereliction. Michael Dear and Adam Moos (1986) examine ghettoization among psychiatric patients in Hamilton, Ontario, emphasizing the mutually constructive nature of individual and society. Both elements are ascribed causality. Two critical facilitative processes—deinstitutionalization and ghettoization—are attributed to the interconnections between capitalist prerogatives, unique and idiosyncratic planner decisions, and the bounded choices of patients. Every act of ghettoizing a psychiatric patient is seen to embody these influences. Barney Warf (1988) collapses these dualisms in a study of the Pacific Northwest lumber industry. A Marxian notion of uneven development is integrated with notions of everyday life and social reproduction. Theory connects everyday life with macroeconomic structures by conceptualizing a ceaseless interplay between these elements. The macro creates the micro; the micro creates the macro. Human actions, now deemed important, transform landscapes within a web of possibilities defined by structural constraints. Such studies are innovative in their unwillingness to reduce cause to either areal-based or macro-scale forces. The importance of individuals is retained even while identifying the context within which human actions take place. A causative whole emerges that recognizes a multiplicity of influences bound in time and space. Such innovative research has, to date, not been applied to the study of neighborhood poverty and dereliction.

DERELICTION AND RACE

Derelict urban neighborhoods often represent the end product of a decline process begun decades earlier. Decline is set in motion by disinvestment, which often snowballs to render neighborhoods useless shells. Such neighborhoods, often adjoining well-maintained areas, become victims of neglect by the complex interconnections of uneven development, race, class, and government actions. Race is an important factor, retarding or facilitating investment as a surrogate variable for the stability of populations. Its influence is reflected in the processes of steering, redlining, and blockbusting. The discussion that follows examines neighborhood decline and the influence of race. Initially, neighborhood decline is discussed in a framework of neighborhood change. The discussion then focuses on the pervasive influence of race on housing markets.

Students of urban decay have identified finite stages through which urban neighborhoods decline to become repositories for the underclass (see, for example, Naparstek and Cincotta, 1976, p. 9; Olson and Lachman, 1976, p. 69; Werner, 1977, p. 12; Downs, 1980, p. 523; Downs, 1981, p. 63; Hoover and Vernon, 1982, p. 166). Despite the fact that much change is cumulative linearly, the notion of staged change is useful. Elaborated here is the Olson and Lachman model, the stages of which they label as the following: (1) healthy and viable; (2) incipient decline; (3) clear decline; (4) heavy decline; and (5) unhealthy and nonviable (1976, p. 69).

Decline proceeds from an initial stage of normalcy where neighborhoods function as its developers intended. There is stability in the sense that the same kinds of people with the same kinds of cultural values seem to be fixed in place although the population itself is in constant flux. The neighborhood experiences a healthy dynamic, with new residents willing to make infrastructural investments. Orthodox thinking has it that the healthiest neighborhoods in urban America have been those dominated by young white families with children enjoying moderate to upper incomes and living in single-family houses: families with access to conventional mortgages and home improvement loans. As property values rise during phase one, homeowners see their equity increasing. For landlords, rents are rising and cash flows are stable. Thriving businesses serve the locality, and city services are dependable. Optimism for continuing prosperity pervades; and in the resident's view, the neighborhood is seen as a good residential environment.

Decline begins in stage two. Anthony Downs sees several separate, but parallel processes operating: (1) a decrease in resident socioeconomic status; (2) ethnic change; (3) building deterioration; (4) increased pessimism regarding the future; and (5) economic disinvestment (1980, p. 523). As housing ages, neighborhoods becomes structurally and functionally obsolete, and physical deterioration begins to be visible. Neighborhood population will have aged, with a large proportion of the original settlers still in residence approaching or beyond retirement age. In contrast, and often in conflict, young families increasingly enter the neighborhood. Most problematical to older incumbents are the young families of different race or ethnicity and/or lower economic class.

Population densities increase as houses are converted to multiple rentals, several families moving into spaces previously occupied by only one. Landlords are increasingly absent, choosing to live outside the community. More investments are seen as speculative, with landlords holding back on building maintenance accordingly. Although property values are stable, and may actually be increasing, there are ominous decisions being made. Realtors may have begun to promote the transition of "old" residents to "new" through blockbusting and other devices. Bankers may have begun to withhold mortgage and home improvement monies, and divert the neighborhood's capital savings toward suburban investments. Public officials, responding to stabilizing tax revenues, may have begun to reduce services, and delay maintenance of streets, parks, schools.

In stage three, renters and absentee landlords become increasingly dominant. Tenant–landlord relations dissolve, with tenants abusing buildings and landlords further disinvesting. Lack of repair, accrued over years if not decades, becomes evident in many structures. Building dilapidation echoes in the litter and debris of public spaces. The employed poor give way to the welfare poor. Blockbusting, built on racial and other fears, will have nearly spent itself, with blacks, Hispanics, or other minorities now comprising a neighborhood majority. Households are larger than ever, with a very high proportion headed by unmarried women. Family incomes are very low and insufficient in the aggregate to sustain traditional neighborhood businesses. Storefronts not already vacant revert to marginal businesses such as bars and nightclubs. Some businesses front for the numbers racket, drug sales, or other elicit activities. Property values drop and community redlining is no longer a conspiracy hidden by the financial community, but a fact known to all. Some houses stand empty. Street crime becomes pervasive.

Figure 5.1   At Eightieth Street on Chicago's southeast side, neighborhoods appeared healthy in the late 1980s.

Stage four differs from stage three in degree rather than in kind. An even larger proportion of an area's buildings stand empty. Many structures, torched by arsonists, await demolition with vacant houses and apartment buildings proliferating. Vacant lots, streets, and alleys increasingly accumulate debris. Most buildings now require major repair, and landlords rent their apartments with difficulty. There is little incentive to maintain property; rather, disinvestment yields capital that can be invested in other housing or economic sectors. A drive through Chicago's southeast side reveals the evidence of this and other previous stages of neighborhood change. Driving north toward the center of the city east of the Dan Ryan Expressway, one can move from neighborhood to neighborhood and see each area progressively deteriorated by stages. Starting at Eightieth Street, one encounters residential blocks perhaps at the end of stage two. Most properties are well maintained in this relatively prosperous black middle-class area that had been nearly all white a mere decade earlier (Figure 5.1). Many properties are protected by massive security fences in a stand against encroaching decay. At Seventieth Street, however, deterioration is clearly problematical in at least one in ten buildings, the effects of early vandalism clearly evident in those vacated (Figure 5.2). Abandoned automobiles are numerous. At Sixtieth Street, more buildings stand vacant than otherwise—most being stripped and otherwise vandalized, as one might expect to see at the end of stage four. At Fifty-fifth Street, the traditional fabric of the city is totally unraveled, with vacant lots rather than standing buildings dominating. A totally derelict landscape of stage five meets the eye in neighborhoods just west of the University of Chicago (Figure 5.3).

The Dual Housing Market

A principal sustainer of American neighborhood decay is racism. Prejudice against blacks and minorities has torn cities apart through the creation of dual housing markets. Assigning blacks and whites to separate housing markets reflects discriminatory practices that have their roots in the early twentieth century. During World War I, with increased black migration to cities, real estate boards created policies to ensure segregation (Still, 1974). Realtors sought to protect property values through maintaining social and economic homogeneity. Thus, the National Association of Real Estate Boards (NAREB), formed in the early 1900s, published a code of ethics that stipulated the need to preserve neighborhood "character." This 1924 ethics code noted that "a realtor should never be instrumental in introducing into a neighborhood a character of property or occupancy, members of any race or nationality, or any individuals whose presence will clearly be detrimental to property values in that neighborhood" (quoted in Zarembka, 1990, p.

Figure 5.2 At Chicago's Seventieth Street (moving toward downtown), vacant, vandalized buildings were problematical.

101). This code, modified in form but not in substance in 1950, continued to push for segregation. While more recently the Fair Housing Act has made it illegal to discriminate in local housing markets, this trend persists. The act, most recently amended in 1968, has failed to curtail segregation because of weak enforcement provision, failure to address the roots of housing discrimination, and lack of enforcement by the executive branch of the federal government (Zarembka, 1990). For example, individuals rarely filed lawsuits when discriminated against, because of the expense of doing so. Moreover, housing discrimination is often subtle and difficult to detect. It is often unknown when a person has been steered or lied to by a realtor.

Figure 5.3   Save for islands of stability like Hyde Park and Bridgeport, most of Chicago's southeast-side residential neighborhoods above Sixteenth Street were well along the way toward total abandonment.

Consequently, of all racial and ethnic minorities, blacks are still the most segregated. Their continued concentration in inner cities is compounded by their low home-ownership rates, high incidence of crowded living conditions, and prevalence of poverty (Pinkney, 1990).

These discriminatory actions stratified populations and maintained property values. To integrate was to threaten middle-income desires for city living and opportunities for builders, developers, and landlords to extract profit. Neighborhoods were carefully cultivated and nurtured; property values reflected collective circumstance. Houses become depreciating assets when nearby parcels are undermaintained, or when housing elsewhere proves technologically superior and more in fashion. As the widely used appraiser text *The Appraisal of Real Estate* (written in 1938) notes, property values decline in response to the "infiltration" of "inharmonious racial groups" (cited in Zarembka, 1990, p. 103). People of "lower economic status and different social and economic background" purportedly weaken neighborhoods, opening the gates for low-income invasion and lessened profit opportunities. The irony of this process is that homeowners, often supporting such practices because of the desire to retain house equity, often lose house value regardless of neighborhood trajectory.

Throughout the twentieth century, home ownership has been represented to Americans as a prime investment opportunity, providing long-term financial security. Equity built up in the real estate of one's home has been promoted as an important form of savings; accordingly, home ownership has been viewed as a mechanism for upward social mobility. Those beliefs have been challenged by social historians Matthew Edel, Elliott Sclar, and Daniel Luria (1984). In the unstable American city, buying a house is an excellent way to provide shelter for oneself and one's family, they assert, but an inadequate means to economic advancement. "Much of what appears as social mobility is interpretable instead as the accumulation of devaluing assets; a process that leaves workers perpetually climbing a down escalator" (p. 9). Home ownership is an individual enterprise, but property values reflect collective social circumstances. Individuals cannot, acting alone, guarantee an external environment hospitable to investment. Houses become depreciating assets when one's neighbors fail to maintain and repair their houses, or when new housing elsewhere proves technologically superior or more in fashion. In the recent market of oversupply, house values have been inherently unstable, with the value of most older homes failing to keep pace with inflation. Even in America's affluent suburbs, the appreciation of housing did not keep pace with the Dow Jones average for stock investment for a previous 30-year period (p. 82).

If a principal cause for American urban decay is to be identified, then it is most certainly racism. Prejudice against blacks and other minorities on the part of whites has torn the traditional city apart through the mechanism of an exaggerated dual housing market. Affluent whites dominate one market. Blacks, discouraged from participating in this market, constitute another, with an arbitrage process operating to relate the two. Anthony Downs (1981, p. 86) has described this process at work. Most whites live in a segregated zone that he terms the "white interior." The outer edge of this housing market is the frontier of suburban new construction. Suburban minorities reside in a parallel segregated zone, the "black interior," separated from the principal market by a transition zone where both white and black households reside. Poorest minorities, including newcomers from outside the metropolis, live in a frontier of initial entry, usually adjacent to a city's central business district or adjacent to downtown industrial zones. Poor whites and most affluent blacks are seen to lie adjacent to the transition zone, with blacks in the zone of transition having incomes greater than their white counterparts.

Average house prices, highest in the zone of construction, fall across the white interior to the zone of transition, effectuating a break between the two housing markets. Toward city center, prices fall once again across the black interior until a zone of abandonment is reached at or beyond the frontier of early entry where houses have little or no long-term value. The two markets exist because more affluent whites are willing to pay a premium to live in racially homogeneous neighborhoods where property values are increasing. At the same time, affluent blacks are willing to pay high prices to gain access to social amenities. Institutions exist to facilitate the transfer of property from whites to blacks in the zone of transition. Realtors, backed by banking interests, buy houses from fleeing whites at low prices and sell to blacks at high prices, arbitrage being the simultaneous or nearly simultaneous purchasing of housing in one market in order to sell in another. House values either side of the transition zone are in constant interplay, creating instability. As long as new construction continues apace at the fringe, the zone of transition will continue to move outward in city space.

Racial prejudice has not only underlain the dual housing markets of cities, but it has boosted house prices and rent levels for blacks wherever they have sought to live. Sellers and landlords (both white and black) usually charge black buyers and renters more than whites. In addition, banks often charge blacks more for mortgage money. Discriminatory pricing is, of course, not the only disadvantage blacks face in their search for housing, but it is fundamental.

In the past, impoverished blacks with no credit ratings had few rental choices. A landlord class emerged to service their needs, but at extravagant prices relative to amount and quality of living space provided. The traditional slum—like Detroit's Paradise Valley, Cleveland's Hough, and New York City's Bedford-Stuyvesant—resulted. Limited black housing was reinforced by racially restricted covenants built into housing deeds, segregation policies of the Federal Housing Administration's mortgage insurance programs, and the separationist code of ethics promulgated by the National Association of Real Estate Boards. Racial covenants were discouraged by Supreme Court ruling in 1948, but integration was not actively encouraged in the mortgage and real estate industries until after the Fair Housing Act of 1968. Court decisions, civil rights legislation, and executive orders in the Department of Housing and Urban Development and other federal agencies have helped to open housing to black renters and buyers. Nonetheless, the dual housing market persists, albeit in changed form.

Overbuilding in the suburbs produced a surplus of houses in the 1960s and 1970s. For every one household formed in the United States between 1960 and 1975, 1.3 new housing units were built (Ley, 1983, p. 298). Oversupply reduced price differentials between the white and black housing markets, accelerating outward movement of the zone of transition. Landlords in the black interior, charging limited rents and faced with increased operating costs, found profit margins eroding. To keep apartments filled, central city landlords turned to less desirable tenants—particularly the welfare poor. In protecting profits, pressed landlords cut costs usually by reducing maintenance and repair. Likewise, real estate speculators reduced down payments on houses for sale, turned to land contracts as opposed to mortgages, and otherwise enticed persons with marginal incomes to home ownership. Covering inflated house payments with difficulty, home-owners also were propelled to neglect maintenance and repair. Thus, behind the rapidly shifting zone of transition moved another frontier of blight and decay. Blacks come to view the outward scramble for improved housing as a continuing and necessary aspect of life. To put down permanent roots here was to surrender to the inevitability of living in derelict zones.

The traditional slum (where the poor were victimized by landlords enjoying substantive control over limited housing supply) has been replaced by a new kind of slum that victimizes both tenant and landlord. It is a place of vacancy where the social fabric and physical infrastructure are unraveling to deaden communities. Realtors, appraisers, loan officers, and others here sustain disinvestment. Working from a base of white prejudice, self-fulfilling market prophecies are created. White homeowners need not be overly sophisticated to see that lower property values and physical decay follow blacks into new neighborhoods. They may not appreciate the underlying dual housing market that produces that change nor recognize that white racism bolsters the system. They may not empathize with blacks who, having paid a premium for housing, can little afford high maintenance costs. They may not appreciate the landlord dilemma of rising costs and need to withhold repairs. Whites, sensing decline beyond their power to control, blame the people who accompany the change.

Minimal new housing in the suburbs has been priced affordable to low-income families. National housing policy (or the jumble of programs masquerading as a program) has emphasized the "trickle down" of older housing. Housing partially used up by more affluent households is passed on when those households opt for newer suburban homes. Low-income families are expected to "filter up" to housing through the machinations of the dual housing market. Filtering occurs when houses decline more rapidly in value than quality, enabling families to enjoy larger, better built, or better designed houses for money previously paid for lesser space. Since the system requires people, both affluent and poor, to move at intervals, it precludes Americans from establishing permanent roots. It discourages intergenerational family stability over time. People are set in motion and needful of improved housing if only to avoid slipping backward on the housing escalator. Suburbanites, moreover, have resisted the encroachment of public housing. Having escaped the instability of central city neighborhoods, they choose not to associate with the poor—especially the minority poor—and legislate accordingly. Suburban zoning and building codes generally preclude the construction of low-priced new housing, forcing reliance on filtering.

Redlining and Blockbusting

Banks and financial institutions substantially influence urban development. In the early 1970s, banks—New York City's especially—began to cut back purchase of municipal bonds, making it more difficult and more expensive for cities to borrow for capital improvements. Banks had accounted for 59 percent of all municipal bond sales in 1971, but only 15 percent in 1975 (Morris, 1978, p. 57). Banks had found devices other than tax-exempt bonds to shield assets from federal taxation. For example, profits were sheltered and tax liabilities cut by establishing branches abroad. Banks, catering to big multinational corporations, positioned themselves to accept corporate deposits outside federal tax jurisdiction. Banks also sought to create scarcity in the bond market in order to drive up interest rates on bonds and notes. Higher interest rates meant larger profits on smaller bond sale volumes, thus releasing money for investment in corporate and federal paper. For the City of New York, municipal debt service jumped, making it the largest item in the city budget (larger even than welfare); and as a result, New York City was brought to the threshold of bankruptcy.

Redlining, however, was the banking practice of the 1960s and 1970s most readily linked to central city decline. The term referred to city maps where loan officers, at banks as well as at savings and loan associations, drew lines around areas where mortgage loans were to be discouraged or disallowed. This act cut off neighborhoods from conventional sources of home financing and loan money for home maintenance and improvement. Financing came to be arranged primarily through land contracts, federally insured mortgages, and other devices. Banks justified redlining as protective action against unnecessary financial risk. "Balanced risk" portfolios, it was argued, demanded that banks limit loans in older urban areas while emphasizing loans in new suburbs. At base was the fear that the value of housing in older neighborhoods would decline faster than the value of covering mortgages. Banks do not price risk so much as they ration funds to avoid risk (Naparstek and Cincotta, 1976, p. 9).

Redlining usually set in motion a self-fulfilling prophecy of inevitable decline. In most cities, banks assessed neighborhoods negatively prior to the actual evidence of blight without reference to the specifics of resident credit ratings, housing conditions, community viability, or business solvency (ibid.). Age of housing was usually a telling criterion for denying an area funds. Anticipation of physical and functional obsolescence set up the very conditions to produce physical decay. More important, however, was race. As blacks were closely associated with poverty and blight, the color of people could trigger "defensive" bank actions helping to set up the very conditions feared. Thus, New York City census tracts with mostly white residents received seven times as many mortgage loans as predominantly nonwhite areas in 1985 and 1986 (Louis, 1989). In 1986, primarily white middle-income areas received three times as many mortgage loans as nonwhite areas of identical income (ibid.). In tracts where housing stock was of the same age, white neighborhoods got two to three times the loan amount as nonwhite areas. Similar results are reported in Atlanta, where white neighborhoods received five times as many mortgage and rehabilitation loans as black neighborhoods of identical income (ibid.). The problem was so pronounced here that prominent, upper-middle-class black politicians were refused loans. Redlining, as a form of racial stereotyping, has helped to sustain neighborhood dilapidation in these cities.

Outright refusal to lend money was and is the simplest form of redlining. Other devices include the use of overly rigid review criteria. For example, houses valued below a minimum loan amount or of too narrow a width or occupying too small a lot would be summarily rejected. In Baltimore in the mid-1970s, lenders would not loan money on houses less than 18 feet wide (most of that city's row houses being less than 14 feet in width) or valued below $15,000 (three-quarters of the city's houses being valued at less than that amount) (Cassidy, 1980, p. 41). The terms on which loans were offered restricted lending. Requiring high down payments, charging excessive interest, setting closing costs excessively high, or limiting mortgages to very short repayment periods precluded buyers from purchasing houses in redlined areas. Properties could be underappraised and the size of the loan limited, making it impossible for buyers to cover purchase costs. Appraisers could be encouraged to follow a narrow interpretation of the "life cycle" principle (that property values must fall automatically with age) or the "neighborhood conformity" principle (that property values must fall in communities with mixed land uses or mixed racial, ethnic, or income groups).

Lenders who redlined their own localities stood accused of ignoring state and federal charter obligations to serve local communities. In the 1970s, depositers living in Northeast central cities tended not to see their savings converted to local mortgage and home improvement loans, thus helping to stabilize local property values. Rather, local savings accounts went to financing new suburban construction, or to building the boom cities of the Southeast and Southwest. In 1976, Chicago's two largest banks—the First National and the Continental—had between them $626 million in savings deposits from the suburbs and $1.7 billion from the central city (Naparstek and Cincotta, 1976, p. 37). While the suburbs received $62 million in home loans, Chicago's neighborhoods received only $5 million—a return of three-tenths of a penny on each savings dollar to the neighborhoods and ten cents on the dollar to the suburbs (ibid.). At the same time, the two banks lost some $163 million on bad loans in speculative real estate trusts (ibid.). Continental lost substantially when various savings and loans defaulted in Oklahoma and Texas in the 1980s, requiring federal bailout. In St. Louis, a study of 92 lenders showed that banks made only 12 percent of their residential loans in the city while savings and loan associations made only 4 percent (Cassidy, 1980, p. 41). In Boston, for every dollar deposited from a central city address only nine cents was returned in mortgages. In suburban Boston, 31 cents was returned to savers (*Redlining*, 1977, p. 38).

A normal real estate market ceases to exist when speculators acquire houses at greatly distressed value for resale to the poor, usually at prices three to four times higher. Land installment contracts come to the fore with third and fourth mortgages held privately and, in common practice, anonymously (Leven, 1972, p. 58). So also do federally insured loans become important. FHA loans limit the lenders risk or stake in a mortgage, thus usually decreasing the lender's resolve to make the mortgage work. Rather than deal with repayment lapses and other problems on a flexible basis (as they do with conventional mortgages), lenders tend to foreclose quickly. "Foreclosure, in turn, may increase the incidence of vacancies, turnover, abandonment and vandalism, further reducing loan availability and feeding the cycle of decline" (*Reinvestment Handbook*, 1978, p. 11). To discourage the abuses of redlining, Congress passed the Home Mortgage Disclosure Act of 1975, requiring most banks and savings and loan institutions to report in annual public statements the number, dollar amounts, and general locations of their residential mortgage and home improvement loans.

The real estate industry provides the mechanism by which real property is exchanged. Banks determine an area's suitability for investment, but realtors actually drive the changes that pit area against area and people against people in the operation of the dual housing market. Instability serves the realtor's interest. The more housing turning over the more commissions to be made. And when houses can be bought cheap and sold dear, the realtor as speculator can turn large profits indeed. Toward this end, unethical realtors have turned to *blockbusting*: the encouraging of panic selling among whites. Blockbusters create an atmosphere of panic through house-to-house canvassing, intensive mailing of circulars, and relentless telephone soliciting. They may locate black families in white neighborhoods to be problematic neighbors. In Chicago of the 1950s and 1960s, more than 100 blockbusters worked the city, "busting" two or three blocks a week (Forman, 1971, p.

88). Although comprising a small minority of Chicago realtors, they nonetheless triggered suburban flight of some 70,000 white families (ibid.).

Realtors of integrity in Chicago and other places—hesitant to engage directly in blockbusting tactics—usually waited short intervals before directing black families to previously white blocks. Their actions, however, differed only in timing and not in kind. Like blockbusters, they practiced "steering." Initially, only whites were encouraged to buy in white neighborhoods. Blacks might even be refused opportunities to inspect houses, and their offers to buy withheld. Once a neighborhood was declared open to blacks, whites would be deliberately directed away, the prejudicial treatment reversed. Today, another kind of "reverse blockbusting" has come to the fore in some cities where affluent whites and blacks are gentrifying central city neighborhoods. Speculators comb neighborhoods just ahead of the restoration movement and make attractive cash offers to owners. In both instances, less affluent black families lose in the exchange of real estate.

Whites vacate central city neighborhoods in anticipation of decline. Threatened by rumors of black encroachment, whites neglect properties fearful that monies spent will be lost. Much of the decline attributed to blacks actually occurs before they move in. Black families, for their part, prove unable to correct structural defects encountered and thus exacerbate disinvestment. For blacks, even more so than for whites, the inevitabilities of decline are immediate. They accept the need to move periodically to keep ahead of the crime-, dereliction-, and poverty-infested zones. The frequent move to upgrade housing has become a part of life for black Americans. Such mobility diverts energy from community, and destroys the concern for locality as place. Disregard for neighborhood only reinforces the propensity to disinvest, heightening the spiral of physical blight.

Blockbusting and redlining are both forms of racism. They have traditionally relegated blacks to second-class housing consumers. The fault lies not so much with blacks as with whites. As Anthony Downs (1970) argues, white society is deeply implicated in the black ghetto. "White institutions created it, white institutions maintain it, and white society condones it" (p. 76). Institutional racism arises when people are placed in subordinate societal positions. Blockbusting is overt in directly playing the interests of whites and blacks against one another. Redlining is covert since it is more easily disguised as action economically justified, and presumably beyond racist motivation. For U.S. central cities, neighborhoods have become little more than zones of passage for people desperately seeking more stable living conditions. Racism has reduced many central city neighborhoods to way stations through which low-income, minority people pass "while working toward the day when they, too, can move out to a better life" (Wilson, 1966, p. 418).

Municipal Government's Role

When racial succession occurs, in-migrating blacks may be more affluent than the whites they replace, although a higher proportion of their incomes will be committed to rents and mortgage payments. This process bodes negatively for future housing maintenance. With transition, household turnover usually brings progressively poorer people. Apartment owners and other landlords, facing shrinking profit margins, initiate disinvestment as vacancies increase and—despite lower assessments and lower tax bills—may withhold tax payments to further reduce costs. As tax collections decline, government acts to cut back neighborhood services including repairs to streets, sewers, parks, schools, and other facilities. Such cutbacks come at the time when effects of physical obsolescence and social stress are greatest. A negative cycle of disinvestment develops with decline in the public sector, paralleling and indeed encouraging further private-sector decline. As Martin Mayer observes, "What has provoked the decline in the physical condition of so many neighborhoods is a process of public disinvestment— a failure to provide adequate police protection, to keep streets and sidewalks clean, to preserve the behavioral (let alone academic) standards of the schools, to maintain the roads, to supply adequate public transportation, even, increasingly . . . to preserve standards of care in water and sewage services" (1978, p. 419).

At the heart of the problem lies the property tax, the traditional bulwark of municipal financing. The fall of property values has more than a personal impact on homeowners and landlords. It is an important cause of the municipal fiscal insolvency threatening the social health of America's central cities. In the late 1970s, the property tax contributed some 82 percent of the $60 billion that localities raised from their taxpayers (Breckenridge, 1977, p. 114). The proportion of city revenues obtained in this manner varied from 99 percent in Boston, 87 percent in Minneapolis–St. Paul, and 70 percent in Baltimore to 58 percent in Chicago and New York City, 56 percent in Detroit, and 50 percent in San Diego (Morris, 1978, p. 72). In New York City, uncollected real property taxes soared in 1976 to some $300 million, approximately half of the budget deficit the city faced the next year (ibid.). In 1980, property taxes yielded more than $3 billion for New York City or about one-quarter of the city's total income from all sources (Listokin, 1982, p. 16). In that year, the property tax was about nine dollars per $100 of assessed value, property being assessed at about 40 percent of its actual value (ibid.).

Critics have increasingly scrutinized the property tax. It is seen by many as regressive, imposing a disportionate burden on low-income families. In areas of declining property values, reassessments downward rarely keep pace with actual values, and property owners face inflated tax bills accordingly. Property taxes are seen to discourage spending on repairs and improvements. Homeowners and landlords who upgrade property potentially increase assessment levels and the amount of taxes owed. Conversely, those who allow properties to decline are rewarded with reduced tax bills. Various studies have established a link between increasing taxes and falling sales prices. In San Francisco, for example, property values were seen to decline by between $14 and $21 for each dollar increase in property taxes (Vaughan and Vogel, 1979, p. 77). As the assessed value of property declines, municipalities have little choice but to increase tax rates in an attempt to sustain tax revenues, putting the less well-to-do in deteriorating neighborhoods at even greater economic disadvantage. Some evidence suggests that it is not the fear of upward reassessment that discourages rehabilitation so much as the tax rate itself. In Chicago and Baltimore in the 1970s, property owners in blighted neighborhoods paid taxes at rates as much as 15 times that of properties in affluent, stable neighborhoods (p. 80).

Many critics of the property tax advocate reform, specifically dividing the tax into separate levies on land and structures. In most cities, tax collectors take two or three times as much tax from buildings as from their sites, which are valuable or not according to location (Breckenridge, 1977, p. 114). Speculators reap rewards from such taxation since they can afford to keep underutilized land off the market until urban growth drives up the price for profit taking. Whereas higher taxes on buildings, as at present, invite disinvestment, higher taxes on land would encourage improvement, or sale to owners willing to make improvements. Landlords who leave slum buildings standing on potentially valuable land would not be protected by the worthlessness of the structure. Reform is justified on equity grounds. Speculators who realize value increments in real estate do so only through the foresight of buying and holding property. "It is entirely appropriate for the community to recapture these unearned increments by taxation, and use them for community purposes" (Netzer, 1980, p. 555).

Declining property tax receipts have led most central city governments to increase reliance on other revenue sources. By the mid-1960s, central city governments in 43 of the nation's largest metropolitan areas were collecting as much as $3.3 billion in property tax revenue (Netzer, 1980, p. 555). A few cities, including Detroit, Louisville, Philadelphia, and Pittsburgh, were also collecting some $242 million in income tax revenue (ibid.). Income taxes enabled governments to tax suburbanites working in the central city. Other cities have introduced sales taxes, targeted the patrons of hotels and motels with special levies, and increased user fees on city services and facilities. Cities have also fallen increasingly dependent on state and federal subsidies not only for capital improvement monies, but to cover ordinary operating expenses as well.

Declining municipal revenues, coupled with inflation and diversion of federal monies into spending on defense, space exploration, and other programs has produced nationwide massive disinvestment of public infrastructure. The nation faces an estimated $3-trillion repair public bill in the 1990s, given decades of postponed or minimal maintenance (Morial, 1986, p. 69). An Urban Institute study of selected cities found a third of them losing some 10 percent or more of their water because of deteriorated pipes (ibid.). For example, about 40 percent of Boston's water use is unaccounted for; New York City loses an estimated 100 million gallons a day from pipeline leaks and breaks (ibid.). In addition, the Environmental Protection Agency estimates that some 21 percent of the nation's water systems do not meet safe drinking standards (p. 70). Nearly half of the nation's wastewater treatment systems are operating at full capacity and, therefore, cannot support further industrial or residential growth (Choate and Walter, 1983, p. 15). The nation's older cities suffer worse. In New York City alone, an estimated $40 billion was estimated in 1981 as necessary to repair, rebuild, or service 1,000 bridges, two aqueducts, one large water tunnel, several reservoirs, 6,000 miles of waterlines, 6,000 miles of sewers, 6,700 subway cars, and 4,500 bases as well as 6,200 miles of paved streets, 17 hospitals, 19 city university campuses, 950 schools, 200 libraries, and hundreds of police and fire stations (Herbers, 1986, p. 158). Federal capital assistance to local governments has encouraged new construction rather than maintenance and repair of existing capital assets. An American Public Works Association survey of city managers found 90 percent freely admitting that federal matching grants for new construction caused them to place low priority on maintenance and repair (Barker and Wise, 1984, p. xix). Beyond the nation's cities, the federal government also has neglected public infrastructure. For example, the 43,000-mile interstate highway system is deteriorating at a rate requiring 2,000 miles of new pavement each year. Lacking adequate funding for regular maintenance, the late 1970s saw more than 8,000 miles of the interstate system, and 13 percent of its bridges, in need of rebuilding (Choate and Walter, 1983, p. 1). Nationwide, the rate of public investment in maintenance of all kinds fell to 2.5 percent of gross national product in 1983, less than half the rate of 1973, with net investment close to zero (Vaughan, 1983, p. 3).

The bureaucratic complexities of municipal government have also taken a toll on central cities and their neighborhoods. Localities must deal with a myriad of city agencies, each of which shifts the boundaries of its service districts to suit its own convenience and fit its own needs. The Rockaway Peninsula of New York City illustrates (Gold, 1980, p. 241). Located on a spit of land on Long Island's south shore near Kennedy Airport, it is reached by causeway and public transit. The site of urban renewal, new public housing

Figure 5.4   New York City's Rockaway reflects a
total bankruptcy of civic spirit and governmental
resolve, its partial abandonment being substantially the
work of misdirected and poorly executed city programs.

has produced a tremendous population increase without benefit of
improved public services (Figure 5.4). Where traditional housing has survived, social service agencies promoted a glut of nursing home and other
domicile facilities, exiling welfare clients there in large numbers. Transportation authorities discouraged the private housing market with prohibitive
transit fares, circuitous routes, and exorbitant bridge tolls. Tax rates were
increased precipitously, decimating the residual business community. The
beach and boardwalk were neglected, and streets and sidewalks deteriorated. Little effort was made to buffer a nearby city garbage dump or control

the truck traffic it generated. The Arverne-Edgemere Urban Renewal Project of the 1960s had been proposed, changed, contested, disapproved, canceled, and then approved again, as the original half square mile of blight grew to several square miles. The City of New York has managed to take a place endowed with outstanding natural amenities (the kind of seashore site that vacation resorts are made of) and convert it into a purgatory for the city's poor. The poor are the losers. "They are relocated from a slum in the Bronx, Brooklyn, or Manhattan into an instant slum, no better than where they came from. [Before] they could ride a train for one fare to a job market in a matter of minutes; from the Rockaways, there is no place to go, no way up, no way out!" (Gold, 1980, p. 241).

Politicians play neighborhoods off against one another in serving vested interests. When General Motors informed the City of Detroit of its intention to move production of Cadillac cars outside the city, Mayor Coleman Young, the city's first black mayor, took action to meet the company's need for space. A rectangular 500-acre site adjacent to a city freeway and served by railroads was selected. One of the city's remaining ethnic neighborhoods, Poletown, was partially leveled, displacing 3,400 people in 1,200 households. More than 100 businesses, 16 churches, several schools, and a hospital were eliminated. Property was condemned under the Michigan "Quick Take Act," which delegated to the city power to seize property for industrial relocation and expansion within 60 days even though price agreements had not been reached with property owners. The city took responsibility for site preparations, including the construction of roads, and relocation costs, homeowners being offered $15,000 in relocation costs, and renters $4,000. The total municipal expenditures on the project amounted to $200 million (Cohen, 1982, p. 3). The site was sold to General Motors for $6.5 million along with a 12-year, 50-percent tax abatement, saving the company $5.4 million annually. Employment at the plant was projected to exceed 6,100 workers, but actual employment stood at about half that figure through the 1980s. Payback for the city was estimated to take 30 years. Whereas General Motors has a new plant and Detroit has preserved something of its employment base, Poletown was doomed. Not enough remains of the community either in social energy or physical structure to warrant survival. Detroit is faced with a neighborhood of abandonment where vitality, although ebbing, once reigned.

Politicians tend to grasp quickly the big project that attracts attention and pretends immediate results. They are less likely to pursue investments in maintenance or rehabilitation where gains over the long term are subtle and difficult to claim. The consequences of deferred maintenance may not appear for six, seven, or eight years, which is a political lifetime. City political systems are structured in short two- or four-year administrations—which is conducive to postponing long-term responsibilities, especially when economic conditions are deteriorating. What suits a politician's short-term time frame, however, may not suit a city's long-term needs. New York City has chosen to neglect public funding of deteriorating inner-city neighborhoods for visible, glitzy projects. Since 1978, the city has helped develop the Midtown Marriot Hotel, the South Street Seaport, the multibillion-dollar Battery Park City Project, and the Jacob Javits Convention Center. The city is currently behind the Times Square redevelopment plan, providing an estimated $650 million in tax subsidies to a project that would change the face of midtown Manhattan (Fainstein et al., 1990). These projects have been supported by two local development agencies—the Urban Development Corporation (UDC) and the Public Developments Corporation (PDC)—that have provided tax subsidies and technical assistance. Such projects, seen as political "coups" by local administrations, have denied public dollars to outlying neighborhoods. Indianapolis has chosen a similar development path, targeting block grants to downtown mall and sports development projects. Whereas 24 percent of block grant dollars nationally went for "affluent development," this local figure averaged 51 percent between 1980 and 1986 (Wilson and Mayer, 1986, p. 11). Conspicuous consumption projects like the Union Station Mall, Hoosier Dome, Claypool Court retailing facility, and Merchants Plaza sprung up within five years. These projects generated "downtown jewels" that strengthened Mayor William Hudnut's local popularity. Here was a mayor who, to many residents, delivered on his promise of rebuilding downtown for middle- and upper-middle-income usage.

The Federal Presence

Federal tax policies have hurt urban neighborhoods in profoundly negative ways. In particular, the income tax has had devastating consequences, encouraging new construction in the suburbs where cheap, open land was available. The tax system has simultaneously favored homeowners over renters, the latter more numerous in central cities. Traditionally, homeowners have received two major tax concessions. First, they have been allowed to deduct mortgage interest and local property taxes from taxable incomes. In 1977, the federal government forgave some $7.6 billion in tax revenue, thereby subsidizing family housing, most of it for the middle and upper classes. The affluent received nearly four times the subsidy of the poor, who received only $2 billion in federal housing assistance payments (Pynoos, Schafer, and Hartman, 1980, p. 17). Second, the value of homeowner housing services has been tax exempt. In the 1970s, these benefits were equivalent to three-quarters of total housing costs to homeowners, and perhaps as much as one-fifth of income (Vaughan and Vogel, 1979, p. xi). In addition, capital gains from the sale of residential property have not been subject to taxation when proceeds were reinvested in another residential property within prescribed time limits. On the other hand, capital gains losses have not been allowed as income tax deductions. Thus, investment capital has been diverted from older neighborhoods where housing is old and likely to decline in value, to new neighborhoods where values are likely to inflate.

Federal tax law has favored suburban businesses over those of the central city. Owners of new commercial buildings have been able to accelerate depreciation, which, early in a building's life, provides larger tax write-offs than straight-line methods allowed on old buildings. It bears emphasizing that accelerated depreciation defers taxes and reduces risk associated with investment by shortening the period of time elapsed before investment recovery. Thus, investors face strong incentives to sell properties early before tax and other benefits lapse. They are also encouraged to build lightly, for buildings need not have long lives to be profitable investments. As the federal tax system has invited deterioration in old buildings through owner neglect, it has set the stage for future decline by encouraging structural impermanence. It has contributed to frequent building turnover and tenure instability. The old-fashioned business values of careful stewardship, conservation, and rational long-range investment management have been subordinated to short-term tax shelter benefits.

As already established, a wide range of federal programs since World War II have variously favored suburban over central city neighborhoods: urban renewal and public housing, and highway development and FHA mortgage insurance, to name a few. These programs variously biased development toward the urban fringe. At least one federal housing initiative, deliberately structured to benefit older neighborhoods, had in fact the exact opposite effect. Destruction was wrought not by intention, but by mismanagement. The Federal Housing Administration had by 1980 some 40 major insurance programs, most of them financing the construction, purchase, or improvement of one- to four-family dwellings. None of these programs insured buyers. The original idea behind the FHA—a Depression-era program—was to bolster lender confidence in making loans to home buyers and landlords to stimulate new construction and local economies. By 1980 there was $87 billion worth of outstanding mortgages insured under FHA rules, and an additional $28 billion under related Veterans Administration policies (Vaughan, 1983, p. 89). Section 235 and related programs, around which a housing scandal of immense proportions evolved, were introduced in the Nixon administration in the late 1960s.

Section 235, intended to promote low-income home ownership, became a program of "urban ruin for profit." It tempted real estate speculators, FHA appraisers, and mortgage lenders to defraud the poor and federal government (Boyer, 1973, p. vii). Speculators bought dilapidated houses and cosmetically rehabilitated them. After FHA appraisers set inflated building values, speculators sought low-income buyers, often falsifying buyer credit histories and personally furnishing down payments. After FHA ap-

Figure 5.5   Fraud associated with the FHA's Section 235 program in the 1960s devastated Detroit, leaving some 13 percent of the city's housing vacant and boarded up.

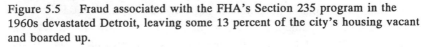

proval (and in most FHA offices, review was very lax), the speculator took his profit and passed the house on to the lender. Section 235 paid all but 1 percent of the interest due on mortgages defaulted. Lenders could turn sizable profits for themselves by discounting loans to unqualified borrowers and foreclosing loans upon default. On a normal $10,000 loan borrowed at 8-percent interest, borrowers received only $9,200. But under Section 235, the FHA insured the full value of indebtedness. When buyers defaulted within the year, lenders stood to collect the full $10,000 face value and $700 in interest. Such lenders received a net realization of $1,500 from a $9,200 advance, or a 17-percent return on a safe investment.

Most houses purchased under Section 235 quickly needed major expenditures for upkeep and repair, which usually exceeded the homeowners' abilities to pay, given low incomes and mortgage obligations. Owners were forced to abandon houses when utilities like heat, water, or electricity failed. Foreclosure often led to abandonment, necessitating the Department of Housing and Urban Development to take possession of empty shells. Although windows might be boarded up and the doors sealed, 235 houses

Figure 5.6   Although the FHA sealed structures taken in mortgage default, the vast majority in cities across the country were so badly vandalized that they did not return to the housing market.

proved easy targets for vandals and arsonists (Figures 5.5 and 5.6). By 1976, some 25,000 dwellings in Detroit—13 percent of the city's total—had been taken over by HUD, with approximately 500 houses per month coming into agency possession. Ten thousand properties were totally vandalized or had been demolished (Leven et al., 1976, p. 180). HUD held 3,600 houses in New York City, 3,000 in Philadelphia, and 4,700 in Atlanta. More than 1.2 million mortgages were insured under Section 235 and related programs, at a total face value of $16.7 billion. More than 166,000 houses were foreclosed in the 1970s, at a loss of $2.1 billion (p. 181).

TENANTS AND LANDLORDS

Federal housing programs since World War II have been slanted toward home ownership, and away from apartment renting. Nonetheless, rental housing (including public housing) sheltered some 29 million households in the United States in 1980, or about one-third of the total (Downs, 1983, p. 2). Eight out of nine occupied rental units were owned by private interests, the ninth being publicly subsidized (ibid.). About 60 percent were in buildings with fewer than five units; and indeed, one third were not apartments at all, but single-family residences or duplexes (ibid). Less than 17 percent lived in buildings containing 20 or more units (p. 13). In 1980, nearly 30 percent of all rentals had been built before 1940, as compared to only 24 percent of the nation's owner-occupied properties (p. 19). However, rental housing was being removed from the market faster than it was being replaced. Between 1970 and 1976, 1.5 million rental units built before 1965 were removed from the nation's inventory, or about 250,000 units each year (p. 40). In addition, more than 360,000 rental units were converted to condominiums and cooperatives (p. 40).

Rents did not increase as fast as consumer income, landlord operating costs, or construction costs during the 1970s and 1980s. Competition from new housing financed by low-interest mortgages depressed rents in the suburbs. The oversupply of new housing in suburbia depressed prices for all housing in the central cities. Nonetheless, new apartment construction continued, especially in the suburbs. There syndicators skimmed the cream off the rental market by building small units attractive to young, upwardly mobile adults (who were looking primarily for short-term housing), and older, retired people (who were looking to escape the responsibilities of home ownership). Neither kind of tenant tended to abuse property. When located in growth areas, such buildings pretended long-term appreciation, with much of the economic reward derived not from operating but from tax sheltering other income. Although the profit rates on rents lagged, the rate of return on equity was excellent, accelerated depreciation and other tax allowances fostering rapid turnover of buildings. With rental housing developed by one group, sold for management to another, and then passed around from management to management, there has been little call for long-term responsibility. Housing is allowed to deteriorate (even encouraged to deteriorate) because the complex edifice of rules intended to stimulate investment also stimulates undermaintenance (Dolbeare, 1976, p. 94).

Rental housing in the central cities—much of it built before World War II—shrank rapidly during the 1960s and 1970s. In Baltimore in the early 1970s, more than one-quarter of the private central city rental inventory was managed by some 50 professional real estate owners, with the largest holding in excess of 1,500 units and the smallest about 100 (Stegman, 1972, p. 27). In New York City, professionals controlled about 30 percent of the rentals (ibid.). The pressure to disinvest central city buildings was immense, especially in neighborhoods behind the zone of transition in the black interior. Good tenants had become increasingly difficult to find, and vacancies were filled more and more by the hard-core poor who little respected property. Management, in big buildings especially, tended to become depersonalized, absentee owners or their agents failing to screen tenants carefully, or supervise them on a day-to-day basis. When problem tenants began to wreck buildings, then disinvestment became mandatory. A vicious circle of decline evolves, with landlord neglect more than matched by tenant destructiveness. Buildings are milked of their value, and when all tax and other advantages of ownership are exhausted, abandonment usually follows.

Rentals in central city neighborhoods are plagued by a constant turnover of tenants. Michael Stegman (1972, p. 59) estimated that during the 1970s the average length of stay for tenants in central city apartments was between two and three years. That meant that between 33 and 50 percent of all tenants moved each year. For about 10 percent of central city landlords, tenant residency averaged one year or less, which meant that at least one-half of their tenantry at the end of a year was completely different from that at the beginning (ibid). Turnover substantially increases the chances of loss by vandalism as well as inflating operating costs. Vacated units need to be cleaned, repaired, advertised, and shown to be filled. Turnover costs, including lost rent and redecorating expenses, can easily total about two year's cash flow, while taking five year's cash flow in the recycling of a badly vandalized unit (Olson and Lachman, 1976, p. 116).

The tenement house movement of the early twentieth century painted a vivid picture of the evil slumlord who overcharged ignorant tenants to the point of callous criminality. The landlord was depicted as beyond the pale of respectable business practice. Underlying the reform impulse was the belief that honest businessmen with well-run rental properties could obtain fair profits from housing the poor. Such was probably untrue then, and it was certainly untrue during the 1960s and 1970s when dereliction in the central cities accelerated so visibly, with abandoned apartment buildings seemingly leading the way toward eventual neighborhood abandonment. In an earlier period when housing was in short supply, landlord abuses of the traditional slumlord type undoubtedly were widespread. But in the era of oversupply characterized by accelerated filtering of housing down to lower-income families, landlords have been constrained. Rather than being victimizers, landlords have come to be victims as well.

Central city landlords face stringent economic realities. They can operate only as long as funds are available in the community for long-term financing. If a landlord pays on his mortgage, pays his taxes, and keeps his building in reasonable repair, will he be able to sell when his tax advantages are exhausted? Will others be able to finance the building to start their round of profit taking? If not, then the landlord is faced with a wasting asset. Money put into the building, even if it is recoverable in terms of immediate operating costs, will not add to his store of potential capital value. Even for new rental facilities, around 60 percent of the nominal rental income is devoted to servicing the mortgage, with an additional 15 to 25 percent going for taxes. Thus between 15 and 25 percent remains for operating costs and profit. The actual proportion of the rent dollar that is within the landlord's short-term competence to spend, or hold onto, is very limited. Imposed priorities often dictate disinvestment with old buildings. "If you do not pay the heating bill—there is immediate tenant complaint—and both criminal and civil procedures may follow. The leaking roof, however, can be met with a hasty inexpensive patch job—rather than more fundamental procedures" (Steinlieb, 1980, p. 56).

Tax delinquency is a certain sign that a structure is being disinvested. Lack of cash flow in a rental building encourages landlords to reduce recurring costs. Failure to pay municipal taxes is an easily initiated form of credit engendering that carries a slow and relatively painless reprimand during the remaining life of an old building. In many cities, tax arrears may build up for as many as five years with little censure. During the Depression of the 1930s, the nation suffered a plague of defaulting property owners unable to maintain mortgage payments in the face of job loss and unemployment. Most cities declared foreclosure moratoriums and then passed stringent legislation slowing the municipal taking of tax delinquent property. These laws greatly aggravated the abandonment problem in America's central cities during the 1960s and 1970s.

Federal rent subsidy programs supported in 1980 some 3 million rental units, or about 11 percent of all renter-occupied units (Downs, 1983, p. 19). This number included some 1.1 million public housing units. Section 8 housing, whereby a private landlord was compensated directly for subsidized portions of a tenant's rent, accounted for another 1.1 million (ibid.). Approximately 30 percent of 9.1 million of the nation's very poor households lived in subsidized rental units (ibid.). Female-headed households represented some 27 percent of all renter households, although members of such households accounted for 41 percent of all renters (p. 25).

Declining maintenance in a central city neighborhood usually appears first in rental housing, and first of all in large apartment buildings under absentee ownership. Dedication to maintaining a building reflects not only the landlord's financial circumstance, the physical condition of the structure, and the level of tenant abuse, but his perception of what other landlords are doing. Because of the way prices are established in a housing market, one person's financial investment in an improvement effects the value of neighboring properties as well. If two neighbors invest, both will receive higher rates of return than previously possible. But if only one invests, and the other does not, then the investor receives a lower rate of return due to the adverse environmental effect of the neighbor's unimproved property. The neighbor, who does nothing, automatically receives a higher rate of return because of the positive environmental effect of the adjacent improvement. Most property owners—especially landlords (and most especially absentee landlords)—usually choose to be "free riders" (Taub, Taylor, and Dunham, 1984, p. 121).

BUILDING ABANDONMENT

Abandoned buildings in our inner-city neighborhoods continue to erode the local social fabric. They signify the ills of neglect, communicating to people the futility of inner-city living. Investors warily eye these eyesores, realizing that one owner's failure to generate profit may portend of things to come. To invest here is to risk losing money. To residents, such buildings stand as metaphors for poverty and grit. They symbolize the social characteristics that propelled generations of inner-city people to leave downtown. To many, abandoned buildings are a sign of irreversible deterioration—a process that has attained a critical internal momentum. It is tied part and parcel to unemployed people, rampant drug abuse, and increasingly scarred infrastructures. In its symbolic qualities, it evokes images of poverty, hardship, and despair. Such a symbolic element, we contend, is a pernicious neighborhood element whose eradication is essential.

Houses and Apartments

Despite its destructive effects, residential abandonment is often difficult to detect. A building may be lived in, but the owner no longer tending or taking responsibility for it. Another building, vacant and totally uninhabitable, may still be on local tax rolls. In New York City, occupied rental buildings are considered abandoned when owners fail for at least three consecutive months to demand rent or institute summary proceedings for nonpayment thereof, and the city determines the building to be a danger to life, health, or safety through owner inaction. Owners may have failed to make repairs, supply janitorial service, purchase heating fuel or other supplies, or pay utility bills (Sternlieb, Hughes, and Bleakly, 1974, p. 55). Again in New York City, vacant buildings are considered abandoned if they are unsealed and unguarded, and if taxes have remained unpaid for at least one year. Abandoned dwellings, therefore, have been removed from the housing market with no intent of immediate reuse.

Residential abandonment in America's urban cities accelerated at an alarming rate through the 1960s and 1970s. By 1975, there were an estimated 199,000 abandoned housing units in New York City, 64,500 in Chicago, 62,000 in Detroit, 33,000 in Philadelphia, and 30,000 in St. Louis (Salins, 1980, p. 35). Between 1973 and 1977, more than 1.1 million home-owned and 1.5 million rental units were removed from the national market (Sternlieb, 1980, p. 9). Nearly one in 25 U.S. residences in 1973 had been scrapped. Nearly one in ten renter-occupied units built before 1939 had been destroyed (p. 16). An estimated 523,000 units were lost yearly to abandonment between 1974 and 1980 (Keune, 1984, p. 486). St. Louis lost 15 percent of its housing to demolition in the 1970s, with an average of 4,000 housing units torn down each year between 1970 and 1976 (Schmandt, Wendel, and Tomey, 1983, p. 3). Nowhere was the scale of abandonment greater than in New York City. Between 1965 and 1968 alone, an estimated 100,000 housing units (5 percent) were abandoned (Dear, 1976, p. 85). Between 1970 and 1984, 294,000 dwelling units were lost, with more than 193,000 units demolished, 98,000 burned out or boarded up, and 3,000 condemned (Stegman and Hillstrom, 1985, p. 224).

In a controversial study, Peter Salins (1980, p. xvi) identifies four specific causes underlying housing abandonment in New York City: (1) the publicly administered shelter allowance programs; (2) rent control; (3) the system for adjudicating landlord–tenant disputes; and (4) the dynamics of the dual housing market. To Salins, abandonment coincided, and continues to coincide, with the poverty phase of racial or ethnic transition. It correlates in time and space with welfare. Where in-migrating populations are dependent on income transfer payments and food stamps, abandonment purportedly follows. He believes that in New York City, rent control produced, and continues to produce, an idiosyncratic pattern of rents that encourages property disinvestment. Such regulations make it difficult, if not impossible, to raise rent to meet rising operating costs. Rents on approximately 60 percent of New York City's 2 million rentals were regulated in the 1970s (Sternlieb, 1972, p. 4). To Salins, shelter allowances produce in tenants, at times, an indifference to building maintenance. In 1975, under the Section 101 program of the Federal Housing Authority, 181,000 households in New York City received an average of $1,000 each, making up the difference between the 25 percent of household income considered an appropriate rent obligation and the fair market rent actually charged by landlords (Vaughan and Vogel, 1979, p. 90). The Section 8 program, inaugurated in 1974, paid eligible landlords a subsidy to make units available at low cost to poor families. Eligible households were those whose incomes did not exceed 80 percent of a neighborhood's median income level. The program also paid moving expenses for people moving to upgraded residences. Approximately one of every ten New York City rental dollars paid to landlords in the late 1970s came from welfare monies (Morris, 1978, p. 24). Rent control and housing allowances together spawned, in Salin's words (1980, p. 54), a "perpetually moving avalanche of devastation."

To Salins, the New York City system of adjudicating landlord–tenant code disputes has been and remains biased against landlords—a legal inheritance of Depression-era landlord abuses. Incentives are provided to create or exaggerate violations in order to avoid rent payment, or to scale back rents at housing court direction. Landlords must absorb significant losses of time and money in countering tenant claims. Problem tenants may prove unevictable in the context of pending claims. These realities enticed, and continue to entice, landlords to seek quick profits in "hit-and-run" or "slash-and-burn" stances. Rental buildings bought cheap are milked for short-run profits. Owners gamble that combinations of low down payments, mortgage payment delinquency, aggressive rent collection, and minimal maintenance will return substantial profits prior to tenant accelerated abandonment. Once depreciation and other tax benefits are exhausted, landlords walk away from buildings, the economic potential of ownership totally exhausted. In 1978, the tax arrears on abandoned property in New York City stood at $1.5 billion, substantially worsening the city's fiscal crisis (Ley, 1983, p. 256).

Nowhere has housing abandonment received more attention than in the South Bronx. Between 1960 and 1975, 250,000 apartments were destroyed despite concerted public efforts to ameliorate housing conditions there. More than $10 billion were spent on public housing and public assistance programs, including those of rent subsidization (Salins, 1980, p. 1). And yet the South Bronx is still a disaster zone (Figure 5.7). Diane Gold describes a typical building of the early 1970s with its "overflowing garbage cans out on the sidewalk in front, broken windows, mailboxes ripped off in the lobby, no front doors, the usual sour run-down building smell, peeling paint, chunks of fallen plaster on the floor, a leaky roof over the stairwell and scraps of old food on the stairs" (1980, p. 191). Residents complained of roaches and rats, faulty toilets, and lack of heat or hot water for months. A key episode in the devastation of the South Bronx was the opening of more than 15,000 apartments in nearby Co-op City in 1958. Central Bronx households moved to Co-op City and those in the South Bronx moved to the Central Bronx, leaving vacant housing, reduced mortgage demand, and a prevalence of

Figure 5.7   In 1988 most of the worst sections of the South Bronx had been leveled, but the decay had by no means been contained despite decades of public pronouncement.

low-income families. The Bronx subsequently lost some 30 percent of this housing inventory (Stegman and Hillstrom, 1985, p. 221).

Where low-income families dominate, different landlord responses engender different outcomes. Responses to changing environmental circumstances may change little or set off a calculated pattern of disinvestment. Immediate profit circumstances are less important than anticipated profit margins in a landlord's decision making. Consequently, aged buildings are not necessarily abandoned first. New buildings in sound condition may be the first to go in a random pattern of building disinvestment. Abandonment, once established, usually spreads by contagion, the negative externalities of disinvested parcels inclining adjacent and nearby neighbors toward similar response. The disease spreads outward in waves of contagion from original epicenters (Salins, 1980, p. xv). Abandonment tends to spread first from one building to another along streets and then across backyards and later across streets (Women's City Club of New York, 1977, p. 58). Abandonment soon infects buildings in a wildfire fashion. Decay coalesces until abandonment becomes visually dominant, the sense of maintenance and orderliness overwhelmed by a sense of dereliction and disorder.

Stores

Retail shops are not immune to dereliction and abandonment. Where cultural, social, and economic change occurs, merchants traditionally have difficulties in adjusting to new tastes, styles, and preferences. Such change, moreover, often reduces local purchasing power and entrepreneurial abilities to sustain profit margins. Investment ordinarily used for new inventory and physical upgrading may be cut back in anticipation of hard times. With realization of economic difficulties, sustained disinvestment is set off that can culminate in a store's closure. As stores close, retail traffic is reduced— a situation that jeopardizes healthier merchants. Reduced street life and vacant buildings invite crime. Vacant storefronts speak not only of reduced business, but imply a decline in community viability. The derelict business thoroughfare, often highly visible, signals to people that an entire area is decaying. Both shoppers and potential residents are discouraged from buying or renting.

Lack of confidence quickly evolves. Normal business replacement is reduced by perceptions of disadvantaged locations, increasing vacancy rates, retail blight, and board-ups. Retailers who continue to hang on have increased difficulties subsisting, peddling wares in a desperate attempt to stay afloat. Business turnover itself increasingly reflects the changing areal character, substituting necessary staple stores for marginal retail outlets. Groceries, hardware stores, and banks are replaced by wig shops, used clothing stores, and junk stores. Such shops do little to complement the surviving retailers. As vacancies mount, buildings are boarded up and vandalism and arson begins to take a toll (Figure 5.8). Buildings are demolished, but usually in a nonselective manner, leaving gaping holes. Vacant lots accumulate litter and rubbish.

Over time, white merchants are replaced by black counterparts. But the latter often find that their businesses are not locally supported. Stores in many black neighborhoods carry a reputation for selling overpriced, shoddy merchandise. Even when a black merchant carries a quality line at competitive prices, many blacks assume otherwise. They doubt that black merchants have access to the best wholesale outlets (Woodstock Institute, 1982, p. 159). Black retailers in central cities almost require national franchise connections in order to command customer confidence. Franchisers, like banks, tend to invest reluctantly in areas of declining affluence and anticipated physical decay. Banks, in pursuing redlining policies, tend to refuse the underwriting of mortgages on such commercial properties.

Chicago's North Lawndale neighborhood offers vivid evidence of commercial decline tied to deindustrialization and white flight. As played out along Ogden Avenue and the other commercial streets, North Lawndale

Figure 5.8   Commercial structures have vanished along the principal shopping street of Chicago's once prosperous Woodlawn neighborhood south of the University of Chicago.

lost 75 percent of its businesses and 25 percent of its employment base between 1960 and 1970. In the next decade it lost another 44 percent of its remaining commercial jobs, and 80 percent of its remaining manufacturing jobs (Chicago *Tribune* staff, 1986, p. 207). There were 30,000 residences in North Lawndale in 1960, but only 16,000 some 20 years later. A survey revealed 9 percent (838) of the area's buildings to be on the verge of collapse, 38 percent (3,432) in need of major rehabilitation, and 3 percent (279) to be abandoned (Chicago *Tribune* staff, 1986, p. 258). Local retailers—serving some 61,500 residents—were comprised of one bank, one supermarket, 48 lottery agents, 50 currency exchanges, 94 licensed bars and liquor stores, and several other marginal establishments (Chicago *Tribune* staff, 1986, p. 28). The area was 97 percent black, with the majority of its households on welfare.

THE THROWAWAY SOCIETY

That Americans tolerate housing abandonment is symptomatic of basic attitudes toward consumption generally. We purchase, we use, and we discard carelessly. Seldom do we examine critically our wastefulness as a society, or even as individuals. Americans suffer from an insidious "throwaway mentality," remarks Gale Cincotta, "that classifies older people, older homes, and older neighborhoods as expendable like pop bottles and used kleenex" (1976, p. 36). In part, wastefulness derives from a modern capitalistic economy that emphasizes conspicuous consumption. Wastefulness is also a cultural legacy, a basic way of looking at the world. The abundant natural resources of the American frontier encouraged capitalist exploitation without fear of short-term retribution. But America is rooted in the industrial slum of the nineteenth-century East as well as the agrarian frontier of the nineteenth-century West. Like the frontier, however, the slum provided little preparation for a subsequent society being neat, orderly, or conserving in outlook.

Today, wastefulness comes to the fore in America's central cities in many forms. Behind the transition zone moves a zone of dereliction where things large and small are consumed and discarded. Abandoned houses and stores stand amid vacant lots, sidewalks, and streets strewn with the debris of a civilization seemingly gone prodigal. The hulks of abandoned automobiles, the shells of cast-off appliances, and assorted debris fill the emptiness. In the worst pockets of discard, rats and roaches compete openly with human beings for sovereignty. Of course, the apologists for capitalism's abuses see such places as both natural and desirable outcomes of economic forces. Derelict places, to them, represent a wasting of land preparatory to economic recycling. Dereliction is seen as a "cleansing" process that anticipates new rounds of investment and profit taking. Critics, on the other hand, see these places as symbols of political failure where problems of injustice, inequality, oppression, and discontent manifest. The debris of modern life accumulates where societal concern is minimal. In a relatively affluent society, where advantages are expected to filter down the hierarchy of advantage, the poor inherit residuals. Poorly served by the public mechanisms of order and neatness, their lot is not only to inherit society's debris, but to accept life in a trash-strewn environment as given.

By the early 1970s, Americans on average were throwing away some 4.5 pounds of junk each day, or almost one ton of trash per year (Still, 1972, p. 132). In 1980, waste per capita had risen to eights pounds per day (Melosi, 1981, p. 192). In the aggregate, New Yorkers daily discarded 24,000 tons of material, or nine times their collective weight in rubbish each year (Pollock, 1987, pp. 5 and 6). There has been a revolution in merchandising in the United States since World War II, and a revolution in packaging to accompany it. Americans, including the poor, now buy most things in self-serve stores. Goods are packaged for ease of handling, the packages themselves intended as point-of-purchase advertisements exciting customers not only to pick up and handle but to buy. Discarded wrappings have produced an explosion of paper, cardboard, cellophane, plastic, and glass. In the early 1970s, Americans were discarding annually 50 billion beverage and food cans, 30 billion bottles and jars, 65 billion metal, glass, and plastic caps (Still, 1972, p. 132). With the packaging bill for 1986 approaching $28 billion, nearly one dollar out of every ten spent on food and beverages in the United States went for packaging. Indeed, Americans spent more for food packaging than the nation's farmers received in net income (Pollock, 1987, p. 8).

And most consumer goods are destined for a one-night stand. That is, they are purchased, consumed, and discarded quickly without regard for any residual value. Only now are Americans becoming cognizant of waste recycling. Less than 2 percent of the steel cans produced in the United States in the 1970s were remelted, and only about 10 percent of the aluminum cans—enough to build 200 Boeing-747 jumbo jets (Nelson, Williams, and Reynolds, 1975, p. 49). Accordingly, the great bulk of the nation's trash goes to landfills and open dumps. In 1968, cities collected and disposed of 140 million tons of waste. If dumped in a single landfill, it would have covered an area estimated at 35 miles square to a depth of 10 feet (Melosi, 1981, p. 191). Many cities have run out of space for dumping. Philadelphia no longer has access to a local landfill and has shipped its wasted as far away as eastern Ohio and southern Virginia in recent years. Between 1980 and 1986, Philadelphia's disposal costs rose from $20 to $90 per ton.

The automobile has symbolized American affluence in the twentieth century like no other consumer good. Purveyor of mobility and independence of action, the automobile is a clear status indicator. The used car, like the used house, has been reserved for the less affluent; and with the decline of public transit in central cities, the used automobile has become a necessity for the poor. To be without an automobile is to be deprived of access to jobs, shopping, and even recreation. Old cars enjoy limited lives in the hands of people with little or no money for repairs. Inoperable vehicles make easy targets for auto strippers (who, while operating illegally, do serve to recycle selected auto parts) and vandals (who pleasure only in destruction). The Sanitation Department removed 31,000 abandoned cars from New York City streets in 1981, 62,000 in 1984, and 129,000 in 1987 (New York *Times*, 1988). Approximately one-sixth were stolen cars. The city faces a greater problem with dead automobiles than it did with dead horses in the preceding century. New York City is not alone. In 1985, 25,000 cars were abandoned in Los Angeles; and in 1986, 36,000 in Detroit (Champaign–Urbana *News-Gazette*).

Unattended automobiles quickly call attention to themselves. Windows and doors may be left open, or license plates may be removed. Perhaps the car simply has not been moved for several days. "In a city that is always on the go, anything static must be dead, and it becomes public domain if

Figure 5.9   By the 1980s, homelessness had become a national disgrace, as shown here in Los Angeles.

no one calls for the body" (Zimbardo, 1973, p. 85). After men and teenage boys strip away the battery, radiator, carburetor, windshield wipers, tires, and other usable parts, children smash the windows and perhaps set fire to the interior. The hulk may then be used as big trash bin, the neighborhood temporarily dumping refuse into it in lieu of the streets. Researchers who have observed unattended cars in central city neighborhoods report that, on average, some two dozen acts over three days will render an automobile totally useless (p. 88).

A depiction of America's decaying central neighborhoods would not be complete without mention of derelict people. Among the abandoned houses and apartment buildings wander men and women variously cast aside by society, victims of the nation's throwaway mentality (Figure 5.9). Traditional vagrants were older males, usually alcoholic and underemployed. They concentrated in places like San Francisco's "South of Market" area, a district of small cheap hotels (which provided intermittent lodgings and served as permanent mailing addresses), saloons (which often furnished free lunches and doubled as informal employment agencies), pawnshops (where emergency funds could be obtained), barber schools (where haircuts were free), and secondhand stores, poolrooms, and missions. Such facilities joined single men with common backgrounds, experience, and problems

(Hartman, 1984, p. 54). Since the 1960s, new varieties of street people have emerged to overwhelm the traditional boweries and skid rows. The chronic drifters now include "deinstitutionalized" mental patients, runaway teenagers, foreclosed or evicted families, the mentally retarded, the physically disabled, abused and battered women, illegal immigrants, and drug addicts.

Perhaps no group epitomizes the throwaway age more than the hundreds of thousands of former mental patients released to their own care. With new drug therapies and soaring operating costs, the mental health profession launched a crusade to integrate patients into local communities. As Michael Harrington observed caustically, "The mentally and emotionally ill as well as the retarded were volunteered by the hale and healthy to help balance the budget" (1984, p. 104). Between 1955 and 1987, the population in the nation's mental hospitals fell from 559,000 to 116,000 (*Newsweek*, 1987, p. 48). During the same period, the number of psychiatric patients in New York's state hospitals declined from 93,000 to about 20,000 (Barbanel, 1987, p. 1E). Rather than isolating patients, treatment now called for integrating patients into local settings. Self-administered antipsychotic drugs, for example, were believed sufficient to permit patients to lead normal lives. By and large, this program has failed. Psychotics, upon release, have tended to withdraw from human contact, failing to regulate themselves medicinally and relapsing into psychosis. By the 1980s about half of the nation's approximately 2 million chronically mentally ill had been reinstitutionalized, but in nursing homes and substandard board-and-care homes rather than hospitals (Harrington, 1984, p. 107). Less than 40 percent of the nation's chronically mentally disabled are housed in public institutions (Dear and Wolch, 1987, p. 203).

The federal government had promised to help local communities shoulder the load of tending the mentally ill. The Community Mental Health Center Act of 1963 promised to subsidize neighborhood facilities for the care of the mentally ill on an outpatient basis. Centers were to tie into a spectrum of redistributive social programs including the Job Corps, Legal Aid, Comprehensive Employment and Training Services, Headstart, and so on. Funds for the centers were not forthcoming and various Great Society programs were cut back or eliminated altogether during the Reagan years. Local infrastructures for mental health care were never replaced. In the 1960s, Illinois moved thousands of mental patients out of state asylums and into privately owned apartment buildings in places like Chicago's Uptown neighborhood. Without alerting city officials, the state shifted much of this financial and custodial responsibility to Chicago's central city, converting sections into outdoor mental wards. Some 7,000 deinstitutionalized patients were shipped to Uptown in one year alone (Marciniak, 1984, p. 23). The city's police came to function as orderlies, its firefighters as emergency nurses.

Housing for single persons has declined precipitously during the 1970s and 1980s. Between 1970 and 1982, New York City lost more than 111,000 single resident occupance (SRO) units, or about 87 percent of the 1970 total. Only 17,200 units remained (Harrington, 1984, p. 117). Most were lost to abandonment, some to condominium conversion. New York City's daily homeless in the early 1980s ranged between 36,000 to 50,000, there being provision for only some 25,000 homeless persons in 55 hotels and nine shelters (Dear and Wolch, 1987, p. 161). Few northern cities have adequate facilities to meet the demands of severe winter nights when just being outdoors is life threatening. Chicago served an estimated 12,000 to 25,000 homeless persons with a mere 1,000 shelter beds (Meyers, 1986, p. 148). In 1984, the Department of Housing and Urban Development conservatively estimated the nation's housing deficit for its "notoriously fugitive" population at 140,000 beds per night (Dear and Wolch, 1987, p. 175). The Supreme Court's 1972 decision declaring unconstitutional many of the nation's local vagrancy laws has made servicing the homeless difficult. They cannot be forced into shelters, nor can city police powers be used, as formerly, to remove them from dangerous situations. Homelessness, by law, was not a public issue and was allowed to proliferate across places.

UNCIVIL BEHAVIOR

Neighborhoods are fundamentally social units that define space, place, and behavior. In healthy neighborhoods, neighbors respect one another as relative equals and are willing to accept and yield to shared norms of behavior (Clay, 1979, p. 5). Peer pressure operates to enforce standards and keep neighborhoods in a kind of social equilibrium. As Phillip Clay observes, important norms govern various aspects of this equilibrium: (1) the extent to which neighbors are expected to be concerned for one another; (2) the degree to which self- and family-discipline are reinforced in social interaction; (3) the extent to which individuals uphold the integrity and image of place; (4) the extent to which positive reinforcements and negative sanctions are directed against outsiders who violate norms; and (5) the extent to which newcomers are integrated into the neighborhood (p. 37). In a healthy neighborhood, people are mutually civil. Behavior rests on assumptions that neighborhood good, and hence individual good, is enhanced by conformance to social norms.

Uncivil behaviors disrupt social equilibrium. In unhealthy neighborhoods, behavior may range from complete indifference to others to overt hostility toward collective norms. Where social controls operate, they are imposed by external actors including police, juvenile authorities, social workers, welfare supervisors. Uncivil neighbors tend not to adhere to community standards of child rearing, property maintenance, and the like. With recently arrived in-migrants, differences may lead to uncivil behavior. When blacks filter into white central city neighborhoods, they usually come as young families with children. White neighbors are often older and in a different life-cycle stage. Antagonisms are partly the result of conflict between generations; between the "impetuousness of youth and the fearfulness of old age" (Clay, 1979, p. 39). But all too frequently antagonisms run far deeper as when suspicion and distrust across divergent social groups prevail.

Central city residents have to make choices when such "alien" people move in. They can flee to the suburbs and avoid potential problems. They can try to integrate newcomers into traditional neighboring patterns. Or they can begrudgingly accept newcomers. Since World War II, most central city whites have chosen to flee. Those who have stood to defend neighborhood have usually resented external "encroachment" but have failed to contest the process. Most Americans loyal to neighborhood ultimately assume stoic stances. They turn away from neighborhood interactions, and focus on protecting house and family. "This self-preservation makes them less caring and socially integrated. In the long run, stoic acceptance is itself uncivil behavior and reinforces decline" (Clay, 1979, p. 39).

Conservatives argue that the family is very much the foundation on which a civilized society is built. "The motivations which drive men and women to do what must be done if society is to prosper—to work, to produce, to delay gratification, to save and invest, to create pleasant, safe towns and neighborhoods, to fight crime and corruption, and to defend the nation when it is attacked—are rooted primarily in the family" (Institute for Cultural Conservatism, 1987, p. 35). Certainly, the family is the primary socializing unit where values are learned. This group contends that the traditional American family seems under assault. They cite a divorce rate nationally running about 50 percent for the generation now under 30 (U.S. Department of Education, 1986, p. 8). Illegitimate birth is common, especially among the central city poor. The proportion of black teenage births out of wedlock jumped from 42 percent in 1960 to 63 percent in 1970 to 89 percent in 1983 (W. Wilson, 1987, p. 28). The single-parent, female-headed household has become common, especially among central city blacks. In 1960, 8 percent of U.S. white and 22 percent of black households were female headed, while in 1980 the percentage stood at 12 percent and 40 percent, respectively (Neckerman, 1987, p. 65). In 1983 the median income of black families headed by women was only $8,000, or 37 percent of the median income of husband-wife black families (Wilson, 1987, p. 26).

Forced into a pattern as AFDC mothers, teenage girls find themselves able to secure societal resources they could not ordinarily acquire: housing and basic medical benefits. It is one course of action that provides for their well-being amid the blockage of conventional paths to material acquisition. In an environment of little hope for future opportunity, jaded perceptions of self and society emerge. Only with difficulty do children develop a sense of upward mobility. Their neglect and poverty, ostensibly entrenched and persistent, reinforce a culture of poverty that feeds back to color future generations. In extreme cases, young boys may make contributions to the household economy through thievery and even drug dealing. By joining a street gang, a son can confer an important benefit on his mother in the form of protection against the risk of rape, mugging, and various rip-offs (Harris, 1981, p. 132). Later, as a "boyfriend in hiding," he can, staying in the same mode, offer protection to and supplement the incomes of other AFDC households. By the late 1970s, AFDC had come to function not as a temporary crutch, but as a regular source of subsistence for an estimated 750,000 U.S. households where opportunities were so scarce (Rein and Rainwater, 1977, p. 20).

In the 1960s, youths aged 14–25 comprised 15 percent of the population, but accounted for 69 percent of arrests in the United States (Harrington, 1984, p. 184). In 1980, 66 percent of all those arrested for urban violent and property crimes were under 25 years of age (W. Wilson, 1987, p. 37). Half of all serious crimes (including murder, rape, aggravated assault, robbery, burglary, larceny, and automobile theft) are committed by youths aged 10–17; and since 1960, juvenile crime has increased at twice the rate of adult crime (Breckenfeld, 1977, p. 115). The 1960s and the 1970s were decades of social liberalization that saw the rise of a "me generation," with its general conviction that old restraints need not apply and that self-expression, if not selfishness, was a moral imperative. When such ideas permeated the world of the youthful poor, they were a major reason for the rise in criminal behavior (Harrington, 1984, p. 184). In addition, the 1960s and 1970s were decades in which an acquisitive materialism flourished, driven as never before by advertising and television programming. Crime was also encouraged by the emergence of youth gangs, whose status in membership hinged on committing aggressive acts against one's community—extreme acts winning the most adulation (Ley, 1974, p. 127).

Nationally, there were 13 million serious crimes reported in 1980 (including 23,044 murders), a 55-percent increase from 1970 (Parenti, 1983, p. 35). The rate of violent crime soared from approximately 150 per 100,000 people to almost 600 between 1960 and 1980 (Clark, 1984, p. 191). As crime increased, so also did the nation's prison population to more than half a million people—a 40-percent increase during the 1970s (Chicago *Tribune* staff, 1986, p. 269). The nation launched a prison building boom with 34 new facilities in 22 states completed in 1984 alone at an average cost of $11 million each. It has been estimated that, for each $100 million spent on prison construction, $1.6 billion will be spent in salaries, operating costs, and debt retirement over the ensuing 30 years (Chicago *Tribune* staff, 1986, p. 269). Rather than attacking the underlying causes of crime (i.e., racial prejudice, unemployment, poverty, lack of education), the nation has chosen to emphasize incarceration—to focus on the individual criminal and ignore the structural defects in society that encourage criminality. Americans have opted for "analgesic" solutions that treat distress rather than cause.

Central cities continue as focal points for criminal activity. Some two-thirds of such arrests take place in areas containing 2 percent of the population. Where is that area?

> Well, it's the same where infant mortality is four times higher than in the city as a whole; where the death rate is 25 percent higher; where life expectancy is 10 years shorter; where common communicable diseases with potential of physical and mental damage are six and eight and nine times more frequent; where alcoholism and drug addiction are prevalent to a degree far transcending that of the rest of the city; where education is poorest—the oldest school buildings, the most crowded and turbulent school rooms, the fewest certified teachers, the highest rate of dropouts; where the average formal schooling is four to six years less than for the city as a whole." (Sternlieb and Burchell, 1973, p. 142)

Crime is epidemic where single-parent households headed by women prevail; mothers being unable to control teenage children. Crime is problematical where uncivil behaviors of all kinds are tolerated as a way of life.

Blacks precipitate more than their share of criminality in central cities, and suffer more as victims. "While blacks account for less than 20 percent of U.S. population, nearly half of all murder victims are black. Blacks are four times as likely as whites to be assaulted, mugged, or raped" (Cassidy, 1980, p. 53). In Chicago, the city's most violent area has overwhelmingly been the black Wentworth Avenue police district on the southside. In 1983, this four-square-mile area (3 percent of city total) had 81 murders (11 percent of city total) and 1,691 aggravated assaults (13 percent of city total) (W. Wilson, 1987, p. 25). Robert Taylor Homes was the most crime-ridden section of all. All of the complexes' 20,000 legal and 5,000 illegal residents were black, with 69 percent of the official population below 18 years of age. Ninety-three percent of the families with children were headed by a single parent. Robert Taylor Homes accounted for 11 percent of the city's murders, 9 percent of its rapes, and 10 percent of its aggravated assaults (ibid.).

Drugs underlie much central city crime—maybe even most of it. Heroin and cocaine effectively mask the deprivation of slum life. As one addict put it, "Man, when you shoot H[eroin], you're no longer in the ghetto. You are in your own world. You can't see the rats. You can't see the roaches. You can't smell the garbage. You're no longer hungry. The holes in your shoes don't bother you. It's your own heaven, and you want to stay there. As long as you stay high, nothing bothers you" (Forman, 1971, p. 131). Having stolen as much as $500,000 to feed his habit, he had spent five years in prison. Now he worried that his seven-year-old son would be into the drug scene "in a year or two." In Baltimore, one study revealed 354 heroin addicts to be responsible for 775,000 crimes in a nine-year period (Meyers, 1986, p. 23). Stealing to feed one's habit becomes a way of life.

With drug dependency—an exaggerated form of narcissistic behavior—energies are channeled toward self-indulgence to the neglect of community. In the Detroit of the early 1970s, an estimated 70 percent of the city's armed robberies and 90 percent of its bank holdups were drug related, the bulk of this crime concentrated among 16–22 year olds. In Detroit and other cities, youth stripped abandoned buildings of copper pipe, wire, and plumbing and electrical fixtures to sustain drug habits. Junkies created atmospheres of fear and intimidation. "Instead of the criminals being regulated by the majority, it is they who establish and control the community's standard of behavior" (Cassidy, 1980, p. 55). Drugs mean violence and high death rates. On three of the South Bronx's worst streets, residents in 1969 had less than a 1-in-20 chance of dying a natural death (H. Leven, 1980, p. 266). In the 1970s, young ghetto males had a 40-percent chance of dying by violence by age 25 (Harris, 1981, p. 132).

Vandalism is a persistent plague in older neighborhoods that precipitates decline and pushes transition zones ever outward. Vandalism encompasses acts of illegal destruction or defacement leveled at property belonging to others (Cohen, 1973, p. 23). Of the total U.S. criminal arrests made in 1980, only 2.4 percent were vandalism related. Police generally tolerate vandals as committing acts too insignificant to divert attention from serious crime. Vandalism is primarily a juvenile offense, those under 18 years of age committing some two-thirds of the offenses (Shannon, 1984, p. 215). Vandalism is often a group ritual—requiring, as it does, a receptive audience. It is an ideal form of rule breaking because it combines a sense of toughness with action, excitement, and the feeling of being in control. For young males, it can be a proving ground of masculinity. Motives range from revenge to drawing attention to specific grievances, to promoting a cause, to challenging or insulting symbolically a particular individual or group, to pleasuring in violent acts and destruction as kinds of play.

Among many central city teenagers, vandalism has become a form of

malicious entertainment spawned by boredom, despair, exasperation, resentment, failure, and frustration (Cohen, 1973, p. 39). It is fostered by
anger and resentment at a quality of life that appears abysmal when compared to the consumption-oriented lifestyles regularly advertised and acted
out around them. Carried along by a kind of mob psychology, gangs of
teenagers frequently wreck abandoned buildings in a process termed by
Vern Allen and David Greenberger (1978, p. 310) "wreckcreation." Pleasure derives from reducing a complex structure to its parts, anticipating
how the process physically unfolds, sharing the novelty of staged destruction, and from the visual, auditory, and tactile-kinesthetic stimuli of the
very act of breakage. When destruction is more complex (versus simple),
more unexpected (versus expected), or more novel (versus familiar), greater
enjoyment is derived (Allen and Greenberger, 1978, p. 312). Wrecking something can be a spectacle and cause for celebration. When done illegally, it
carries risks that amplify exhilaration. Fire is especially dramatic. In 1986,
juveniles accounted for 40 percent of all U.S. arson arrests, with children
under ten accounting for 7 percent of total (New York *Times*, 1987a). There
were 111,000 confirmed or suspected arson fires in 1986, down 34 percent
from the 1977 peak of 167,500. Nonetheless, this act caused 705 deaths and
$1.6 billion in property damages. Sixty percent of the fires were in vacant
buildings (ibid.).

The nation has witnessed massive neighborhood destruction as a result
of persistent vandalism over time—an apparent reversal of the instinct against
fouling one's own nest. Many central city poor—particularly the abject black
poor—nominally identify with places inhabited. Although they perpetually
look forward to better housing, they recognize that all housing within reach
carries social stigma. If private, it is old, obsolete, and barely functional.
If public, it is poorly designed to minimum standards. Housing is not something coveted and prized so much as it is despised as symbolic of one's
poverty and lack of opportunity. Today's poor, moreover, are frequently
transplanted from rural places (especially the South) and do not have a
tradition of directly confronting oppression through active political participation. They frequently resign themselves to the fate of their condition,
distrusting the political process that could potentially mitigate poverty and
neglect. Anger and resentment often gets displaced, focusing on vague
actors and groups rather than local and distant institutions that perpetuate
poverty.

Graffiti art is both a blunt exercise in rule breaking and a means of hu-
manizing dehumanized spaces (Figure 5.10). As its production carries risks,
it offers excitement as a kind of mild vandalism. Youth gangs can define
turf. Indeed, most aggressive wall markings are located near edges of gang

Figure 5.10   Racism rears its head in an uncivil gesture of bigotry. Graffiti can be many things, including a despoiler of place as here in rural Kentucky. Such prejudices, brought to the central city, have underlain its decline.

territories, in the "marchlands" between zones of influence. At territorial cores, assertive behavior toward rivals is unnecessary and graffiti obscenities are almost absent (Ley, 1974, p. 217). Individuals use graffiti to build a sense of self-importance: one's work displayed publicly in competition with other graffiti artists. Graffiti can change the meaning of a place by demonstrating the interloper's power over socially sanctioned jurisdiction. As it raises the individual's sense of importance, it diminishes the community's importance as a locus of caring. Graffiti artists assert a deliberate contempt for social propriety. As with any form of vandalism, no matter how trivial, the costs mount up. In 1982, the New York City Transit Authority calculated graffiti-related costs at $10 million: half in maintenance costs for cars, tunnels, and stations and half in revenues lost from passengers diverted to other forms of travel (Francis, 1983, p. 17).

SCORNING THE UNDERCLASS

Prior to World War II, the very poor—both black and white—were located largely in rural America. Especially impoverished were southern sharecroppers and tenant farmers, with sharp economic and social distinctions separating them from the landowning class (Daniel, 1985). For the urban poor, largely white, the gradients of social stratification were not so sharp. Working-class families in tenements and row houses were scarcely distinguishable from shopkeeper and artisan neighbors in districts that gradually merged, in an intricately stepped hierarchy, from working-class neighborhood to lower middle class, to middle, to upper middle, and so on to wealthy neighborhoods (Leven, 1972, p. 64). In many ethnic areas, economic classes mixed in close proximity in communities of interest defined by language and often religion. There the predominantly white urban poor occupied positions of dignity and social responsibility. By the 1960s, the rural poor had moved to the cities, the blacks among them encountering severe discrimination. White ethnics, who had worked hard to shed stigmas of foreignness, were particularly defensive of their neighborhoods and their prerogatives as upwardly bound Americans. By the 1970s, a vast gap had developed between the white laboring classes, quickly fleeing to the suburbs, and the black poor—largely, erstwhile rural in-migrants relegated to blighted zones.

Central cities subsequently spawned a largely black "underclass" that currently persists. Its recent history, rooted in unemployment and underemployment, shows little economic progress. Unemployment rates in excess of 7 percent during times of economic recovery and expansion are among the highest structural unemployment levels in recent American history. During the 1950s unemployment averaged 4.2 percent, 4.8 percent during the 1960s, and 6.2 percent during the 1970s. But in the early 1980s it climbed to 8.5 percent (Meyers, 1986, p. 94). Each recession and economic recovery left the country progressively worse off. For blacks in the early 1980s, the unemployment stood at 15.3 percent (more than double that of whites), and for black teens it stood at 38 percent (Meyers, 1986, p. 94). Blacks had entered a depression equal to that of the 1930s. Unskilled jobs have been evaporating in urban America—a result of deindustrialization. The four largest Northeast cities (New York, Chicago, Philadelphia, and Detroit), accounting for one-quarter of the nation's central city poor, lost more than 1 million manufacturing, wholesaling, and retailing jobs between 1967 and 1976 alone, just as minority populations were expanding there.

Blue-collar employment decline in central cities has been partly offset by growth of "knowledge-intensive" fields like finance, brokerage, accounting, consulting, advertising, and law. Between 1970 and 1984, for example, New York City lost 492,000 industrial jobs with low educational requirements while gaining 239,000 with high requirements (W. Wilson, 1987, p. 40). However, relatively few blacks were called upon to participate in the new economy. Instead, employers relied primarily on white females. Service-sector growth coincided with the mass conversion of white housewives "from baby production and services in the home to the production of services and information away from home" (Harris, 1981, p. 136). More white females had high school and college degrees, spoke standard English, and had fewer difficulties working in subordinate positions with white male supervisors.

Although most central city blacks work, each succeeding crop of job-seeking teenagers finds it difficult to find jobs that pay more than welfare. Increasingly, central city blacks are forced to take the welfare route. This passage by circumstance sustains actions and values that the broader society finds abhorrent. Rooted in despair and minimal opportunity, ethics of work avoidance and profligacy emerge that become seen as individually chosen and selected. The embracing of welfare and "leisure lives" are believed signs of irresponsibility and self-generated pathological lifestyles. To the middle class, the ethic of work avoidance has come to the fore. Central city blacks are seen as rejecting employment at hand while embracing welfare and leisure activities. A new kind of dandyism purportedly has emerged. Unrecognized in this stigmatization is the context of constraint and antiblack attitudes that debilitates human pride. Institutionalized barriers to out-migration, securing better housing, and obtaining better paying jobs generate frustration and anger that can quickly turn to despair. Poorly provided political outlets to express discontent compound despair that can yield fatalist, apathetic, and discouraged people. This despair is exacerbated by a society that emphasizes lifestyles and values that the low income have great difficulty attaining.

Like most Americans, slum dwellers take many values from the media, especially from television. Television's message is one of unfettered consumption. To be a conspicuous consumer is to be accorded social status and prestige. Television's message is one of heightened reality, obtained not from being attuned to life's subtleties, but to a quest for intensive experiences. Television, by emphasizing the socially novel, has asserted the importance of instantaneous consumption in various forms of everyday life. For groups unable to follow this path, anger and resentment follow. In the process of sensationalizing to sell products and inform consumptive behavior, move-over, tragic snippets of life are portrayed as commonplace events. Emphasis on crime has made criminality seem expected and acceptable in certain circumstances. Crime stories currently dominate much of television's dramatic fare. In 1987, the $1.5 million spent per episode of *Miami Vice* nearly equaled the entire annual budget for the real Miami vice squad. So also has television news reporting come to emphasize crime along with the violence of traffic accidents and disasters both natural and man-made. Americans once experienced their cities directly. Today that experience is largely mediated through electronic communications. Television has become the window through which people see a selection of experiences, carefully chosen to hold their attention. They do not interact directly with the subjects of those experiences, and therefore their judgments about them are secondhand (Pasquariello, Shriver, and Geyer, 1982, p. 172). Television reduces viewers' inclination to really know places as objects of affection.

This transmission of social values has reinforced poverty and generated increased rates of city deprivation. One urban pathology increasingly visible as an outgrowth of sustained poverty is hunger. In a striking pattern of neglect, urban neighborhoods exhibit enlarging numbers of hungry children. This upsurge follows a period of intensive federal involvement in local affairs that all but wiped out urban malnutrition. In New York City, approximately 700,000 children are currently growing up in poverty—more than 37 percent of the city's children (Johnson, 1990). Since 1975, the local consumer price index has risen 127 percent, dramatically outpacing the buying power of the minimum wage. The poorest tenth of city renters in 1987 spent 85 percent of their income on rent, leaving little for food and other essentials. At a time when government assistance was most in need, help has disappeared. Under the Reagan administration, the federal government cut programs for the poor by $57 billion between 1982 and 1985 (ibid.). Food stamp and child nutrition programs were slashed by $6.8 billion and $5.2 billion, respectively. These cuts, coming just after the devastating economic consequences of the early 1980s recession, swelled the number of local hungry children. Ironically, these events, as mentioned above, occurred after a sustained and successful federal initiative to wipe out hunger. In 1980, the federal government was spending $13.4 billion on food and nutrition programs (ibid.). School breakfasts, lunches, and food stamps were targeted to the poor. These programs today have been virtually eliminated. While the average New York City family of four spends $536 a month on food, the maximum food stamp benefit is $331 (ibid.). Such hunger exacerbates suffering and limits individual potentialities. Children with this affliction have higher rates of absenteeism, poorer self-image, and greater difficulty staying alert and awake in school. Hunger thereby intensifies the very condition—poverty—that constrains individual life chances.

All major U. S. cities have abandoned neighborhoods. Their erosion and decline result from neglect wrought by the private sector and ill-considered public-sector programs. No other fully industrialized society, either capitalist or socialist, tolerates such widespread decay and despair. It is a national disgrace. Natural disaster or acts of war have never rendered such widespread urban devastation. Americans cope with hurricanes, tornadoes, floods, and other catastrophes. Communities, dazed and disorganized, always collect themselves in the face of such disasters and rebuild quickly. San Francisco rebounded from earthquake and fire in 1906—a twentieth-century phoenix risen from its ashes. The strategy of recovery was direct: protect remaining human resources, reopen lines of communication and supply, start visible action quickly, make everyone's image and expectations clear and secure (Lynch, 1972, p. 195). But Americans have not reacted similarly to the processes of decay attacking their cities.

Dereliction in a capitalist nation is certainly intelligible and unsurprising. Clearly, it has become commonplace. But neighborhood poverty and dereliction is the result of legal codes, public policies, and private initiatives that Americans have the power to change. It is not a natural process. Dereliction is tragically wasteful—not only for those caught firmly in the syndrome of poverty, but for all Americans. Needlessly lost material and energy resources decay built environments. Human potentialities go unfulfilled. Lives are squandered in enclaves of neglect that are human constructions capable of being eradicated or perpetuated. To treat these enclaves as natural and inexorable is to lose sight of their human-crafted essence. The economic prowess of capitalism may explain urban neighborhood dereliction, but it is no excuse.

6

Rural Decline

America is not really an urbane nation. While most of her people live in metropolitan areas and the vast majority reside in places larger than 5,000 people, most Americans still look to rural America for a sense of rooted-ness. Escape to the pseudo-pastoralism of suburbia speaks of a kind of pro-vincial-mindedness wrought by earlier generations on the nation's farms and in her small towns. Since World War II, affluent Americans have dis-carded central city instabilities for the presumed safety of rural-like subur-ban settings. As an ideal, the image of rural America has been distorted. The vision, obscured by nostalgic longings culturally inbred in America's sub-urbs, sees rural places as little changed and little changing. In an urban world of constant flux, rural America appears to be established, fixed, perman-ent, anchored—a refuge from modern-day turmoils. Clearly, the vision is an illusion, for changes in rural America are profound. Those who would seek refuge there, beware!

FARMING IN ECLIPSE

Farming, fishing, and forest–mineral extraction have traditionally under-lain the U.S. rural economy, the rural pastness with which Americans read-ily associate. America was once rooted in farms and small farm trade cen-ters. Vast changes, however, have swept across the agrarian scene during recent generations, leaving in their wake much dereliction. Farmers, wit-nessing a revolution in mechanization and chemical applications to agricul-ture, have experienced growing scale and specialization of farming. Capital has been substituted for labor, undermining rural populations amid expand-ing farm output. Farms consist of day-to-day managed land involving individuals

197

or corporations conducting agricultural operations on an annual cycle. In defining farms, the Census Bureau since 1974 has set a minimum of ten acres for size, and a minimum of $1,000 for product sales (Larson, 1981, p. 148). The number of places designated as farms declined from 6.2 million in 1940 to 2.4 million in 1981 while the average size of farms increased from 175 to 428 acres (Korsching, 1986, p. 2). Farmer numbers declined even faster: a 70-percent loss between 1940 and 1974 (Larson, 1981, p. 151). By 1982, people living on farms had declined to 5.6 million, or only 2.4 percent of the nation's total population (Shaffer, Salant, and Saupe, 1986, p. 2).

Farm production has been concentrated in fewer and fewer hands. Whereas in 1939 the largest 5 percent of the nation's farms accounted for 38 percent of the nation's farm output, in 1982 they accounted for 50 percent (Korsching, 1986, p. 3). Indeed, the 17,000 farms with gross annual sales of more than $500,000, comprising the top 1 percent nationally in 1980, produced about 27 percent of the nation's farm commodities (Leistritz et al., 1986, p. 127), with the smallest 50 percent accounting for less than 3 percent (Jackson, 1980, p. 76). Land ownership has become even more concentrated. In 1974, farms with 2,000 or more acres represented 3 percent of total farms, but 46 percent of farmland (Vogeler, 1981, p. 72). Large-scale "factory" farms differ from traditional family operations in that they are dependent on hired labor that is typically socially disadvantaged—sharp divisions evolving in areas with big farms between a small landowning and reasonably prosperous elite, and a large mass of laborers who live only slightly above the subsistence level (Leistritz et al., 1986, p. 127). Little mobility exists in such rural caste systems.

The symbiosis between big business and big government has propelled the drift toward bigness in farming. Whereas few large corporations run farms directly (since, in fact, nonfamily corporations operated only 0.3 percent of the nation's farms in 1985 and owned only 1.6 percent of the farmland), they do dominate the financing and marketing of agricultural products as well as the manufacture of equipment and the provisioning of farm supplies and services (Pasley, 1986, p. 24). Farming itself simply does not return large enough profits. Implement manufacturers, hybrid seed suppliers, fertilizer and pesticide producers of irrigation technologies—all have pushed farmers toward larger-scale production. Banks, for their part, have encouraged more aggressive farmers to enlarge land ownerships to accommodate bigness of operation. Corporate oligopolies control distribution of most farm commodities and their conversion into finished consumer products. For example, by the 1970s four firms had come to control production of 87 percent of the nation's breakfast cereal, and 85 percent of the bread and prepared flour (Shover, 1976, p. 181).

Federal involvement in agriculture over the past 50 years has accelerated concentration, especially through commodity price stabilization (using allotments and other support mechanisms) and subsidization of research and innovation adoption through state university and farm extension programs. Federal programs have aided middle- and upper-income farmers primarily. Agricultural price supports for wheat, corn, soybeans, rice, cotton, tobacco, sugar, milk, and selected other commodities provide farmers with guaranteed incomes by covering differences between actual market prices and specified target prices. Payments in the early 1980s were limited to $20,000 per farmer per year (far more than the average $5,400 made to AFDC recipients) (Beeghley, 1983, p. 45). The total cost of guaranteeing farmer incomes—$3.3 billion in 1979—rose to $13.3 billion in 1983 (ibid.). Agricultural extension agents focused on the top quarter of all producers (Belden and Forte, 1978, p. 487). While the number of farms in the United States fell from 6 million to 2.9 million between 1945 and 1971, annual appropriations for extension work increased from $38 million to $322 million (ibid.).

Bigness has brought specialization. As sociologist Marion Clawson (1980, p. 68) reminds us, two generations ago the typical farmer grew his own seeds, grew feed for his draft animals, produced his own fertilizer in the form of manure, harvested his own crop, and carted it to market. He was often his own blacksmith, shoeing his horses and repairing his machinery. Nonfarm specialists now perform many of these tasks. Today, farmers buy most of what they need to operate. Generations ago, the cost of purchased inputs was approximately half of the value of farm outputs, the value added by farmers being half or more of the gross production. Today, production costs are approximately three-quarters of gross output (ibid.). Such specialization has diverted employment away from farms and into towns and cities.

Farm yields have jumped. American farmers consumed only 10,000 tons of chemical fertilizer in 1945 compared to 400,000 tons in 1965 (Jackson, 1980, p. 24). This fortyfold increase in energy-intensive enrichments (and fertilizer production has come to absorb some 20 percent of the natural gas annually consumed in the United States) brought a doubling in crop production (ibid.). In Illinois, for example, farms averaged 50 and 95 bushels of corn in 1945 and 1965, respectively (ibid.). The push to increase yields over the short run has wrought serious problems in many areas, such as soil erosion, water depletion, and salinization.

Farmers may still control land, but they do not control farm capital, technology, and, of course, market. Some farm operators have become totally dependent on agribusiness, their roles reduced to that of wage earners on their own properties. They work with only the appearance of being owners. By the 1980s, all sugarcane and sugar beets were grown under contract, as were 95 percent of the nation's vegetables for canning and freezing and 85 percent of its citrus (Stockdale, 1982, p. 321). Geographer Ingolf Vogeler observes that as farmers "continue to buy more machines or use more hired labor, rely more on borrowed capital, and lose control over long-term management decisions, they cease to be family farmers and become instead outdoor production workers similar to industrial workers" (1981, p. 12). Although farm productivity per worker outstrips industrial productivity several times, the farmer's income is well below that of industrial workers. As political economist James Iron adds, American farmers have been "squeezed, bled, induced to work hard for little" (quoted in Vogeler, 1981, p. 289).

Despite the growing dominance of agribusiness, the myth of the traditional U.S. family farm persists. The reality of farming, however, is that fiscal survival requires embracing commercialization and larger scales of production. Increasingly, farmer survival is not predicated on land ownership so much as on the wages paid through contract arrangements, off-farm employment, or debt assumption. Today's family farm, often legally incorporated for income and inheritance tax purposes, must function like a corporation. Farmers borrow money to put in crops, paying off debts in whole or in part depending on production costs and prevailing commodity prices. Each year, farmers gamble all or nearly all of their equity on input cost, market, and weather. No other industry has workers relying on loans to sustain employment. Farmers are vulnerable for they have few of the businessman's benefits—neither employment security nor freedom and the possibility of lavish income (Pasley, 1986, p. 24).

Through the 1970s, farm families relied heavily on increasing land values to help pay debts and get new loans. Farms were mortgaged to enable farmers to increase size of operations. During the 1970s, farmers experienced a boom as food prices soared with inflation, and overseas demand for American agricultural commodities grew. From 1950 to 1980, exports increased from 8 percent to 24 percent of gross farm income, and foreign markets came to absorb the production of two of every five acres (Korsching, 1986, p. 4). When inflation slowed in the 1980s and foreign demand declined in response to a rising dollar and increased agricultural production abroad, the farm economy deflated, sending land values through the floor. Farm income dropped by nearly one-third. At the same time, a series of good harvests flooded markets for most commodities which drove prices down below average production costs in many sectors, and falling land values pushed farmer debt-to-asset ratios to dangerously high levels (Agnew, 1987, p. 197). By the mid-1980s, some one-third of all farmers in the North Central states were experiencing serious cash flow problems. Even by 1975, farm debt stood at 159 percent of farm-generated income (up from 96 percent in 1960), and 80 percent of farm household income (up from 58 percent) (Vogeler, 1981, p. 31). Off-farm employment emerged as critical to farm solvency.

MEASURES OF RURAL DECAY

Changes in farming have been paralleled by a massive abandonment of farmland, especially in areas of rough terrain and less fertile soils. In the Southern Piedmont, 10 million acres—an area one-fifth the size of Iowa—passed out of farmer ownership across 89 counties from Charlotte, North Carolina, to Birmingham, Alabama, between 1939 and 1974 (Hart, 1980, p. 492). "Roughly two-fifths of this land was wooded, and presumably had contributed only minimally to farm production, but the loss of four and one-half million acres of harvested cropland plus one and a third million acres of other cleared farm land is genuinely staggering," geographer John Hart writes (ibid.). Kentucky's 218,000 farms in 1950 were reduced to 110,000 in 1978. The decline was most dramatic in the eastern mountains where number of farms dropped from 65,000 to 17,000 over the same period (Kentucky Heritage Council, 1984, p. 530).

Except for a slight drop in the 1920s, farmland acreage had increased in the conterminous United States until the 1950s when 40 million acres were lost (Hart, 1964, p. 1). By the 1970s, however, 3 million acres yearly were being converted to nonagricultural uses—a loss equal in size to Vermont, New Hampshire, Massachusetts, Rhode Island, Connecticut, New Jersey, and Delaware combined (Herbers, 1986, p. 138). Highways covered 21 million acres, and reservoirs and other impoundments another 10 million acres (ibid.). Most startling, about 2,000 acres of prime farmland was being consumed by urban sprawl daily (Jackson, 1980, p. 23). Between 1969 and 1978, farmland decreased by some 88 million acres, or nearly 10 million acres annually (Fletcher and Little, 1982, p. 84).

Most farmland abandoned in anticipation of urban growth stands idle prior to development, sometimes for decades. Land usually passes into the hands of speculators when inflated tax assessments, based on anticipated "highest" uses, make farming unprofitable. In New England, farmland conversion to nonagricultural uses has been so widespread that the region now imports some 80 percent of its food (Jeffords, 1984, p. 6). In the South, Florida lost nearly 15 percent of its agricultural land in the 1970s alone (ibid.). In 1983 some 78 million acres of farmland lay idle in the United States, with only 16 million of those acres in federal conservation reserve programs (New York *Times*, 1987b). A sense of impermanence casts a pall over rural areas where speculation dominates landholding. Farmers are too few to maintain the traditional supply and marketing infrastructures, and land is too fragmented to farm profitably. The temptation to sell prime farmland for nonagricultural purposes at nonagricultural prices has been very strong in recent decades. Between 1971 and 1977, capital gains on the physical assets of farmers, in fixed dollars, outstripped net income from actual farming two-and-a-half times over (Jackson, 1980, p. 77).

Abandoned farmland reverts to grass, scrub, or forest. To the conscientious farmer, the scenes invoke notions of dereliction. Landscapes appear unkempt, ragged, messy. No longer are fields manicured to precision or field margins carefully trimmed. Vegetation spreads wildly toward some new climax, the gardener's impulse replaced by natural selection. In reality, the new scene is far from disordered. Natural processes play out in measured ways, although ways not always satisfying to the cultured eye. For less fertile land poorly suited to farming, the reemergence of forest, savannah, or prairie is indeed a form of rejuvenation. In fallow conditions, land may achieve better and higher use despite its slovenly appearance. Eliminating destructive acts of exploitative farming with associated soil erosion, water depletion, and alienation of wildlife is a form of restoration. Land left alone restores itself. In the city, by comparison, land is too fragmented, subsurfaces too disturbed, and pedestrian traffic too intense for vacant spaces to be significantly self-reclaiming. Urban land abandonment speaks strongly of dereliction, but in the countryside it may not.

Even abandoned buildings in rural areas may carry different meanings from those in the city. In an urban setting, decay and abandonment creates more of the same, given the close proximity of properties. Dereliction spills over in the close interdependency of properties. Owners react to the actions (or inactions) of neighbors investing (or disinvesting) according to the perceived neighborhood change. In the countryside, space serves as a buffer where buildings stand relatively isolated. With diminished negative spillover, dereliction appears contained. Where land reverts to nature, abandoned structures appear to revert to nature also, in a kind of slow cleansing. Where vacant farmsteads stand in the wake of farm consolidation, they take the form of isolated relics easily romanticized (Figure 6.1). Old and abandoned farm buildings and equipment may strike harmless nostalgic poses in their decay. Derelict buildings in rural areas often communicate positively as ruins.

Buildings vacated in rural America speak of people who have fled to urban lives. Between 1920 and 1970, farmer net out-migration totaled 48.7 million. Between 1960 and 1970, alone, it dropped from 15.6 million to 8 million—nearly a 50-percent decline (Vogeler, 1981, p. 3). Between 1940 and 1970, 4.5 million blacks migrated to northern and western cities, the proportion of blacks living in metropolitan areas increasing from 27 percent

Figure 6.1   In areas of fertile soils, relic farmsteads speak of farm consolidation and related population loss.

to 74 percent between 1910 and 1970 (p. 80). Rural black land ownership in the United States declined by 330,000 acres per year from 1954 to 1969 (p. 80). In 1920, 75 percent of southern blacks lived in rural areas, with 57 percent on farms (Leistritz et al., 1986, p. 125). Thirty-five percent of southern farms were operated by blacks (ibid.). In 1980 only 13 percent of employed blacks in the United States lived in rural areas, and less than 1 percent were employed in agriculture (ibid.). By 1960 there were already 1 million blacks in New York City, some 890,000 in Chicago, 670,000 in Philadelphia, 560,000 in Detroit, and 335,000 in Los Angeles. By contrast, the largest southern concentrations were in Houston and Atlanta, with 215,000 and 186,000 blacks, respectively (Bell, 1978, p. 183).

In areas where abandoned agriculture land is widespread, out-migration has tended to leave a residual of poverty in its wake—poverty now several generations old in many places. In areas like the Adirondacks of Upstate New York, many farmers who had clung to subsistence-scale operations through World War II found their rundown farms next to worthless. Their skills proved equally useless in the urban economy already glutted by would-be workers looking for jobs. Cash reserves exhausted, men found themselves unable to supplement farm incomes by selling their labor locally. "Unable to get out of debt, unable to get out of farming, and unable to get money out of their farms, many families were locked into dead-end farming at subsistence levels or below" (Fitchen, 1984, p. 50). Poverty attracts poverty. Additional poor families are attracted by the cheap housing, low land values, and low taxes. Buildings consequently deteriorate, having value only as basic shelter capable of minimizing cash flow. Appearances are not important. Substandard, deteriorated housing is readily accepted if, through ownership, residential security is guaranteed for the foreseeable future. House upgrading is usually piecemeal, repairs and improvements made only infrequently when time, money, materials, and optimism coincide. Relatives and neighbors may help. Improvements may require years to complete or may never be completed, given economic constraints—giving to houses and yards a permanent makeshift look. Gerry-built houses and mobile homes may cluster on properties reflecting kinship and friendship tries. Stacks of weathered materials salvaged and hoarded may give properties a disordered appearance, especially to those whose sensibilities are formed in big-city suburbs. To the rural poor, however, such clutter symbolizes conservation within difficult times—the seizing of life's meager opportunities.

The legacy of severe poverty often breeds an acquisitive orientation to material items through a heightened quest to possess (Fitchen, 1984, p. 85). Acquisition becomes important to one's sense of security (Figure 6.2). The poor are often quick to buy cheap articles on impulse to satisfy whims.

Figure 6.2   Rural poverty often reflects in the accumulation of cast-off farm equipment, inoperable automobiles, and stacks of various materials hoarded against the uncertain future.

Much-desired items may be purchased, perhaps sacrificing needed house or other repairs. As sociologist Janet Fitchen observes, commodities—once owned—quickly lose their emotive value: "The promise of happiness remains unfulfilled—and the quest is on for something else, more, better" (ibid.). Consequently, among the poor, feelings of material deprivation often remain unassuaged—a nagging appetite never satiated. Women collect boxes of used clothing, stacks of magazines, discarded furniture. Men collect cars, car parts, appliances, hardware. Automobiles bought cheaply may quickly prove unusable; and thus, collecting standby cars inside yards is justified in terms of replacement parts. Car repair and sale may supplement incomes, and cars awaiting attention may be viewed as a kind of "bank account" (p. 99). Car repair provides men with a means of using and displaying skills, and car repairing in rural America is an important activity binding men together socially through reciprocal assistance. Cars rot slowly into hulks often buried in entanglements of nature's obscuring and healing vegetation.

In some U.S. regions, especially in Appalachia, slovenly habits of trash discard appear newly ubiquitous. Rooted in a highly mobile frontier culture with origins, perhaps, in a Celtic Europe of centuries past, rural people create midden piles out of dooryards. Cabins are surrounded by debris, including the shells of derelict cars casually thrown into ravines. Photographed in the mountains of Eastern Kentucky in the early 1970s is a roadside where chickens pick carefully through refuse discarded on the public way (Figure 6.3). The people of Appalachia took such habits with them to the nation's industrial cities. Widespread trashing suggests a minimal concern for maintenance and a substantial problem of community breakdown.

Joint efforts to rehabilitate houses and repair automobiles may be the only community initiatives that rural poverty areas enjoy. As farming declines and residents out-migrate, formal social, educational, and religious institutions evaporate. Rural neighborhoods cease to exist; post offices, telephone exchanges, school districts, and local governments fold. Such places no longer house people or provide services. "No longer is farming the common interest it once was, providing for daily and seasonal patterns of conversation and communal action. No longer is there an annual round of activities to give meaning and regularity to interaction. No longer are there public places and public activities for the entire community" (Fitchen, 1984, p. 45). Governmental and other functions are left to larger jurisdictions based at a further distance.

WASTING THE LAND

Property can be idled, farm buildings vacated, and communities abandoned and still the land abides. Only when the land itself is wasted can

Figure 6.3   In the past, trash disposed of along eastern Kentucky's public roads biodegraded. In the modern age of packaging, trash accumulates, threatening public health where localities are too poor to afford systematic cleanup.

dereliction truly be said to characterize a rural setting. Land can be returned to farming, new buildings constructed, and new communities established. But should the soil be wasted and made unfit, then society's options for reuse are substantially restricted. During the 1970s, erosion nationwide removed an estimated 5.3 billion tons of soil annually from privately owned farmland (Fletcher and Little, 1982, p. 88). On average, 4.7 tons of topsoil eroded from each cropped acre each year (ibid.). When land planted in grasses is subtracted, the average figure rises to 5.8 tons, substantially above the 5 tons per acre figure that the Department of Agriculture considers the rate of loss sustainable without threatening future productivity (ibid.). About one-third of all U.S. cropland is eroding at rates above the tolerance, with some 48 million acres—or some 10 percent of the total—losing as much as 14 tons per acre per year (ibid.) An estimated 225 million acres of land in the American West has undergone severe desertification due to lowered water tables, reduction of surface water, salinization, and/or severe soil erosion (p. 101). Overdraft of the Ogallala Aquifer that underlies much of Central Kansas, for example, is epidemic. The number of wells grew from 250 in 1950 to 2,850 in 1980; the aquifer, once 58 feet thick, is now less than 8 feet thick (Sheridan, 1981, p. 27).

Approximately 1.3 billion acres of land are held in private ownership in the United States today. Of that land, some 26.3 million acres or 2 percent is in residential use, owned by some 50 million people (Vogeler, 1981, p. 67). Some 40 million acres or 3 percent is used for commercial or industrial purposes, held by some 3 million owners (ibid.). That leaves some 1.2 billion acres in farmland, ranchland, and forestland, held by some 7.5 million entities, including individuals and corporations (ibid.). Across these various categories, some 3 percent of owners hold 95 percent of private land, or 55 percent of total acreage both private and public in the United States (Meyer, 1979, p. 49). Railroad, timber, and energy companies are major land and resource owners. Four railroads hold 23 million acres in surface and mineral rights, while the 12 largest timber companies control 35 million acres (Vogeler, 1981, p. 67). In the 1980s, oil companies controlled vast land holdings: Exxon some 40 million acres and Amoco some 28 million acres, for example (Meyer, 1979, p. 47). Only two federal agencies—the Bureau of Land Management and the U.S. Forest Service—control more land than Exxon (Vogeler, 1981, p. 67). Large coal corporations own vast tracts. Amax Coal Company owns over 100,000 acres of prime farmland in the cornbelt of Indiana and Illinois—land that in 1977 produced more than 13 million tons of meat (ibid.). In Appalachia, coal companies own 67 percent of the land in Logan County, West Virginia; 59 percent of the land in Harlan County, Kentucky; and 58 percent of the land in Wise County, Virginia (Subcommittee on Energy and the Environment, 1981, p. 110).

Mineral extraction—especially open pit and strip mining—can desolate an area and, indeed, a whole region like Appalachia (Figure 6.4). Until recently, the accepted practice was to mine accessible deposits cheaply with little regard for environmental and social costs. Spoils were left lying in ridges interspersed by brackish ponds and lakes. Through 1965, an estimated 3.2 million land acres had been affected in such a manner (Wali and Kollman, 1977, p. 111). By 1974, 20 of 25 states with strip mines had adopted reclamation laws, although most were imprecise in goals and standards. In Ohio, for example, reclamation meant "backfilling, grading, resoiling, planting, and other work to restore an area of land . . . so that it could be used for forest growth, grazing, agricultural, recreational or wildlife purpose, or some other useful purpose of equal or greater value" (LaFevers, 1977, p. 18). The Missouri law required that at least 75 percent of a stripped area be restored to a rolling topography suitable for farming (ibid.). By 1980, about 95 percent of the coal (or some 770 million tons mined by stripping) was covered by reclamation laws (Subcommittee on Energy and the Environment, 1981, p. 110).

The federal government has moved to clean up mine spoils. The Abandoned Mine Reclamation Fund, financed through fees collected from coal

Figure 6.4   Auger mining, as shown in 1972, had decimated the Walker Valley at the edge of Hazard, Kentucky. Valley walls have slumped, obscuring completely the floodplain.

mine operators, accumulated some $386 million through 1980 (Subcommittee on Energy and the Environment, 1981, p. 237). Even when land is restored to conditions approximating original configurations, it may take centuries to fully restore fertility. Crop yields from carefully restored ground approach only 70 percent of previous productivity (p. 167). Strip mining, in destroying agricultural resources, immediately displaces people and disrupts community infrastructures. Stripping destroys rural neighborhoods much as urban renewal destroys urban neighborhoods. Exploitation of land and human beings often goes hand in hand. Appalachians have proved powerless against coal company political power wielded in state legislatures. Ian Barbour (1980) writes that a society pursuing only affluence destroys human community and natural resources. "People find themselves alienated from nature and each other" (Barbour, p. 98).

DECLINING SMALL TOWNS

Rural economic changes have precipitated substantial population decline in America's rural villages and small towns. Art Gallaher and Harland

Padfield (1980, p. 11) see the dying small community as the secular phenomenon of the industrial age. Small settlements fade as containers for economic and population growth. Modern farm economy has reduced both farmer numbers and small-town support structures. Between 1979 and 1983, retail sales in Iowa declined 17 percent, substantially retrenching small-town main streets (p. 277). In 1984 alone, Iowa retailers suffered $38 million in sales losses, resulting in some 4,000 business closings (p. 277). During 1986 and 1987, one-third of 600 farm implement dealers in Iowa and Nebraska quit business (Robbins, 1988). In this process, lost small-place functions are frequently captured by larger places as retailers and wholesalers, enjoying economies of scale, assume the residual business of declining localities. Small-town businesses, once lost, tend not to be reestablished. Functions, once gone, tend to be gone forever (Figure 6.5).

The scale of integration necessary to forge community completeness is increasing everywhere. That is, the numbers of people, the organization mass, and the differentiations of functions and structures necessary to economic and political life are being raised to higher powers (Ford, 1978, p. 119). Localities, relatively autonomous at one time, are being absorbed more substantially into urban fields of influence. For example, small-town local institutions depend heavily on outside funding and direction that restricts local decision making. Indeed, the shift of economic power from local to

Figure 6.5   Small-town Main Streets all across the nation were in rapid eclipse in the 1980s, as in Upstate New York's New York Mills.

regional to national agencies has created a public affairs vacuum in many localities. Collective action through voluntary associations, for example, has become highly specialized and fragmented, and more expressive (related, for example, more to the needs of fellowship) than task oriented (Ford, 1978, p. 119). Economy in decline pretends community in eclipse. Agents of larger society may attack local problems vigorously, but with an emphasis on public relations rather than genuine citizen participation. Problems of distant bureaucracy undermine the sense of community. Whole categories of local institutions wither, in a loss or extinction of social forms that—like the loss of genetic forms in nature—tends to be permanent.

Naive small-town politics and a general condition of powerlessness have hampered local improvement efforts (Padfield, 1980, p. 161). Rural people tend to blame themselves for their problems rather than looking to the larger social system—especially the structuring of the American economy. Urban places, more occupationally and organizationally diverse, are more likely to enact substantive improvement schemes. Sparsely populated areas tend to lag behind, accepting the urban lead. Although farm and small-town geographical isolation has been reduced through the present decade, there still operates a kind of psychological isolation among rural people. "Similar television, radio, movie, magazine, and newspaper availability does not guarantee similar impact. Individuals can be selective—watching, listening to, and reading those materials that are most in keeping with their prior beliefs, and interests" (Willits, Bealer, and Crider, 1982, p. 73).

Farm and small-town life has traditionally promoted frontier-inspired values: the sanctity of private property, the importance of individualism, the belief in progress. As a foil for individualism, the belief in a stable and fixed rural society made it possible to emphasize near-anarchic individualism without risking destruction of social fabric (Robertson, 1980, p. 218). There is irony in all of this, for the small rural community has proved extremely vulnerable to the social and economic consequences of rural resource exploitation: exploitation championed by the intense valuing of private property, individualism, and progress. The small town appears destined to become a casualty of the very ideals and forces that created it (Padfield, 1980, p. 164).

When the local economy falters, small-town demographic makeup changes. Youthful wage earners seek employment elsewhere, especially in cities, leaving older populations in place. When median age of residents reaches approximately 35, deaths begin to exceed births and decline becomes as much a function of low birth rates as out-migration (Bertrand, 1980, p. 197). Often out-migration is matched by in-migration, but of a less educated and more disadvantaged population attracted to cheap housing. Like rural precincts where farmland is being abandoned, this new small town needs continued community services but is less able to pay. Poverty, emergent over time, soon drives out remaining wealth and people with high income potential. This impoverished population utilizes a declining physical infrastructure with little promise that decay will ever be reversed.

Farm consolidation also precipitates small-town decline in town. Walter Goldschmidt (1978), working for the Department of Agriculture, established in the 1940s a tie between the size of an area's farms and town viability. In a comparative analysis of two California farm towns—one dominated by big corporate farms and the other by small family farms—he established that the towns supported by small farms had twice as many business establishments. This town type did 61 percent more retail trade. Its small farms supported approximately 20 percent more people at measurably higher levels of living. In the small farm community, independent entrepreneurs comprised more than half of the population, as against less than one-fifth for the large farm place where nearly two-thirds were lowly paid farm laborers. Public facilities (streets, sidewalks, sewers, etc.) were more extensive and better maintained, and the small farm community had more institutions for democratic decision making and broader community citizen participation. One assumes, therefore, that as farm consolidation changes a town's economic base (as small farms give way to large), towns can be expected to diminish in social energy. It is the nineteenth-century populist warning that capitalist transformation of agriculture obliterates rural America's democratic and egalitarian promise (Vail, 1982, p. 28). Agribusiness proponents in Congress pressured Goldschmidt's superiors to suppress his research, eventually closing the Bureau of Economics that employed him. The bureau's mission, to examine the social consequences of industrial farming, was never resumed by the Department of Agriculture; and indeed, little social justice research of any kind was conducted by the agency until the 1970s.

On average, one small business forcibly closes every time a town's hinterland loses six farm families to farm consolidation (Vogeler, 1981, p. 252). Larger farms use fewer total inputs per unit of output, and tend to look to distant suppliers and market outlets to further economies of scale. Once a town's retail and wholesale businesses begin to decline, ripple effects tend to accelerate closures. Small-town businesses are highly interdependent. Should a farm town's grain elevator close, economic viability of the remaining businesses is weakened. Farmer traffic to town is reduced, and the trade at local cafes, hardware stores, and the like declines. Bank deposits fall and community bankers are less able to make business loans. Empty storefronts depress property values. Usually, the specialized professionals— especially dentists, doctors, and lawyers—are the first to leave. "They move to larger places or centralized clinics on the correct assumption that a regional clientele will seek them out" (Wilkinson, 1974, p. 46). Next the large dry-goods stores close along with sellers of expensive specialty items such as jewelry. Duplicate businesses are driven out by contracting customer competition. If there are two hardware stores, one may go under; if there are three groceries, one or two may close (ibid.). Car dealers, turning from selling to repairing autos, make cars available only on order. The range of goods and services and the inventories retained decline, undercutting the town's ability to compete with other places.

Loss of central place functions can decimate physical infrastructure, especially at a town's center. As demonstrated in a 1967 photograph, the town of Tuscola in East Central Illinois had a viable Main Street anchored at its principal intersection by a small hotel (Figure 6.6). The same intersection photographed in 1976 was a very different scene (Figure 6.7). Not only had Tuscola lost functions to Champaign–Urbana some 30 miles to the north, but most of its residual retail activity had relocated to a peripheral highway strip. The town's Main Street, once symbolizing the place, became a ghost of its former self. Tuscola's plight reflects a retrenching process that has affected most of America's small towns over the past few decades.

As railroad companies aggressively competed for control in the late nineteenth and early twentieth centuries, redundant small towns cropped up in many localities. The speculative promise of most places, however, went essentially unfulfilled (Hudson, 1985). The nation has been left with an

Figure 6.6   Main Street at Tuscola, Illinois, in 1967.

Figure 6.7   Tuscola's Main Street in 1976.

oversupply of towns—an excess now made especially acute by federal agricultural policies that promote farm consolidation in viable agricultural areas and land abandonment elsewhere. As Kenneth Wilkinson observes,

> The land and economy of the United States will not support as many small towns as they did before. It is very difficult not to see the future as a long drawn-out struggle for community survival, lasting for half a century, in which some battles may be won but the war will be lost. A future in which most such towns will become isolated or decayed, in which local amenities must deteriorate, and in which there will finally be left only the aged, the inept, the very young—and the local power elite. (Wilkinson, 1974, p. 39)

Few towns respond well to decline. Most choose not to plan for orderly transition, and only accept their plight with resignation. Railroads found it easy to stake out new grids of streets and start up at 4- to 5-mile intervals towns where only vacant space had been. But it is very difficult to end a town where land is owned, structures are real, and vested interests both private and public are intensely competitive in circumstances of shrinking wealth. It is far easier to despoil towns by allowing decline to wreak havoc beyond cooperative channels of control.

Most rural communities are at an old growth stage. Marion Clawson writes, "Like old persons approaching the end of life, such communities may best simply enjoy such life as they have, relaxing in the pleasure of their existence while it lasts, and accepting the future as inevitable" (1980, p. 79). Disengagement theory posits a need for mutual and synchronized disengagement between individuals and society—a necessary prelude to and a kind of preparation for death (Wylie, 1980, p. 239; Cumming and Willing, 1961). Withdrawal is an intrinsic developmental stage often desired by the elderly. In this regard, declining villages and small towns may provide compatible environments for growing old. The desired withdrawal of old age may be enhanced in an environment that is itself withdrawing from society. "Continuity may be more easily achieved in a familiar environment, an environment in which one's roots run very deeply and which itself is besieged with terminal decline" (Wylie, 1980, p. 240).

Not all towns need die. Some larger towns, especially county political seats—continue to absorb the functions of smaller nearby places. Towns near large cities thrive as suburban or exurban homes for commuters. Some towns may succeed at attracting tourists or second-home owners. For some places, industry may stimulate growth. New industries usually locate in large, sophisticated urban centers where work skills, risk capital, and esoteric technical supports are readily found. With time, production processes become standardized as larger scales of production are reached to serve expanding markets. Aging industry slides down its "learning curve" toward lower skill requirements as new machines more fully automate work. Mature industries thus seek (indeed, are forced to seek) cheap labor markets. For American firms, cheap labor may be had overseas, and it may be had in nonmetropolitan America. But highly routinized factory work may prove a mixed blessing for small towns. Wilbur Thompson (1977) asks why small towns attract slow-growing and poorly paying industries. "Small places find that they must run to stand still, as their industrial catches seem to come to these out-of-the-way places only to die" (p. 95). Manufacturing jobs represented 50 percent of all nonmetropolitan employment growth in the 1960s as corporations sought out a "low-wage, underemployed, rural and heavily female labor force with 'better' work attitudes (less affected by unionization, less demanding about working conditions, and more willing to take dead end jobs without pension and health benefits)" (Tabb, 1984, p. 13).

DECLINING ROADS AND RAILROADS

Rural America is burdened with a deteriorating transportation infrastructure. Interstate highway construction consumed most of the nation's fiscal and technological resources for road building in the 1960s, 1970s, and 1980s. Rural roads were generally ignored under federal guidelines that made one-third of the nation's rural roads ineligible for federal subsidy. Rural governments, moreover, found themselves with shrinking tax bases amid declining populations and large numbers economically dependent (the aged, the juvenile, and the uneducated). Across much of rural America in the 1980s, oiled or other hard-surfaced roads reverted to gravel or dirt. Closed bridges precipitated road closings and disrupted well-integrated road networks. In the 1980s, 9 percent of U.S. rural bridges collapsed, 29 percent were structurally deficient, 24 percent posted against excessive weight, and 38 percent were functionally obsolete (Kaye, 1982, p. 157). Seventy-five percent of U.S. rural collector routes were found to be in fair or poor condition (Chicoine, 1986, p. 145). Operating costs of autos on such low-quality aggregate roads, compared to hard-surfaced roads, have been estimated at an additional seven cents per mile (p. 146).

Local highway authorities have had difficulty maintaining infrequently traveled roads. Some 71 percent of total rural U.S. mileage carries only 13 percent of rural traffic (Chicoine, 1986, p. 144). Roads must be maintained to accommodate farm trucks and school buses, the latter necessitated by the nearly universal consolidation of rural schools. Roads are vital to long-distance nonfarm commuting in towns and cities. To maintain roads, rural governments must either raise taxes, reduce maintenance, or abandon bridges and rights-of-way; and accordingly, most rural highway authorities have chosen retrenchment, facilitating a cumulative process of stagnation and decay. Not only are America's rural roads deteriorating, but public road transport is declining as well. Even before the Reagan administration collapsed rural transportation links by deregulating intercity bus service, only 40 percent of towns between 2,500 and 10,000 in population (and only 15 percent of those under 2,500) enjoyed scheduled bus connection (Kaye, 1982, p. 157).

Rural road deterioration and the accompanying rise of rural inaccessibility has been greatly exaggerated by the simultaneous dismantling of the nation's railroads. Certainly, America's railroads were substantially overextended, precipitating the development of superfluous towns. Some 6,000 separate railroad corporations built lines after 1840 in an uncoordinated drive to profit. Most railroads were constructed not to produce transportation efficiency so much as to generate profits from the financial manipulation of stocks and bonds. By the 1960s some 500 separate railroads survived, although the great bulk of the nation's rail mileage was concentrated in the hands of some two dozen companies.

During the 1970s the rate of return on the investments of class-I railroads averaged only 2.8 percent (MacAvoy and Snow, 1977, p. 3). Profits from railroading have long been depressed—a function of strict government regulation of freight rates, high rates of taxation, archaic work rules built into union contracts, and competition from other transportation modes variously subsidized by the federal government. With very low rates of return, disinvestment of physical plant and diversion of assets into other businesses has long characterized the railroad industry. Consequently, much of the railroad infrastructure of the United States is outmoded and inefficient, further reducing the railroad industry's competitive stance. The rail share of intercity freight ton-miles fell from 54 percent in 1947 to 35 percent in 1970. Trucks, on the other hand, increased their share from 5 percent to 16 percent, and pipelines from 10 percent to 22 percent (p. 14).

Disinvestment creates a predictable sequence of events leading to abandonment. Deferred maintenance brings reduced service frequency and constraints on high-speed use. Severe damage to connecting bridges via floods or storms may catalyze desires to cease operations. When scrap value of lines prove higher than costs of rehabilitation, abandonment is economically justified. Between 1916 and 1969 the Interstate Commerce Commission (ICC) authorized the abandonment of 56,805 miles of track (Allen, 1974, p. 5). During the 1970s, abandonment accelerated. Just under one-half of U.S. trackage was unfit for high-speed operation, with the typical freight car filled to capacity for only 23 days a year (MacAvoy and Snow, 1977, p. 64). By decade end, deferred maintenance stood at an estimated $7.5 billion (p. 65).

In transporting people, one railroad car can do the work of 50 automobiles. Railroads also consume one-sixth the energy of trucks in transporting freight (Parenti, 1983, p. 124). And yet the federal government continues to subsidize highway transportation while neglecting railroads. Congress put $118 billion into transportation between 1946 and 1973 without any of it going to the railroads (Runke and Finder, 1977, p. 34). Proposals to abandon trackage are generally met with public apathy even though, for small towns, rail abandonment usually means higher transportation costs (Allen, 1974, p. 143). Community goods formerly supplied by rail may increase in price, and jobs may be lost as employers curtail operations due to rising expenses. Towns may encounter difficulties in attracting employers—especially manufacturers—without real connectivity. Rail abandonment changes road use by trucks, increasing road wear and inflating highway repair costs.

The Interstate Commerce Commission established in 1972 the "thirty-four car rule," which has become a principal standard for determining rail line viability. A line on which annually less than 31 carloads are originated or terminated per mile of line is presumed unprofitable (U.S. Department of Transportation, 1976, p. 97). The ICC shifted such burden of proof required from the railroad to abandonment protesters. Railroads desirous of abandoning lines can discourage, and do discourage, patronage that reduces traffic below the 34-car minimum. For example, railroads may refuse to service trackside customers who fail to generate more than a minimum number of carloadings or terminations per week. By eliminating low traffic branches or feeder lines, traffic is reduced on trunk lines as well—which leads to abandonment. Whole railroad systems have been disemboweled in order that holding companies might transfer assets and operating capital into more lucrative enterprises beyond transportation. Increased small-town isolation has been part of the social cost paid.

SENSE OF COMMUNITY AND RURAL VIABILITY

The Agriculture Act of 1970 and the Rural Development Act of 1972 promised a revitalized rural America (Beckman, 1977, p. 55). The former directed executive agencies to locate and maintain new federal offices and facilities in sparsely populated areas. The latter declared Congress's intention to promote "a sound balance between rural and urban America" by creating new aid programs that would produce new rural jobs. Traditional commodity price stabilization and other federal farm policies, helping to consolidate farmsteads, has had little effect on blunting rural decline. This process continues to be endemic to rural America. Farmers and small-towners have lost political influence with declining numbers—a fate sealed by the reapportionment of Congress and the state legislatures in the 1960s. For example, 81 small towns in Connecticut had 43 percent of the seats in the state's lower house before 1965, and 14 percent after (Ladd, 1969, p. 84). Thus rural people have lost the power to reverse negative federal and state policies and to pass new beneficial legislation even when they agree as to what that legislation should be.

Federal neglect of the small town has helped engender rural decline. Tax policies favor large landowners and wealthy investors. Technology—much of it created by federally subsidized research and development activity—serves principally larger producers. Critics argue that national gains from farm concentration have reached a point of diminishing return. Most of the economies derived from size can be achieved on small farms, they maintain. Wendell Fletcher and Charles Little (1982, p. 60) argue that a 175-acre wheat–barley farm in the Northern Plains returns 90 percent of the economies of a 1,475-acre farm. Ingolf Vogeler (1981, p. 100) argues that large farms only appear efficient because capital-intensive mechanization replaces labor, which makes for higher worker yields. They are efficient at making profits, largely by disregarding social and environmental production costs. Once economies of size are reached, however, large-scale farmers are no more efficient in terms of input cost per unit output. Small-scale farmers are, indeed, more efficient because they have higher yields per acre with their labor-intensive methods. By not displacing as much labor with machines, family farmers provide greater employment opportunities. "Collectively, they allocate societal resources more rationally than large-scale producers" (Vogeler, 1981, p. 100).

A slightly "inefficient" agricultural sector, in a technical sense, may achieve higher social justice and increase overall economic "efficiency." That is, fewer people will be on welfare in cities. Fewer Americans, suffering unemployment, will reduce the extremes of affluence and poverty. Federal policy changes could reorient the nation from the community-killing agriculture of the past to a community nurturing agriculture. As Wendell Berry writes, "The standard of the exploiter is efficiency, the standard of the nurturer is care. The exploiter's goal is money, profit; the nurturer's goal is health—his land's health, his own, his family's, his community's, and his country's" (1977, p. 7). Suggested changes to federal farm policy include the following: revising income tax laws that presently favor tax-loss farming and absentee ownership; restricting corporate or foreign ownership of farmland; modifying federal price support payments to remove the advantages accruing to large-scale operations; and assisting farmers on small farms to achieve economies of scale through cooperatives (Larson, 1981, p. 175).

Public debate on rural issues has been submerged by the big business interests and big government that propel the nation ever onward toward increased urbanization. Wendell Berry asks us to consider what happens when farm people are forced to take up off-farm work, or move to the city.

> The immediate result is that they must be replaced by chemicals and machines and other purchases from an economy adverse and antipathetic to farming. This means that the remaining farmers are put under yet greater pressure to abuse the land. If under the pressure of an adverse economy, the soil erodes, soil and water and air are poisoned, the woodlands are wastefully logged, and everything not producing an immediate economic return is neglected, that is apparently understood by most of the society as merely the normal cost of most kinds of production. (Berry, 1988)

Rural America is seen by most Americans as expendable, having value only as a labor and raw-materials exporter.

Two small-town types seem to be thriving in the 1990s. First, as already mentioned, there are the small places near cities that function more like suburbs, a large proportion of their residents commuting to nearby employment nodes. Second, there are those rural communities embodying cultural systems that override the capitalist impulse to value only profits. In central Illinois, where the authors presently live, one can drive through neighboring towns that are similarly advantaged geographically but very unalike in evident prosperity. Both have been established at similar times; both enjoy the same railroad and highway connections; both are rooted in the same farm economy; both will have the same soil and other environmental resources. And yet, one place will be alive and growing while the other is dormant. In the growth place, the traditional range of central place functions will be thriving: a cafe, supermarket, soft-goods or other specialty stores, a newspaper, a bank, and the full range of automobile and farm implement dealers all locally owned. The dormant place will be but a shell of its former self, with a marginal convenience store, a grain elevator, and perhaps a funeral home, probably all owned by outsiders. In the former place, maintenance levels are high and a sense of orderliness prevails.

Differences in orderliness can be observed in neighboring towns all across the Middle West. Borrowing the concept of the "covenanted" community from historian Page Smith (1966, p. vii), rural sociologist Sonya Salamon (1985, p. 325) finds the variances in local prosperity to be linked to cultural factors—especially ethnic identity as embodied in inheritance patterns, family goals, and church affiliation. *Covenanted towns* are based on a relatively homogeneous ethnic group built around one or more strong, communally-organized church congregation. In east central Illinois, it is the German-, Dutch-, and Scandinavian-based Catholic, Lutheran, and Reformed churches that provide the social glue. People are willing to make economic sacrifices in order to perpetuate the traditional order of family, church, and town. *Cumulative towns* merely grow and decline through the accretion and loss of individuals or individual families impelled solely by economic motives. People value little the institutions of community there.

In the rural midwestern covenanted communities, there abides a strong tradition of family farming. Land is to be passed across generations. In cumulative towns, on the other hand, land is treated more as investment to be bought and sold, each generation left on its own to rise or fall in farming. Around covenanted towns, the farms tend to be small and operator owned. Around cumulative towns, the farms tend to be large but absentee owned. Whereas farm families in the covenanted communities support their towns (even when prices are more favorable in cities at a distance), families in cumulative places orient their business wherever short-run advantage may be had. They owe little loyalty to local merchants. Cumulative towns are dying today because individual priorities have not included social investment in community preservation.

Such observations reinforce A.B. Hollingshead's (1937, p. 180) earliest conclusions. In studying rural Nebraska churches established on the nineteenth-century frontier, he found some 70 percent of the congregations organized by more individualistic denominations—like the Baptists, Methodists, and Presbyterians—to have been dissolved, but only 15 percent of the Evangelical, Lutheran, or Roman Catholic churches (p. 190). The latter churches functioned as community integrators. They tended to stabilize various European immigrant colonies of landholding farmers, whose farms tended to pass across generations. Americans moving westward from the East and the South, on the other hand, casually formed and dissolved churches as they casually bought and sold farms, having approached the frontier as individuals and joined religious congregations compatible with individualism. Independence meant freedom to move and abandon enterprises (Rohrer and Quantic, 1980, p. 150).

In covenanted communities, change is resisted by the local social fabric. There is a basic commitment to sustain farms and family-owned land (Salamon, 1985, p. 325). Each generation replicates the tenure ladder, with children climbing upward by utilizing parental sponsorship and support (Rogers and Salamon, 1983, p. 529). Children not continuing in farming may be supported in town businesses. In cumulative communities, change is openly embraced, with farming approached primarily as a business enterprise and land viewed primarily as an investment. Operations are run unsentimentally for profit.

In the covenanted communities, rural Americans are now discovering that smallness pays. Smallness works when reinforced by *gemeinschaft*, the society of close personal connections (Furay, 1977, p. 59). By holding land in usufruct for future generations, farmers of covenanted communities have struck on a means of enriching themselves far beyond the pecuniary rewards of the marketplace. They have surrounded themselves with stable physical and social environments. They have proved that the small community need not die or live solely by the grace of nearby big cities.

Many commentators promote a kind of "U.S. rural triage" that advocates the neglect of declining small towns (Daniels and Lapping, 1987, p. 275). Developmental effort should be focused, they argue, on places expected to function as growth poles, where infrastructural economies of scale, agglomeration economies in a diversity of labor markets, and diffusion outward of economic benefits to peripheral areas might be obtained. It is clear that the U.S. rural triage is occurring independent of such policy efforts being used. Rural America is undergoing vast change precipitated primarily by agricultural concentration. Only those places readily drawn into urban commuter fields or sustained as covenanted communities are alive and thriving. Elsewhere one finds increasing isolation, increasing land degradation, and increasing poverty among declining populations. Rural America—the traditional guardian of such values as individualism, independence, and progress—is falling victim to her own ideals. Rural America's decline has contributed directly to problems elsewhere, especially in the nation's central cities. Unable to thrive on farms and in small towns, tens of millions of rural people have fled to the cities undereducated, underskilled, and otherwise poorly prepared, especially in the emergent postindustrial order. The rapidly growing urban underclass is one result. As a society we should have asked ourselves whether such a transformation was indeed necessary. Has it proved desirable? As the nation's agricultural resources dwindle under the strain of modern farming, and as rural communities evaporate through related population loss, cities struggle under other burdens directly imposed—for example, the operation of the dual housing market with the flight of affluent classes to suburbia. Like dominoes toppling, the changes in rural America rumble through the system.

7

Renaissance?

The forces of land development, driven by revolutions in transportation and communication, have wrought substantial reorganization of America's geography over the past half-century. In this remaking of America, substantial economic imbalance and social inequality have been introduced, bringing along widespread landscape dereliction. The continued pyramiding of wealth and power, accelerated population sorting by economic class and social status, and quickened land and other resource wastefulness are important dimensions of what may yet lead to U.S. political crisis. America's industrial cities have been growing old. Poor people—especially poor blacks—have concentrated in areas of physical decay where unemployment and underemployment offer little hope of improvement. Suburbs wastefully consume space, spiraling land prices upward to isolate further the most affluent from the least affluent. In the suburbs, Americans are spacing themselves farther and farther apart, with fewer occupants per housing unit, fewer housing units per acre, and greater distances between developed areas (Herbers, 1986, p. 159). Well beyond the new suburbs, much of rural and small-town America languishes in states of decay. While Americans have been under-utilizing and abandoning the old, they have been creating a new nation with extravagant investment and maintenance requirements per capita.

Policies are needed at the national, state, and local levels that would stabilize declining areas, while at the same time positively addressing growth issues. The nation must learn to anticipate and manage the changes wrought by its relatively free market economy. In past decades, the agents of development in the United States have pushed to consolidate power. They have increasingly removed their decision making from popular influence. Businessmen, politicians, and planners, congeal around projects "co-opting agreeable representatives of public opinion, outmaneuvering attempts at

223

organized opposition, fragmenting criticisms and overwhelming it with expert knowledge" (Marris, 1974, p. 156). Certainly, change must be expected and even encouraged. But should not the change process respect the viewpoints of diverse agendas? Should not managers reconcile diverse social objectives such that the best of the past merges with the best that innovation offers? The search for adequate means of managing urban decline remains a tortuous one. Some signs of renaissance, however, may offer encouragement.

ENCOURAGING ECONOMIC GROWTH

Much governmental response to change in the 1960s and 1970s, especially at the federal level, promoted economic inefficiency by way of adjustment. Free-market capitalism had offered a practical means for an underpopulated nineteenth-century nation to develop rapidly its abundant resources. But in a mature twentieth-century economy where physical resources were substantially committed—some irreversibly so—the nation had begun to stretch the economic carrying capacity of its resource base. Most Americans had come to live affluent lives, no longer concerned with obtaining essential comforts. The U.S. agenda had become one of protecting its advantages. Government spending and regulation and corporate oligopolistic practice led to a national economy volatile and insecure in a world of increasing interdependence. As Russel Barsch and Jeffrey Gale (1982, p. 55) observe, risk had become an enemy rather than an opportunity in the new international reality. As government used its resources to insure industries, firms, cities, and regions against economic failure—insulating them from market forces—inefficiencies were introduced. Market discipline—risk of failure—no longer operated to stimulate innovation as industries externalized their technological disadvantages. As inefficiencies accumulated,increased public investment was required to prevent widespread job loss and unemployment (ibid.). Ultimately, inefficiencies overwhelmed many industries and areas, and plant closings resulted.

A healthy economy requires governmental involvement not to insure firms and places against risk, but to stimulate risk taking. Private initiatives carry social costs requiring governmental oversight and regulation. Profit pursuits and the pursuit of optimum social value do not necessarily coincide. To producers, the important activities are the profitable ones, and activities that cannot be assigned profit implication are often neglected. Social costs generated go unassigned, with government necessarily intervening to ameliorate the neglect. Capitalist initiative responds to market demand; and if demand is insufficient within a locality to bring about balanced development, then entrepreneurs will tend to set up export activities. Areas, instead of being raised to new richer internal equilibriums, are further weakened by having new elements of imbalance grafted onto already out-of-date structures. "Agriculture, instead of being made healthier and richer, will be ruined by the exodus of manpower and the land will be abandoned; the local industries, instead of being diversified in terms of local needs, undergo specialization and impoverishment; local or regional autonomy, instead of being reinforced, will be diminished even more" (Gorz, 1970, p. 39). Again, government necessarily intervenes to ameliorate the imbalance.

Local communities have sought to promote community welfare through economic growth. Cities and towns have subsidized firms through programs like low-interest loans, tax increment financing, property tax abatements, and low utility rates. Communities commonly assemble and clear land, construct buildings for lease, improve roads, and enhance public infrastructure. "Enterprise zones"—a development device designed to stimulate economic activity in declining areas—won widespread popularity in the 1980s. As originally conceived by geographer Peter Hall, enterprise zones were to be freed of many locally imposed taxes, zoning restrictions, and other regulations. Federal and state governments were also to provide major job-creation incentives, including reduction in social security payroll taxes on employees, reduction in capital gains tax rates, accelerated depreciation on assets, and subminimum wage rates for young workers (Gold, 1982, p. 2; Pasquariello, Shriver, and Geyer, 1982, p. 72).

Housing development has also been stimulated to promote community welfare. This development purportedly generates a range of economic multipliers, including enhancing tax ratables, expanding retailing facilities, and replenishing the construction industry. Housing quality, moreover, structures an area's socioeconomic composition and labor force characteristics that attract certain industrial types. Consequently, industrialists are often given preference for new land tracts—ones that will provide both jobs and shoulder a large local tax burden. They are perceived as the cure for many local ills, and attracting them tends to preoccupy most municipalities. Where inducement programs are deficient relative to nearby municipal offerings, revision is believed crucial to community well-being.

With depleted resources, city governments have had to be increasingly imaginative. Declining revenues have necessitated search for programs that minimize direct expenditures. Moreover, cities often have severe constraints built into their charters, curtailing options that are often perceived as desirable. Detroit, for example, is limited in its possibilities for conducting money-generating enterprises. The Michigan state constitution prevents municipal ownership of private stock or from establishing city-owned banks. The constitution limits the role of public credit, and restricts the kinds of taxes that can be collected. Industrial land assemblage—for example the leveling of Detroit's Poletown for a new General Motors plant—required innovative public–private sector relationships. Detroit's felt need was to employ skilled and semiskilled workers at or near their accustomed wage, taking advantage of the area's metalworking technology concentration. In the early 1980s, while private interests held several smaller tracts between 15 and 40 acres in size, the city controlled only one industrial site as large as 60 acres—a meager land base on which to rebuild a ravaged city economy (Luria and Russell, 1984, p. 276).

Besides assembling building sites, Detroit and other cities have offered corporations low-interest bonds to construct industrial facilities. Bonds for commercial projects rose sharply from $6.2 billion in 1975 to $44 billion in 1982 (Logan and Molotch, 1987, p. 177). Since development bonds are tax exempt, the federal treasury is the real subsidy source. Federal tax loss stood in 1983 at an estimated $7.4 billion (ibid.). In some instances, plants are placed under ownership of quasi-governmental, nonprofit organizations in order to spare corporate occupants local property taxes as well. However, bonds generally are designed to be retired through property tax increases anticipated as a result of new development. Tax increment redevelopment may be the most significant economic growth initiative pursued by central city governments in recent decades. Since new capitalization ultimately pays for itself in higher property tax revenues, cities have been encouraged to use part of this anticipated tax "increment" to fund revitalization in advance.

City governments often spend their energies chasing large industries, even though these types of employers usually perpetuate low-skill and low-wage conditions. Large national and international corporations tend not to put roots down in communities. As Randolph Langenbach writes, "What is needed are jobs with a future, jobs with which the employee can achieve an identity. To be worthy of enticement to a particular city, industries must offer a chance for career advancement and some prospect for permanence. To realize this goal, cities should encourage not merely the relocation of large, already established industries, but the founding of small new businesses" (1977, p. 7). Inexpensive industrial floor space within former factories and mills is one kind of resource that old industrial cities can use to such end. Such space usually requires little capital outlay to be made productive, and usually allows for easy expansion. As Jane Jacobs (1961) was arguing even in the 1960s, new ideas—no matter how profitable they may ultimately be—cannot withstand the chancy trial of error and experimentation in the high-overhead economy of new construction. "Old ideas can sometimes use new buildings. New ideas must use old buildings" (p. 188).

Economist David Birch (1979) points to the benefits of small enterprises in promoting economic development. Birch argues that economic growth is fueled by new business formation. Study of business growth in selected localities shows that firms with less than 20 employees generate as much as two-thirds of all new jobs, and that small independent firms create slightly more than half of new jobs added (p. 36). Risks in starting new businesses are great. In 1983, some 600,000 new U.S. enterprises were incorporated, 30 percent never to open and 70 percent to fail within five years. Nonetheless, over the three years, 1980–82, new small companies generated 2.7 million jobs at a time when large established firms were shedding 1.7 million workers (Davidson and Pryde, 1982, p. 96).

The sort of city growth that smallness suggests not only coexists with central city neighborhood revitalization, but in many ways depends on it (Schwartz, 1982, p. 272). Small businesses need entrepreneurial skills that community organizations can cultivate in its members. Neighborhoods, in turn, help shape the work attitudes that employees bring to a job. Social conditions surrounding a workplace affect property values and the willingness of lenders to provide capital to businesses. Through the 1960s and 1970s, government programs to foster economic development in central cities did not pay adequate attention to such total growth environments. Transfer payments were made to the poor on terms that weakened further the frail family and social fabrics of central city communities. Schools and training programs taught skills needed by large manufacturers and not the skills and sense of social responsibility needed by struggling small-scale entrepreneurs. Programs have ignored the development of human capital for locally controlled development and long-run growth.

Central City Revitalization: An Overview

Stabilization of social and physical infrastructures is a requisite step in stimulating economic recovery in central cities. Until recently, most residential real estate markets have tended to cycle only once, with real estate interests creating, maintaining, but eventually discarding residential assets. This process has changed with the recent rise of gentrification. By 1975, nearly three-quarters of the nation's urban places of more than half a million people had experienced private housing renovation at the neighborhood scale. Taking all cities above 50,000 population, nearly half reported such activity, affecting an estimated 55,000 renovated housing units (Black, 1975, pp. 3 and 7). By 1979, 86 percent of all cities with more than 50,000 people had revitalizing neighborhoods (Black, 1980, p. 8).

Neighborhoods appear to rebound in at least three stages (see Gale, 1980, p. 95; Schill and Nathan, 1983, p. 29). Stage one involves an influx of "risk-oblivious" households. They are young, relatively affluent single persons or childless couples who purchase homes amid neighborhood decline. Many may be homosexual or interracial couples who seek places of social diversity and social acceptance. They "conquer" turf to impose their values on place. Often, these "pioneers" are members of the artistic and design professions and, accordingly, have an eye for and an appreciation for outdated but once architecturally fashionable housing. They overlook "the obvious risks to their person, their property and their pocketbooks" (Gale, 1980, p. 105). First-stage movers mix readily with nearby low-income populations, forging mutual respect based on nonconformist behavior. Geographer Roman Cybriwsky (1978, p. 18) terms such places "urban villages."

Stage two attracts "risk-prone" buyers. Local newspaper, magazine, and media discovery of an area facilitates realtor and speculator interest. Exchange value (what a property is worth on the real estate market) looms as important as use value (the satisfactions that a property generates), as an area is increasingly eyed through lenses of potential profitability. A second wave of householders, aware of the risks in buying and occupying older property, nevertheless accept these risks in the face of low property prices and the high equity growth potential (Gale, 1980, p. 105). These are people attracted by neighborhood proximity to work—especially downtown office jobs—and nearby amenities, like panoramic downtown or waterfront views and cultural districts. Many residents invest "sweat equity" as well as capital by doing much of the property refurbishing themselves. Second-stage movers less easily assimilate into neighborhoods. They learn to ignore or adjust to discontented neighbors amid increased resentment over increasing property taxes and rents resulting from upgrading. Most risk-prone resettlers are from other cities or neighborhoods and are not part of a reverse suburban migration. Many are previous renters and, through renovation, buy their first home. Some intend to be long-term residents, but others see their investments as speculative, intending to sell property at inflated prices. Cybriwsky (1978, p. 18) terms second-stage areas "defended neighborhoods."

Stage three attracts "risk-averse" buyers. With renovation rapidly accelerating, neighborhoods come to enjoy a thoroughly middle-class identity. Cautious households, previously fearful of investing, now replace many early pioneers. Professionals, corporate managers, and empty-nester older couples increasingly enter the neighborhood. More are from the suburbs since housing can now be purchased with conventional mortgages. More residents, considering themselves permanent, show interest in supporting community organizations. Many organizations promote the locality as a physically distinctive place. Residents advocate historic or landmark district status as a means of protecting local ambiance. They actively lobby for better police and fire protection, street and sidewalk improvements, and other public facilities. The new community interest hinges on enhancing property values. The place has "gentrified." It is, in Cybriwsky's words "a fashionable inner-city district" (1978, p. 18).

Scholars link housing supply, house prices, and gentrification in explaining intercity differences in neighborhood revitalization. Geographer Brian Berry (1980, p. 20) starts from the premise that replacement housing units (a product of the relationship between rate of new housing construction and rate of household growth) is critical in understanding rates of local housing abandonment and rehabilitation. In the mid-1970s, massive rehabilitation coincided with declines in new house construction, and a related rapid rate of house price inflation. It was in those cities where rates of replacement supply were least that revitalization made greatest impacts, especially in neighborhoods where professional or managerial jobs located close by supported large numbers of young college-educated singles. Decreasing availability of suburban land for development, inflating suburban housing costs, rising transportation costs, and increased commuting time are seen as having subsequently inclined more Americans toward central city residences in the 1980s (London, 1980, p. 84). Anthony Downs (1981, p. 66) lists the factors underlying central city revitalization, first by metropolitan context (Table 7.1) and then by neighborhood context (Table 7.2).

Clearly, changing demographics are driving the revitalization of U.S. central cities. For one thing, household numbers competing for housing have grown. Between the mid-1950s and the mid-1980s, household numbers in the nation have more than doubled amid a population increase of less than one-quarter (Schill and Nathan, 1983, p. 17). Between 1960 and 1980, single-person households jumped from 13 percent to 23 percent of total (ibid.). Young people were moving away from home and marrying later. A soaring divorce rate was breaking up households, and the number of widowers and widows living alone was increasing with longer life expectancies (Schill and Nathan, 1983, p. 18). In 1960, 38 percent of women over 16 years old held jobs; this percentage increased to 52 percent by 1980 (ibid.). Childless couples had fewer reasons to avoid city life. Between 1970 and 1977, one- and two-person urban households increased 19 percent while all other households decreased 4 percent (Downs, 1981, p. 77). Small gentry households tended to be relatively affluent, employed in white-collar jobs lodged in central business district service, information processing, and management activities.

The energy crisis of the 1970s modified American living styles that further induced gentrification. Between 1973 and 1975, purchasing power of the dollar shrank nearly 20 percent, the volume of household savings and other wealth declining some 12 percent and household debts rising more than 18 percent (Gappert, 1979, p. 46). Many Americans began to see inexpensive inner-city housing in a new light. Americans increasingly rec-

Table 7.1   City and Metropolitan Factors Underlying Revitalization

Factor	Operation
Demand Side	
Strong downtown business district with growing employment	Creates demand for housing close to downtown jobs
Rising real incomes	Increase households' ability to rehabilitate housing
Formation of many small, childless households	Increases households that need less space, are oriented to urban amenities, and do not need public schools
Rapid in-migration of households	Increases demand for good-quality housing
No in-migration of poor households	Permits older neighborhoods to stabilize
Supply Side	
Long commuting times to downtown business district	Make living near downtown more desirable
Strong restrictions on suburban development	Limit suburban housing and jobs, enhancing city housing and jobs
Rapid increases in prices of suburban housing	Make city housing more attractive
Loose housing market	Enables poor households displaced by revitalization to find adequate housing, possibly reducing resistance to revitalization
Uncontrolled rents	Encourage property maintenance and investment in new rental units
Easy condominium conversion	Increases owner occupancy

Source: Downs, 1981, p. 66.

Table 7.2   Neighborhood Factors Underlying Revitalization

Factor	Operation
Demand Side	
Proximity to amenity such as lakefront, ocean-front, park, or downtown	Enhances long-term value
Good public transportation	Enhances convenience, especially for households with more than one worker
Access to high-quality public or private schools	Enhances attractiveness to households with school-age children
No nearby public housing with school-age children who would dominate the public schools	Enhances attractiveness to households with school-age children and incomes high enough to support renovation
Perception of community as safe	Enhances attractiveness as place to live
Proximity to revitalized neighborhoods	Creates expectations that revitalization will work here as well
Supply Side	
Single-family housing	Simpler to rehabilitate than multi-family housing, fewer management problems
Housing with interesting architec-tural features such as high ceilings, fireplaces, carved woodwork	Attractive to young households, which are most likely to rehabilitate
Brick housing	Easier to rehabilitate than frame housing, easier to care for, lasts longer
Multifamily housing suitable for condominium ownership	Owner-occupied property better maintained and residency more stable than rented property
Financial institution willing to provide mortgages and home-ownership loans	Makes ownership and rehabilitation easier
Commitment by local government to upgrade infrastructure and public services	Reassures private investors of long-term value of homes
Strong neighborhood organization dominated by homeowners	Creates pressure on local government to enforce housing codes and improve public services
Housing and other structures in relatively good condition	Encourages private investment by owners and lenders

Source: Downs, 1981, p. 76.

ognized old buildings as potentially more energy efficient and longer lived than new "ticky-tacky" creations. Most older houses use shutters, blinds, curtains, draperies, and awnings to reduce summer heat gain. Terrace or row houses in older northern urban districts share walls that minimize heating and cooling costs. Variously, the old house is proving to be more energy affordable. Heating oil in 1981 cost eight times what it had a decade earlier; natural gas had quintupled in price (Goetze, 1983, p. 71).

Revitalization has emerged because clever entrepreneurs have been able to profit from meeting new housing demands. One unanticipated benefit has resulted: reuse of existing structures has conserved land, raw materials, and energy. These are resources that the nation has found to be in finite supply. Every building represents a resource stockpile. Cities contain extensive infrastructures of buildings, pipes, reservoirs, conduits, streets, and parks whose reproduction elsewhere would be formidably expensive. Can the nation afford to treat its cities as expendable resources? Can America afford to rebuild itself every generation? The existing housing stock is the largest single component of the nation's collective wealth—a substantial resource base that ought to be protected. By 1970, the estimated value of U.S. residential structures was nearly $700 billion or some 30 percent of the value of all reproducible assets (Dolbeare, 1976, p. 96). In 1970, approximately 35 percent of the nation's housing stock was older than 35 years (ibid.).

THE FEDERAL ROLE

Federal government has affected central city revitalization through a tangle of programs—the more significant, perhaps, administered by the Department of Housing and Urban Development. The Section 235 and Section 236 programs survive from the Housing Act of 1934. The former provides mortgage, interest reduction, and operating subsidies to reduce rents for low-income households. Although revised in the 1970s, the Section 8 program also dates from the 1930s, the government paying landlords the difference between actual market rents (up to a determined "fair market" maximum) and the rental contributions of tenants (normally 30 percent of household income). Subsidies are usually administered by local public housing authorities. In addition, the program provides a guaranteed rental stream to developers who will build or rehabilitate housing for low-income people. By 1979 Section 8 was, in the aggregate, as large as the public housing program, with 840,000 units occupied and an additional 430,000 committed for or actually under construction (Struyk, 1980, p. 164). However, need far exceeded supply as an estimated 1.6 million households were eligible for Section 8 benefits nationwide. In New York City, for example, the program covered only some 2 percent of eligible households (Bowsher, 1980, p. 1). Section 202, a related program established in 1959, directs long-term loans to private nonprofit sponsors in order to finance rental or cooperative housing facilities for elderly and handicapped persons.

In the Johnson administration's War on Poverty, the Economic Opportunity Act of 1964 and the Demonstration Cities and Metropolitan Development Act of 1966 (the Model Cities Program) established new central city decline initiatives. A cabinet-level Department of Housing and Urban Development (HUD) was created to administer new and previously mandated housing activities. Title VI of the subsequent Community Economic Development Amendment encouraged self-help among urban and rural low-income residents. It sought to encourage people in economically depressed localities to break cycles of poverty by investing in permanent economic benefits (Berndt, 1977, p. 52). Central were the community development corporations: nonprofit, locally based entities through which federal monies were to be channeled toward job creation, job training, and housing rehabilitation. The Vietnam War not only diverted attention from this social agenda, but—more importantly—diverted money.

Between 1954 and 1973, Washington made 58,000 housing rehabilitation grants totaling $169 million, and approved low-interest loans on some 69,000 dwellings with a value of approximately $295 million (Vaughan and Vogel, 1979, p. 92). Section 312 of the 1964 Housing Act made funds available for residential, mixed-use, and nonresidential development in areas certified by local governments. By 1980, some 80 percent of the annual $84 million available under the program was being directed toward multifamily housing (Keune, 1984, p. 487). Between 1966 and 1973, $350 million was distributed across some 258 local code-enforcement programs, bringing an estimated 250,000 buildings nationwide up to code at least temporarily (Vaughan and Vogel, 1979, p. 92). In 1960, money spent on repairing existing housing stock consumed only 20 percent of the nation's total housing expenditure; but by 1970 it had risen to 33 percent, and to 42 percent in 1980 when Americans spent close to $45 billion on home improvements (Keune, 1984, p. 486).

The 1974 Housing and Community Development Act brought "revenue sharing" to the nation. This involved making block grants to local governments for a wide range of improvement projects, the philosophy being that local communities understood local needs and were best qualified to administer funds. Programs like urban renewal, model cities, water and sewer line subsidization, open space procurement, and housing rehabilitation were subsumed. Block grants were an important program fixture. Intended primarily for private and public housing rehabilitation, they were distributed mainly to low- and moderate-income areas. Block grants also could be used to fund public service jobs up to a limit of 10 percent of municipal payroll. In 1986 alone, this program channeled some $3.1 billion to local communities (Morial, 1986, p. 55). Communities were required to generate redevelopment plans with some type of citizen participation. Community organizations, including neighborhood clubs or action groups, were given an opening through which planning bureaucracies might be influenced.

The 1970s also brought the Neighborhood Housing Services program (NHS) and urban homesteading. NHS was a joint effort between HUD and the Federal Home Loan Bank Board. Local partnerships were promoted between areal residents, lenders, and local government. Five basic elements were envisioned: (1) physical infrastructural preservation; (2) code enforcement and facility upgrading; (3) enhanced local lending and; (5) greater supervision of government spending. This was to be accomplished through subsidizing financial lending, setting up a high-risk revolving loan fund, creating nonprofit corporations, and the like. The Pittsburgh NHS, begun in 1969 as a local experiment in neighborhood revitalization, made nearly 400 loans through 1975, totaling nearly $1 million (*Neighborhood Preservation*, 1976, p. 4). Staff services included rehabilitation counseling, loan referral, loan servicing, budget counseling, supplying of tools, and supervising construction work. By 1977, there were 35 NHS programs active in the nation.

Urban homesteading was another program begun at the local level and later boosted by federal action. For the 1960s, Philadelphia, Wilmington, and Baltimore among other cities began distributing city-owned houses to individuals who agreed to renovate and reside within them. Section 810 of the 1974 Housing and Community Development Act created a national demonstration program transferring HUD-, VA-, and Farmers Home Administration-held properties to local governments to be revitalized through homesteading. By 1984, some 107 cities were participating (Keune, 1984, p. 487).

Of all the federal initiatives encouraging central city revitalization, none achieved the visibility of the 1977 Urban Development Action Grant (UDAG) program. UDAG targeted communities with sluggish population growth or decline, large per-capita income disparities, large poverty populations, and large blocks of substandard houses (Morial, 1986, p. 54). It provided capital for developments that promised job increases and enlarged local tax bases. By 1980, nearly 700 grants across 400 cities had been authorized, totaling $1.3 billion. Cities then were able to create some 160,000 temporary construction jobs, retain 92,000 old jobs, and create 200,000 permanent openings (Holcomb and Beauregard, 1981, p. 14).

By 1986, some $3 billion were used to fund 2,000 UDAG projects (Morial, 1986, p. 53). Minorities filled some 38 percent of the approximately 405,000 new jobs (Morial, 1986, p. 53). Some 80,000 new housing units arose under these projects, with 40 percent of them occupied by low- and moderate-income residents. (Figure 7.1). More than 30 percent of UDAG monies funded industrial projects; and nearly 40 percent, commercial ventures such as retail and office buildings, shopping centers, hotels, and nursing homes.

The Economic Development Administration (EDA) complemented the UDAG program by spending $175 million to rebuild urban public infra-structures in 1986 (Morial, 1986, p. 56). Grants went to construct and rehabilitate industrial parks, water and sewage systems, and ports. EDA monies also funded revolving loan funds in selected cities to nurture small and minority businesses. Similarly, the Small Business Administration made loans for building rehabilitation both to individual entrepreneurs and to local non-profit development corporations (Cassidy, 1980, p. 279).

Federal commitment to revitalizing U.S. central cities has shifted in response to the variable ideologies of presidential administrations. Although bol-stered by the civil rights movement, liberal concern for central cities took a back seat to the Vietnam War. The subsequent rise of conservative politics greatly diminished public resolve to attack dereliction. Increasingly, the nation has turned from federal spending to reliance on the private sector to solve this ill. UDAG funds, for example, declined from $440 million to

Figure 7.1   St. Louis Place on that city's northside was financed in part by an Urban Development Action Grant (UDAG). The new development fills gaps created by abandoned housing.

$235 million between 1981 and 1985. The program was virtually elimi-
nated thereafter (Morial, 1986, p. 55). Federal housing assistance and job
training funds were cut by more than 50 percent and 60 percent between
1982 and 1986 (p. 8). Crime-fighting assistance to state and local governments was only one-fifth its level in 1986 relative to 1975 (p. 9). This shift
was less an austerity program than a redirection of spending priorities favoring military and defense spending. Federal spending increased as a percentage of gross national product from 22.9 percent in 1980 to 23.3 percent
in 1986.

While some federal urban programs have existed for more than half a
century, others have quickly come and gone, downscaled and subsumed by
more ideologically acceptable programs. None have been fully funded to
meet the needs assigned. Generally, most have suffered from bureaucratic
waste and lack of careful coordination. As the federal government has
never fully committed itself to solving urban ills, the best that can be said
is that federal programs have been suggestive of solutions left unfulfilled.
The nation seems perpetually caught between the liberal impulse to use
government excessively and the conservative predilection to overempha-
size market forces. The pendulum continues to shift. Unfortunately, initiatives such as the Neighborhood Housing Services and the Urban Development Action Grant programs, which pragmatically mixed liberal and
conservative stances, have proved to be short-lived.

INITIATIVES FROM CITY GOVERNMENTS

City revitalization programs have tended to grow from opportunities created
by state and federal funding, with subtle variations across cities identifiable. Locally administered housing codes have been a major tool, growing
from 50 to over 5,000 cities between 1954 and 1968 (Listoken, 1985, p. 3).
More than 85 percent of cities larger than 50,000 currently use this tool
(ibid.). Their influence, however, has been suspect. Housing codes work
when local governments and courts oversee compliance. By the 1980s, it
was clear that most central city code programs were ineffective. Lack of
funding, fragmented administration, and overly complex rules combined to
weaken effectiveness. Housing inspection carried little glamour. As critics
observed, the typical inspection program tended to be cluttered with tire-
some little details. They were often manned by "dull, narrow-minded civil
servants and second-class professionals, relegated to basements and drab
corners of municipal office buildings" (Hartman, Kessler, and LeGates, 1980,
p. 560).

Local housing courts have been reluctant to impose criminal or even civil
sanctions, viewing themselves essentially as "compliance boards of last

resort" (Nachbaur, 1974, p. 217). Landlords obtain continuances by making "good faith" token repairs. Fines in most cities have been low, often less than the cost of enforcing compliance. They have amounted more to code-violation licensing fees. Landlords milk their buildings, spend only what is necessary, and wring profits from undermaintenance. Even where local administrators and courts have worked vigorously to police housing codes, the effect is often to sustain decline. When the costs of meeting code prove prohibitive, landlords become more inclined toward disinvestment, tax delinquency, and abandonment. Housing meant in theory to "trickle down" to low-income families is removed from the market. Paradoxically, this accelerates building destruction. As code enforcement appears to be practical only in stable localities, many cities vary codes from neighborhood to neighborhood as reflects stability. Other cities vary only the intensity of their single code enforcement geographically.

Zoning ordinances have come under widespread criticism recently. They are seen to have a standardizing effect, producing homogeneous, commonplace landscapes. Originally, housing and zoning ordinances were intended to stimulate safe and sanitary cities with stable property values. But standards have been pushed higher and higher over time; and, couched in increasingly restrictive terms, codes have come to safeguard the vested interests of labor unions, material manufacturers, government agencies. Unions guarantee that only their certified craftsmen work; manufacturers impose exaggerated technical requirements that enhance profits; elaborate inspection and certification procedures inflate bureaucratic empires. In sum, rehabilitation is made more difficult. The inflated costs of required labor and material plus the cumbersome approval process nearly precludes rehabilitation of old buildings in some places.

Bureaucracies frequently frustrate rather than facilitate. Developers frequently face a complex obstacle course at city hall. The St. Louis case is instructive (Leven, 1972, p. 62). For a building permit, one must appear in person at a crowded permit office where the first of many long lines await. Visits to various other offices are required to prove property ownership, prove tax payment, and receive plan approval. After several weeks, city inspectors arrive to evaluate the rehabilitation site, after which the petitioner, if granted a building permit, launches another round of office hopping and line waiting. Many cities, such as Denver, have streamlined such procedures, aided by computerized data banks. For each urban land parcel, computers tell the building type, the number of housing or commercial units contained, vacancies, tenure type, assessed value, and price at last market sale (Goetze, 1983, p. 102). This has been the exception, however. New technologies have revolutionized government service only where the will to facilitate rather than frustrate prevails.

Figure 7.2   Missouri's Redevelopment Law (Chapter 353) underlay development in the 1970s of Laclede's Landing, an entertainment and office district
on the St. Louis waterfront.

Through the 1970s, American cities were notoriously slow acting on delinquent taxes. In Cleveland, city and county officials followed a 15-step
procedure. In one case described by Susan Olson and Leanne Lachman
(1976, p. 39), a property delinquent in 1965 first appeared on an auditor's
advertisement in 1967. In 1970, a delinquent land certificate went to a
prosecutor who filed for foreclosure in 1971. A court-issued decree of sale
was made in 1973, and the property placed on the market in 1974, some
nine years after the owner first defaulted on his taxes. By law, property in
Cleveland that did not sell for the full amount of taxes, assessments, costs,
and penalties at the first sheriff's sale would be held for a second auction,
adding to the adjudication process as much as another two years. Such a
legal system poses problems. Landlords stop paying taxes in an effort
to squeeze profits from their buildings, and housing abandonment often
ensues. In 1966 there were 8,200 tax-delinquent parcels in Cleveland; in
1974 there were 11,000, or nearly 7 percent of the city's total (Olson and
Lachman, 1976, p. 1).
    States began to extend accelerated foreclosure powers to cities during the
1970s. St. Louis created a Land Reutilization Authority empowered by the
state to manage, transfer to other city agencies, or sell delinquent properties. Foreclosure procedures were streamlined with most delinquent proper-

Figure 7.3   Whole new neighborhoods were created in the 1980s in the St. Louis Central West End, many built by suburban developers enticed into the central city for the first time. Here the city has created a new park around which to focus development.

ties passing to city control within three years. First, the city was allowed to bring suit against properties as against property owners. Second, the city was allowed to treat delinquent parcels in rem as a class, as against treating each parcel individually. Housing obtained by St. Louis went initially into its homesteading program, buyers leasing units until units were brought up to code when titles were issued. Ten states had empowered in rem programs by 1985; courts in most cities appointed receivers to abate hazardous conditions and manage properties, expenses being covered by building profits earned. Shortfalls constituted liens, and property owners were thus required to satisfy receiver claims, refusal leading to foreclosure and transfer of ownership. New York City shortened its in rem process to approximately 30 months. In 1982, approximately 70,000 housing units had been foreclosed, with New York City acting as the receiver for most. In 1987, 30,000 parcels or some 3.5 percent of the all properties in the city were under the control of the Division of Real Property (Listokin, 1985, p. 12).

No metropolis suffered a more severe decline in its central city than St. Louis. During the 1970s, the city's population declined some 27 percent from 622,000 to 453,000 people (Schmandt, Wendel, and Tomey, 1983, p.

63). But perhaps no city has more successfully innovated toward reversing its decline. Besides legislation creating the city's Land Reutilization Authority, the Missouri Legislature in 1969 launched three other significant initiatives. The Land Clearance Act enabled St. Louis to create a Land Clearance Authority charged with leveling buildings in selected zones. Activity came to focus immediately south and north of the central business district, where large sport and convention facilities have been developed. The Planned Industrial Expansion Act authorized issuance of revenue bonds to finance land, buildings, and equipment for businesses expanding in or relocating to the central city. But by far the most significant legislation was the Missouri Redevelopment Law, known as the Chapter 353 program.

Chapter 353 gives powers of eminent domain to private redevelopment corporations created by the city. Once formed, a redevelopment corporation can acquire by condemnation any property within its designated territory. The law also provides 25 years of partial real estate tax abatement. For the first ten years, the redevelopment corporation pays only the tax assessed prior to redevelopment. For the next 15 years, taxes are paid at half the newly assessed rate on both land and buildings. In addition, the city negotiates with developers about improvements to streets, sewers, water lines, and other public utilities. In many instances, maintenance of the public infrastructure is contracted to the redevelopment corporation on a renewable basis. Thus, private capital and government combine in "joint ventures" directed toward revitalizing city sections. By 1980, some 47 separate redevelopment projects had been launched in St. Louis (65 percent of them located in or adjacent to the central business district) at a cost of more than $300 million (Mandelker, Feder, and Collins, 1980, p. 27).

Critics of St. Louis's redevelopment corporations claim that much of the early investment—largely in bank and office buildings, hotels, mixed residential and commercial developments, and shopping centers—would have been made despite public subsidy (Figure 7.2). For example, Busch Stadium was constructed under a Chapter 353 subsidy. It has been only in the 1980s that neighborhood-oriented redevelopment corporations have substantially begun to impact residential areas in St. Louis through building rehabilitation, new "infill" construction, and large planned-unit developments at the scale of suburban subdividing. This development, hinged substantially on the creation of office jobs in downtown, likely would not have been forthcoming without public subsidy—including that focused in the central business district (Figure 7.3). Critics also decry lost property taxes. They predict that, by the end of the 1990s, the city will have "mortgaged" its future completely, revenue-generating power becoming subservient to private developers. St. Louis schools appear especially threatened by an eroding tax base due to property tax abatement. Defenders of the redevelopment corporations argue, however, that the city's revenue base is sufficiently diverse to recoup foregone revenue through nonproperty taxes.

HISTORIC PRESERVATION

Historic preservation is a recent government initiative to revitalize urban neighborhoods. Its expressed goal is to preserve and maintain historic landscapes and their artifacts through provision of rehabilitation incentives. In this program, neighborhoods are systematically packaged for conspicuous consumption, with upgrading as the end product. The past, seen as interwoven into landscape, is commodified and made a salable item. Preservation was long considered a luxury that only affluent communities could afford. Today, preservation takes place as a restructuring tool alongside other developmental options. Old places—the containers of relic fabric residual from the past—are taking on new life. Changes in U.S. tax laws, patterns of housing consumption, and renewed opportunities for profitably developing urban real estate have played major roles.

The National Historic Preservation Act of 1966 set the tone for modern preservation. It created the National Register of Historic Places to inventory nationwide significant buildings and historic districts. By 1970 there were approximately 2,000 entries on the National Register, and by 1980 almost 20,000 (Schill and Nathan, 1983, p. 24). A preservation fund provided grants-in-aid to state preservation programs (where the inventorying was actually conducted), as well as financial assistance for limited restoration work and property acquisition. A new cabinet-level body, the Advisory Council on Historic Preservation, advised the president on preservation matters and coordinated federal preservation activities. A review process was introduced to appraise potentially destructive federal activities on National Register properties. In 1976, this oversight was extended to embrace all properties potentially eligible for the register.

Federal effort was paralleled by local level preservationist efforts. In 1965, fewer than 100 communities protected historic neighborhoods through district zoning. By 1980, nearly 1,000 localities had designated one or more historic districts (Schill and Nathan, 1983, p. 24). Some 600 cities and towns had adopted architectural controls, and appointed oversight boards or commissions to review requests to demolish, modify, or undertake new historic district construction.

New York City's Landmark Preservation Commission (LPC), established in 1965, oversees four historic categories: (1) aesthetic or historical districts; (2) symbolic landmarks; (3) significant open spaces; and (4) public scenic landmarks. Such properties, once designated, "cannot be altered, demolished, or reconstructed in any way (including such minor changes as adding a new sash, door, air conditioner, business sign, etc.) without first obtaining from LPC an appropriate certificate" (Listokin, 1982, p. 5). As of 1981 the commission oversaw 41 historic districts with some 16,000 buildings, about 600 landmark structures, and approximately 30 interior and scenic landmarks (ibid.). Furthermore, the commission made grants to repair low- and moderate-income properties in historic districts, funded preservation research and public education programs, and monitored related city agency actions. Finally, the commission oversaw the selling and buying of development rights whereby zoning allowances were transferred from historically significant properties to other locations.

Historic district zoning, like zoning generally, has ensured that contiguous properties have compatible uses. It has sought to minimize market externalities or spillover damages from contiguity (Gold, 1976, p. 353). It seeks to lower uncertainty regarding future land uses by variously restraining development. By so labeling areas, zoning not only verifies exchange and use values, but creates them. Once a historic district is set apart from the other spaces of a city, a basis for defining social status accrues. The property resources of the zone are seen to be in finite supply—a basis for symbolizing status. Once revitalized, historic districts clearly symbolize material success. Examples of increased property values within historic districts are widespread. Between 1955 and 1972, property values rose 200 percent in the Beacon Hill and Back Bay areas of Boston, as against 126 percent for the city as a whole (Wolf, 1981, p. 322) (Figure 7.4). Prior to historic designation, Beacon Hill and Back Bay property values had increased by 61 percent between 1946 and 1955. Citywide, this figure was 66 percent (Wolf, 1981, p. 322). In "Old Town" Alexandria, Virginia, unrestored building values increased about 3.5 times its former value through the 1970s to a level approximately 2.5 times the value of similar structures outside the historic district (Schill and Nathan, 1983, p. 29) (Figure 7.5).

Tax reform was an important impetus to historic preservation. The 1976 Tax Reform Act extended several tax benefits to renovators of certified historic commercial buildings. They could either amortize the costs of rehabilitation over five years or accelerate depreciation on total value of improvements. Owners could also obtain tax credits for the cost of rehabilitation. "A developer who in 1975 undertook new construction would have saved between 4 and 9 percent in taxes compared to one who rehabilitated an existing property. In 1977, however, after passage of the act, an owner of a certified historic building would have saved between 13 and 28 percent by renovating" (Schill and Nathan, 1983, p. 25). The act disallowed for tax purposes any expense deductions incurred in demolishing historic build-

Figure 7.4   Boston's Beacon Hill was an early central-city historic preservation success, coming shortly after World War II.

ings and accelerated depreciation on new replacement buildings. In the first three years, more than 750 buildings were renovated nationwide with over $425 million invested (ibid.).

Although certified historic structures were not eligible, the Revenue Act of 1978 included a 10-percent investment tax credit for rehabilitation of commercial and industrial buildings 20 or more years old. The 1981 Economic Recovery Act offered rehabilitation incentives on older and historic buildings, replacing the 1976 and 1978 incentives with a single three-tier tax credit: (1) 15 percent for 30-year-old commercial structures; (2) 20 percent for those 40 years old; and (3) 25 percent for certified historic buildings. By 1983, some 2,600 properties worth $2.2 billion had been certified for use of various rehabilitation tax incentives (Ainslie, 1984, p. 300).

Preservation incentives are played out at the local level in numerous ways. In Pittsburgh's historic districts of the 1970s, developers could acquire abandoned buildings for as little as $8,000 and rehabilitate them into market-value housing at a cost of some $40,000 per unit. For the typical three-unit building, this involved a total development outlay of approximately $120,000, and an investment tax credit of $30,000 (O'Bannon, 1984, p. 379). One firm rehabilitated more than 100 buildings, saving over $450,000 through tax credits. While this seemed a substantial loss for the federal

Figure 7.5   Alexandria, Virginia's historic district—pictured here in the early 1980s—serves nearby Washington, D.C., as a bedroom community.

treasury, the firm grew from 5 to 150 employees, in effect creating each new job for $3,000 worth of tax credit. The company paid state and city income taxes, business taxes, and sales taxes in addition to its $1-million payroll. It also paid approximately $200,000 per year in property taxes on formerly vacant and vandalized buildings (ibid.).

Historic preservation is based in a popular grass-roots reaction to the squandering of the built environment's resources. Aided and abetted by the National Trust for Historic Preservation established in 1949, historic preservationists developed local political clout through mobilizing neighborhood groups to promote local self-interests through conservation. Perhaps the work of St. Louis's LaFayette Square Restoration Committee illustrates. When the committee was formed in 1969, the LaFayette Square neighborhood surrounding a nearby 30-acre park was badly blighted. Part of the neighborhood had been slated for clearance to accommodate a new freeway. Many houses stood vacant and vandalized. When we visited in 1971 to photograph familiar old houses (see Figure 1.6), we thought that we were seeing it for the last time. However, the Restoration Committee's lobbying efforts thwarted the proposed freeway. The St. Louis Plan Commission produced a plan for historic zoning. The committee launched a revolving fund with money obtained from the National Trust and local banks. With the fund, the committee made emergency building repairs and sold them to new owners interested in restoration. In its first 18 months, the committee acquired 12 properties and resold six at prices approximating their costs (Galbraith, 1976, p. 325). Several corporations were convinced to aid employee house purchases by backing mortgages. By 1977, membership in the LaFayette Square Restoration Committee included more than 300 families.

St. Louis's preservation was assisted by the city's tradition of private streets. Indeed, the LaFayette Square success was spawned from Benton Place, a private street immediately adjacent to the area's park on the north. Private streets in St. Louis are blocked off at one end to prevent through traffic, and street ownership (often including boulevarded park space) is guaranteed by adjacent property deed restrictions. Indentured deed restrictions require the formation and maintenance of incorporated street associations that levy property assessments and oversee street maintenance. Associations are taxed by the city for provision of police, fire, water, sewage, and other public services. In sum, the private street creates a covenant among property owners for maintenance of its public spaces.

GENTRIFICATION AND INCUMBENT UPGRADING

The process of gentrification has restructured numerous urban neighborhoods across the United States. This process has involved outside investors repairing properties and buildings for financial gain. Thus, speculators and developers often buy up properties in this process and sell expensively or build repair structures themselves. Called cynically "private urban renewal," "reinvasion," or "reverse blockbusting," a substantive bidding-up of property values accompanies successful gentrification. Usually, extraordinary increases in real estate taxes accrue, which landlords pass along to renters through hefty rent increases. In Philadelphia's Queen Village, tax assessments rose by an average of 129 percent during the 1970s, with increases in contiguous areas averaging only 17 percent (Levy and Cybriwsky, 1980, p. 149). Property owners, initially resistant to the ills of gentrification, eventually feel the pinch through increased local property taxes. Increased assessed valuation of property means higher tax bills. In dramatically upgrading neighborhoods, this increase can be prohibitive and force owners to sell. Consequently, long-term residents often find themselves displaced by gentrification. It therefore represents a form of revitalization that directly benefits a select group—newly arrived households—to the detriment of long-term inhabitants.

Critics condemn gentrification as a destroyer of low- and moderate-in-

Figure 7.6   South Baltimore, where incumbent upgrading has successfully stabilized blue-collar communities, may be a future target for gentrification.

come neighborhoods (Figures 7.6 and 7.7). Geographers Neil Smith and Michele LeFaivre (1984) call the process "devitalization." "Summer chairs on the sidewalk, televisions out on the stoop, and children's street games are replaced," they write, "with herringbone pavements, fake gas lamps, wrought iron window railings, and a deathly hush on the street" (p. 43). Neighborhoods in this situation are destroyed by economic forces that allow the affluent to impose their will on the less affluent. The market becomes a mechanism that accords preferential treatment to the wealthy, allowing them to pick and choose desired neighborhoods. The indigent can only observe, wait for the market to impose its will, and hope to find suitable alternative accommodations.

Gentrification involves a residential sorting process by which Americans have been reordering themselves geographically. Attracted by urban pioneer and affluent reconquest ethics, gentrifiers are affluent Americans desirous of urban lifestyles. They are no longer content to live in scattered urban enclaves or in the "sterility" of suburbia, and come to places that are packaged and marketed as safe central city havens. Generally, gentrification skims the cream of a city's older, surviving housing stock, taking those areas originally developed for the upper-middle and upper classes—districts with pleasing architecture and natural amenities. Usually selected are

Figure 7.7   South Baltimore of the 1980s enjoyed a vigorous street life reflective of a healthy neighborhood.

neighborhoods convenient to employment, especially to jobs in central business districts. Declared historic districts in many cities, they stand in stark contrast to those neighborhoods where housing abandonment has produced vacancy if not total dereliction. But, as critics note, they also stand in contrast to vulnerable working-class neighborhoods easily victimized by the machinations of property value inflation. Once gentrification becomes entrenched, developers seek to spread it into the best of the city's remaining neighborhoods that are often working-class sections.

Critics also decry gentrification as an unauthentic form of urban revitalization. Residents are purportedly attracted by the novelty and excitement of the city, but once there, they choose to experience it vicariously and passively, through grillwork, curtained windows, and door locks. Affluent urbanites, like many of their suburban counterparts, privately surround themselves in material wealth. Missing is the active street life, the intensive neighboring, and the concern for community outside of preoccupation with house equity. *Gesellschaft* replaces *gemeinschaft*. Affluent urbanites are seen as using the city as an entertainment commodity, of operating from a voyeuristic attitude like "going to a circus" (Allen, 1984, p. 36). "Tourists in the city (and some would add the gentrifiers as 'resident tourists') do tend to see the 'natives' as actors against a romantic scenery in a kind of theatre-in-the-round. The actors sometimes come forth and interact with the spectators, surprising, delighting, and sometimes embarrassing them, but always leaving them with a feeling that they have 'participated'" (ibid.). As suburbanites are seen to quest for romantic small-town values buffered from parochial rural concerns, so affluent urbanites are seen to quest for urbanity buffered from urban diversity.

Initially, working-class neighborhoods often welcome gentrifiers. New residents do not seem threatening, and their investments appear to enhance aesthetics. A threshold is reached, however, beyond which incumbent residents become increasingly defensive and concerned about loss of neighborhood fabric (Levy and Cybriwsky, 1980, p. 150). Some become bitter when friends are forced to move or when grown children, raising their own families, cannot afford to live nearby. This bitterness is compounded by property value increases that bring with it larger tax burdens. The growing realization of residential dislocation brings a surprising array of responses, ranging from fatalist acceptance to overt confrontation. While some passively submit to the whims of "natural change," others mobilize and seek to contest the process. As displacement begins, upgraders—difficult to dislike as one's next-door neighbors—come to be disliked in the aggregate as an anonymous class representing forced change.

Although large numbers of people have been forcibly displaced by gentrification in recent years (annual estimates having ranged up to 900,000), it is not evident that most have been disadvantaged by the process (Knox, 1982, p. 335). Michael Schill and Richard Nathan (1983) sampled both stayers and movers associated with nine gentrified neighborhoods in five American cities. Only 23 percent of those who moved did so because of displacement. "Of those displaced, however, only 16 percent indicated that their current home was worse than the one they lived in before they were displaced. Sixty-seven percent of the displaced households reported that their housing actually improved. When asked to compare their old and their current neighborhoods, 56 percent of the displaced households rated the new neighborhoods as better than the old" (p. 7). In addition, housing costs increased for displaced households moving for other reasons. The elderly, considered by most critics of gentrification to be its real victims, were not affected in numbers larger than other age groups. Although recognizing problems, Schill and Nathan conclude that the advantages of gentrification outweigh its disadvantages. Other analysts have reached similar conclusions (see: Grier and Grier, 1980; Gale, 1980). In contrast, a multitude of other scholars are more critical of gentrifications (cf. Cybriwsky, 1978; Beauregard, 1986; Hartman, Kessler, and LeGates, 1980; Smith, 1982). They see displacement as an inequitable outcome of affluent households' forcing long-term residents from community. In effect, the economic sphere subsumes the social sphere as a determinant of people's right to reside. The fact that households have long-term attachment to place and local institutions becomes secondary to household economic clout to buy into areas. Cybriwsky (1978), for example, detailed the severe emotional grief associated with forced removal from one Philadelphia neighborhood. Displacees experienced the loss of social worlds at the hands of gentrifiers.

Cities have sought to curb displacement only when overt resident abuses like tenant beatings, physical threats, and harassment have been documented. Harassment has been especially problematical where rent controls prevent landlords from raising rents. Common harassment strategies have been identified: cutting off heat and utilities, allowing garbage to accumulate, neglecting maintenance, failing to make necessary repairs, engaging in verbal and physical abuse, and setting fires. In 1983 alone, more than 3,000 cases of harassment were reported in New York City (Marcuse, 1986, p. 162). Apartment conversion to condominiums created substantial difficulty in some cities during the 1970s, reducing rental unit supplies to critically low levels. Some 396,000 units were converted, or approximately 1.3 percent of all U.S. rental units. However, in Washington, D.C., conversions reached upwards of 8 percent. Condominium conversions displaced households on limited and/or fixed incomes, diverted capital and entrepreneurial effort away from housing renovation and new construction, and encouraged speculation. In depressed markets, apartments renting at $125 a month were worth from four to six times the annual gross rent (or $12,000 to $18,000 per unit); but marketed as condominiums, they might bring ten times that amount (Goetze, 1983, p. 30). Conversions usually occurred when depreciation and interest deductions ceased to afford owners sufficient tax shelter.

It is doubtful whether city revitalization will ever turn the metropolis inside out, with the affluent dominating central city living and those in the suburbs languishing in poverty. This is what urban gentrification would accomplish if pushed to the extreme. It is far more likely that markets for gentrification will prove limited. There are measures that cities can take to encourage incumbent upgrading as opposed to gentrification. For example, local lenders can be catalyzed to make more home-improvement loans in older neighborhoods. Michael Schill and Richard Nathan (1983, p. 140) outline the following. Rent supplements might be tried, along with "first right of refusal" ordinances that allow tenants to purchase rental units in the face of condominium conversion. Mortgage subsidies and aid in forming limited-equity cooperatives are other ways of helping. Most importantly, cities can stabilize property taxes through abatements. Cities can build or subsidize new housing for low- and moderate-income families as infill on vacant land in older neighborhoods. Such measures are most meaningful in places where a strong sense of community exists, bolstered by local institutions with strong interests in locality. Where locality-based community has been missing, neighborhoods have been especially vulnerable to both reinvestment-related and disinvestment-related displacement. More affluent incumbents have tended to take their money and run to the suburbs as circumstances invited.

While gentrification and incumbent upgrading have accelerated in recent years, most central city neighborhoods continue on the downward spiral of decay and abandonment. Those that have stemmed decline—like the Italian Hill in St. Louis, the Polish suburb of Hamtramck near Detroit, the now Hispanic Boyle Heights in Los Angeles—have blunted the deterioration by concerned community action. Social cohesiveness provides a focus around which notions of community are asserted. The case of Edgewater on Chicago's northside is instructive. Sustained decline set in by the early 1950s, most noticeable among the tall apartment towers overlooking Lake Michigan that once so forcefully symbolized luxury and leisure. By the 1960s, newcomers of wide racial and ethnic diversity had appeared: Greeks, Armenians, Rumanians, Koreans, Japanese, Chinese, Filipinos, Cambodians, Hispanics. Edgewater was never really its own place. Linked with nearby Uptown as a planning district, it was variously divided by city bureaucracies into a confusing set of service areas. Clear territorial claims were not asserted until creation of the Edgewater Community Council in the 1960s. The council's immediate goal was establishment of block or neighborhood clubs, which, as they strengthened, would form and focus the council's program toward specific revitalization goals. Apartment conversion to condominiums positively reinforced the emergent sense of community. As renters were replaced by owners, buildings increasingly functioned as "vertical neighborhoods" equivalent to the "horizontal neighborhoods" organized back from the lake.

Ed Marciniak (1984, p. 79) evaluates Edgewater's apparent success at stemming decline. Activists operating through block clubs and the Edgewater Community Council pressured the city to enforce building, zoning, and fire codes. Lobbying brought additional "beat" policemen to the streets, a special program eliminating street-corner prostitution. Various city services were monitored, as, for example, garbage collection and street and alley cleaning. Local chambers of commerce were activated and pressure brought to increase off-street parking in commercial areas. The city was persuaded to modernize mass transit stations. Commitments by leading institutions to invest in local rehabilitation projects were publicized. Cleanup and beautification campaigns were launched, neighborhood celebrations were held, and permanent signs erected to identify neighborhoods. New traffic patterns were devised, with many residential streets closed to through traffic. Arson was reduced through citizen surveillance. But, as Marciniak concludes (p. 80), these rather standard approaches to revitalization produced results disproportionately small to the efforts invested.

The big payoffs came as a result of several major offensives. First, citizens organized to elect reform candidates in several of the city's northshore wards. The Democratic political establishment had long endured by mustering on election day voters from the halfway houses, nursing homes, sheltered care facilities, flophouses, boarding and rooming houses for the elderly poor, and residential hotels. Marciniak quotes a former precinct captain: "It's a hellish circle of vice and poverty. I know. I was part of it. One of my rooming houses furnished each voter a dirty bed in a dingy room. A day labor agency supplied temporary labor and a check at the end of the work day. The nearby bar cashed the check that same evening and catered to alcoholic needs while streetwalkers hung around to pick up any remaining change. On election day my victory margin was twenty-to-one" (1984, p. 80). To ensure the vote, politicians had a vested interest in protecting landlords, tavern keepers, and the operators of day labor agencies from being cited for violating health, safety, fire, building, or other codes.

Second, not-for-profit day labor offices were established that not only paid higher wages to laborers, but, contrary to established practice, charged no finding fee to employers who hired clients into permanent jobs. Third, the Edgewater Community Council mobilized voters to rid neighborhoods of unruly bars, package liquor stores, and other contentious land uses that attracted soliciting, narcotics, and violence (Marciniak, 1984, p. 82). Fourth, crime was confronted head-on through citizen patrols staffed by volunteers in radio-equipped cars. Fifth, an escort service was created to protect crime witnesses against intimidation when appearing in court. As Marciniak argues, "A sure sign that neighborhood deterioration has started is the unwillingness of residents to complain about unlawful activity or to come to the rescue of someone in trouble. . . . No neighborhood," he continues, "can last long when its social climate is uncaring, irresponsible or isolationist" (p. 87). Sixth, and very important for Edgewater, was a moratorium obtained on the further licensing of sheltered care facilities. Seventh, city officials agreed not to saturate the community's housing market with subsidized housing. In the early 1980s, Chicago's northshore—the neighborhoods of Lakeview, Rogers Park, Edgewater, and Uptown—contained 9 percent of the city's population, but held 33 percent of its Section 8 housing (p. 99). Finally, the council induced locally based institutions, such as Chicago's Loyola University, to invest locally rather than moving facilities elsewhere.

Incumbent upgrading appears to be successful in Chicago's Edgewater, but gentrification may already be hard on its heels. Renters have given way to owners through extensive conversion of apartments to condominiums,

producing inflated property values. To protect and enhance property, affluent residents have turned against the less affluent by attacking the institutions that permitted low-income residency. Residential displacement has
increasingly unfolded. The neighborhood currently shows visible signs of
gentrification: trendy restaurants, boutiques, overpriced specialty stores, and
the like. The irony here is that incumbent upgrading may fail to halt neighborhood upgrading and be destroyed by its own success. Incumbent upgrading often sets the stage for gentrification.

In some environments, incumbent upgrading has not been successful.
Cincinnati's Over-the-Rhine district has languished for decades despite efforts
at stabilization. Out-migrating German and Italian residents were increasingly replaced by thousands of unskilled Appalachian whites and urban
renewal–displaced blacks. The area became a low-income repository for
poor whites, blacks, and elderly German families. More than 100 businesses left the area between 1972 and 1978, leaving nearly 30 percent of
its storefronts empty (Schill and Nathan, 1983, p. 81). By 1981, nearly 40
percent of the Over-the-Rhine's housing units were vacant (ibid.).

Phyllis Myers and Gordon Binder (1977, p. 27) review the unsuccessful
attempt to revitalize Cincinnati's Over-the-Rhine. This neighborhood, marked
by entrenched poverty, could not effectively upgrade under federal model
cities funds. Resources were squandered. At issue was a patchwork ameliorative approach that could not halt persistent decline. Under Community
Development Corporation sponsorship, a revitalization plan was imposed
that was sloppy and lacked significant resident input. Outside plans dictated shoddy rehabilitation, poor workmanship, and insensitivity to local
needs. For example, wallboard was incorrectly applied and it ultimately
weakened buildings; sandblasting similarly damaged fragile brick and sand-
stone facades. Moreover, one local group—People Against Displacement—
opposed rehabilitation on the grounds that it would bring gentrification.
They successfully leveraged the passing of a city antidisplacement ordinance. Locals won the right to use up the area's declining physical resources. From a high of nearly 6,000 in 1960, the area's population fell to
below 2,100 in 1980 (Myers and Binder, 1977, p. 28). Value of building
repairs consequently fell from $389,000 to $6,000 between 1970 and 1973
(p. 27). Abandonment of the neighborhood appeared inevitable.

COMBATING WHITE FLIGHT

The American penchant to avoid trouble by moving to new places continues to plague central cities. Massive white out-migration to suburbs lies
at the crux of contemporary city troubles. This process has been institu-

tionalized in the structuring of real estate markets and mortgage financing, in the conduct of government—and, indeed, everywhere that racism has been tolerated. Unfortunately, racism has been tolerated almost everywhere in American society. Americans who have "made it" disparage association with those who have not; and accordingly, the upper and middle classes have traditionally sought to demonstrate their successes by segregating themselves. "It is much easier to pass on cherished values to one's children if they are raised in schools and neighborhoods where only children from families with similar values are found" (Downs, 1970, p. 139). And personal security is much greater where one lives in an area "where nearly all others accept the same standards of public deportment" (ibid.). Blacks have been too readily stereotyped by whites who impart poverty traits to all blacks. By associating blacks with depressed property values, whites set up self-fulfilling prophecies that can totally deflate landscapes.

How might cities be stabilized against racism's erosion of neighborhood? Neighborhoods in transition need to be made equally attractive to blacks and whites alike. It can also be argued that they should be made equally attractive to blacks and whites of varying income levels. The immediate goal, however, would be to keep white households moving into a neighborhood at a sufficient rate to maintain its integration (Downs, 1981, p. 99). Oak Park, Illinois—one of Chicago's older western suburbs—began experimenting with integrative programs in the late 1960s (Goodwin, 1979, p. 80). The zone of transition, with its wake of depressed property values, was steadily approaching across the adjacent Austin city neighborhood to the east. Between 1966 and 1973, Austin changed from white to black at a rate of 37.5 blocks per year (Taub, Taylor, and Dunham, 1984, p. 46). Indeed, a general two-step succession process had been under way for decades, with higher-status white Protestants first fleeing before lower-status white Catholics, and the latter group then fleeing before blacks (deVise, 1977, p. 1).

The black transition in Austin was first felt in the schools. Young black families replaced older white households. In 1970, there were 84 percent more children under 18 years of age in the tracts turned black than there had been ten years previously (Goodwin, 1979, p. 80). The white assumption was that Austin was going to be "overwhelmed." "It existed at a cognitive level that might be characterized as 'everyone knows.' It was possible and even usual to talk about the predicted or feared effects of changing community racial composition without ever making explicit mention of race, which was clearly unnecessary for mutual understanding" (p. 107). Fear of declining property values and crime was widespread. Various civic groups organized in Austin to combat the negative effects of change. However, fragmented by the cross-cutting boundaries of governmental agencies, political resolves proved impossible. Austin residents simply lacked sufficient channels to government. The Organization for a Better Austin, for example, was frustrated in its opposition to local redlining and local FHA mortgage-financing policies—especially the latter agency's approval of buildings with extensive code violations.

Carole Goodwin (1979) evaluates Oak Park's apparent departure from the historical patterns of rapid and total block-by-block racial turnover. In 1968, Oak Park passed a fair-housing ordinance prohibiting discrimination in home and apartment advertising, sales, rentals, and financing. It outlawed the panic peddling associated with blockbusting. Block clubs were organized under the auspices of a Beautification Commission intended "to strengthen the mechanics of informal social control and lead to improved maintenance of homes and property" (p. 188). A Community Relations Commission followed in 1971. Its Oak Park Housing Center strove to attract both white and black residents to Oak Park through use of brochures and newspaper advertisements that strengthened the city's image as an integrated place. It sought to encourage prospective black residents to locate throughout Oak Park and not just in blocks adjacent to Austin. It initiated a community education program alerting residents to harmful real estate practices, provided legal referral services to those who had suffered discrimination, and provided a forum for the exchange of ideas regarding neighborhood stabilization. In 1972 the village board banned "for sale" and "sold" signs from residential property other than condominiums and newly constructed houses, and it outlawed redlining. Oak Park began licensing apartments in 1974 with mandatory inspections. The exteriors of residences were routinely inspected also, and owners notified of needed repairs. An alley inspector was hired to watch for debris accumulation, improperly disposed garbage, and illegally parked automobiles.

The temporary blunting of the dual housing market and its encroaching transition zone can be variously explained. Foremost was the community's reputation as an affluent and historically distinct suburb. The prevalence of "prairie school" architecture—much of it designed by Frank Lloyd Wright—made Oak Park a "notable" place. This distinctiveness translated into higher property costs that limited less affluent housing demand. Oak Park, moreover, had substantial local community control. Local leaders were able to take initiative to direct both the rate and the direction of black in-migration. As Goodwin (1979, p. 208) concludes, Oak Park was able to forge a new identity for itself rather than having an undesired one thrust upon it. Local community control hinged on Oak Park's having an autonomous government responsive to its citizens. It was able to relate in its various departments and readily respond to community need. A strong tradition of activism and volunteerism underlay a political culture territorially focused. Government's role, limited by constitutional restrictions and political realities, was also augmented by private and quasi-public institutions. They provided the critical resources—including loans, technical assistance, and counseling programs—that sustained the physical and social fabric of a heterogeneous neighborhood.

At least two noteworthy proposals designed to deflate racism in the housing market were rejected in metropolitan Chicago. First, in 1969 Judge Richard Austin ordered the Chicago Housing Authority to build new public housing units in white neighborhoods, thus ensuring that no neighborhood would be immune from both class and racial integration. The uproar that followed put a stop to all local public housing construction. Second, home equity insurance to be financed by a special homeowner property tax in affected neighborhoods was recently rejected (Johnson, 1988). The program was to compensate those suffering from declining property values. To be eligible for compensation, it was proposed that homeowners pay for appraisal by a city-sponsored commission and agree not to sell for five years. Those who could not obtain the appraised price at time of sale would appeal, have their properties inspected for maintenance level, and receive the difference in compensation. Here again the idea was to remove the element of fear. The plan was attacked as insulting to blacks by giving life to the fallacy "that blacks and other minorities bring down property values" (ibid.).

Despite decades of experimentation, the nation has still not developed satisfactory revitalization tools. Some federal programs have not only failed to generate revitalization, but substantially contributed to decay. Other programs, showing promise, have been aborted as the political-ideological pendulum swung from liberal to conservative. In America's central cities, gentrification has offered a form of revitalization that has directly benefited a small group. This process has effectively upgraded areas but to the detriment of many residents. Displacement of the less affluent and destruction of community have been negative side effects. Racism may be declining across the United States, but its strength suffices to drive persistent white flight. The engine of land development in America is a strong one. It need only be turned from generating economic imbalances and social inequities toward resolving them.

Decay is what the affluent walk away from and what the poor are left with. Writing of planners, Kevin Lynch has noted, "They do not know how to deal with waste—old farms and scrub growth, derelict mines and buildings, vacant lots, abandoned tenements, accumulated solid waste, old railroad yards" (1972, p. 190). For America's central cities, planning for shrinkage rather than expansion has been overly traumatic. Government has not known how to turn the processes of change to advantage. The learning process has been long and painful. Unable to preserve the traditional city, the building up of a new kind of city was long delayed. Developers have only slowly responded to central city needs, faced as they were with an abundance of suburban opportunities. Urban obsolescence has not been well managed, and cities have not grown old gracefully. Prolonged decline reflects a societal neglect, an emphasis on the suburban over the urban landscape. Resources concentrate in suburbia as profits and lifestyles are chased there to the detriment of central cities. The irony of urban revitalization is that in its latest form—gentrification—it tends to benefit a small elite urban class. Packaged as the salvation of city woes, it selectively restructures and offers little prospect for improving the quality of life of most urban residents.

8

Community and the Built Environment

Dereliction is poignantly amplified when contrasted with the counterforces of orderliness and maintenance. Stable and revitalized places successfully resist decay despite aging and obsolescence. What is it that enables some places to resist or reverse eroding change? What is it that invites a sparing of and a caring for cultural landscape? The concept of community, we feel, holds the answer. Viable built environments reflect constructive sociability. People who share a strong sense of community tend to invest emotion, time, energy, and money in their places. Neglect surfaces where sense of community is substantially diminished. Sense of community may hold the key to urban landscape revitalization, and may be necessary to sustain the successes of the new suburban and rural landscapes.

In emphasizing the individual, Americans have tended to lose sight of community. In America's past, frontier isolation from seats of established social order invited a self-help ethic. A revolt against real and imagined political tyranny during colonial times facilitated the drive to self-assertion. Capitalism provided the economic engine for subduing a continent by emphasizing prerogatives of individual initiative through private property. And yet in America, as everywhere, community defined at various scales has always been requisite to individual satisfaction if not success. Shared community interests provide the contexts for individual aspiration and fulfillment. In promoting individual welfare, we as a nation have lost sight of individualism's collective legitimization (Elkins and McKitrick, 1954; Doyle, 1978, p. 156). We value the individual only because collectively we have decided to do so. America's historical dream was one of rough equality in communities of self-sufficient and self-governing freeholders. It was a dream of European peasant origins that valued hard work, frugality, and independence "bound by a deep, strong sense of life in common, sustained by familial ties and religious beliefs" (Boyte, 1984, p. 54). On the frontier, settlers strove to establish a sense of neighborhood through mutual sharing, helping, and individual action. Local and nongovernmental institutions such as churches, aid societies, fraternal orders, and social clubs quickly evolved requisite to civility.

COMMUNITY DEFINED

While definitions of community vary (see Sjoberg, 1965, p. 115), most establish three criteria as important. As Art Gallaher and Harland Padfield state succinctly, community is "a social unit existing for a purpose in a particular place" (1980, p. 1). Marion Clawson (1980, p. 55) elaborates from his bias as an economist. Community is a set of social relationships or roles among people who are related geographically through production and consumption of goods and services. Calvin Redekop (1975, p. 136) emphasizes the cultural. In community, people in a place bond through shared belief, attitude, and intentionality. David Popenoe (1985, p. 6) highlights the social, emphasizing the regularizing of practical activity interconnections. Sociologist Talcott Parsons (1960, p. 250) refers to community as a social system that has a historical referent and from which role relationships develop. These three dimensions—the social unit, the purpose, and the place—highlight a shared reality where interconnections forge bonds of cooperation and reciprocity.

Jane Jacobs (1961, p. 135) early linked landscape vigor with community. She saw local community as chains of influential persons through whom messages passed, bonding aggregates of people together—the key people shortening the linkages of communication and providing tighter group integration. Social links required the growth of trust carefully nurtured over time. Disrupted, a city's social networks do not heal quickly, for people take years to build significant relationships with one another through propinquity. Severed from established social ties, people become ineffectual, their skills as communicators transferring to other settings with difficulty. For localities to function in self-government, continuity in social networks had to be fostered. "The networks are a city's irreplaceable social capital. Whenever the capital is lost, from whatever the cause, the income from it disappears, never to return until and unless new capital is slowly and chancily accumulated" (p. 138). Critical to neighborhood survival and city vitality was the druggist, grocer, apartment house superintendent, or housewife who made a deliberate effort to know and be known in everyday life. Critical also were the priest or minister, policeman, and local politician who operated within lines of established authority, taking jurisdiction for people in a place.

Sociologists distinguish two community types. The German word *gemeinschaft* applies to the first type: the traditional, territorially based community valued by Jane Jacobs. Place is primary. Within circumscribed space, people are thrown into frequent, highly personalized interactions. Limited spatial mobility fosters a parochialism that encourages intensive local social relations. Primary relationships of family and kin group, and secondary relationships of church, school, and business, anchor local socialization patterns. Fear of retribution disciplines those who deviate too far from established norms. "Relationships are developed on a face-to-face basis, in small groups, in naturalistic ways; they evolve slowly and last, all because of the relative permanence of the people" (T. M. Smith, 1982, p. 128).

In many places, mobility has overcome the dependency on such based social networks. The second community type, termed *gesellschaft*, refers to this newer areal form. It reflects those communities that have a nominal aggregate sense of place, shared customs and traditions, and constant neighboring and local socialization patterns. These characteristics flow out of the modern individualist penetration of everyday life—an ethic that has increasingly guided individuals to follow a particular life path. The roots of modern individualism lie in the Protestant Reformation and the view that man faces God individually. Suppliants encounter the infinite and the incomprehensible not through the mediation of organized churches, but as separate and isolated beings (Wachtel, 1983, p. 61). In their separateness, individuals profess community loyalties for purposes of self-interest. The German word *gesellschaft* applies to such communal arrangements of limited liability. Modern communities attract participants by offering rewards and gratifications. The individual easily withdraws from social relationships that do not reward, and forms other alliances. Limited-liability communities thrive to the extent that members share physical landscapes and have similar material goals.

For the upper middle classes, work is what gives life meaning and puts the individual in social context. Work defines who one is. Clearly, sense of position no longer hinges on locality and neighboring ties, but on white-collar careers. Work is a definer of one's character, position, and identity (Wachtel, 1983, p. 156). As women have entered the workforce and have left child rearing to day-care centers and schools, locality-based community has eroded even faster. Diminished here are the neighboring ties forged around child rearing. Decline of gesellschaft has ostensibly been less pronounced in low- and moderate-income areas, where activity patterns are less far-flung. But even blue-collar workers orient more to jobs in today's corporate world. If not loyalty to corporation, then loyalty to union or trade is characteristic. With gesellschaft, intense local socializing is rarely important to sense of self. Locality is "eclipsed" (Stein, 1961). The most meaningful relationships are not those shared through propinquity, but those of joint enterprise. People collaborating together at work or at play develop close relationships, but usually stop short of intimate personalization. Since commitment is limited, the costs of withdrawal are low (Wireman, 1984, p. xxi). In modern society, people play highly specialized roles. "By promoting a plurality of individual worlds, specialization dissolves the continuity of persons, their sense of living a common life and having common concerns" (Haworth, 1966, p. 19). The values shared are highly general-ized and communicated impersonally, thus to obscure underlying layers of diverse if not conflicting opinion. In a locality, material possessions come to symbolize social worth more than actual knowing through direct association. "Appearential" ordering comes to the fore (Lofland, 1973, p. 82). What neighbors appear to be—and not what they are—forms shared satisfactions.

With the breakdown of traditional communal ties and the rise of communities of limited liability, locality has taken new meaning. Localities have become places for concentrating like activities and like people in a world of increasing specialization. For generations, Americans have been busy sorting themselves geographically according to class and status. Suburban neighborhoods have been contrived for more affluent groups, each of which display their architecture, landscaping, and other material possessions in the celebration of values shared. Evacuated central city neighborhoods have become repositories for society's less affluent. Thus, spatial segregation has liberated America's affluent citizens from responsibility for the disadvantaged, who no longer live nearby. Spatial segregation isolates fragments, and makes the unsavory disappear from sight. Within new suburbs, private space has been emphasized over public, and neighbors remain estranged through lack of common experiences, despite the superficial appearances of civility that material possessions pretend. The impersonalized world of the consumer dominates—social worlds engineered primarily by the logic of the marketplace: malls, shopping centers, convenience stores, singles bars (Gottdiener, 1985, p. 272). The modern metropolis is a bundle of geographically separated facilities and services that economically bind individuals who dwell in atomistic life spaces (Popenoe, 1985, p. 91).

Socially homogeneous neighborhoods consolidate social structure by limiting intergroup contact, guaranteeing the separate existence of social worlds with distinctive value orientations (Ley, 1983, p. 159). In selecting a neighborhood, people purify life experiences and reduce fear of the unknown (Sennett, 1970, p. 30). Community stands as a kind of reference group with which individuals and families see themselves sharing common cause. Therein lies the sense of solidarity. The houses people live in and the things they have and use provide the vital messages of apparent commonality. As means of evading experiences that threaten, socially homogeneous neighborhoods provide bulwarks against disorder. Avoidance of the negative anchors the new sense of community. "Communally painful experiences, unknown social situations full of possible surprise and challenge, can be avoided by the common consent of a community to believe they already know the meaning of these experiences" (Sennett, 1970, p. 38). Increasingly, Americans are a people afraid of social worlds they cannot absolutely control.

Diminished community orientation spells trouble for America. In unstable central city neighborhoods, transiency erodes sociability. When one's neighbors are forever on the move, situated near one for only a few months or even weeks, then neighboring bonds are necessarily weak if not impossible. A constant succession of neighbors almost necessitates mutual suspicion and social distance. As few households are known to one another, people legitimize each other's conduct with great difficulty, always assuming and expecting the worse. Anonymity gives people immunity from moral controls. Missing is the gossip, ridicule, and ostracism by which traditional communities keep members controlled. As planner Walter Firey observed in his study of Boston's declining central neighborhoods, "In the absence of any rewards for proper behavior there is an actual weakening of moral inhibitions and an atrophy of conceptions of right and wrong. Such norms, however well rooted they may have been in individual consciousness, tend to deteriorate when the individual is removed from the social context of reward, punishment, and reinforcement in which they were originally defined" (1947, p. 315). Traditional courtesies and civilities are dropped under the strain of alienation. When social risks appear too great, stances of avoidance are assumed (Karp, Stone, and Yoels, 1977, p. 108). In city neighborhoods, the individual's sense of civic virtue hinges not on cooperating with neighbors, but on leaving them alone.

Localities devoid of community must rely on social enforcers: persons specially trained—police, judges, social workers, and educators—to impose behavioral norms. Residents become pawns of bureaucracies that labor impersonally on their behalf. Authority, rather than welling up intrinsically through social consensus, is imposed externally. Once institutionalized at a distance, decision making may suppress local initiatives—local perceptions and inclinations giving way totally to a cosmopolitan outlook. The vacuum of collapsed community invites outsiders to transform places not only politically, but economically and physically as well. In declining central cities (as in declining small towns), residual populations lack the know-how, political and business connections, and the wealth to deflect (let alone reverse) negative change. Localities devoid of community organization easily become pawns of other places.

People without a strong sense of local community rely on attachments to larger social constructs: the city, the nation, or simply mass society. Although experiencing increased dependency on outsiders, locals may create myths of local autonomy. They may see themselves as effective actors in the new, enlarged social sphere. Common interests are assumed. Tied vicariously to larger social networks, locals may deny their powerlessness until crisis brings a rude awakening. Failure to stop urban renewal, the construction of a freeway, or the locating of a prison, a waste dump, or some other noxious facility may demonstrate forcefully the weaknesses of the locality. Then, what feeble energy survives in community networks may be dissipated completely by individual alienation. Alienated people who see themselves dominated by forces beyond their control succumb to resignation. Community—taken for granted at one time—is now mourned and forgotten.

People project themselves beyond locality toward higher poles of affection. Most Americans today seem content to look beyond their neighborhoods for life's anchors. Areal attachments are increasingly the city, region, or nation. Regularly the city rises to celebrate itself in staged media events. Especially important are the rituals of professional sports (even though teams be manned by mercenaries from other places), which focus attention on cities defended day to day, and season to season. People only recently arrived in a city who are energetically cheering a televised baseball, basketball, or football team in a singles bar symbolize this new kind of community to America. Through sports, Americans forge areal attachments that transcend any emotive connection to neighborhood. As James Robertson observes, professional sports capsulate many American values in their pretended representation of community.

> Basketball uses some of the peculiarly American imagery and idealism of lines— there are foul lines (as there are in baseball) and court lines which must be crossed—but in football the entire game is built around the frontier, the line, the boundary. Football ritualizes the moving frontier, and the teamwork, cooperation, and individual heroism necessary to move that frontier; simultaneously, it also ritualizes the teamwork, cooperation, and individual heroism necessary to resist the moving frontier (football players are pioneers and Indians at the same time). (Robertson, 1980, p. 252)

Mass entertainment further distracts the city dweller from the local scene. "Thus the urbanite," Dennis Clark notes, "leaps from the springboard of home directly into the mainstream of metropolitan life. There is no intervening communal structure to organize opinion, refine desires, develop responsibility and provide an organic community framework for reference to urban affairs" (1960, p. 61). The modern American seeks community vicariously, participating in rituals only suggestive of community.

EXCHANGE VALUES VERSUS USE VALUES

People value places both for what they can be used for in a monetary sense and for what they can be used for in a social sense. Places have, as we have said, both exchange and use values (Lefebvre, 1973). In the United States, the former has dominated definitions of community, for places tend to be governed by economic interests centered on the exchange values of land parcels measured as "rent," embracing purchase expenditures as well as payments to landlords (Gottdiener, 1985, p. 102). Thus the people who aggressively dream, plan, and organize themselves to make money from property transactions have dominated those who strive to preserve the local bonds of community. Widespread acceptance of the impersonal, self-equilibrating market obscures the socialness of locality, and places become mere instruments and not ends in themselves. As John Logan and Harvey Molotch write, "Efforts to make place serve use values are therefore noticeable as 'interfering' in the 'normal' urban processes. Whereas buying and selling real estate needs no special justification, regulating that buying and selling for the benefit of residents requires special political action and ideological mobilization" (1987, p. 47).

Working-class neighborhoods have had difficulty preserving use values. Such residents are rarely organized politically to control or even substantially influence land development, unlike their European counterparts. This population has maintained a sharp separation between the realm of work and that of home and neighborhood. In contrast to Europe, the American political system provides little security backup for workers in the form of income maintenance, public medical care, and stable (nonmarket) housing. In America, economic insecurities are compounded by active promotion of an "ideology of consumerist individualism" (Logan and Molotch, 1987, p. 110). Traditionally, migrants to industrial cities were treated merely as "labor" and given little buffering from an economic system conceived in Darwinian terms. Foreign immigrants, for example, were thrown onto the resources of family and neighborhood, although church, aid society, and other institutions did follow many groups from Europe to cater to their needs. Certain other groups—for example, out-migrating southern blacks— were less fortunate and had no such protection to fall back on.

It is not surprising that neighborhoods came to provide degrees of security for people of like origins, language, religion. Nor should it surprise anyone that group conflicts frequently set neighborhood against neighborhood, as insecure people sought to defend status and resources. Monied interests often facilitated intergroup and interneighborhood conflict. Unstable land values linked to territorial succession brought (as they continue to bring) profits to speculators. American consumers, acting individually to protect equity in property, move frequently. Old stock, white Americans give way to "hyphenated" white Americans who give way to nonwhite Americans. Poor blacks, who have tended to climax this march to progress, frequently give way to the devastation of dereliction. Ethnic neighborhoods, largely of working-class consistency, are ever-shifting manifestations destined to dissipate over time in America's traditional scheme of city building.

As long as basic racial and other social prejudices divide Americans, ethnicity as a basis for community bonding will remain ever problematical. The impulses to defend local communities are constantly offset by real estate counterforces, especially where class and status differences are used by speculators to lever change. Only where an ethnic community is vigorously growing through sustained in-migration or natural population increase (or both) will energies prove adequate to defend turf. Ethnicity does have implicit in it, however, certain stabilizing impulses. Ethnic communities serve an important buffering function, easing newcomer assimilation. Neighborhood provides sense of physical and psychic security as a dependable environment loaded with familiar social landmarks. One encounters here predictable actors engaged in comprehensible activities and behaviors. People share signs of commonality, whether skin color, language, dialect, or taste in clothing. People are easily categorized, behavioral expectations enhanced, and the risks of everyday life reduced.

As residents of ethnic neighborhoods increasingly assimilate, energies that sustain the closed community tend to dissipate. In cities, "urban villages" erode as families increasingly adopt materialistic values and symbols. Residents are then inclined toward suburbia where real estate equity is more readily protected, where personal property is believed safeguarded against vandalism and theft, and where job opportunities are greater. Outmigrants mix in the suburbs, to the dissolution of ethnic uniqueness. In old neighborhoods, ethnic ways are largely vestigial—mere reminders of a lost solidarity. Assimilation has long been assumed in the United States and the exotica of ethnic variety seen as not only temporary, but expendable. "Americanization" programs in public schools, trade unions, and large corporations accelerated the process. To hold good jobs, Americans of all kinds have found speaking correct English, dressing in good taste, and adhering to mainstream courtesies absolutely necessary.

Churches often anchor residual ethnic communities against total dissipation, congregations and ethnic communities becoming synonymous. A covenant of religious tie offers unification, allowing populations to embrace English, forsake customary dress, diet, and amusement, and still retain some sense of ethnic belonging. Church congregants find fellowship beyond theological guidance. Members go to church to be with people (to see and be seen); these associations are also played out in the neighborhood beyond.

Stores are patronized, contracts offered, employees promoted with implications of mutual support. Of course, churches bolster not only city neighborhoods against the forces of decay, but also rural neighborhoods and small towns. As already demonstrated, covenanted places retain sufficient economic energy to abide total absorption into larger, external economic and social spheres.

Examples of city neighborhoods sustained by church-inspired covenants are numerous. Sociologist Roger Ahlbrandt's (1984, p. 5) study of neighborhood involvement in Pittsburgh discloses the city's Roman Catholic parishes as bastions of residual community feeling. Questioned as to social involvements, church-attending homeowners tended to be more involved with their neighborhoods than others. Neighborhoods with high percentages of Catholics expressed high levels of attachment, satisfaction, and happiness. Ahlbrandt concludes, "The institutional base—particularly the presence of a strong organization, such as the Catholic Church—provides a mechanism which draws people inward and helps to create and maintain [a] neighborhood's social fabric" (p. 187).

A church may provide a kind of social glue for an ethnically based community, but its effectiveness as preservation agent depends on local economic viability (Steinberg, 1981, p. 53). When property values erode and local employment collapses, no amount of church-encouraged sociability will sustain community bonding. In the 1970s, many central city churches stood isolated amid the vacant lots of abandoned neighborhoods. Churches caught before the sweep of central city change found themselves quickly outliving useful purpose. When Detroit's Roman Catholic bishop consolidated dozens of city parishes that closed churches in the late 1980s, he acted in recognition that central city communities had simply evaporated. Without sufficient parishioners and adequate monies to sustain vigorous parish life, the churches stood symbolic of lost neighborhood and the triumph of exchange over use values.

NEIGHBORHOOD AS PLACE

Neighborhoods have long intrigued sociologists and planners, the former looking to comprehend the social segmentation implicit, the latter to apply proper development tools (see Keller, 1968; Downs, 1981). The viable neighborhood is seen to have a unique essence and character. It has boundaries beyond which resident affections lapse. Churches, schools, and the like are seen to anchor neighborhoods socially, with residents sharing common ties through institutionally sustained social networks. Residents daily share public spaces. Foremost, however, neighborhoods are defined by neighboring: relations built around the unavoidable fact of propinquity.

Neighboring plays out across back fences, sidewalks, local stores, and wherever neighbors interact. For neighborhoods to work (indeed, for neighborhoods to exist), neighbors must agree on what constitutes acceptable public behavior. Sandra Schoenberg and Patricia Rosenbaum write, "Safe passage through the streets is a general need that residents of most neighborhoods attempt to enforce. Safe passage is constructed on the identification of strangers and the *ad hoc* surveillance by community leaders who make their presence known. Other types of public agreements deal with the maintenance of property, the disposal of garbage, the behavior of children, and the type of visiting allowed in the streets" (1980, p. 32).

Norms are a matter of expectation. Neighbors have to be assured of one another in order to face the future comfortably. Expectations turn on past behavior. Where neighbors are similar in income, occupational ambition, education, ethnicity, or race, material symbols of conformity usually prove sufficiently reassuring. Even where differences abide and neighbors are socially segmented, successful neighboring can hinge around shared values openly expressed. For example, an area's residents may determine to live in an "integrated" neighborhood or maintain physical neighborhood infrastructure order to protect equity. Expectations hinge on the future view. As neighbors leave, what is the likelihood that they will be replaced in kind? As Anthony Downs (1981, p. 35) notes, neighborhood residents can never fully control their future. They can, however, affect the larger community's view of current maintenance levels by how highly they praise living there. Positive promotion invites positive results.

In blue-collar areas, healthy neighborhoods excite vigorous street life. To the outsider—especially those from middle-class suburbs—first impressions may suggest crowding and confusion, and even chaos. Geographer Roman Cybriwsky writes of Philadelphia's Fairmount neighborhood:

> In good weather, and especially after dinner, the streets and sidewalks . . . are crowded with people. Residents sit outside their doors and greet passing neighbors who frequently take walks in search of conversation. Children play hopscotch, stick ball, and street hockey wherever there are vacant parking spaces, or tour the neighborhood on bicycles. Street corners belong to teenagers who hang out in large groups. The neighborhood has its "public characters" who are nearly always around. During hot summer weather bar patrons take their drinks outside and form tight clusters. (Cybriwsky, 1978, p. 24).

Familiarity with such places brings order to view. A social organization is seen to prevail, which Cybriwsky describes as follows, "There is a time and place within the neighborhood for different people and their activities, and residents know where and when they may do what without infringing on others" (1978, p. 24).

In a study of neighborhood satisfaction, Angus Campbell and his colleagues (Campbell, Converse, and Rodgers, 1976, p. 115) found that expressed contentment with life increased only slightly with the amount of education, occupational level, and affluence of respondents. Very low income people could be astonishingly satisfied with their residential circumstances. The low levels of education among their subjects suggested to these researchers that ignorance might indeed be bliss—constricted horizons leading to a kind of blind and unquestioning satisfaction with a status quo. Faced with urban instability, the American poor seem to prefer stability in whatever form, comfort being born of inertia. "Beyond a certain initial point of familiarity, satisfaction with a situation increases as one becomes increasingly accommodated to it," they write (p. 163). Stability—the prospect of being left content among one's kind in a place of comfortable familiarity—apparently ranks high in America's central cities if not in its suburbs and small towns. The good neighborhood is a stable one where neighboring evolves naturally among people accustomed to one another and unthreatened by prospects of imminent change. Among the poor, who obtain little status from their jobs or from being employed, a stable neighborhood of long-term attachments can produce their only sense of self-worth.

Whereas sociologists have learned much about neighboring, the fact remains that planners, architects, and other designers have found it difficult to plan neighborhoods. An area's physical layout can facilitate neighboring, but crucial is the predisposition to neighbor predicated on mutual trust born of sharing behavioral norms. Accordingly, the mere segregating of people categorically by class and status is the most widely practiced neighborhood planning strategy in America today. Nonetheless, the search for ideal physical neighborhoods persist, much of it directly descended from the seminal efforts of such planners as Ebenezer Howard (1945) and Clarence Perry (1939). Perry (1939, p. 45) formulated principles regarding size, boundaries, open space, facility location, and internal street configuration. The ideal neighborhood, as he advocated, should house a population sufficient to support an elementary school, the actual area embraced depending on population density. The neighborhood should be bounded on all sides by arterial streets that would provide access but also allow through traffic to bypass. The area should be laced with parks and recreational grounds. The school and other public and quasi-public institutions should be centrally located, but shopping facilities should be peripheral in conjunction with those of adjoining neighborhoods and shared major arteries. Internal streets, while functional, should discourage through traffic. Such principles have been adopted in most recent U.S. "new town" and "planned-unit" developments over recent decades.

Today, emphasis is given more to the socioeconomic aspects of neighborhood planning: sufficient economic base to support local services; sufficient credit to build and maintain housing stock; sufficient political power to garner and sustain public services; sufficient jobs locally (or in easy access) to support local income levels (Wireman, 1984, p. 39). Use values have come to the fore: effective schools responsive to local needs; attractive, clean, and safe play areas close to homes; quick access to emergency health care; local surveillance of and control over behavior in public spaces (ibid.). And the bedrock attribute of the successful neighborhood remains security. Residents must feel personally safe when they publicly encounter one another and strangers on the streets. Surveillance and the individual willingness to take jurisdiction over one another's behavior is key (Jacobs, 1961, p. 36). True, well-designed neighborhoods require economic capital in order to thrive; but, as has too often been forgotten in the past, they require social capital as well.

COMMUNITY DEVELOPMENT

Community development on a firm neighborhood basis requires cooperative institutions and individuals who recognize and value the communal nature of social life. In the 1980s, more Americans seemed committed to the search for community through neighborhood involvement. Rooted in the civil rights and consumer rights movements, and bolstered by the ethic of historic preservation, the quest for local community appears to be a reaction against the isolation and impersonality of modern life. It is, according to Graham Finney, a thrust to recapture the small community, "to exercise control over what happens closest to where one experiences most deeply what is occurring in his or her world" (1977, p. 198). It is, according to Daniel Yankelovich (1981), a cultural transformation generating a new social ethic. In an ongoing study of American's expressed life satisfactions, Yankelovich found the percentage of respondents claiming to be "deeply involved in the search for community" to have increased from 32 percent to 47 percent between 1973 and 1980 (p. 251). More and more Americans, he asserts, were coming to realize that they had many acquaintances but few close friends—an emptiness requiring correction.

Commitment and satisfaction are two different animals, however. Areal commitment appears not to be positively related to satisfaction (Ahlbrandt and Cunningham, 1979, p. 41). People can be committed to their local community but judge its physical conditions and social resources to be poor. High levels of satisfaction may lull residents into complacency. Indeed, many middle-class Americans—especially suburban residents—take for granted local social infrastructures. In affluent areas, residents tend to resign neighborhood affairs to elected and appointed government officials, to church leaders, and to the other private authorities who provide daily leadership. Only when serious problems arise do residents politically organize on behalf of place, and then usually on an ad hoc basis for the duration of the perceived crisis. Strong dissatisfaction, on the other hand, encourages defeatist attitudes. In slums, residents frequently assume powerlessness and defer crisis to politicians and bureaucrats. When issues rise to invite involvement, turned-off Americans tend to remain uninvolved. Drives to increase neighborhood satisfaction, however, can be used successfully as a mechanism to increase resident commitment even in the face of complacency and defeatism. At least, that is one of the important assertions of this book.

Resident bonding through community commitment rests on certain preconditions. A study of public–private partnerships in urban revitalization by the Committee for Economic Development identified six foundations (Ledebur, 1982, p. 207). First, a place must enjoy a civic culture that fosters a sense of community and encourages citizen participation. Second, people must share common local visions that enjoin different groups to cooperate in defining common goals. Third, "building-block" organizations are necessary to blend individual self-interests with broader interests, and translate mutually held goals into effective action. Fourth, key groups need to be "networked" such that communication is facilitated, especially when differences need to be mediated. Fifth, leadership needs to be prized, and new leaders encouraged for their entrepreneurial abilities. Sixth, individuals and groups must be simultaneously adaptive to changing circumstances and promote a sense of continuity supportive of sustained enterprise.

Sense of duty orients individuals to community goals, providing the glue of neighborhood bonding. Community thrives around ideas of discipline, responsibility, and obligation. Lawrence Haworth writes,

> Duty and obligation connote the individual's taking a distinctive stance in the world, one characterized by centering his life on something outside himself, toward which he directs his efforts. His posture is that of one who understands that the meaning of events consists in their impact upon the world, not himself, and who conducts his affairs with an eye to their ramifications in the world. He acts for the sake of something which transcends him but which he regards as preeminently valuable, and his affairs gain significance from their tendency to sustain that value. In this way, people freely take on duties and obligations and become, for their effort, "moral creatures." (Haworth, 1966, p. 60)

Those who embrace self-interest and ignore civic duty become what Peter Colwell (1976, p. 72) calls "free riders": people who coast on other's actions. Through the inertia of unenlightened self-interest, communities pull apart and are developmentally hindered. Without "civic culture," which values obligation beyond self, community languishes.

Ethnic communities—even those firmly anchored in institutional covenants—are usually not permanent. Clearly, drive for personal and family security tied to property equity has proved stronger. When ethnic communities defend themeselves territorially against intruding others, they usually dissolve in the face of individual self-interest. In the central city, previously committed people depart, leaving only free riders in the social vacuums created. So also has social class proved problematic in sustaining neighborhood stability. Neighborhoods can be built to attract specific social classes; but again, real estate dynamics fragment class commonalities by manipulating perceptions that associate race and class. Nonetheless, class awareness tied to the issue of property equity may prove in the future to be the rallying point around which to organize local-based community. As Lawrence Haworth argues, "If the city is to become a community, then the inhabitants must identify the settlement itself as the focal point of their individual lives" (1966, p. 87).

Future community visions might well center on the physical manifestations of neighborhood: the built environment. Common cause requires a common object of affection toward which sense of duty can be directed. The most viable object—one that totally surrounds and encompasses neighborhood residents—is the physical neighborhood itself. As Haworth reaffirms, "The common cause that unifies the inhabitants of a city should be, simply, the city" (1966, p. 87). Such thinking goes against many of the accepted values of a capitalistic society. American economists generally view the welfare of the individual (or the household) as the ultimate entity of concern, and the functioning of places as merely instrumental (Katzman, 1982, p. 27). Places are mere context. But places are indeed instruments of individual well-being; and as such, they should be given careful attention in the enhancing of human satisfaction. Manipulating place can become the rallying ground on which community commitment is achieved. Community can be shaped on the anvil of place—place created and place maintained. The built environment symbolizes society and helps configure it through manipulation of the physical world. People form and are formed by their physical surroundings. Clear recognition of this fact portends much for the community movement.

People base aspects of their personal identity on place attributes: places lived in, places idealized, places craved, and even places loathed. While symbolic interactionists examine how meaning is produced through direct human interaction, students of environmental cognition emphasize how people communicate indirectly through messages embedded in their surroundings. Combined, Linda Stoncall (1983) argues, these two approaches lay a foundation for analyzing the interpersonal, subjective consciousness of communities. "Looking at individuals interacting, viewing their surroundings in varied ways, and promoting some of the surroundings as symbolic representations of their community leads to a social psychological approach to community," she writes (p. 184). Turning this observation to the issues at hand, we will observe that communities of shared interest do play out in physical worlds selectively configured to promote community goals. Deliberate concern with environment as symbol can provide the common vision appropriate not only to stabilizing communities, but to stabilizing the built environment itself—built environment and community symbiotically configured. We need not only to understand how this works from the point of view of social psychology, but to take these comprehensions and apply them.

In focusing resident interest and affection communally on the built environment, a variety of organizational vehicles already have proved locally useful. In St. Louis, private streets have been found to be marvelously resilient in the face of devastating decay and abandonment. Property owners, bound by legal covenants, take responsibility for shared communal spaces, and arbitrate one another's care of private property. Neighborhood bonds here are anchored in maintaining neighborhood as physical environment. Such block associations, by committing individual households to group effort, enable individuals to influence changes around their property; and to a signif-icant degree, property owners control areal externalities. Sense of duty, responsibility, and obligation are directed to the neighborhood through self-interest: the protection of equity in property. Even would-be free riders are carried along into the fray through legal mandate. Neighborhoods organized around legal covenants will be watched, guided, and directed by those who have the most immediate stake in their futures (Eager and Hyatt, 1979, p. 100).

Condominium associations perform the same functions at the scale of building or building complexes. They collect member assessments and make public rules. Associations can use the courts to enforce rules as, for example, by placing liens on delinquent property or errant members. The ability of Chicago's Edgewater area to resist seemingly inevitable urban decay hinged in no small degree on converting apartment buildings to condominiums. Owners projected concern for their buildings onto the neighborhood beyond through the mechanism of a voluntary neighborhood association, a community group not grounded in legal covenant but formed strictly through volunteer commitments. Through volunteered effort, pressure was brought to bear on city government, reversing many policies detrimental to locality property values. Through volunteerism, the neighborhood was promoted as a distinctive place worth preserving.

Tenants can also bind themselves together in legally covenanted associations. Codes of conduct regarding public spaces can be communally enforced through contracted tenant obligation. Tenant associations in public housing projects have proved successful. Planner Oscar Newman (1980, p. 111) writes of New York's Lefrak City, a 32-acre complex of 20 eighteen-story apartment buildings in Queens. Aggressive fair-housing organizations had directed minority residents to Lefrak City, causing project management to drop tenant screening procedures and to alter selection criteria. Administrators backed away from keeping the project integrated at a 2:1 white-to-black ratio as originally planned. By 1976, with 70 percent of residents black, the project began to experience high vacancy rates as middle-income residents, both black and white, began to out-migrate. To fill vacancies, the project began leasing to large families and those with rent supplements. Tenants were accepted despite prior histories of vandalism, neglect of children, and nonpayment of rent. Graffiti soon covered the walls inside and out. Damage to doors, windows, mailboxes, elevators, waste disposal facilities, and laundry areas increased faster than repairs could be made.

Tenants of Lefrak City formed a tenant association and used it to institute a tenant selection program guaranteeing orderly residents. Through the association, authorities were persuaded to evict troublesome neighbors. Although many chose not to engage directly in building politics, membership fees, the required participation in periodic elections, and the required donating of time to the work of the association kept all involved. At Lefrak City, tenants patrolled hallways and outdoor areas, guarded entrances, and otherwise assumed jurisdiction over public places (Newman, 1980, p. 111). Such active participation simultaneously policed the premises and fueled resident pride of place.

Voluntary associations have been most widespread in promoting locality-based communities in the United States. In revitalizing neighborhoods, these associations have lobbied government, solicited banks and other businesses for investment capital, used federal programs to direct investment, and promoted general resident welfare. Perhaps most useful, voluntary associations have sponsored revolving funds for the renovation and recycling of properties, as in St. Louis's LaFayette Square area. Here again, focus has been placed on the built environment—especially its upgrading with the prospect of equity enhancement. Community volunteerism has been organized hierarchically in many cities, block and neighborhood groups sending representatives to umbrella organizations representing an entire city section like Chicago's Edgewater. Such community organizations have engaged in municipal politics, electing aldermen or other representatives to city government. Community organizations in cities like Baltimore have linked in citywide political coalitions. Such organizations provide the networking whereby local concern is channeled into effective action. Networks keep the lines of communication open that enable community sentiment to focus effectively when issues arise.

Community leadership is vital. Residents predisposed to community action, sharing common visions, and linked organizationally are only as effective as leadership permits. Necessary are people capable of articulating ideas, molding consent, and representing the group will to others beyond. Necessary are people willing to commit themselves to the defining of goals and goal implementation, people who enjoy the challenges of organizing, directing, and motivating. Leadership, however, needs to be cultivated within groups. Community action in America (at least that outside established mechanisms of government) usually proves short-lived—ad hoc efforts organized around single issues producing little if any permanent infrastructure. Leaders quickly come and go with the transience of public issues. To achieve permanency, leaders must promote institutionalized continuity. New interests must be developed as old ones wane.

Enduring community groups are those that elect their own leaders, administer their own programs, prove self-supporting financially, set their own budgets, and provide highly visible services. They are organized from the bottom up, and not from the top down. Starting in the 1960s, federal urban revitalization programs sought to impose community on localities from above. By the mid-1970s, some 186 different programs spread over 21 federal agencies mandated community participation in plan formulation (Porter, 1976, p. 17). The citizens assembled to input local views rarely represented constituencies. Local politicians frequently chafed at their perceived exclusion and often became antagonistic. Organized community groups were rarely given veto powers and often found their advice unheeded. Almost universally, federally subsidized urban redevelopment was run from city hall, with Washington exercising veto power. Community participation was, in fact, a sham. Most efforts to halt urban decline during the 1960s and 1970s were marked by failure to define national policy in terms responsive to varied local needs.

Grass-roots organizing seems imperative to sustaining urban places. Local-based communities need to be indigenously cultivated. Arthur Naparstek and Gale Cincotta observe, "If we are to speak realistically of precon-ditions required for effective change, it must be recognized that the neighborhood—not the sprawling, anonymous metropolis—is the key. In real terms, people live in neighborhoods, not cities. Their investments, both emotional and economic, are in neighborhoods, not cities. And the city can-not survive if its neighborhoods continue to decline" (1976, p. 8). Lawrence Haworth (1966) argues that local community needs institutionalization. "The process of ordering neighborhood affairs should become as settled and fixed a facet of neighborhood life as are the processes by which children are educated and the material necessities of life provided" (p. 111). Community councils should be permanent rather than ad hoc creations formed to meet specific problems. They should be permanent fixtures, run by local interests, and overseen by broader regulatory agencies.

THE ROLE OF LOCAL GOVERNMENT

It may be naive to think that, one day, communities will thrive in the United States at the local level. It may be even more naive to believe that Americans will turn enthusiastically to local governments anchored in such communities. Nonetheless, it seems appropriate for this discussion to push ahead, encouraged by the premise that, indeed, grass-roots democracy does have a future in America. We will argue that community-responsive government, if not community-based government, will be necessary to eliminate and prevent future dereliction, especially in urban America. Dereliction cannot be solved by isolated acts of property owners or tenants. Coalitions are needed to tackle shared problems like environmental decay and public neglect. No arena for community action is more important than that of government. No activity energizes local communities as effectively as politics.

Locality-based government rests on the premise that local problems need local resolution. Only those problems appropriate to city, regional, state, or federal levels should be left to decision makers there. At issue is the principle of subsidiarity captured by the phrase "no bigger than necessary." "Nothing should be done by a higher or larger organization that can be done as well by a lower and smaller one" (Greeley, 1977, p. 133). Such thinking contrasts with the New Federalism espoused in the 1970s and 1980s, which merely divested federal government of whole categories of urban responsibility, dumping problems on ill-prepared local governments. The argument for locality-based government holds that each level of government has its proper role and that those roles need to be carefully interpreted (Pasquariello, Shriver, and Geyer, 1982, p. 95). As most problems faced by city neighborhoods originate elsewhere, active governmental hierarchies (various levels effectively orchestrated) are vital to the maintenance of neighborhood integrity. At each level, moreover, equity needs to be a guiding principle. Government resource distribution, private-sector restructuring, and the like need to be closely scrutinized as processes generating benefits for some and costs for others. Locality-based community here is tied part and parcel to local democratic representation, concern for the range of local populations, and participatory political processes.

Douglas Yates (1982, p. 134) has been a persistent advocate of local government. He calls for cities to increase local responsiveness by decentralizing government by the following steps: intelligence gathering (officials stationed in neighborhoods to temper public opinion); consultation and advisory planning (councils organized to draw out public opinion); program administration (locals used as agents of city programs); administrative accountability (locals used directly to administer programs locally); political accountability (officials elected at the local level to formulate policy); and authoritative decision making (elected local officials directly overseeing local programs). Decentralization, Yates concludes (ibid.), increases administrative attentiveness and responsiveness to neighborhood needs. It reduces distance between citizens and their government and increases citizen feelings of political efficacy. It stands to enhance democracy by developing local leaders and by providing wider opportunities for local citizen involvement (Steinberger, 1985, p. 65). At the same time, the regulatory function of state and federal governments is recognized as crucial. The key is to capture the wishes of locals to direct the path of neighborhood change and to ensure that equity considerations are met.

Arthur Naparstek and Gale Cincotta (1976, p. 77) outline three decentralization strategies that lead to increased grass-roots power: (1) decentralizing services to neighborhoods for efficiency and administrative convenience (i.e., neighborhood police and fire stations); (2) decentralizing multifunctional services into the same community center to increase citizen convenience and faster response (i.e., neighborhood multiservice centers); and (3) placing mayoral outreach programs in neighborhoods to facilitate citizen access (i.e., "little city halls"). Naparstek, like Yates, recognizes as important the regulatory role of state and federal governments. For grass-roots political participation to work, government oversight is required. These actions guard against local economic elites' manipulating government to achieve hidden agendas (see Logan and Molotch, 1987).

Meeting in Philadelphia in 1976, the Alliance for Neighborhood Government—a coalition of neighborhood groups from all over the United States—adopted a "Neighborhood Bill of Responsibilities and Rights" (*Neighborhood Preservation*, 1976, p. 123). The document stipulated that people can and should govern themselves democratically. It asserts the rights of neighborhoods to determine their own goals consistent with broad civil ideals of justice and human equality, to define their own governing structures and operating procedures, to control private and public resources necessary for supporting neighborhood decisions, to influence decisively the planning and implementation of government actions and private institutions, and to have the information necessary to carry out these rights. The "bill"—a philosophy for grass-roots decision making—is intended to help neighborhoods control their own destinies. Recognizing that U.S. business and political leaders have used the pretext of scientific management and more efficient administration to obtain control of neighborhood affairs, the Alliance for Neighborhood Government champions grass-roots activism to reverse elitist abuses.

The drive for local empowerment has led advocates in Congress to propose a federal Community Preservation Act (Institute for Cultural Conservatism, 1987, p. 130). The proposed legislation would enable urban neighborhoods to define themselves as legal entities empowered to fight crime, control development, establish enterprise zones, and set standards for architectural quality and building maintenance. The cause has been taken up by the political right. "The more local the level at which a problem can be dealt with or a decision taken and implemented, the more likely it will be to reflect reality, accord with local circumstances, directly involve the people affected, lead to effective action, and preserve that most important of liberties, liberty in the way we live our daily lives" (Institute for Cultural Conservatism, 1987, p. 23). We would call, further, for according political power to local groups that have historically been politically muted or disenfranchised. Such residents, disproportionately found in decaying neighborhoods, need to influence more firmly the course of local change through influencing policy decisions and resource allocation procedures. Whether communities choose to promote areal stability or gentrification, local decision-making input and control of public resources is needed.

Affluent suburbanites already enjoy degrees of local autonomy. It is time to extend the same privileges to those in the central cities—especially the poor and politically dispossessed. The roots of suburbanization lie in affluent people's escaping the problems of the central city, including those created by unresponsive political machines and associated bureaucracies. The balkanization of suburbia has tended to produce small political units responsive to local needs: both the needs of the more affluent classes willing and able to seek more pastoral residential precincts and those of the developers who create and market the containing physical infrastructures. Suburbanites tend to associate with their local governments in personalized ways. Officials tend to be approachable, and resident complaints tend to be answered.

Widespread adoption of hierarchical or federal systems of city governance does not appear imminent. Many central city neighborhoods, impacted by decay, lack the adequate social capital to function effectively in a political manner. In cities where blacks and other minority groups have realized office by playing the established political game, it is not likely that they are eager to dilute their new power by substantially changing the game rules. The creation of locality-based communities is necessary—a process of community forming in which minority politicians take a leadership role. The decentralizing of governmental bureaucracies appears to be a logical first step toward generating social capital at the neighborhood level capable of sustaining locality-based government in the future.

Political decentralization would gradually follow bureaucratic decentralization, Naparstek argues (1976, p. 82). Initially, advisory neighborhood boards would be created to work with city administrators in identifying and correcting local problems. Local service areas would be made coterminous with city neighborhoods. Reconstituted as neighborhood councils, boards would be ultimately vested with local legislative and executive powers; their members would be elected, with one member serving as neighborhood mayor. Neighborhood managers would work with councils overseeing local programs administratively. In turn, neighborhood councils would elect representatives to a reconstituted city council that would function as a council of neighborhoods, one representative serving as mayor. A city manager might retain administrative authority over citywide programs, and coordinate neighborhood-level programs where necessary. Councils at the neighborhood level would be authorized to raise revenue, receive budgeting grants from the city government, and spend those monies in ways appropriate to local agendas.

The quest for neighborhood rights and governance runs counter to American legal tradition. In 1868, John Dillon, chief justice of the Iowa Supreme Court, articulated what came to be known as the "Dillon Rule." "According to Dillon, local governments are merely creatures of the state governments and, as such, can be created and destroyed at will. They have no residue of sovereignty, no inherent rights, no claim to special recognition or protection" (Steinberger, 1985, p. 73). An essentially centralist's position, it implicitly denies the need for local self-government. Subsequent political movements—the rise of political machines, the Progressive response, the New Deal, the civil rights movement—either ignored or were inimical to notions of community (ibid.). Professing to champion democracy, the United States has not embedded in its legal system the apparatus requisite to prompting and sustaining local democracy. In large measure, ours is not a participatory democracy where citizens are invited to involve themselves in local problems. Following James Madison's advocacy of representative democracy, our governmental compacts often restrain citizen input into politics. A political system dominated by a plurality of hierarchically organized interest groups, all competing with one another in the political marketplace, is merely a variety of elite rule (p. 65).

ADVOCATING LOCALITY-BASED COMMUNITY

We believe that community empowerment of all citizens offers the best opportunity to fight urban decay: landscape made an object of local will. Where local communities function with substantial political clout, attention will ostensibly turn to stewarding the built environment. We believe this to be the case for two reasons. First, goals, values, and sense of place would be interwoven into local physical fabrics. It is here that lives are made, friendships forged, and community shared. Second, economic prosperity is often tied to local built environment. Collective attempts at preservation follow from the individual initiative to retain house equity. Property owners realize that collective local circumstances shape property worth, and organized efforts to forge desirable physical fabrics benefit individual owners. Individual gain, therefore, comes from properly choreographing the larger collectivity. The need is to provide localities with the power, resources, and technical expertise that would permit *all* residents to participate politically in this endeavor.

There was a time when most Americans thought of themselves as members of some inwardly focused community. People considered themselves part of a rural neighborhood, small town, or city neighborhood. The degree to which this place functioned as fully integrated was unimportant. What counted was that local problems would generate a collective response. Whether or not a person actually participated in community did not matter. Comforting was the realization that options existed to follow kinship, friendship, and acquaintance ties toward fuller community participation. Life in America was, therefore, rooted in localities of various sizes and descriptions. People shared a range of local values. Selected behavioral norms might be violated (especially in private), but they stood as ideals to govern public intercourse. Codes of conduct, although shifting over time, provided anchorage. Americans in most localities were programmed toward civility. To violate local norms invited ostracism. People, dependent on the neighboring goodwill, tended to conform. Of course, traditional communities— especially the covenanted ones—could tyrannize through enforcing their rigid behavioral standards. Security of community here rarely came without tension.

Against the impulses of community stood individualistic tendencies. With so many localities offering so many opportunities, Americans frequently found it expedient to move. Ties of family, friends, and neighbors moved toward the ephemeral in a nation of constant movers. However, even the most mobile of drifters could find solace in the local communities that sustained themselves. Most communities maintained cores of people relatively fixed in place.

New technologies—the telephone, the automobile, the airplane, the radio, the television, and so on—changed (and ultimately destroyed, in many places) the apparent need for local-based community (Meyrowitz, 1985). Improvements in transportation and communication—intended to bond places closer together—stimulate commerce generally, and award the specific investors in the new technologies. Although innovations were not intended to discourage and break down community, they often did. Automobiles enabled owners to travel and lose emotional commitment to neighborhood. New opportunities were created beyond the dictates of locally sanctioned codes of conduct. As places became outwardly directed, binding social fabrics invariably unraveled. Sometimes decline brought a reweaving of residual threads into larger fabrics: the rural neighborhood reoriented to town, or the urban neighborhood submerged in the amorphous city. Even where city neighborhoods survived, they were easily overwhelmed by the realities of social change (new social groups replacing old), of economic change (new employment bases replacing old), or political change (new power bases replacing old).

Thus, Americans have recently experienced the rise of nonplace communities of the limited-liability kind. For many, a sense of belonging does not attach to locality, but is defined around shared interests spatially diffuse. People relate to one another through shared values—especially values of consumption. One's place of work and place of recreation contribute much to a sense of identity. At work and play, interpersonal relationships tend to be experienced firsthand. In one's neighborhood, interpersonal relationships may be largely symbolic, signified indirectly through the display of property.

These changes have been aided and abetted by the American economic system. Modern capitalism is the engine that has propelled such change. The high value given to private property and the quest for its unencumbered use in profit taking have been crucial. Exchange values dominate over use values in the configuring of local spaces: most localities lack the wherewithal to withstand market pressures for land. Communities thus emphasize the private, personal prerogatives of entrepreneurs (increasingly redefined by the corporate mold) and their right to move capital in search of lower operating costs. They emphasize a mobile labor force (labor viewed only as a cost of production) willing to move in the face of job loss, job shift, and new job creation. American capitalists, consequently, have never been in the business of creating and sustaining permanent places as human habitats. They rarely seek to ensure community stability. Always, they have been in the business of making profits.

The American way to profit has been configured by a legal system that encourages rapid change and promotes bigness. Accelerated depreciation and other tax allowances and deductions have, through the 1980s, encouraged new construction over old, usually to the benefit of big investors over small. Government programs (especially at the federal level)—besides encouraging widespread automobility through highway construction—encouraged suburban growth through subsidizing middle- and upper-class residential construction. Rather than confronting directly problems of unemployment, poverty, inadequate housing for low-income groups, and crime (among other social problems), Americans have attempted to subsume such difficulties with an expansive economy. Economic growth has become the watchword since World War II, the assumption being that growth will produce affluence—enough affluence to "trickle down" to society's deprived.

The tyranny of geographical space continues to dominate one segment of America's population: her poor—especially the minority poor (blacks and Hispanics) warehoused in decaying cities. A segregated "underclass" has emerged. The habitats of the poor are crumbling around them—a situation that accelerates oppression and self-depreciating criminality, people turning on their surroundings to further demean their prisons of space and resources. Here is anomie, not community. Its roots lie in unemployment, underemployment, blockage of aspirations, inadequate education, and the effects of institutionalized racism. Anomie is visibly reflected in derelict urban landscapes. Its extent is vast—too much for a nation that prides itself as world leader and model for future world generations.

People trapped in poverty have little basis for community bonding. Their wealth is insufficient to trigger concerns for property. The material surroundings stigmatize them. There is little on which to base pride of place; and there is, accordingly, little solace in place identification. This "underclass" lacks the social capital to bond. Attempts at community building fail because of fatalist and defeatist attitudes. This despair is undiminished by nominal public charity. Moreover, a fatalist dependency evolves—a willingness to be dependent rather than assertive. The poor fail to control their lives; thus, they walk a path of self-contempt. In a final irony, isolation prevents them from connecting with the American mainstream. Not only have the affluent fled the environment of the poor—collapsing their residual communities behind them—but so also have family-sustaining job opportunities. In sum, lack of community results from and sustains poverty. Slums are perpetrated as storehouses for society's least desirable.

Locality-based communities appear to be both an antidote against environmental decay and a catalyst for reclaiming decayed places. Built environments are human constructs. They reflect a society's values and its ability to organize toward sustaining those values. Society structures landscape and is itself structured by landscape—the material world being laden with symbolisms that help to pattern human behavior. Landscape maintenance reflects a society's state of health. In a democracy, landscape vibrancy results from active planning for change and effective resource use. The realm of politics is crucial here, providing outlets for local citizen decision making and control of resource allocation. The local political realm, we believe, must involve all residents in performing these functions. The obvious gain in efficiency that empowering communities will bring needs to be supplemented with concerns for equity. The issue of who benefits is as important as the degree to which people benefit. Without this additional concern, the locality-based community concept becomes just another mechanism for exchange-value advocates to dominate local restructuring agendas. The excitement of streamlining planning and resource distribution procedures, therefore, must be complemented by concerns for costs and benefits incurred.

Totalitarian regimes bring order to landscape by centrally imposing values of control. Orderliness in place reflects successful control: the power of the state clearly symbolized, especially in public spaces. In a democracy, power is diffuse. The tolerance for disorder is necessarily broad to encompass diverse interests. In the United States, where governmental powers are restricted, individual residents are given substantial power to configure private property. Business interests—especially those of urban elites—concentrate on a control of property that justifies proposed developments as environmentally cleansing, much as totalitarian political regimes justify their building programs. Stability, orderliness, and maintenance can also spring from local-based community—especially those where bonding plays out around issues of property protection. Local-based community in urban America has been difficult to sustain, given centralized political power. Nonetheless, it is the potential seed that offers hope for reversing dereliction.

9

Conclusion

Dereliction has always been part of the American scene. Europeans cut down forests and broke land with wasteful extravagance in securing footholds in the New World. The harvesting of the sea, the exploitation of the soil, and the relentless quest for furs, minerals, and other valuables left paths of destruction that totally disrupted native ecologies held stable by the aboriginal populations. North America would never again be in any sense pristine. The importation of European capitalism would consume the continent, shaping and creating but also disrupting and despoiling. The westward march of the frontier was one of environmental exploitation where individuals and corporations sought opportunity in developing farms, mines, towns, and cities. Overall it was a conquering marked by profligacy and waste. Americans "commodified" the physical environment by reducing development to a privatized and wealth-creating undertaking.

Environmental abuse was justified in the name of progress. New development and destruction of the old proceeded simultaneously. Built environments unfolded that initiated a subjugation of land and resources in the name of economic growth and progress. Cities and towns evolved as capitalist growth points, where land, labor, and capital were efficiently harnessed to spur wealth production. Imposed on the land were grids of roads and streets and networks of canals and railroads on which change was actively promoted. Architecturally, America became an ephemeral land of accelerating redevelopment: material culture being used up and replaced or, alternatively, discarded the same as nature. Changes in transportation and other technologies wrought new places—which left the old often isolated and in decline. Once thriving villages withered when bypassed by railroads. Once thriving towns declined when bypassed by highways. For every action, there was a reaction; and in the reaction, dereliction often lurked.

283

DERELICTION AND CHANGE IN AMERICA

Everything in landscape carries social meaning. What then is it that dereliction traditionally has symbolized in America? Most Americans have seen dereliction as temporary, inevitable, squalid, and a precondition to renewal. It is overt degradation, but something short-lived and functionally important as a cleansing agent. It was therefore seen to be useful in the evolution of new things and, accordingly, could be tolerated in at least modest doses for limited periods of time. Chronic dereliction, however, had to be escaped; but then, old places were easily abandoned for new, and dereliction readily evaded thereby. For most Americans, dereliction spoke of change, which in turn pretended progress—a safe assumption in a nation of seemingly unlimited resources and technological potential. As America matured, most places got bigger and better; and positive assumptions about dereliction, for most people, were validated most of the time.

Change is integral to the American way of life. America is never finished, and deliberately so. It is a nation with landscapes in perpetual states of emerging and occluding. American places are basically ephemeral, for not even successful places escape constant tinkering. Places that function well turn profits for their owners, satisfy their occupants, and permit the acquiring of suitable life chances. But they are as vulnerable to shifts of technology, cycles of capital investment, competitions of vested interests, and passing fads of taste as any other kind of place. Successful places are creatures of the marketplace and can be victimized by economic and cultural shifts like other commodities. America is not a place for those who value landscape stability.

America's built environments are expected to be used up. Systems for repair and periodical renewal tend not to be built into new construction. Maintenance tends not to be planned. Americans build in the cheapest way and then neglect maintenance. Having extracted value from a place, Americans typically move on to extract value elsewhere. They seek to "filter up" to better places, passing down old landscapes to those coming behind. No place can remain the same for long, given this game of musical chairs— which, as a kind of sport, has long been the real national pastime. Change stands as a self-fulfilling prophecy in the United States. The only circumstance that does not change is change itself, which marches relentlessly along. Newness is prized in a blind future-orientation. The quest for modernism in recent generations has rejected the past out of hand—for, as obsolescence is expected, obsolescence is obtained.

America is not a conserving nation. The idea of stewarding natural and built environments is not deeply inculcated in the American mind. As a society, we make less than optimal use of resources already invested in landscapes, readily tapping new resources elsewhere instead. America is not set up to run as a steady-state economy. We do not consider ourselves integral with nature. The thirst for material happiness, profit taking, and subsequent hypermobility fuels a form of disquieting alienation that penetrates everyday life. Americans know that their economy must constantly expand or it will collapse, and places are constantly restructured to meet this requirement. Landscape and place are annihilated by the never-ending quest to unearth wealth. In the process, past and future concerns become subordinated to present drives and imperatives. The richness of life, its past relics, and its future aspirations are flagrantly discarded by a society viewing life through a materialist lens.

Every generation has known its derelict zones, but never before has dereliction become so widespread and visible. The pace of change has accelerated, and displacement been made more profound. American profit pursuits now transcend national boundaries, ensnaring growing numbers of people in the capital–wage relations of deindustrialization. Impermanence has become epidemic. With highly mobile firms and labor forces, the nation's industrial geography is in a clear and unmistakable state of flux. The shift from railroad- and pedestrian-oriented landscapes to those of excessive automobility explains much. The automobile has given Americans increased mobility and made possible the accelerated creation of suburbs. The automobile, improved telecommunications, and air travel have fostered a decentralized economy. Capital has been liberated to seek investment opportunities where labor and other productive factors are cheapest. The growth of big business and big government has fostered concentrated decision making and made economic development less responsive to local needs. The nation finds itself intertwined in a rapidly integrating worldwide economy as it faces a new "postindustrial" era.

In recent decades, tremors from America's great unresolved social dilemma—racial inequality—have racked the nation. The withdrawal of affluent whites from central cities—subsidized by federal transportation, housing, and taxing policies—reflects an entrenched racist dimension in American society. Dual housing markets with expanding zones of transition have wrought gross instability, intensifying decline, and wholesale neighborhood abandonment. The civil rights movement momentarily restricted overt discriminatory practices like racial separation of schools, housing, and employment opportunities. Less obvious discriminatory processes, however, have persisted. Redlining, blockbusting, and realtor steering continue to flourish. These institutionalized practices sustain the isolation of a poverty-stricken underclass in the inner cities. Racism's final phase in America is still a long way off.

The loss of a stabilizing political compass led the nation into a disastrous adventure in Vietnam. The war diverted federal monies from social programs designed to eradicate social inequalities. It sapped the nation's economy by committing investment capital to nonproductive war instruments. A defense establishment was reinforced at the expense of upgrading social welfare. A heightened military posture contributed substantially to feelings of national insecurity; atomic war threatened a kind of ultimate dereliction. Shifts in the balance of trade, federal spending deficits, and an overly strong dollar in the 1970s and early 1980s negated the promises of superabundance made by liberal and conservative growth coalitions after World War II. America began to experience job loss and declining standards of living relative to other nations. The 1980s emergence of strong Japanese and West German economies threatened to reduce America to second-rate status. Suddenly, America's derelict zones came to symbolize profound problems.

America had always been able to ignore dereliction in her landscape. It was usually isolated, small scale, and closely tied geographically and temporally to visible new improvements. Derelict things were assumed away as temporary manifestations awaiting redevelopment. This despoliation was justified as necessary to modernization and growth; as transitional between the end of one phase of development and the beginning of another. So long as the nation grew rapidly, optimism jaundiced America's perceptions. When Americans saw abandoned factories, deteriorated slums, rundown towns, and neglected farms, they persisted in seeing a transient phenomenon. Dereliction represented a temporary fallow stage in the recycling of capitalist landscapes. It was ephemeral and of little consequence. Disinvestment, underutilization, vacancy, abandonment, and outright degradation were ignored. In confronting the common vagrant, for example, Americans typically looked the other way, stepped around, and went off about their normal business. Their reaction to derelict landscapes has been similar.

Today, dereliction is no longer confined to out-of-the-way places bypassed by the march of progress. It pervades urban centers and subsumes whole regions. It is difficult to avoid. Dereliction operates at a massive scale, defined in cities not by the block or by the street but by the square mile. Derelict zones have come to sustain large low-income populations whose social pathologies are increasingly difficult to contain. Curative processes of the past no longer seem to offer solutions; dereliction appears to have become unstoppable. Where landscapes and buildings stand abandoned for decades, rebirth cannot so readily be assumed. Especially discouraging is recognition that many recent ameliorative programs have compounded the crisis—urban renewal, public housing, the War on Poverty among them. The American economy no longer pretends a superabundance with which to solve social and environmental problems. Dereliction has become truly frightening.

Avoiding Dereliction

Affluent Americans have recently developed a hypersensitivity to dereliction. They have increasingly escaped obsolescence, oldness, and pastness, through out-migration. They have opted for newness—if not modernity—as a hedge against seemingly inevitable decline, which is seen as dark, foreboding, inevitable, and threatening to consumption lifestyles. If one cannot escape dereliction, then, as with death, one can at least strive to evade and postpone it. Evasion has led to a whole new sorting out of the American people. Affluent Americans have separated themselves from the lesser sorts seen as the carriers of decline. The affluent escape to places where property equity can be sustained. American society has stratified geographically and socially as never before—a nation dividing against itself. In the drive for newness, Americans close out the unpleasant realities of life in favor of the happy view. Geographical separation from problems has become America's biggest sustainer of optimism.

Americans have an array of possible ways to interpret and respond to dereliction. For example, they can conceptualize dereliction as simultaneously problem and opportunity. A first step involves developing a tolerance for old things. Respect for the old necessitates an informed sense of history. Awareness of things past can excite pleasure, especially in landscapes that display temporal depth. Age, whether rendered in surface patina or reflected in total ruin, takes on aesthetic value. Moreover, since old things cannot be created anew but only spared, pastness in the built environment is always a limited resource. Positive social status is easily ascribed to rare things when the context is correct. Antiquity stabilized and conserved can be a positive status referent, as witnessed in the burgeoning gentrification movement. In these developments, an emergent awareness exists that the past need not be utterly rejected.

Increased concern for maintenance and orderliness offers a counterforce to dereliction. Built-in systems for maintenance promise to extend structural life. Constructing more durable and energy-efficient buildings and providing for their constant monitoring and periodic repair prolongs use. To this end, tax laws are necessary that will encourage building upgrading and repair. Further, accelerated depreciation and other tax benefits need to be extended to new and old construction alike. A society can cope with dereliction by effectively managing its built environment. It can plan growth to maximize resource utilization—not only new resources obtained from nature, but old resources already invested in built infrastructure.

Shrinkage of urban infrastructure can be planned in order that spillover and other effects of abandonment be minimized. Cities can practice "triage" by funneling capital investment and operating monies into easily salvageable neighborhoods, withdrawing such support from areas less salvageable. By concentrating people and activities, cities can be made more efficient in their functioning even amid derelict spaces. Cleared land, protected from economically marginal land uses, can be made to represent a kind of community savings account set aside for significant future development. Government, however, must intervene in real estate markets. Private market processes alone are insufficient to confront infectious decay. Orderliness is a communal value outside the ability of private interests to attain, especially under grossly unstable conditions of urban fiscal distress. Traditionally, urban investment has stimulated higher density land uses. Clustering, for its part, is predicated on focused intensification in a context of overall thinning.

Emergent U.S. central city revitalization in the 1980s required substantial governmental involvement as, for example, the imposition of historic districts and the empowering of development corporations. Communal compacts of various sorts were established to forge future growth agendas. To sustain this process, we must continue to recognize the importance of place renewal and maintenance. Government can be a critical facilitator through the prudent use of its financial and political resources. Government funds—including block grants, homesteading resources, housing subsidies, and the like—can stabilize declining areas. Political processes, moreover, can bring low-income people into the planning process and heighten their awareness of options at their disposal. In effect, government's provision of technical assistance, financial resources, and planning expertise may stem dereliction.

Locality-based community is vital to stabilizing urban neighborhoods. The creation of place-concerned institutions is a starting point for facilitating turnaround. What could be more appropriate than politically institutionalized communities that make place creation and place maintenance a central concern. Stabilized and revitalized neighborhoods require that strict attention be paid both to exchange and use values as they translate into the physical infrastructure of built environment. The human habitat contains and symbolizes community. Lack of interest in the functioning and symbolization of place invites dereliction. Indeed, derelict zones may be defined as places lacking positive social symbolization and constructive use since they lack a sustaining community of interest.

Values Manifested

What do the realities of dereliction in today's America say about Americans? Certainly, dereliction speaks of individualism. Most Americans seek individual solutions in dealing with environmental decay. Having found it difficult to sustain communities based on ethnicity, for example, ethnic

Americans now flood the suburbs. Only the affluent and better-educated gentry have recently succeeded in forming and sustaining communities in central cities, their successes based firmly on issues of equity—enhancement through property protection. Only in the elite suburbs (and perhaps in elite resorts) are people seemingly totally safe from dereliction. Part of the attraction of big-city suburbia is the existence of its small-scale, autonomous municipalities that remain responsive to resident needs in matters of stabilizing property values and other social issues. In more affluent suburbs, lifestyles clearly dictate concern with use values as well as with exchange values—values communicated in landscape through high-style architecture, landscaping, and other amenities covered by zoning ordinances, deed restrictions, land use covenants, and other mechanisms of communal control.

Community, however, is not overtly a central concern in suburbia. The benefits of stability in place are still seen to accrue to the individual. But whereas elites seek to manipulate for profit the spaces of less affluent classes, they obtain for themselves—through control of government in suburban exclaves—police powers with which to stabilize and enhance their own spaces. In this regard, more affluent and better-educated Americans (and therefore the more politically savvy) have long benefited, in fact, from the advantages of locality-based community. Most elites advocate full rights in private property ownership, unfettered market freedom, and independence from governmental control (although governmental subsidy of private initiatives usually is welcomed). Nonetheless, elites readily surrender such rights to government in the creation of their own residential communities. Through community they seek to maximize their individual lives.

By contrast, exchange values dominate use values in the bulk of America's central city neighborhoods (and, indeed it could be argued, in most of the nation's small towns and rural precincts as well). "Economic space" prevails over "life space." In their nation's economic organization, most Americans function like pawns in a gigantic chess game. Individuals may be represented collectively in city councils, state legislatures, and Congress, with elected officials passing an electorate's muster; but the United States is not an economic democracy. True, entrepreneurs adhere to market processes; but in today's age of oligopolies, corporate entrepreneurs greatly restrict the range of options brought to the marketplace. Americans consume what they are offered. Americans enjoy access to an unparalleled range of goods and services; this, however, does not negate the fact that America's marketplace options are constricted.

Americans are content to reproduce these guiding political and economic processes. Relatively few seek to adjust the rules by which the game of life is played. They have allowed themselves to be reduced from citizens to clients. Government bureaucracies and big corporations define the fabric of everyday life. American individualism is preserved primarily in the selection and process of consuming things. For America's more affluent, levels of consumption have reached hedonistic proportions. The less affluent, on the other hand, can only emulate this process. America of the twentieth century has seen the triumph of a consumer ethic; the engine of American society runs to use things up, often wastefully. This is accepted as consumptive expectations are fulfilled.

Success in America is a drive to get one's "rightful" share. A sense of social progress derives when individuals collectively think of themselves as successful consumers. Newness imparts an allusion of success. It pretends progress, for it enables consumption in new and innovative ways. Newness consumed, especially early on in an innovation phase, suggests an advantage over others; and accordingly, status attaches through the mere fact of adoption. As a sense of success derives from embracing newness, so also does it derive from rejecting oldness—especially the obsolete. In the need to abandon, dereliction looms an unfortunate by-product. Most successful Americans view most old places as repositories for the unsuccessful; and indeed, many old places have become just that in the United States. But much that is new in the built environment is not better than the old, but merely different. Indeed, much new construction in the nation is decidedly inferior to the old by design, workmanship, and quality of materials used. The drive for newness in the built environment actually offers less to many people who only *think* they are getting more.

People become readily adapted to their surroundings—especially those who consider themselves powerless in the prevailing schemes of entrepreneurship and governance. Human adaptability is a great sustainer of dereliction in America. So widespread has dereliction become—so indelible has it grown in so many places—that Americans who cannot escape its debilitating effects increasingly come to accept it as a necessary condition. The succumbing to dereliction as a natural accompaniment of life bodes ill. A society both forms and is formed by the physical habitat it occupies, for, as we have argued previously, the built environment is indeed a repository of symbolisms whereby people communicate. The values and tastes that play out in the landscape serve to mold behavior, reinforcing people's beliefs, attitudes, and intentionalities relative to one another. By their physical structuring, landscapes provide degrees of freedom vis-à-vis a population's functioning as social entity. But the symbolic constraints are more important. When does dereliction become a way of life and not just a condition of life for those surrounded by the slovenliness of decaying and disordered habitats?

Acceptance of dereliction counters much of the traditional spirit of America. The drive to self-improvement diminishes when one's surroundings constantly communicate failure. The work ethic languishes in favor of consumerist stances often reduced to extreme forms of narcissism, including that of drug abuse. Work avoidance looms as dereliction's accompaniment, inviting downward spirals of negative self-absorption. Parasitic dandyism emerges where alienation has not squelched the success drive. Dereliction negates basic assumptions around which the mainsprings of America have long been tightly wound. Dereliction negates a sense of progress, a sense of a better future. Warehoused in degrees of poverty, residents of America's derelict zones languish in a hopelessness that for many has become chronic. Hopelessness breeds anomie. Anomie fosters criminality and other behaviors seen as deviant by America's majority, who find it increasingly difficult to isolate themselves from the turmoils implicit in their society.

Dereliction reflects selfishness. It mirrors competitive social, economic, and political realities that spawn clear winners and losers. Derelict zones have served successful Americans as important reference places, reminding of advantages won and misfortunes avoided. They enable the successful to measure personal good fortune against the misfortunes of others, embodying symbols of material impoverishment long transcended. The successful see misfortune and, having held it at a distance in their own lives, use the experience to bolster their sense of worth. Derelict landscapes offer a mirror. They are the psychological antipodes of America's privileged places. Dereliction makes the pretensions of status very real in demonstrating all that the elites have conquered.

TOWARD A SENSE OF CONTROL

How much dereliction can America tolerate? At what point will dereliction pose a threat to the social fabric of the nation? Americans have felt themselves an exceptional people immune from the forces of decline played out around them, past and present. The American propensity to ignore decline—particularly its physical landscape manifestations—has been part of this syndrome. At what point, however, does a degraded, disordered built environment begin to send truly negative messages about who we are as a people? When do these messages begin to undermine our fundamental sense of confidence as a nation? With America's central cities in substantial disarray and rural and small-town America rapidly declining, that point of national disillusionment may not be far away. In the future, we as a society will reach a kind of threshold. We will be forced to make a real commitment to wise resource management, minimizing dereliction in the process. Before then, however, we will probably accelerate further the drive to exploit environments, reducing them to even greater degrees of slovenliness and depredation. Whole categories of American place will suffer chronic abuse for which, by the overwhelming scale of the problem, there will be no apparent easy remedy.

The positive view for America is one of enhanced place consciousness where landscapes are valued for wide-ranging social meanings. This view, however, necessitates a dramatic shift in American attitudes toward the importance of built environments. Landscapes do not evolve naturally, driven by unseen and uncomprehended forces. People—particularly influential elite opinion makers and decision makers—form landscapes through various institutional arrangements predicated on self-interest. The majority, acting as clients and customers, accept, abide, or reject landscapes according to individual proclivities. It is in the role of passive consumers that Americans orient themselves to landscape—which accordingly tends, in many circumstances, to be an oppressive orientation. We believe that this can change with the realization that landscapes should be humane forms, structured to reflect the individual needs of all. Everyone should be able to extract necessary materialist, emotive, and aesthetic sustenance. There are, unfortunately, many people today whose sentiments and needs go totally ignored. They reside in landscapes fully shaped by other people. These people need to be heard. Derelict landscapes need to be restructured to end their deprivation, suffering, and disquieting silence.

By building a sense of community around issues of environmental concern, localities stand to defend themselves against unwarranted wastage. Defending built environments at the local scale requires resident influence over—if not control of—land use. Local political agendas must be constructed around deed restrictions, around covenants shared in communal property management, or through the use of police powers such as zoning. Governments influence stability in land use through tax policies, capital budgeting, and the rendering of services—which necessitates a degree of local governmental control if local values are to be upheld. In localities managed by impersonal bureaucracies, people often find themselves manipulated by business or other interests linked to distant politicians. Much landscape dereliction in the United States rests on local inabilities to resist and counter detrimental external forces.

Locality-based communities may not be able to halt decline externally induced. A corporation's decision to close a local plant, for example, is often beyond local abilities to reverse. But communal action based on local interests can ameliorate losses. Conserving stances can be taken to retard an area's dissipation, enabling locals to regroup themselves and renew the community's functioning along positive lines of innovation. Mass wastage need not be assumed. What locals cannot accomplish acting as individuals under free-market circumstances, they may well accomplish with community action. Mobilized communities can stabilize property values, rebuild public and private infrastructures, and capitalize new building projects and the like. These community acts would both reflect and invite vigor. Landscape growth and decline cycles are expected under capitalism, and some dereliction is a logical outgrowth. Nonetheless, dereliction need not generate intensive physical and resource collapse that leaves widespread poverty and despair in its wake. Local coalitions can blunt this process with aggressive actions that assert the need to restore humane and livable environments.

Much recent landscape change has been wrought by forces regional, national, and even international in scope. Local communities cannot hope to stand alone against such impelling change. How, therefore, are local problems to be formulated and solved set against these broader contexts? For the city, should centralized agencies impose paternalistic solutions to problems professionally conceived? Or should locality-based communities link together in federated systems of problem solving, guaranteeing grassroots views? By the 1980s, many of the nation's central cities were literally ungovernable over extensive sections of their territory. Centralized bureaucracies failed to safeguard still livable neighborhoods. We believe that cities ought to be politically restructured to foster degrees of local control over local concerns. Neighborhoods need to be extended the meaningful responsibilities of self-governance. New political communities need to be created where social vacuums now languish. But success at preventing and curing dereliction through locality-based community will hinge on linking those communities to higher levels of urban and regional governance. Local voices need to be heard in the planning process; broader government structures need to provide resources and assure equity considerations. This balanced perspective ascribes tasks to rebuilding neighborhoods across the array of spatial scales. To rely exclusively on broader-level government or local-based actors is to invite abuse and inequality in restructuring.

Change brings dereliction when owners and managers of local resources pursue short-run economic returns. Since the Depression, the American tax system—through accelerated depreciation and other mechanisms—has promoted extreme shortsightedness in business. Dereliction accompanies accelerated change when overcapacities are encouraged, inviting a wasting of still functional infrastructure. Dereliction comes to the fore when governments prove unable to ameliorate such change. Dereliction remains a chronic problem when people evade, adapt, and otherwise refuse to change the institutions that perpetuate syndromes of change for change's sake. Dereliction can be controlled only to the extent that Americans prove willing to monitor change and alter institutions that produce needless waste.

Americans need not always be jockeying for position in a ceaseless quest for security ever located beyond the horizon. They need not be perpetually fearful of losing by standing still in places of developed affection. They need not fear putting down roots. Instead, they can come to enjoy a new kind of freedom: the freedom to stay put. Americans have long safeguarded their rights—especially their sense of independence, which was clearly translated into love of mobility. The right to move and move frequently, however, has been transformed into need. Succeeding in America requires constant attention to escaping decay and decline. Environmental degradation looms problematical not only to the poor who abide in it as habitat, but to the affluent who aim continually to avoid it. A kind of frontier operates in America today. It is not the frontier of new opportunities claiming undeveloped spaces. It is the frontier of unresolved problems denying and threatening personal opportunities through decay and decline. It is an invidious frontier that pushes Americans constantly from place to place.

LEARNING FROM DERELICTION

Do Americans still want the always shifting, unstable landscapes that have characterized their nation over past decades? Or have Americans tired of the kaleidoscope of places that is an America ever changing? Perhaps Americans are ready to seek more stability by putting down roots in places affectionately held. Perhaps Americans are ready for built environments where innovation preserves the best of the past. Perhaps they are ready for places where positive change comes incrementally, configured out of stewarding impulses. New starts on unsullied ground made sense in a young country with abundant land and other resources. But in a mature nation with rapidly dwindling resource stocks, wasteful adolescent behaviors make little sense.

We will not be naive and assert that Americans will soon change their fundamental values or alter their entrepreneurial instincts so as substantially to eradicate wasteful landscape change. Americans tend not to see problems (or act to solve problems that they do see) until crises are reached. We have argued above that dereliction has indeed reached a crisis point in America. As students of landscape, we all have to recognize this crisis and search for solutions. At issue is physical and human degradation that has slowly engulfed our cities and beyond. People and environments have been left behind in an era of seeming affluence that only benefits selective landscapes and populations. Capitalist development has proceeded along uneven paths of development, which now threaten America through profound imbalance and inequity.

Scholars can shape a dialogue regarding dereliction's implications for

American society. We hope this book contributes to that end. Much remains to be learned, however, let alone communicated. Have we yet measured dereliction in all its varied forms? Have we fully comprehended how various kinds of people see or conceptualize dereliction and act on their comprehensions? Academics need to probe further the who, where, when, and how of dereliction, seeking to understand more fully why its various manifestations are so widespread in America. We believe dereliction reflects basic values that guide Americans. Dereliction can be a prism through which to refocus inquiry on the cultural bases of Americanism. We can further investigate dereliction as a means of better knowing how America works. For the geographer, dereliction is a social and spatial process. Areal containers of neglect are generated, both structured by and structuring social processes. These containers are sociospatial entities formed by the interconnections of society, its institutions, and individual biographies. Their ceaseless interplay generates zones of disinvestment simultaneously forging and reflecting society.

Americans traditionally have sought opportunities around which to define personal successes. The move to new places and the quest for new things built around new beginnings carries the very essence of much of American history. But America does not sum up to cumulative success linearly defined. America is an accumulation of successes and failures—a nation where progress has been honed as much on false starts, misdirected adventures, and outright bankruptcy as anything else. Concern with dereliction gives us an opportunity to explore this other dimension of America being obscured by the boosters, apologists, and champions of the ever optimistic. Concern with dereliction offers a kind of realism that looks beyond America's successful to embrace fully her unsuccessful, as well. If we look only to the derelict-free zones of America in explaining and justifying ourselves as a nation, we will tell a story filled with illusions. Confronting derelict zones forces us more substantially to comprehend what it means to be American.

This scholarly sortie into America's derelict zones has produced some very personal comprehensions for its authors. As children we entered worlds believed essentially changeless. Cues taken from adults suggested that individual lives changed slowly, inexorably, and by extension of established trends. Progress was linear. It was an optimistic view that history did not really double back on itself, that most people and places did not retrograde, and that those who did were fundamentally flawed and could be blamed for their own misfortunes. We expected a certain world to continue forever. It was a world of streetcars, small corner grocery stores, and an eight-team American League. As adults, we now realize that things do change, that change is not always for the better, and that indeed it is often for the worse.

We think back to the Detroit and the New York City we individually knew as children, and the places that nurtured our parents. Can we honestly say that these new, substantially remade cities are today better places? We conclude that they are only different. Uneven development filtered through the lens of local conditions continues to produce poverty and dereliction amid wealth and prosperity. Inner-city revitalization has usually pushed dereliction to less visible locations, generating easily identifiable "progress" and concealing its symbiotic partner: dereliction. We argue, then, that tied part and parcel to capitalist development is the production of renewed and derelict landscapes. Their spatial patterns change, their shuffling is ceaseless, but their emergence is constant.

We are astounded by the scale of geographical displacement that has occurred over our lifetimes. America is a mosaic of interconnected places constantly changing as economic conditions dictate new patterns of investment, labor migration, infrastructural construction, and so forth. Farms, rural neighborhoods, towns, and cities become interwoven through a connected ensemble of capital, labor, and resource flows. Amid global, regional, and local uneven development, some of the places prosper and others suffer. The magnitude of prosperity and suffering, moreover, are transmitted through local institutions. They define where these benefits and costs will localize. Local populations, actively interpreting these costs and benefits through local meanings and symbols, respond in frequently unique and novel ways to sustain or blunt these processes.

It follows that no class of place has universally prospered in terms of the time-honored criteria of population increase, economic growth, and political viability. Farms have disappeared at an ever-increasing rate, and with them most farm towns have declined. Shifting employment bases have left urban neighborhoods abandoned or in the process of being abandoned. If we compared all named places in the United States as they were at the end of World War II with their present condition, we would find, we believe, the vast majority to be lesser places today. Many have suffered from one or another form of chronic dereliction. They have physically eroded, with expectations for the future substantially diminished. Such decline was not something that most Americans expected half a century ago. They saw American landscapes evolving gently, naturally, and inevitably out of a less disquieting past.

As a nation we continue to reconfigure ourselves geographically. People, enterprise, and wealth concentrate in outer metropolitan rings. As a result of this refocusing, derelict landscapes have evolved, both of city center and beyond the suburbs in the countryside. The images of 50 years ago that promised a utopian future have proved misleading. True, our cities have been reorganized around networks of freeways and masses of tall buildings configured in modern styles of architecture. But the images of the utopian future were incomplete. They did not show that for every successful new landscape there would be many unsuccessful old ones. They did not show that behind the stylish facade of a modern America would languish a derelict America. How enthusiastically did America anticipate a new beginning after World War II! How flawed the result.

For ourselves—students of landscape history—these have been exciting decades. Documenting the ongoing changes in America's built environment has proved stimulating. But the waste implicit in that change has been immense—a fact that Americans need to owe up to fully. Social problems borne of the displacements caused are now most critical. Should the scholar's enthusiasm to observe and analyze perhaps give way to the impulse to reform? Should the stance of the basic researcher perhaps give way to that of the advocate? These have been interesting decades in which to live. Probably never before in American history has so much changed so drastically so quickly. The generation of our elders has seen extraordinary transformation. Will succeeding generations be able to abide the same with grace? Will they learn to demand increased humaneness in their built environments. Will they learn to diminish wastefulness and eliminate dereliction? Indeed, we wonder what our children and grandchildren will think when they look back to assess the landscapes of their lives and ours.

Bibliography

Adams, Carolyn T. 1982. "The Flight of Jobs and Capital: Prospects for Grassroots Action." In John C. Raines, Lenore E. Berson, and David M. Gracie (eds.), *Community and Capital In Conflict: Plant Closings and Job Loss*. Philadelphia: Temple University Press. Pp. 3–36.

Adams, J. 1970. "Residential Structure of Midwest Cities." *Annals of the Association of American Geographers*, 60, pp. 37–62.

Adams, William Y. 1980. "The Dead Community: Perspectives from the Past." In Art Gallaher, Jr., and Harland Padfield (eds.), *The Dying Community*. Albuquerque: University of New Mexico Press. Pp. 23–56.

Agnew, John A. 1981. "Homeownership and Capitalistic Social Order." In Michael Dear and Allen J. Scott (eds.), *Urbanization and Urban Planning in Capitalist Society*. London and New York: Methuen.

———. 1984. "Devaluing Place: 'People Prosperity Versus Place Prosperity' and Regional Planning." *Environment and Planning D: Society and Space*, 1, pp. 35–45.

———. 1987. *The United States in the World Economy: A Regional Geography*. Cambridge, UK: Cambridge University Press.

Ahlbrandt, Roger S. Jr., 1984. *Neighborhoods, People, and Community*. New York: Plenum Press.

Ahlbrandt, Roger S. Jr., and James V. Cunningham. 1979. *A New Public Policy for Neighborhood Preservation*. New York: Praeger.

Ainslie, Michael L. 1984. "Statement about Appropriations for Preservation." In Russell V. Keune (ed.), *The Historic Preservation Yearbook*. Bethesda, MD: Adler and Adler. Pp. 300–320.

Allen, Benjamin J. 1974. "The Economic Effects of Rail Abandonment on Communities: A Case Study." Unpublished Ph.D. dissertation. University of Illinois.

299

Allen, Irving L. 1984. "The Ideology of Dense Neighborhood Redevelopment." In Bruce London and J. John Palen (eds.), *Gentrification, Displacement, and Neighborhood Revitalization*. Albany: State University of New York Press. Pp. 27–42.

Allen, Vernon L., and David B. Greenberger. 1978. "An Aesthetic Theory of Vandalism." *Crime and Delinquency*, 24, pp. 309–21.

Anderson, Martin. 1986. "The Federal Bulldozer." In James Q. Wilson (ed.), *Urban Renewal: The Record and the Controversy*. Cambridge, MA: MIT Press. Pp. 496–508.

Aponte, Robert, and Kathryn Neckerman. 1987. "Joblessness versus Welfare Effects: A Further Reexamination." In William J. Wilson (ed.). *The Truly Disadvantaged: The Inner City, the Underclass, and Public Policy*. Chicago: University of Chicago Press. Pp. 93–106.

Arieli, Yehoshua. 1964. *Individualism and Nationalism In American Ideology*. Cambridge, MA: Harvard University Press.

Bagdikian, Ben H. 1978. "The Black Immigrants." In Richard D. Rodefield et al. (eds.), *Change in Rural America: Causes, Consequences, and Alternatives*. St. Louis: Mosby.

Baldassare, Mark. 1984. "Evidence for Neighborhood Revitalization: Manhattan." In Bruce London and J. John Palen (eds.), *Gentrification, Displacement, and Neighborhood Revitalization*. Albany: State University of New York Press. Pp. 90–102.

Banfield, E. 1970. *The Unheavenly City*. Boston: Little, Brown.

Barbanel, Josh. 1987. "Cycles of Concern: Societies and their Homeless." New York *Times*, November 29, p. 1-E.

Barbour, Ian G. 1980. *Technology, Environment, and Human Values*. New York: Praeger.

Barker, Michael, and Robert N. Wise (eds.). 1984. *Rebuilding America's Infrastructure: An Agenda for the 1980s*. Durham, NC: Duke University Press.

Barsch, Russel, and Jeffrey Gale. 1982. "U.S. Economic Development Policy: The Urban–Rural Dimension." In F. Stevens Redburn and Terry E. Buss (eds.), *Public Policies for Distressed Communities*. Lexington, MA: Lexington Books. Pp. 39–62.

Bassett, K., and J. Short. 1980. *Housing and Residential Structure*. London: Routledge and Kegan Paul.

Bauer, Douglas. 1981. "Why Big Business Is Firing the Boss." New York *Times Magazine*, March 8.

Beauregard, Robert A. 1986. "The Chaos and Complexity of Gentrification." In

Neil Smith and Peter Williams (eds.), *Gentrification of the City*. Boston: Allen and Unwin. Pp. 33–55.

---. 1989. Economic Restructuring and Political Response. Beverly Hills, CA: Sage.

Beckman, Norman. 1977. "Government's Role In Population Movement: Policy by Indirection." In Herrington J. Bryce (ed.), *Small Cities in Transition: The Dynamics of Growth and Decline*. Cambridge, MA: Ballinger. Pp. 51–71.

Beeghley, Leonard. 1983. *Living Poorly In America*. New York: Praeger.

Belden, Joe, and Gregg Forte. 1978. "A New Direction II: Rejuvenating the Small Family Farm." In Richard H. Rodefeld et al. (eds.), *Change in Rural America: Causes, Consequences, and Alternatives*. St. Louis: Mosby. Pp. 487–93.

Bell, Daniel. 1973. *The Coming of Post Industrial Society*. New York: Penguin.

———. 1978. *The Cultural Contradiction of Capitalism*. New York: Pantheon.

———. 1984. *The Cultural Contradictions of Capitalism*. New York: Basic Books.

Berndt, Harry E. 1977. *New Rulers in the Ghetto: The Community Development Corporation and Urban Poverty*. Westport, CT: Greenwood Press.

Berry, Brian J. L. 1980. "Inner City Futures: An American Dilemma Revisited." *Transactions of the Institute of British Geographers*, New Series, 5, pp. 1–28.

———. 1985. "Islands of Renewal in Seas of Decay." In P. Peterson (ed.), *The New Urban Reality*. Washington, DC: Brookings Institution.

Berry, Wendell. 1977. *The Unsettling of America: Culture and Agriculture*. New York: Avon.

———. 1988. "Living Well on the Good Land." *New York Times*, July 10, p. 2F.

Bertrand, Alvin L. 1980. "Ethnic and Social Class Minorities in the Dying Small Community," In Art Gallaher, Jr., and Harland Padfield (eds.), *The Dying Community*. Albuquerque: University of New Mexico Press. Pp. 187–205.

Birch, David. 1971. "Toward a Stage Theory of Urban Growth." *Journal of the Institute of Planners*, 37, pp. 78–87.

———. 1979. *The Job Generation Process*. Cambridge, MA: MIT Program on Neighborhood and Regional Change.

Black, J. Thomas. 1980. "Private-market Housing Renovation In Central Cities: An Urban Land Institute Study." In Shirley B. Laska and Daphne Spain (eds.), *Back to the City: Issues in Neighborhood Renovation*. New York: Pergamon Press. Pp. 3–12.

Blaikie, Piers, and Harold Brookfield (eds.). 1987. *Land Degradation and Society*. New York: Methuen.

Bluestone, Barry. 1982. "Deindustrialization and the Abandonment of Community." In John C. Raines, Lenore E. Berson, and David M. Gracie (eds.), *Com-*

munity and Capital in Conflict: Plant Closings and Job Loss. Philadelphia: Temple University Press. Pp. 38–61.

Bluestone, Barry, and Bennett Harrison. 1982. *The Deindustrialization of America: Plant Closings, Community Abandonment, and the Dismantling of Basic Industry.* New York: Basic Books.

Boulding, Kenneth E. 1968. *Beyond Economics: Essays on Society, Religion, and Ethics.* Ann Arbor: University of Michigan Press.

Bourne, Larry, and John R. Hitchcock. 1978. *Urban Housing Markets: Recent Directions and Research and Policy.* Toronto: University of Toronto Press.

Bowles, Samuel, David M. Gordon, and Thomas E. Weiskopf. 1983. *Beyond the Wasteland: A Democratic Alternative to Economic Decline.* Garden City, NY: Anchor.

Bowsher, Prentice. 1980. *People Who Care: Making Housing Work for the Poor.* Washington, DC: Jubilee Housing.

Boyce, Byrl N. 1975. *Real Estate Appraisal Terminology.* Cambridge, MA: Ballinger.

Boyte, Harry C. 1984. *Community Is Possible: Repairing America's Roots.* New York: Harper and Row.

Branson, William H. 1984. "The Myth of Deindustrialization." In Richard B. McKenzie (ed.), *Plant Closings: Public or Private Choices?* Washington, DC: Cato Institute.

Breckenfeld, Gurney. 1977. "How Cities Can Cope with Shrinkage." In *How Cities Can Grow Old Gracefully.* Subcommittee on the City, Committee on Banking, Finance, and Urban Affairs, House of Representatives, 95th Congress, 1st Session. Washington, DC: U.S. Government Printing Office. Pp. 105–17.

Brenner, Harvey. 1976. *Estimating the Social Costs of National Economic Policy: Implications for Mental Health and Clinical Aggression.* Washington, DC: U.S. Government Printing Office.

Brittan, Arthur 1973. *Meanings and Situations.* London: Routledge and Kegan Paul.

————. 1977. *The Privatized World.* London: Routledge and Kegan Paul.

Brown, H. 1980. "Work Groups." In Graeme Salaman and Kenneth Thompson (eds.), *Control and Ideology in Organizations.* Cambridge, MA: MIT Press.

Bunce, H. 1980. "The Spatial Dimension of the Community Development Block Grant Program: Targeting and Urban Impacts." In Norman Glickman (ed.), *The Urban Impacts of Federal Policies.* Baltimore: Johns Hopkins University Press.

Bunge, William, and R. Bordessa. 1975. *The Canadian Alternative: Survival Expectations and Urban Change.* Toronto: York University, Department of Geography.

Burch, William R., Jr. 1981. "Boom, Bust, and Maintenance: Cycles of Illusion and Reality in American Communities," In Edward J. Miller and Robert P. Wolensky (eds.), *The Small City and Regional Community.* Stevens Point, WI: Foundation Press.

Burtless, Gary. 1987. "Inequality in America: Where Do We Stand?" *Current*, no. 297, November, pp. 4–10.

Campbell, Angus, Philip E. Converse, and Willard L. Rodgers. 1976. *The Quality of American Life: Perceptions, Evaluations, and Satisfactions.* New York: Russell Sage Foundation.

Campbell, Colin. 1987. *The Romantic and the Spirit of Modern Consumerism.* Cambridge, UK: Basil Blackwell.

Carter, Everett. 1977. *The American Idea: The Literary Response to American Optimism.* Chapel Hill, NC: University of North Carolina Press.

Cassidy, Robert. 1980. *Livable Cities: A Grassroots Guide to Rebuilding Urban America.* New York: Holt, Rinehart, and Winston.

Castells, M. 1979. *The Economic Crisis and American Society.* Princeton, NJ: Princeton University Press.

Cater, J., and T. Jones. 1989. *Social Geography.* London: Edward Arnold.

Catlin, S. 1981. "The Use and Misuse of Community Development." *Administrative Science Quarterly*, 26, pp. 545–62.

Cawelti, John G. 1965. *Apostles of the Self-made Man.* Chicago: University of Chicago Press.

Center for Urban Studies. 1977. *Redlining and Disinvestment as a Discriminatory Practice in Residential Mortgage Loans, Part II.* Chicago: University of Illinois.

Champaign–Urbana *News-Gazette.* 1987. September 16, p. D2.

Chicago *Tribune.* 1988. "Poverty Edges Up in 1987, U.S. Says." September 1, sect. 1, p. 5.

Chicago *Tribune* Staff. 1986. *The American Millstone: An Examination of the Nation's Permanent Underclass.* Chicago: Contemporary Press.

Chicoine, David L. 1986. "Infrastructure and Agriculture: Interdependencies with a Focus on Local Roads in the North Central States." In Peter F. Korsching and Judith Gildner (eds.), *Interdependencies of Agriculture and Rural Communities in the Twenty-first Century: The North Central Region.* Ames: Iowa State University Press. Pp. 141–63.

Choate, Pat, and Susan Walter. 1983. *America in Ruins: The Decaying Infrastructure.* Durham, NC: Duke University Press.

Christoffel, Tom, David Finkelhor, and Dan Gilbarg (eds.). 1970. *Up against the American Myth.* New York: Holt, Rinehart, and Winston.

Cincotta, Gale. 1976. "Testimony." *Proceedings.* Committee on Banking, Housing, and Urban Affairs, U.S. Senate, 94th Congress, 2nd Session, June 14. Washington, DC: U.S. Government Printing Office.

Cipolla, Carlo M. 1970. *The Economic Decline of Empires.* London: Methuen.

Clark, Daniel. 1984. *Post-industrial America: A Geographical Perspective.* New York: Methuen.

Clark, Dennis. 1960. *Cities in Crisis: The Christian Response.* New York: Sheed and Ward.

Clark, G. 1989. "Pittsburgh in Transition: Consolidation of Prosperity in an Era of Economic Restructuring. In Robert A. Beauregard (ed.), *Economic Restructuring and Political Response.* Beverly Hills, CA: Sage.

Clark, G., and M. Dear. 1984. *State Apparatus: Structures and Language of Legitimacy.* Boston: Allen and Unwin.

Clawson, Marion. 1980. "The Dying Community: The Natural Resource Base." In Art Gallaher, Jr., and Harland Padfield (eds.), *The Dying Community.* Albuquerque: University of New Mexico Press. Pp. 55–88.

Clay, Phillip L. 1979. *Neighborhood Renewal: Middle-class Resettlement and Incumbent Upgrading in American Neighborhoods.* Lexington, MA: Lexington Books.

Cochran, Thomas C. 1985. *Challenges to American Values: Society, Business, and Religion.* New York: Oxford University Press.

Cohen, Armand. 1982. *Poletown, Detroit: A Case Study in "Public Use" and Reindustrialization.* Cambridge, MA: Lincoln Institute of Land Policy.

Cohen, R. B. 1971. "Multinational Corporations, International Finance, and the Sunbelt." In D. C. Perry and A. J. Watkins (eds.), *The Rise of the Sunbelt Cities.* Beverly Hills, CA: Sage. Pp. 211–26.

Cohen, Stanley. 1973. "Property Destruction: Motives and Meanings." In Colin Ward (ed.), *Vandalism.* London: Architectural Press. Pp. 23–53.

Cole, Robert C. 1979. *Work Mobility and Participation: A Comparative Study of American and Japanese Industry.* Berkeley: University of California Press.

Colwell, Peter F. 1976. *An Economic Analysis of Residential Abandonment and Rehabilitation.* Washington, DC: National Bureau of Standards.

Conlan, T. J. 1984. "The Politics of Federal Block Grants: From Nixon to Reagan." *Political Science Quarterly,* 99, pp. 247–70.

Conrad, Peter. 1984. *The Art of the City: Views and Versions of New York.* New York: Oxford University Press.

Cox, Kevin R., and Andrew Mair. 1988. "Locality and Community in the Politics of Local Economic Development." *Annals of the Association of American Geographers*, 78, pp. 307–25.

Cumming, Elaine and Henry Willing. 1961. *Growing Old.* New York: Basic Books.

Cybriwsky, Roman. 1978. "Social Aspects of Neighborhood Change." *Annals of the Association of American Geographers*, 68, pp. 17-33.

Cybriwsky, R., et al. 1986. "The Political and Social Construction of Revitalized Neighborhoods: Society Hill, Philadelphia, and False Creek, Vancouver." In Neil Smith and Peter Williams (eds.), *Gentrification of the City.* Boston: Allen and Unwin.

Dahl, Robert. 1961. *Who Governs?* New Haven, CT: Yale University Press.

Dahmann, Donald C. 1981. "Subjective Indicators of Neighborhood Quality." In Denis F. Johnson (ed.), *Measurement of Subjective Phenomena*. Washington, DC: Bureau of the Census.

Daniel, Pete. 1985. *Breaking the Land: The Transformation of Cotton, Tobacco, and Rice Cultures since 1880.* Urbana: University of Illinois Press.

Daniels, Thomas L., and Mark B. Lapping. 1987. "Small Town Triage: A Rural Settlement Policy for the American Midwest." *Journal of Rural Studies*, 3, pp. 273–80.

Davidson, Steven D., and Paul L. Pryde. 1982. "Capital and the Economic Development of Distressed Communities: The Role of Federal Development Financial Programs." In F. Stevens Redburn and Terry F. Buss (eds.), *Public Policies for Distressed Communities*. Lexington, MA: Lexington Books. Pp. 93–105.

Dear, Michael. 1976. "Abandoned Housing." In John S. Adams (ed.), *Urban Policymaking and Metro Dynamics*. Cambridge, MA: Ballinger. Pp. 59–100.

———. 1981. "Social and Spatial Reproduction of the Mentally Ill." In Michael Dear and Allen J. Scott (eds.), *Urbanization and Urban Planning in Capitalist Society*. London and New York: Metheun.

Dear, M., and A. Moos. 1986. "Structuration Theory in Urban Analysis, 2: Empirical Application." *Environment and Planning A*, 18, pp. 351–74.

Dear, Michael, and Jennifer R. Wolch. 1987. *Landscapes of Despair: From Deindustrialization to Homelessness*. Princeton NJ: Princeton University Press.

DePalma, Anthony. 1988. "Pace of Building Abandonment Tumbles." New York *Times*, July 10, p. 1-RY.

de Tocqueville, Alexis. 1956. *Democracy in America*. New York: Mentor.

"Detroit's Heroin Subculture." 1978. *Newsweek*. September 28.

deVise, Pierre. 1977. *The Annexation of Oak Park by Chicago*. Chicago: Chicago Regional Hospital Study, Working Paper No. 8.

Dicken, P. 1986. *Global Shift*. London: Harper and Row.

Dicken, P., and P. E. Lloyd. 1990. *Location in Space*. New York: Harper and Row.

DiGiovanni, Frank F. 1984. "An Examination of Selected Consequences of Revitalization in Six U.S. Cities." *Urban Studies*, 21, pp. 245–59.

DiGiovanni, Frank F., and Nancy A. Paulson. 1982. "The Social Neighborhood: An Unspecified Factor in Homeowner Maintenance?" *Urban Affairs Quarterly*, 18, pp. 235–54.

Dolbeare, Cushing. 1976. *Neighborhood Preservation*. Committee on Banking, Housing and Urban Affairs, U.S. Senate, 94th Congress, 2nd Session, June 14. Washington, DC: U.S. Government Printing Office.

Domhoff, G. William. 1983. *Who Rules America Now?* New York: Simon and Schuster.

Downs, Anthony. 1970. *Urban Problems and Prospects*. Chicago: Markham.

———. 1979. "Key Relationships between Urban Development and Neighborhood Change." *Journal of the American Planning Association*, 45, pp. 462–72.

———. 1980. "Using the Lessons of Experience to Allocate Resources in the Community Development Program." In Jon Pynoos, Robert Schafer, and Chester W. Hartman (eds.), *Housing Urban America*. New York: Aldine. Pp. 522–35.

———. 1981. *Neighborhoods and Urban Development*. Washington, DC: Brookings Institution.

———. 1983. *Rental Housing in the 1980s*. Washington DC: Brookings Institution.

Doyle, Don H. 1978. *The Social Order of a Frontier Community, Jacksonville, Illinois, 1825–70*. Urbana: University of Illinois Press.

Duncan, J., and D. Ley. 1982. "Structural Marxism and Human Geography: A Critical Assessment." *Annals of the Association of American Geographers*, 72, pp. 30–59.

Dye, Thomas R. 1986. "Community Power and Public Policy." In Robert J. Waste (ed.), *Community Power: Directions for Future Research*. Beverly Hills, CA: Sage. Pp. 29–51.

Eager, Robert C., and Wayne S. Hyatt. 1979. "Neighborhood Revival through Community Associations." In Stanley Berman, David Clurman, and Lewis R. Kaster (eds.), *New Tools for Recycling Properties: Real Estate Conversions and Rehabs*. New York: Harcourt, Brace, Jovanovich.

Edel, Matthew, Elliott Sclar, and Daniel Luria. 1984. *Shaky Palaces: Homeownership and Social Mobility in Boston's Suburbanization*. New York: Columbia University Press.

Edwards, R.C., Reich, M., and T. E. Wieskopf. 1978. *The Capitalist System*. Englewood Cliffs, NJ: Prentice-Hall.

Elkins, Stanley, and Eric McKitrick. 1954. "A Meaning for Turner's Frontier." *Political Science Quarterly*, 69, pp. 321–53 and 565–602.

Elazar, D. J. 1972. *American Federalism: A View from the States*. New York: Crowell.

Etzioni, Amitai. 1983. *An Immodest Agenda*. New York: McGraw–Hill.

Fainstein, Norman, Susan S. Fainstein, and Alex Schwartz. 1990. "Economic Shifts and Last Use in the Global City: New York, 1940–1987." In R. Beauregard (ed.), *Atop the Urban Hierarchy*. Lanham, MD: Rowman and Littlefield.

Fainstein, S. 1974. *Urban Political Movements*. Englewood Cliffs, NJ: Prentice-Hall.

Feagin, Joe R. 1984. "Sunbelt Metropolis and Development Capital: Houston in the Era of Late Capitalism." In Larry Sawyers and William K. Tabb (eds.), *Sunbelt/Snowbelt: Urban Development and Regional Restructuring*. New York: Oxford University Press. Pp. 99–127.

Finkler, Earl, and David C. Peterson (eds.), 1974. *Nongrowth Planning Strategies: The Developing Power of Towns, Cities, and Regions*. New York: Praeger.

Finkler, Earl, William J. Toner, and Frank J. Popper. 1976. *Urban Nongrowth: City Planning for People*. New York: Praeger.

Finney, Graham S. 1977. "Building from Strength in Mature Cities." In *How Cities Can Grow Old Gracefully*. Subcommittee on the City, Committee on Banking, Finance, and Urban Affairs, U.S. House of Representatives, 95th Congress, 1st Session. Washington, DC: U.S. Government Printing Office. Pp. 195–206.

Firey, Walter. 1947. *Land Use in Central Boston*. Cambridge, MA: Harvard University Press.

Fitch, James M. 1982. *Historic Preservation: Curatorial Management of the Built World*. New York: McGraw-Hill.

Fitchen, Janet. 1984. *Poverty in Rural America: A Case Study*. Boulder, CO: Westview Press.

Fletcher, W. Wendell, and Charles E. Little. 1982. *The American Cropland Crisis*. Bethesda, MD: American Land Forum.

Ford, Arthur M. 1973. *Political Economics of Rural Poverty in the South*. Cambridge, MA: Ballinger.

Ford, Thomas R. (ed.). 1978. *Rural USA: Persistence and Change*. Ames: Iowa State University Press.

Forman, Robert E. 1971. *Black Ghettos, White Ghettoes, and Slums*. Englewood Cliffs, NJ: Prentice-Hall.

Fox, Richard W., and T. J. Jackson Lears (eds.). 1983. *"Introduction."* In *The Culture of Consumption: Critical Essays in American History, 1880–1980*. New York: Pantheon Books. Pp. ix–xvii.

Francis, Dorothy B. 1983. *Vandalism: The Crime of Immaturity*. New York: Dutton.

Franklin, John H. 1956. *The Militant South*. Boston: Beacon Press.

Fried, Marc. 1966. "Grieving for a Lost Home: Psychological Costs of Relocation." In James Q. Wilson (ed.), *Urban Renewal: The Record and the Controversy*. Cambridge: MIT Press. Pp. 359–79.

Friedman, Lawrence M. 1980. "Public Housing and the Poor." In Jon Pynoos, Robert Schafer, and Chester W. Hartman (eds.), *Housing Urban America*. New York: Aldine. Pp. 473–84.

Friedmann, John. 1982. "Life Space and Economic Space: Contradiction in Regional Development." Unpublished manuscript quoted in Barry Bluestone and Bennett Harrison, *The Deindustrialization of America*. New York: Basic Books.

Furay, Carol. 1977. *The Grass-roots Mind in America: The American Sense of Absolutes*. New York: New Viewpoints.

Galbraith, Carol. 1976. "Conservation: The New Word for Old Neighborhoods." *Connecticut Law Review*, 8, pp. 312–33.

Gale, Dennis E. 1980. "Neighborhood Resettlement: Washington, DC." In Shirley B. Laska and Daphne Spain (eds.), *Back to the City: Issues in Neighborhood Renovation*. New York: Pergamon Press. Pp. 95–115.

Gale, S., and E. G. Moore. 1975. *The Manipulated City*. Chicago: Maaroufa.

Gallaher, Art, Jr., and Harland Padfield (eds.). 1980. *The Dying Community*. Albuquerque: University of New Mexico Press.

Gappert, G. 1979. *Post-affluent America*. New York: Franklin Watts.

Giddens, A. 1981. *A Contemporary Critique of Historical Materialism*. London: Macmillan.

———. 1985. "Time, Space, and Regionalization." In Derek Gregory and John

Urry (eds.), *Social Relations and Spatial Structures*. New York: St. Martin's Press.

Gilbert, Neil. 1987. "The Unfinished Business of Welfare Reform." *Society*, 24, pp. 5–11.

Gilder, G. 1981. *Wealth and Poverty*. New York: Basse.

Glickman, N. 1987. "Cities and the International Division of Labor." In Michael P. Smith and Joe R. Feagin (eds.), *The Capitalist City*. Cambridge, UK: Basil Blackwell.

Goetze, Rolf. 1983. *Rescuing the American Dream: Public Policies and the Crisis in Housing*. New York: Holmes and Meier.

Gold, Andrew. 1976. "The Welfare Economics of Historic Preservation." *Connecticut Law Review*, 8, pp. 348–69.

Gold, Diane F. 1980. *Housing Market Discrimination: Causes and Effects of Slum Formation*. New York: Praeger.

Gold, Steven D. 1982. *State Urban Enterprise Zones: A Policy Review*. Denver: National Conference of State Legislatures.

Goldschmidt, Walter. 1978. *As You Sow*. Montclair, NJ: Allheld, Osmun.

Goodwin, Carole. 1979. *The Oak Park Strategy: Community Control of Racial Change*. Chicago: University of Chicago Press.

Gordon, D. 1978. "Capitalist Development and the History of American Cities." In William K. Tabb and Larry James (eds.), *Marxism and the Metropolis*, New York: Oxford University Press.

Goro, Herb. 1970. *The Block*. New York: Random House.

Gorz, Andre. 1970. "Private Profit versus Public Need." In Tom Christoffel et al. (eds.), *Up Against the American Myth*. New York: Holt, Rinehart, and Winston. Pp. 33–47.

Gottdiener, Mark. 1985. *The Social Production of Urban Space*. Austin: University of Texas Press.

Greeley, Andrew M. 1977. *Neighborhood*. New York: Seabury Press.

Grier, George, and Eunice Grier. 1980. "Urban Displacement: A Reconnaissance." In Shirley B. Laska and Daphne Spain (eds.), *Back to the City: Issues in Neighborhood Renovation*. New York: Pergamon Press. Pp. 252–68.

Grimsby, William G. 1966. "Housing Markets and Public Policy." In James Q. Wilson (ed.), *Urban Renewal: The Record and the Controversy*. Cambridge, MA: MIT Press. Pp. 24–49.

Hall, Peter. 1966. *The World Cities*. New York: McGraw-Hill.

Hall, Robert E. 1980. *The Importance of Lifetime Jobs in the U.S. Economy.* Washington, DC: National Bureau of Research.

Hamnett, C. 1984. "Gentrification and Residential Location Theory: A Review and Assessment." In David Herbert and Ron Johnston (eds.), *Geography in the Urban Environment, Progress in Research and Application.* Chichester, UK: John Wiley.

Harrington, Michael. 1984. *The New American Poverty.* New York: Holt, Rinehart, and Winston.

Harris, Marvin. 1981. *America Now: The Anthropology of a Changing Culture.* New York: Simon and Schuster.

Harrison, Bennett, and Barry Bluestone. 1989. *The Great U-Turn: Corporate Restructuring and the Polarizing of America.* New York: Basic Books.

Hart, John F. 1964. "Abandonment of Farmland in Kentucky." *Southeastern Geographer,* 4, pp. 1–10.

Hart, John F. 1968. "Loss and Abandonment of Cleared Farm Land in the Eastern United States." *Annals of the Association of American Geographers,* 58, pp. 417–40.

———. 1980. "Land Use Change in a Piedmont County." *Annals of the Association of American Geographers,* 70, pp. 492–527.

Hartman, Chester. 1984. *The Transformation of San Francisco.* Totowa, NJ: Rowman and Allanheld.

Hartman, Chester, Robert P. Kessler, and Richard T. LeGates. 1980. "Municipal Housing Code Enforcement and Low-income Tenants." In Jon Pynoos, Robert Schafer, and Chester W. Hartman (eds.), *Housing Urban America.* New York: Aldine. Pp. 560–73.

Harvey, David. 1981. "The Urban Process under Capitalism: A Framework for Analysis." In Michael Dear and Allen J. Scott (eds.), *Urbanization and Urban Planning in Capitalist Society.* London and New York: Methuen. Pp. 91–121.

———. 1985. *Consciousness and the Urban Experience.* Baltimore: Johns Hopkins University Press.

Hawley, Amos H., and Sara M. Mazie (eds.). 1981. *Nonmetropolitan America in Transition.* Chapel Hill: University of North Carolina Press.

Hawley, F. Frederick. 1987. "The Black Legend in Southern Studies: Violence, Ideology, and Academe." *North American Culture,* 3, pp. 29–52.

Haworth, Lawrence. 1966. *The Good City.* Bloomington: Indiana University Press.

Hayes, Dennis. 1978. *Repairs, Reuse, Recycling: First Steps toward a Sustainable Society.* N.p.: Worldwatch Institute.

Hayes, Linda S. 1982. "Youngstown Bounces Back." *Fortune*, December 17. Pp. 102–96.

Heidenheimer, Arnold J., Hugh Heclo, and Carolyn T. Adams. 1975. *Comparative Public Policy*. New York: St. Martin's Press.

Herbers, John. 1986. *The New Heartland: America's Flight beyond the Suburbs and How It's Changing Our Future*. New York: Times Books.

Herzog, L. A. 1990. *Where North Meets South*. Austin: University of Texas.

Hill, Richard C. 1983. "Crisis in the Motor City: The Politics of Economic Development." In Susan Fainstein et al. (eds.), *Restructuring the City: The Political Economy of Urban Redevelopment*. New York: Longman.

———. 1984. "Economic Crisis and Political Response in the Motor City." In Larry Sawers and William K. Tabb (eds.), *Sunbelt/Snowbelt: Urban Development and Regional Restructuring*. New York: Oxford University Press. Pp. 313–38.

Hirschman, Albert O. 1970. *Exit, Voice, and Loyalty: Response to Decline in Firms, Organizations, and States*. Cambridge, MA: Harvard University Press.

Hodge, David C. 1981. "Residential Revitalization and Displacement in a Growth Region." *Geographical Review*, 17, pp. 188–200.

Hoffer, Eric. 1964. *The Ordeal of Change*. New York: Harper Colophon.

———. 1969. *The Temper of Our Time*. New York: Harper and Row.

———. 1982. *Between the Devil and the Dragon: The Best Essays and Aphorisms of Eric Hoffer*. New York: Harper and Row.

Holcomb, H. Briavel, and Robert A. Beauregard. 1981. *Revitalizing Cities*. Washington, DC: Association of American Geographers.

Hollingshead, A. B. 1937. "The Life Cycle of Nebraska Rural Churches." *Rural Sociology*, 2, pp. 180–91.

Hoover, Edgar M., and Raymond Vernon. 1982. "How Neighborhoods Evolve." In Ronald H. Baylor (ed.), *Neighborhoods in Urban America*. Port Washington, NY: Kennikat Press. Pp. 157–66.

Howard, Ebenezer. 1945. *Garden Cities of Tomorrow*. London: Faber and Faber.

Hudson, John. 1985. *Plains Country Towns*. Minneapolis: University of Minnesota Press.

Hughes, James W., and Kenneth D. Bleaky, Jr. 1975. *Urban Homesteading*. New Brunswick, NJ: Rutgers University, Center for Urban Policy Research.

Hunter, Albert. 1974. *Symbolic Communities*. Chicago: University of Chicago Press.

Illinois Advisory Committee to the U.S. Commission on Civil Rights. 1981. *Shutdown: Economic Dislocation and Equal Opportunity.* Chicago: Illinois Advisory Committee.

Jackson, Kenneth T. 1985. *Crabgrass Frontier: The Suburbanization of the United States.* New York: Oxford University Press.

Jackson, Wes (ed.). 1980. *New Roots for Agriculture.* Lincoln: University of Nebraska Press.

Jacobs, Jane. 1961. *The Death and Life of Great American Cities.* New York: Vintage Books.

Jacoby, L. R. 1972. *Perception of Air, Noise, and Water Pollution in Detroit.* Ann Arbor: University of Michigan, Department of Geography.

Jakle, John A. 1985. *The Tourist: Travel in Twentieth Century North America.* Lincoln: University of Nebraska Press.

Jeffords, James M. 1984. "The Loss of U.S. Cropland: Whose Issue Is It"? In Frederick R. Steiner and John E. Theilacker (eds.), *Protecting Farmlands.* Westport, CT: AVI. Pp. 3–14.

Johnson, C. 1990. "Still Hungry after All These Years." *City Limits*, March, pp. 14–16.

Johnson, Dirk. 1988. "Plan to Insure Home Value Brings Chicago Racial Rift." *New York Times*, February 9, p. 9-Y.

Johnson, Kenneth M. 1985. *The Impact of Population Change on Business Activity in Rural America.* Boulder, CO: Westview Press.

Judd, D. 1979. *The Politics of American Cities.* Boston: Little, Brown.

Kain, J. F. and J. M. Quigley. 1970. "Evaluating the Quality of the Residential Environment." *Environment and Planning*, 2, pp. 23–32.

Kamara, Jemadari. 1983. "Plant Closings and Apartheid: The Steel Connection." *Antipode*, 15, pp. 40–41.

Karp, David A., Gregory P. Stone, and William C. Yoels. 1977. *Being Urban: A Social Psychological View.* Lexington, MA: Heath.

Katzman, Martin T. 1982. "The Case Against Bailing Out Distressed Areas." In F. Stevens Redburn and Terry F. Buss (eds.), *Public Politics for Distressed Communities.* Lexington, MA: Lexington Books.

Kaye, Ira. 1982. "Transportation." In Don A. Dillman and Daryl A. Hobbs (eds.), *Rural Society in the United States: Issues for the 1980s.* Boulder, CO: Westview Press. Pp. 156–63.

Keller, Suzanne. 1968. *The Urban Neighborhood: A Sociological Perspective.* New York: Random House.

Kentucky Heritage Council. 1984. "Saving Kentucky's Countryside." In Russell Keune (ed.), *The Historic Preservation Yearbook*. Bethesda, MD: Adler and Adler. Pp. 485–93 and 529–31.

Keune, Russell V. (ed.). 1984. *The Historic Preservation Yearbook*. Bethesda, MD: Adler and Adler.

Kleinfield, N. R. 1988. "Reinventing a Company Town." *New York Times*, March 27, p. 4F.

Kluckholn, Clyde C. 1961. "The Study of Values." In Donald N. Barrett (ed.), *Values in America*. Notre Dame, IN: University of Notre Dame.

Knox, Paul. 1982. *Urban Social Geography*. New York: John Wiley.

Korsching, Peter F. 1986. "Foreword: Agriculture and Commercial Interdependencies." In Peter F. Korsching and Judith Gildner (eds.), *Interdependencies of Agriculture and Rural Communities in the Twenty-first Century: The North Central Region*. Ames: Iowa State University Press. Pp. 1–11.

Kotler, Milton. 1969. *Neighborhood Government: The Local Foundations of Political Life*. Indianapolis: Bobbs-Merrill.

Kravitz, Alan S. 1977. "The Other Neighborhoods—Building Community Institutions." In *How Cities Can Grow Old Gracefully*. Subcommittee on the City, Committee on Banking, Finance, and Urban Affairs, U.S. House of Representatives, 95th Congress, 1st Session, Washington DC: U.S. Government Printing Office. Pp. 91–96.

Ladd, Everett C. 1969. *Ideology in America: Change and Response in a City, a Suburb, and a Small Town*. Ithaca, NY: Cornell University Press.

LaFevers, James R. 1977. "Effects of Legislative Change on Reclamation." In John L. Thomas (ed.), *Reclamation and Use of Disturbed Land in the Southwest*. Tuscon: University of Arizona Press. Pp. 18–25.

Lake, R. W. 1983. *Readings in Urban Analysis*. New Brunswick, NJ: Rutgers University, Center for Urban Policy Research.

Langenbach, Randolph. 1977. *A Future from the Past: The Case for Conservation and Reuse of Old Buildings in Industrial Communities*. Washington, DC: Department of Housing and Urban Development.

Lappe, F. M., and J. Collins. 1978. *Food First: Beyond the Myth of Scarcity*. New York: Random House.

Larson, Olaf F. 1981. "Agriculture and the Community." In Amos H. Hawley and Sara M. Mazie (eds.), *Nonmetropolitan America in Transition*. Chapel Hill: University of North Carolina Press. Pp. 147–93.

Lasch, Christopher. 1978. *The Culture of Narcissism: American Life in an Age of Diminishing Expectations*. New York: Norton.

Laska, S. B., J. M. Seaman, and D. R. McSeveney. 1982. "Innercity Reinvestment: Neighborhood Characteristics and Spatial Patterns over Time." *Urban Studies*, 19, pp. 155–65.

Laska, Shirley B., and Daphne Spain. 1979. "Urban Policy and Planning in the Wake of Gentrification: Anticipating Renovators' Demands." *Journal of the American Planning Association*, 45, pp. 523–31.

Laurie, Taylor. 1973. "The Meaning of Environment." In Colin Ward (ed.), *Vandalism*. London: Architectural Press. Pp. 54–63.

Lears, T. J. Jackson. 1983. "From Salvation to Self-realization: Advertising and the Therapeutic Roots of the Consumer Culture, 1880–1930." In Richard Fox and T. J. Jackson Lears (eds.), *The Culture of Consumption: Critical Essays in American History, 1880–1980*. New York: Pantheon Books. Pp. 1–38.

Lefebvre, Henri. 1973. *The Survival of Capitalism*. London: Allison and Busby.

Leistritz, F. Larry, et al. 1986. "Impact of Agricultural Development on Socioeconomic Change In Rural Areas." In Peter F. Korsching and Judith Gildner (eds.), *Interdependencies of Agriculture and Rural Communities in the Twenty-first Century: The North Central Region*. Ames: Iowa State University Press. Pp. 109–37.

Ledebur, Larry C. 1982. "The Reagan Revolution and Beyond." In Paul R. Porter and David C. Sweet (eds.), *Rebuilding America's Cities: Roads to Recovery*. New Brunswick, NJ: Rutgers University, Center for Urban Policy Research. Pp. 191–208.

Leven, Charles L. 1972. *Urban Decay in St. Louis*. St. Louis, MO: Institute for Urban and Regional Studies.

Leven, Charles, James T. Little, Hugh O. Nourse, and R. B. Read. 1976. *Neighborhood Change: Lessons in the Dynamics of Urban Decay*. New York: Praeger.

Levin, Hannah. 1980. "The Struggle for Community Can Create Community." In Art Gallaher, Jr., and Harland Padfield (eds.), *The Dying Community*. Albuquerque: University of New Mexico Press. Pp. 257–77.

Levy, Paul R. 1980. "Neighborhoods in a Race with Time: Local Strategies for Countering Displacement." In Shirley B. Laska and Daphne Spain (eds.), *Back to the City: Issues in Neighborhood Renovation*. New York: Pergamon Press. Pp. 288–301.

Levy, Paul R., and Roman A. Cybriwsky. 1980. "The Hidden Dimensions of Culture and Class." In Shirley B. Laska and Daphne Spain (eds.), *Back to the City: Issues in Neighborhood Renovation*. New York: Pergamon Press. Pp. 138–55.

Lewis, H. Lapham, Michael Pollan, and Eric Etheridge. 1987. *The Harper's Index Book*. New York: Henry Holt.

Lewis, Oscar. 1959. *Five Families: Mexican Case Studies in the Culture of Poverty*. New York: Basic Books.

———. 1969. "The Culture of Poverty." In Daniel P. Moynihan (ed.), *On Understanding Poverty*. New York: Basic Books. Pp. 187–200.

Lewis, R. W. B. 1955. *American Adam, Innocence, Tragedy, and Tradition in the Nineteenth Century*. Chicago: University of Chicago Press.

Ley, David. 1974. *The Black Inner City as Frontier Outpost: Images and Behavior in a Philadelphia Neighborhood*. Washington, DC: Association of American Geographers.

———. 1983. *A Social Geography of the City*. New York: Harper and Row.

———. 1985. "Alternative Explanations for Inner City Gentrification: A Canadian Assessment." *Annals of the Association of American Geographers*, 75, pp. 238–58.

Ley, David, and Roman Cybriwsky. 1974. "The Spatial Ecology of Stripped Cars." *Environment and Behavior*, 6, pp. 53–68.

Listokin, David. 1982. *Landmarks Preservation and the Property Tax: Assessing Landmark Buildings for Real Estate Taxation Purposes*. New Brunswick, NJ: Rutgers University, Center for Urban Policy Research.

———. 1985. *Housing Receivership and Self-help Neighborhood Revitalization*. New Brunswick, NJ: Rutgers University Press, Center for Urban Policy Research.

Littman, Daniel A., and Myung-Hoon Lee. 1984. "Plant Closings and Worker Dislocation." In Richard B. McKenzie (ed.), *Plant Closings: Public or Private Choices?* Washington, DC: Cato Institute. Pp. 127–54.

Lofland, Lynn. 1973. *A World of Strangers*. New York: Basic Books.

Logan, John R., and Harvey L. Molotch. 1987. *Urban Fortunes: The Political Economy of Place*. Berkeley: University of California Press.

London, Bruce. 1980. "Gentrification as Urban Reinvasion: Some Preliminary Definitional and Theoretical Considerations." In Shirley B. Laska and Daphne Spain (eds.), *Back to the City: Issues in Neighborhood Renovation*. New York: Pergamon Press. Pp. 77–92.

London, Bruce, and J. John Palen (eds.). 1984. *Gentrification, Displacement, and Neighborhood Revitalization*. Albany: State University of New York Press. Pp. 4–26.

Louis, E. T. 1989. "Still Locked In: Bank Loans and Minority Communities." *City Limits*, February, pp. 12–16.

Lowenthal, David. 1966. "The American Way of History." *Columbia University Forum*, 9, pp. 27–32.

————. 1985. *The Past Is a Foreign Country*. Cambridge, UK: Cambridge University Press.

Luria, Dan, and Jack Russell. 1984. "Motor City Changeover." In Larry Sawers and William K. Tabb (eds.), *Sunbelt/Snowbelt: Urban Development and Regional Restructuring*. New York: Oxford University Press. Pp. 271–312.

Lynch, Kevin. 1972. *What Time Is This Place?* Cambridge, MA: MIT Press.

Lynd, Staughton. 1982. *The Fight against Shutdowns: Youngstown's Steel Mill Closings*. San Pedro, CA: Singlejack Books.

Macauley, Rose. 1953. *Pleasure of Ruins*. London: Weidenfelt and Nicolson.

MacAvoy, Paul W., and John W. Snow (eds.). 1977. *Railroad Revitalization and Regulatory Reform*. Washington, DC: American Enterprise Institute for Public Policy Research.

McDonald, Forest. 1988. "Prologue." In Grady McWhiney, *Cracker Culture: Celtic Ways in the Old South*. Tuscaloosa: University of Alabama Press. Pp. xxi–xliii.

McKenzie, Richard B. 1984a. "Business Mobility: Economic Myths and Realities" In *Plant Closings: Public or Private Choices?* Washington, DC: Cato Institute. Pp. 11–23.

————. 1984b. "The Case for Plant Closures." In *Plant Closings: Public or Private Choices?* Washington, DC: Cato Institute. Pp. 205–19.

McQuade, Walter. 1966. "Urban Renewal in Boston." In James Q. Wilson (ed.), *Urban Renewal: The Record and the Controversy*. Cambridge, MA: MIT Press. Pp. 259–77.

McWhiney, Grady. 1988. *Cracker Culture: Celtic Ways in the Old South*. Tuscaloosa: University of Alabama Press.

Mandelker, Daniel R., Gary Feder, and Margaret Collins. 1980. *Reviving Cities with Tax Abatement*. New Brunswick, NJ: Rutgers University, Center for Urban Policy Research.

Marciniak, Ed. 1984. *Reversing Urban Decline*. Washington, DC: National Center for Urban Ethnic Affairs.

————. 1986. *Reclaiming the Inner City*. Washington, DC: National Center for Urban Ethnic Affairs.

Marcuse, Peter. 1986. "Abandonment, Gentrification, and Displacement: The Linkages in New York City." In Neal Smith and Peter Williams (eds.), *Gentrification of the City*. Boston: Allen and Unwin. Pp. 153–77.

Marris, Peter. 1974. *Loss and Change*. New York: Pantheon Books.

Marsh, Ben. 1987. "Continuity and Decline in the Anthracite Towns of Pennsylvania." *Annals of the Association of American Geographers*, 77, pp. 337–52.

Maslow, Abraham. 1968. *Toward a Psychology of Being.* Princeton, NJ: Van Nostrand.

Matrullo, T. 1989. "Waterfront Dollars." *City Limits,* December, p. 6.

Mayer, Martin. 1978. *The Builders.* New York: Norton.

Meehan, Eugene J. 1985. "The Evolution of Public Housing Policy." In J. Paul Mitchell (ed.), *Federal Housing Policy and Programs, Past and Present.* New Brunswick, NJ: Rutgers University Press, Center for Urban Policy Research.

Melosi, Martin V. 1981. *Garbage in the Cities: Refuse, Reform, and the Environment, 1880–1980.* College Station: Texas A & M University Press.

Meyer, Peter. 1979. "Land Rush." *Harpers' Magazine,* January, p. 49.

Meyers, Edward M. 1986. *Rebuilding America's Cities.* Cambridge, MA: Ballinger.

Meyrowitz, Joshua. 1985. *No Sense of Place: The Impact of Electronic Media on Social Behavior.* New York: Oxford University Press.

Middleton. Michael. 1980. "Perspective on Preservation." In *Preservation: Toward an Ethic in the 1980s.* Washington, DC: National Trust for Historic Preservation. Pp. 70–74.

Miller, Arthur. 1973. *The Death of a Salesman.* New York: Viking Press.

Miller, Herbert. 1971. *The Children of Frankenstein: A Primer on Modern Technological and Human Values.* Bloomington: Indiana University Press.

Mills, C. Wright. 1951. *White Collar.* New York: Oxford University Press.

Mollenkopf, J. 1978. "The Pontius Politics of Urban Development." In William K. Tabb and Larry Sawers (eds.), *Marxism and the Metropolis.* New York: Oxford University Press.

Molotch, Harvey, L. 1976. "The City as a Growth Machine: Toward a Political Economy of Place." *American Journal of Sociology,* 82, pp. 309–31.

Moncrief, Lewis W. 1973. "The Cultural Basis of Our Environmental Crisis." In Ian G. Barbour (ed.), *Western Man and Environmental Ethics: Attitudes toward Nature and Technology.* Reading, MA: Addison-Wesley. Pp. 31–42.

Moore, William. 1969. *Vertical Ghetto: Everyday Life in an Urban Project.* New York: Random House.

Morial, Ernest N. 1986. *Rebuilding America's Cities.* Cambridge, MA: Ballinger.

Morris, Richard S. 1978. *Bum Rap on America's Cities: The Causes of Urban Decay.* Englewood Cliffs, NJ: Prentice-Hall.

Muller, P. 1981. *Contemporary Suburban America.* Englewood Cliffs, NJ: Prentice-Hall.

Murray, C. 1984. *Losing Ground: American Social Policy, 1950–1980.* New York: Basic Books.

Myers, Phyllis, and Gordon Binder. 1977. *Neighborhood Conservation: Lessons from Three Cities*. Washington, DC: The Conservation Foundation.

Nachbaur, William T. 1974. "Empty Houses: Abandoned Residential Buildings in the Inner City." In George Steinlieb and Virginia Paulus (eds.), *Housing, 1971–72*. New York: AMS Press. Pp. 193–241.

Naparstek, Arthur J., and Gale Cincotta. 1976. *Urban Disinvestment: New Implications for Community Organization, Research, and Public Policy*. Washington, DC: National Center for Urban Affairs.

Neckerman, Kathryn. 1987. "Poverty and Family Structure: The Widening Gap between Evidence and Public Policy Issues." In William J. Wilson (ed.), *The Truly Disadvantaged: The Inner City, the Underclass and Public Policy*. Chicago: University of Chicago Press. Pp. 63–92.

Neighborhood Preservation. 1976. Committee on Banking, Housing and Urban Affairs, U.S. Senate, 94th Congress, 2nd Session, June 14. Washington, DC: U.S. Government Printing Office.

Nelson, John P., John N. Williams, Jr., and Thurston H. Reynolds III. 1975. *The Impact of Litter*. Frankfort, KY: Legislative Branch Research Commission.

Netzer, Dick. 1980. "Effects of the Property Tax in Urban Areas." In Jon Pynoos, Robert Schafer, and Chester W. Hartman (eds.), *Housing Urban America*. New York: Aldine. Pp. 547–59.

Newman, Oscar. 1973. *Defensible Space: Crime Prevention through Urban Design*. New York: Collier Books.

———. 1980. *Community of Interest*. Garden City, NY: Anchor.

Newsweek. 1983. August 15, p. 17.

———. 1987. "Forcing the Mentally Ill to Get Help." November 9, p. 48.

New York *Times*, 1987a. November 1, p. 29-Y.

———. 1987b. November 10, p. 13-Y.

———. 1988. January 17, sec. 4, p. 26.

O'Bannon, Patrick W. 1984. "Tax Incentives and Preservation in Pennsylvania: Some Results." In Russell V. Keune (ed.), *The Historic Preservation Yearbook*. Bethesda, MD: Adler and Adler. Pp. 378–80.

O'Connor, J. 1973. *The Fiscal Crisis of the State*. New York: St. Martin's Press.

Olson, Susan, and M. Leanne Lachman. 1976. *Tax Delinquency in the Inner City: The Problem and its Possible Solutions*. Lexington, MA: Lexington Books.

Packard, Vance. 1960. *The Waste Makers*. New York: David McKay.

Padfield, Harland. 1980. "The Expendable Rural Community and the Denial of

Powerlessness, " In Art Gallaher, Jr., and Harland Padfield (eds.), *The Dying Community*. Albuquerque: University of New Mexico Press. Pp. 159–85.

Parenti, Michael. 1983. *Democracy for the Few*. New York: St. Martin's Press.

Parsons, Talcott. 1960. "The Principal Structures of Community." In Talcott Parsons (ed.), *Structural Processes in Modern Society*. New York: Free Press. Pp. 250–79.

Pasley, Jeffrey L. 1986. "The Idiocy of Rural Life." *New Republic*, December 8, pp. 24–27.

Pasquariello, Ronald D., Donald W. Shriver, Jr., and Alan Geyer. 1982. *The City: Theology, Politics, and Urban Policy*. New York: Pilgrim Press.

Peet, R. 1975. "Inequality and Poverty: A Marxist-Geographic Theory." *Annals of the Association of American Geographers*, 65, pp. 564–72.

Perry, Clarence A. 1939. *Housing for the Machine Age*. New York: Russell Sage Foundation.

Perry, D. 1987. "The Politics of Dependency in Deindustrializing America: The Case of Buffalo, N.Y." In Michael P. Smith and Joe R. Feagin (eds.), *The Capitalist City*. Cambridge, UK: Basil Blackwell.

Perry, D., and A. Watkins. 1977. "People, Profit, and the Rise of Sunbelt Cities." In D. C. Perry and A. J. Watkins (eds.), *The Rise of the Sunbelt Cities*. Beverly Hills, CA: Sage.

Philadelphia City Planning Commission. 1984. "North Philadelphia Plan: A Guide to Revitalization. Technical Report, City of Philadelphia.

Pinkney, A. 1990. *The Myth of Black Progress*. New York: Cambridge University Press.

Piven, F. F., and R. A. Cloward. 1977. *Poor People's Movements*. New York: Pantheon.

Pollock, Cynthia. 1987. *Mining Urban Wastes: The Potential for Recycling*. N.p.: Worldwatch Institute.

Popenoe, David. 1985. *Private Pleasure, Public Plight: American Metropolitan Community Life in Comparative Perspective*. New Brunswick, NJ: Transaction Books.

Popper, Frank J. 1985. "The Environmentalist and the LULU," *Environment*, pp. 27, 7–11, 37–40.

Porter, Paul R. 1976. *The Recovery of American Cities*. New York: Sun River Press.

Pred, A. 1984. "Place as Historically Contingent Process: Structuration and the Time Geography of Becoming Places." *Annals of the Association of American Geographers*, 74, pp. 279–97.

Prouty, L. Fletcher. 1987. Letter to the New York *Times*. October 21, p. 22-Y.

Pynoos, Jon, Robert Schafer, and Chester W. Hartman (eds.). 1980. *Housing Urban America*. New York: Aldine.

Raines, John C. 1982. "Economics and the Justification of Sorrows." In Raines, Lenore E. Berson, and David M Gracie (eds.), *Community and Capital in Conflict: Plant Closings and Job Loss*. Philadelphia: Temple University Press. Pp. 282–311.

Rainwater, Lee. 1980. "The Lessons of Pruitt-Igoe." In Jon Pynoos, Robert Schafer, and Chester W. Hartman (eds.), *Housing Urban America*. New York: Aldine.

Ravitz, Abe C. 1956. "Timothy Dwight: Professor of Rhetoric." *New England Quarterly*, 29, pp. 63–72.

Rawlings, Charles W. 1982. "The Religious Community and Economic Justice." In John C. Raines, Lenore E. Berson, and David M. Gracie (eds.), *Community and Capital in Conflict: Plant Closings and Job Loss*. Philadelphia: Temple University Press. Pp. 136–51.

Redekop, Calvin. 1975. "Communal Groups: Inside or Outside Community" In Jack F. Kinton (ed.), *The American Community: Creation and Revival, A Multidisciplinary Perspective*. Aurora, IL: Social Science and Sociological Resources. Pp. 135–61.

Redlining and Disinvestment as a Discriminatory Practice in Residential Mortgage Loans. 1977. Chicago: University of Chicago, Center for Urban Studies, Pt. 1.

Reich, Charles. 1970. *The Greening of America*. New York: Random House.

Reich, Robert B. 1983. *The Next American Frontier*. New York: Penguin.

Rein, Martin, and Lee Rainwater. 1977. "How Large Is the Welfare Class." *Change*, September, pp. 20–23.

Reinvestment Handbook. 1978. Harrisburg, PA: Commonwealth of Pennsylvania, Department of Community Affairs.

Relph, Edward. 1987. *The Modern Urban Landscape*. Baltimore: Johns Hopkins University Press.

Revere, Espeth. 1984. *Housing in Crisis: Report of the Data Base Study Group in the Housing Abandonment Task Force*. Chicago: Woodstock Foundation.

Robbins, William. 1988. "After a Year of Subsidized Gains, Signs of New Hope." New York *Times*. February 14, p. 4-E.

Robertson, James O. 1980. *American Myth, American Reality*. New York: Hill and Wang.

Rodnick, David. 1972. *Essays on an America in Transition*. Lubbock, TX: Caprock Press.

Rogers, Susan C., and Sonya Salamon. 1983. "Inheritance and Social Organization among Family Farmers." *American Ethnologist*, 10, pp. 529–50.

Rohrer, Wayne, and Diane Quantic. 1980. "Social and Demographic Processes of Declining Nonmetropolitan Communities in the Middle West." In Art Gallaher, Jr., and Harlan Padfield (eds.), *The Dying Community*. Albuquerque: University of New Mexico Press. Pp. 133–57.

Rokeach, Milton. 1973. *The Nature of Human Values*. New York: Free Press.

Runke, James F., and Alan E. Finder. 1977. *State Taxation of Railroads and Tax Relief Programs*. Lexington, KY: Council of State Governments.

Russett, B. 1970. *What Price Vigilance?* New Haven, CT: Yale University Press.

Ryan, William. 1971. *Blaming the Victim*. New York: Pantheon Books.

———. 1987. "Ethnic Determinants of Farm Community Character." In Michael Chibaik (ed.), *Farmwork and Fieldwork*. Ithaca, NY: Cornell University Press. Pp. 168–88.

Salamon, Sonya. 1985. "Ethnic Communities and the Structures of Agriculture." *Rural Sociology*, 50, pp. 323–40.

Salins, Peter D. 1980. *The Ecology of Housing Destruction: Economic Effects of Public Intervention in the Housing Market*. New York: New York University Press.

Salter, Christopher L. 1983. "The Cowboy and the City: Urban Affection for Wilderness." *Landscape*, 27, pp. 43–47.

Santmire, H. Paul. 1973. "Historical Dimensions of the American Crisis." In Ian G. Barbour (ed.), *Western Man and Environmental Ethics: Attitudes toward Nature and Technology*. Reading, MA: Addison-Wesley.

Sawhill, John C. 1981. "Preserving History and Saving Energy: Two Sides of the Same Coin." In Diane Maddox (ed.), *New Energy from Old Buildings*. Washington, DC: National Trust for Historic Preservation. Pp. 19–27.

Schafer, Robert. 1980. "Discrimination in Housing Prices and Mortgage Lending." In Jon Pynoos, Robert Schafer, and Chester W. Hartman (eds.), *Housing Urban America*. New York: Aldine. Pp. 294–308.

Schill, Michael H., and Richard P. Nathan. 1983. *Revitalizing America's Cities: Neighborhood Revitalization and Displacement*. Albany: State University of New York Press.

Schmandt, Henry J., George D. Wendel, and E. Allen Tomey. 1983. *Federal Aid to St. Louis*. Washington, DC: Brookings Institution.

Schoenberg, Sandra P., and Patricia L. Rosenbaum. 1980. *Neighborhoods That Work: Sources for Viability in the Inner City*. New Brunswick, NJ: Rutgers University, Center for Urban Policy Research.

Schultz, Charles. 1984. "Industrial Policy: A Digest." In Richard B. McKenzie (ed.), *Plant Closings: Public or Private Choices?* Washington, DC: Cato Institute.

Schwartz, Edward. 1982. "Economic Development as if Neighborhoods Mattered" In John C. Raines, Lenore E. Berson, and David M. Gracie (eds.), *Community and Capital in Conflict: Plant Closings and Job Loss.* Philadelphia: Temple University Press. Pp. 257–81.

Sennett, Richard. 1970. *The Uses of Disaster: Personality, Identity, and City Life.* New York: Alfred Knopf.

Shaffer, Ron, Priscilla Salant, and William Saupe. 1986. "Rural Economics and Farming: A Synergistic Link." In Peter F. Korsching and Judith Gildner (eds.), *Interdependencies of Agriculture and Rural Communities in the Twenty-first Century: The North Central Region.* Ames: Iowa State University. Pp. 55–72.

Shakrow, Don M., and Julie Graham. 1983. "The Impact of the Changing International Division of Labor on the Labor Force in Mature Industrial Regions." *Antipode*, 15, pp. 18–22.

Shannon, Lyle W. 1984. "The Role of Vandalism in Delinquent Careers." In Claude Levy-Leboyer (ed.), *Vandalism: Behavior and Motivations.* Amsterdam: North–Holland. Pp. 215–28.

Sheridan, David. 1981. *Desertification of the United States.* Washington, DC: U.S. Government Printing Office.

Short, J. 1989. *The Humane City.* New York: Basil Blackwell.

Shover, John L. 1976. *First Majority; Last Majority.* Dekalb, IL: Northern Illinois University Press.

Siegfried, Andre. 1927. *America Comes of Age.* Translated by H. H. Hemming and Doris Hemming. New York: Harcourt, Brace.

Sjoberg, Gideon. 1965. "Community." In J. Gold and W. L. Kolb (eds.), *Dictionary of Sociology.* London: Tavistock.

Slayton, William. 1966. "The Operation and Achievements of Urban Renewal Programs." In James Q. Wilson (ed.), *Urban Renewal: The Record and the Controversy.* Cambridge, MA: MIT Press. Pp. 189–229.

Smith, C. 1988. *Public Problems: The Management of Urban Distress.* New York: Guilford.

Smith, Neil. 1979. "Toward a Theory of Gentrification: A Back to the City Movement by Capital and Not People." *Journal of the American Planning Association*, 45, pp. 538–48.

———. 1982. "Gentrification and Uneven Development." *Economic Geography*, 58, pp. 139–55.

Smith, Neil, and Michele LeFaivre. 1984. "A Class Analysis of Gentrification" In Bruce London and J. John Palen (eds.), *Gentrification, Displacement, and Neighborhood Revitalization.* Albany: State University of New York Press. Pp. 43–63.

Smith, Page. 1966. *As a City upon a Hill: The Town in American History.* New York: Alfred Knopf.

Smith, T. Michael. 1982. "Becoming a Good and Competent Community." In Paul R. Porter and David C. Sweet (eds.), *Rebuilding America's Cities: Roads to Recovery.* New Brunswick, NJ: Rutgers University, Center for Urban Policy Research. Pp. 123–42.

Smith-Kline Forum for a Healthier American Society. 1980. Advertisement: "America's Most Critical Choice." *Newsweek,* September 15.

Solomon, Arthur P. 1974. *Housing the Urban Poor: A Critical Evaluation of Federal Housing Policy.* Cambridge, MA: MIT Press.

Squires, Gregory D. 1982. " 'Runaway Plants,' Capital Mobility, and Black Economic Rights." In John C. Raines, Lenore E. Berson, and David M. Gracie (eds.), *Community and Capital in Conflict: Plant Closings and Job Loss.* Philadelphia: Temple University Press. Pp. 62–97.

Srinivasan, M. S. and S. Srinivasan. 1986. *Maintenance Standardization for Capital Assets: A Cost–Productivity Approach.* New York: Praeger.

Starr, Michael E. 1984. "The Marlboro Man: Cigarette Smoking and Masculinity in America." *Journal of Popular Culture,* 17, pp. 45–57.

Starr, Roger. 1977. "The Changing Life of Cities" In *How Cities Can Grow Old Gracefully.* Subcommittee on the City, Committee on Banking, Finance, and Urban Affairs, U.S. House of Representatives, 95th Congress, 1st Session. Washington, DC: U.S. Government Printing Office. Pp. 47–51.

Stegman, Michael A. 1972. *Housing Investment in the Inner City: The Dynamics of Decline; A Study of Baltimore, Maryland, 1968–1870.* Cambridge, MA: MIT Press.

Stegman, Michael A. and Doug Hillstrom. 1984. *Housing In New York.* New York: Department of Housing Preservation and Development.

Stein, Maurice. 1961. *The Eclipse of Community.* New York: Harper Torchbooks.

Steinberg, Stephen. 1981. *The Ethnic Myth: Race, Ethnicity, and Class in America.* Boston: Beacon Press.

Steinberger, Peter J. 1985. *Ideology and the Urban Crisis.* Albany: State University of New York Press.

Sternlieb, George. 1972. *The Urban Housing Dilemma: The Dynamics of New York City's Rent Controlled Housing.* New York: Housing and Development Administration.

————. 1980. *The Maintenance of America's Housing Stock*. New Brunswick, NJ: Rutgers University, Center for Urban Policy Research.

Sternlieb, George, and Robert W. Burchell. 1973. *Residential Abandonment: The Tenement Landlord Revisited*. New Brunswick, NJ: Rutgers University, Center for Urban Policy Research.

Sternlieb, George, and James W. Hughes. 1977. "New Regional and Metropolitan Realities in America." In *How Cities Can Grow Old Gracefully*. Subcommittee on the City, Committee on Banking, Finance, and Urban Affairs, U.S. House of Representatives, 95th Congress, 1st Session. Washington, DC: U.S. Government Printing Office. Pp. 3–30.

Sternlieb, George, James H. Hughes, and Kenneth Bleakly. 1974. *Housing Abandonment in Pennsylvania*. New Brunswick, NJ: Rutgers University, Center for Urban Policy Research.

Stewart, George R. 1968. *Not So Rich as You Think*. New York: Houghton Mifflin.

Still, Bayard. 1974. *Urban America: A History with Documents*. Boston: Little, Brown.

Still, Henry. 1972. "Littered Land." In Robert K. Yin (ed.), *The City in the Seventies*. Itasca, IL: Peacock. Pp. 130–36.

Stockdale, Jerry D. 1982. "Who Will Speak for Agriculture?" In Don A. Dillman and Daryl A. Hobbs (eds.), *Rural Society in the United States: Issues for the 1980s*. Boulder, CO: Westview Press. Pp. 317–27.

Stone, Clarence N. 1986. "Power and Social Complexity." In Robert J. Waste (ed.), *Community Power: Directions for Future Research*. Beverly Hills, CA: Sage.

Stoneall, Linda. 1983. *Country Life, City Life: Five Theories of Community*. New York: Praeger.

Storper, M., and A. J. Scott. 1985. "Production, Work, Territory: Contemporary Realities and Theoretical Tasks." In Allen J. Scott and Michael Storper (eds.), *Production, Work, Territory*. Boston: Allen and Unwin.

Storper, Michael, and Richard Walker. 1983. "The Theory of Labor and the Theory of Location." *International Journal of Urban and Regional Research*, 7, p. 3.

————. 1984. "The Spatial Division of Labor: Labor and the Location of Industries." In Larry Sawyers and William K. Tabb (eds.), *Sunbelt/Snowbelt: Urban Development and Regional Restructuring*. New York: Oxford University Press. Pp. 19–47.

Struyk, Raymond J. 1980. *A New System for Public Housing*. Washington, DC: Urban Institute.

Subcommittee on Energy and the Environment, Committee on Interior and Insular

Affairs, U.S. House of Representatives, 96th Congress, 2nd Session. 1981. *Oversight Hearings on the Surface Mining Control and Reclamation Act of 1977*. Washington, DC: U.S. Government Printing Office.

Sumka, Howard J. 1980. "Federal Antidisplacement Policy in a Context of Urban Decline." In Shirley B. Laska and Daphne Spain (eds.), *Back to the City: Issues in Neighborhood Renovation*. New York: Pergamon. Pp. 252–68.

Summerson, John. 1963. *Heavenly Mansions and Other Essays on Architecture*. New York: Norton.

Tabb, William K. 1984. "Urban Development and Regional Restructuring, An Overview." In Larry Sawyers and William K. Tabb (eds.), *Sunbelt/Snowbelt: Urban Development and Regional Restructuring*. New York: Oxford University Press. Pp. 3–15.

Taub, Richard P., D. Garth Taylor, and Jan D. Dunham. 1984. *Paths of Neighborhood Change: Race and Crime in Urban America*. Chicago: University of Chicago Press.

Taylor, Ralph B. 1986. *Urban Neighborhoods: Research and Policy*. New York: Praeger.

Therkildson, Paul T. 1964. *Public Assistance and American Values*. Albuquerque: University of New Mexico, Division of Government Research.

Thompson, K. 1980. "Organizations as Constructors of Social Reality (I)." In Graeme Salaman and Kenneth Thompson (eds.), *Control and Ideology in Organizations*. Cambridge, MA: MIT Press.

Thompson, Wilbur R. 1977. "The Urban Development Process." In Herrington J. Bryce (ed.), *Small Cities in Transition: The Dynamics of Growth and Decline*. Cambridge, MA: Ballinger. Pp. 95–112.

Thurow, Lester C. 1980. *The Zero-Sum Society: Distribution and the Possibilities for Economic Change*. New York: Basic Books.

———. 1985. Quoted in Thomas C. Cochran, *Challenges to American Values: Society, Business, and Religion*. New York: Oxford University Press.

Tobin, G. A. 1976. "Suburbanization and the Development of Motor Transportation: Transportation Technology and the Suburbanization Process." In Barry Schwartz (ed.), *The Changing Face of the Suburbs*. Chicago: University of Chicago Press.

Toffler, Alvin. *Future Shock*. New York: Bantam Books.

Toner, William J. 1974. "Introduction to Nongrowth Economics." In Earl Finkler and David C. Peterson (eds.), *Nongrowth Planning Strategies: The Developing Power of Towns, Cities, and Regions*. New York: Praeger. Pp. xiv–xxv.

Toynbee, Arnold. 1947. *A Study of History*. New York: Oxford University Press.

Tuleja, Tad. 1985. *Beyond the Bottom Line: How Business Leaders Are Turning Principles into Profits.* New York: Facts on File.

Turner, Jonathan, and David Musick. 1985. *American Dilemmas: A Sociological Interpretation of Enduring Social Issues.* New York: Columbia University Press.

Udall, Stewart L. 1968. *1976: Agenda for Tomorrow.* New York: Harcourt, Brace, and World.

U.S. Census Bureau. 1980. *Census of Population and Housing.* Department of Commerce.

U.S. Department of Education. 1986. *The Family: Preserving America's Future; A Report of the Working Group on the Family.* Washington, DC: U.S. Government Printing Office.

U.S. Department of Transportation. 1976. *Railroad Abandonments and Alternatives: A Report on Effects Outside the Northeastern Region.* Washington, D.C.: U.S. Government Printing Office.

Vail, David J. 1982. "Family Farms in the Web of Community: Exploring the Rural Political Economy of the United States." *Antipode,* 14, pp. 26–38.

Van Allsberg, M. 1974. "Property Abandonment in Detroit." *Wayne Law Review,* 20, pp. 25–37.

van Duijn, J. J. 1983. *The Long Wave in Economic Life.* London: Allen and Unwin.

Vaughan, Roger J., 1983. *Rebuilding America,* Vol. 2: *Financing Public Works in the 1980s.* Washington, DC: Council of State Planning Agencies.

Vaughan, Roger J. and Mary E. Vogel. 1979. *The Urban Impacts of Federal Policies,* Vol. 4: *Population and Residential Location.* Santa Monica, CA: Rand Corporation.

Vernon, Raymond. 1960. *Metropolis 1985.* Cambridge, MA: Harvard University Press.

———. 1966. "The Changing Economic Function of the Central City." In James Q. Wilson (ed.), *Urban Renewal: The Record and the Controversy.* Cambridge, MA: MIT Press.

Vogeler, Ingolf. 1981. *The Myth of the Family Farm: Agribusiness Dominance of U.S. Agriculture.* Boulder, CO: Westview Press.

Wachtel, Paul L. 1983. *The Poverty of Affluence: A Psychological Portrait of the American Way of Life.* New York: Free Press.

Wali, Mohan K., and Alden L. Kollman. 1977. "Ecology and Mining or Mining Ecology?" In John L. Thames (ed.), *Reclamation and Use of Disturbed Land in the Southwest.* Tucson: University of Arizona Press. Pp. 108–15.

Walker, R. 1981. "A Theory of Suburbanization: Capitalism and the Construction of Urban Space in the United States." In Michael Dear and Allen J. Scott (eds.), *Urbanization and Urban Planning in Capitalist Society.* London and New York: Methuen.

Wallerstein, Immanuel. 1983. *Historical Capitalism.* London: Verso.

Wanniski, Jude. 1979. *The Way the World Works.* New York: Basic Books.

Warf, B. 1988. "Regional Transformation, Everyday Life, and Pacific Northwest Lumber Production." *Annals of the Association of American Geographers,* 78, pp. 326–46.

———. 1989. "Progress Report: Locality Studies." *Urban Geography,* 10, pp. 178–85.

———. 1990. "The Reconstruction of Social Ecology and Neighborhood Change in Brooklyn." *Environment and Planning D: Society and Space,* 8, pp. 73–96.

Warsaw, Robin. 1988. "Restoring Housing in Philadelphia." New York *Times.* August 5, p. 35 Y.

Waterman, Alan S. 1984. *The Psychology of Individualism.* New York: Praeger.

Webber, M. J. 1982. Agglomeration and the Regional Question," *Antipode,* 14, pp. 1–11.

Weber, Max. 1930. *The Protestant Ethic and the Spirit of Capitalism.* New York: Scribners.

Weeks, D. R. 1980. "Organization and Decisionmaking." In Graeme Salaman and Kenneth Thompson (eds.), *Control and Ideology in Organizations.* Cambridge, MA: MIT Press.

Weinstein, J. 1968. *The Corporate Ideal and the Liberal State.* Boston: Beacon Press.

Werner, Frances E. 1977. *Redlining and Discrimination Practice in Residential Mortgage Loans.* Chicago: University of Illinois, Center for Urban Studies.

Widrow, W. 1987. "Dispelling the Myths of Housing Vouchers." *Shelterforce,* 10, no. 4, September/October, p. 15.

Wilkinson, Kenneth P. 1974. "Consequences of Decline and Social Adjustment to It." In Larry R. Whiting (ed.), *Communities Left Behind: Alternatives for Development.* Ames: Iowa State University Press. Pp. 43–53.

Williams, Michael R. 1985. *Neighborhood Organizations: Seeds of a New Urban Life.* Westport, CT: Greenwood Press.

Willits, Fern K., Robert C. Bealer, and Donald M. Crider. 1982. "Persistence of Rural/Urban Differences." In Don A. Dillman and Daryl A. Hobbs (eds.), *Rural Society in the United States: Issues for the 1980s.* Boulder, CO: Westview Press. Pp. 69–76.

Wilson, David. 1987. "Urban Revitalization on the Upper West Side of Manhattan: An Urban Managerialist Assessment." *Economic Geography*, 63, pp. 35–47.

———. 1989. "Toward a Revised Urban Managerialism: Local Managers and Community Development Block Grants." *Political Geography Quarterly*, 8 no., 1, pp. 21–41.

———. 1991. Urban Change, Circuits of Capital, and Uneven Development." *The Professional Geographer*, 43, pp. 403–15.

Wilson, D., and D. Mayer. 1986. *Tax Abatements, Targeting Strategies, and Equity*. Discussion paper H1, Geography Department, Indiana University, Indianapolis.

Wilson, James Q. 1966. "Planning and Politics: Citizen Participation in Urban Renewal." In *Urban Renewal: The Record and the Controversy*. Cambridge, MA: MIT Press. Pp. 407–21.

———. 1975. *Thinking about Crime*. New York: Basic Books.

Wilson, William J. 1987. *The Truly Disadvantaged: The Inner City, the Underclass, and Public Policy*. Chicago: University of Chicago Press.

Wireman, Peggy. 1984. *Neighborhoods, Networks, and Families: New Forms for Old Values*. Lexington, MA: Lexington Books.

Wolf, Peter. 1981. *Land Use in America: Its Value, Use, and Control*. New York: Pantheon Books.

Wolfe, Alan. 1981. *America's Impasse: The Rise and Fall of the Politics of Growth*. New York: Pantheon Books.

Women's City Club of New York. 1977. *With Love and Affection: A Study of Building Abandonment*. New York: Women's City Club of New York.

Wong, K. K., and P. E. Peterson. 1986. "Urban Response to Federal Program Flexibility." *Urban Affairs Quarterly*, 21, pp. 293–309.

Woodstock Institute. 1982. *Evaluation of the Illinois Neighborhood Development Corporation, Background Report*. Chicago: Woodstock Institute.

Wylie, Jeanie. 1989. *Poletown: Community Betrayed*. Urbana, IL: University of Illinois Press.

Wylie, Mary. 1980. "The Dying Community as a Human Habitat for the Elderly." In Art Gallaher, Jr., and Harland Padfield (eds.), *The Dying Community*. Albuquerque: University of New Mexico Press. Pp. 237–56.

Yankelovich, Daniel. 1981. *New Rules: Searching for Self-fulfillment in a World Turned Upside Down*. New York: Random House.

Yates, Douglas. 1982. "Neighborhood Government." In Ronald H. Baylor (ed.),

Neighborhoods in America. Port Washington, NY: Kennikat Press. Pp. 131–41.

Yin, Robert K. 1982. *Conserving America's Neighborhoods*. New York: Plenum Press.

Zais, J. P. 1976. "Housing Allowances: Ongoing Experiments and Policy Options." In Robert Mendelson and Michael Quinn (eds.), *The Politics of Housing in Older Urban Areas*. New York: Praeger.

Zarembka, A. 1990. *The Urban Housing Crisis*. New York: Greenwood.

Zelinsky, Wilbur. 1975. *The Cultural Geography of the United States*. Englewood Cliffs, NJ: Prentice-Hall.

Zimbardo, Philip G. 1973. "A Field Experiment in Auto Shaping." In Colin Wood (ed.), *Vandalism*. London: Architectural Press. Pp. 85–90.

Zucker, Paul. 1968. *Fascination of Decay: Ruins, Relict, Symbol, Ornament*. Ridgewood, NJ: Gregg Press.

Index

About the Authors

John Jakle is a professor of geography and landscape architecture and head of the Department of Geography at the University of Illinois, Urbana-Champaign. His interests spread across historical, cultural, and urban social geography with focus on interpreting the American landscape as built environment. Among his other books are *Common Houses in America's Small Towns, The Visual Elements of Landscape, The Tourist: Travel in Twentieth Century North America,* and *Human Spatial Behavior: A Social Geography.*

David Wilson researches the internal structure of cities, social and political processes within cities, and U.S. housing and urban policy. He has published in such journals as *Urban Geography, Economic Geography, Political Geography Quarterly, Journal of Urban Affairs, Environmental Management, The Professional Geographer,* and *Society and Space.* He is assistant professor of geography at the University of Illinois, Urbana-Champaign.